STRONG MANAGERS, WEAK OWNERS

THE POLITICAL ROOTS OF
AMERICAN CORPORATE FINANCE

STRONG MANAGERS,
WEAK OWNERS

THE POLITICAL ROOTS OF
AMERICAN CORPORATE FINANCE

Mark J. Roe

PRINCETON UNIVERSITY PRESS   PRINCETON, NEW JERSEY

Copyright © 1994 by Princeton University Press
Published by Princeton University Press, 41 William Street,
Princeton, New Jersey 08540
In the United Kingdom: Princeton University Press,
Chichester, West Sussex
All Rights Reserved

Library of Congress Cataloging-in-Publication Data
Roe, Mark J., 1951–
Strong managers, weak owners : the political roots
of American corporate finance / Mark J. Roe.
p.   cm.
Includes bibliographical references and index.
ISBN 0-691-03683-7
1. Corporations—United States—Finance.
I. Title.
HG4061.R58   1994   658.15—dc20   94-12179   CIP

This book has been composed in Caledonia

Princeton University Press books are printed
on acid-free paper and meet the guidelines
for permanence and durability of the Committee
on Production Guidelines for Book Longevity
of the Council on Library Resources

Printed in the United States of America

1   3   5   7   9   10   8   6   4   2

Contents

Preface

WHAT FOLLOWS is frankly fragmentary. I try here more to suggest new lines of research and thinking about the American public corporation than to provide an exhaustive treatment of the viewpoint I present. The American firm and the structure at its top—where the board of directors, shareholders, and senior managers interact—is not just the result of an efficiency-driven economic evolution. It is, more than has yet been acknowledged, also the result of American politics, particularly the politics that influenced and often dictated the way financial intermediaries—banks, insurers, pension funds, and mutual funds—moved savings from households to firms.

In the 1980s, many of the largest American firms restructured, often painfully. Many became more efficient and productive; some became less so. The relationships among shareholders, boardrooms, and senior managers were in upheaval, and still are. Proposals have arisen to change the way the three interact—some by giving shareholders greater voice in the corporate boardroom, some by giving them less. Often unnoticed is that the controversies of the 1980s and 1990s have been shaped by political decisions, many made long ago. These decisions may eventually be reversed, but a stable reversal (and an understanding of why some reversals will be hard to achieve), must deal with the forces—many of which were political—that created the modern American firm and its boardroom. While today's political forces differ from the past's, we can see why, if the past is any guide, broad changes in corporate governance are not in the cards without becoming a political issue. Corporate forms are malleable, and politics helps to shape them. The political history I give in this book suggests that if today's activism, which is visible but low, becomes a fundamental challenge to accepted ways of doing things, the fight will move from the economic to the political arena, where politics will settle it.

This history matters because corporate governance—the relationship among a firm's shareholders, its board of directors, and its senior managers—matters. And corporate governance matters because management matters. Technologies establish the frontier of what the firm can do; management determines how close the firm gets to that frontier.

That corporate governance matters can be seen in the 1990s' newspaper headlines of turmoil in corporate boardrooms; CEOs' tenure has become insecure, and activist boards are holding some firms' CEOs accountable for their firms' performance. The form of today's accountability is new, but the substance is not: the hostile takeovers of the 1980s were also fights about how to govern large firms at the top. And international competition makes governance decisions more visible, because governance failures show up more quickly than they once did, not only in headlines of corporate failure, but in closed factories and lost jobs.

Economic theory once treated the firm as a collection of machinery, technology, inventory, workers, and capital. Dump these inputs into a black box, stir them up, and one got outputs of products and profits. Today, theory sees the firm as more, as a management structure. The firm succeeds if managers can successfully coordinate the firm's activities; it fails if managers cannot effectively coordinate and match people and inputs to current technologies and markets. At the very top of the firm are the relationships among the firm's shareholders, its directors, and its senior managers. If those relationships are dysfunctional, the firm is more likely to stumble.

Viewing the firm as a governance structure is no longer novel: Ronald Coase won a Nobel Prize in part because of his conception in the 1930s of the firm as balancing off the gains from an internal governance structure against the gains from market trades, and generations of economists have since furthered his analysis. Economists now understand how complex firm structures can help to avoid agency costs—mismanagement in more ordinary talk. Business historians have shown how specialized management made American business succeed early in this century. Technological innovation alone was not enough to ensure competitiveness. The basic technologies were available in several nations during the early part of the century; but the United States was the first to develop a managerial structure to exploit them.

Making products in a large firm requires a complex command and control structure, which can break down, continuing to send the same commands even when markets are asking for change. At the top of the firm's command and control structure is the boardroom, where two important decisions are made: the basic allocation of a firm's resources and the choice of its top managers. Although boards of directors rarely innovate and some boards may not even understand the technologies on which a firm's business is based, when the board chooses the personnel at the top and when it makes basic capital allocations, it deeply affects whether the firm succeeds or fails.

Corporate governance matters most for big firms that have large sunk organizational and physical capital and compete in imperfect product markets. For them, the signals of change from product markets or capital markets are at first weak and do not show up in lost profits right away. The 1990s upheavals in General Motors, Sears, American Express, Westinghouse, Kodak, and IBM, all of whose problems dated back at least a decade, show how firms can slowly slide toward failure without product markets' forcing improvement. Their failures are partly failures of governance—the process by which boards and senior managers reacted to (or ignored) the early market messages.

True, poor governance did not create these firms' initial problems. Increasing international competition and regulatory decisions changed GM's auto market; changing financial technologies challenged American Express's franchise; new video technologies threatened Kodak; the personal computer challenged IBM. Although errors of business judgment induced a few declines, when those judgments were first made, many of the bets were good ones that in the end just didn't pay off. But although poor governance did not spark failure, better governance might have snuffed out the fire when it was a spark and not a conflagration. Economic and technological change set up the problem, but corporate governance—how and whether those at the top of the firm reacted—influenced whether the firms succeeded despite the challenge.

Society wins if governance works. When it works, boards evaluate managers' reactions to problems before product market competition seriously hurts the firm. Although shareholders profit first from good governance, their profits are not the "bottom line" for public policy here: poor management imposes costs on the firm's employees, its suppliers, its customers, and its communities. Closed factories and lost jobs are resources wasted; if mediocre managers—or good managers whose hands are tied by dysfunctional relationships with their boards and stockholders—close some of those factories and lose some of those jobs, when better management could have cost-effectively modernized and avoided obsolescence, then corporate governance matters.

The distinctive governance structure of the large American firm—distant shareholders, a board of directors that has historically deferred to the CEO, and powerful, centralized management—is usually seen as a natural economic outcome arising from specialization: shareholders would specialize in risk-bearing but wanted diversification, and firms needed specialized, professional management. Both shareholders and managers wanted to exploit technologies that demanded large-scale operations. Thus technology and economics impelled the large firm to evolve to have distant shareholders and centralized management. While not wrong, the evolutionary argument is incomplete. Foreign systems show that specialization and diversification could have been achieved other than with the American distant shareholder structure. The American corporate structure has not yet been fully examined as a political outcome, and that is the distinctive analysis that I make in this book. American corporate structures are in considerable part the result of political decisions, many long forgotten, about the organization of financial intermediaries. Had those decisions differed, today's governance structures could have been different. American democracy affected American finance, which in turn affected the structure of America's large public firms (just as politics in other nations affected the structure of their large firms). American politics deliberately weakened and shattered financial intermediaries, thereby making managers more powerful than they otherwise had to be.

Interest group fights helped shape the outcome—fights between rival financial institutions in the distant past and, more recently, fights led by managers. At other times a public policy rationale—usually of dealing with a financial abuse—was in play. The rival interest groups were sometimes evenly divided, allowing lawmakers to play one off against the other; at other times, lawmakers had several solutions to a public policy problem, several ways of dealing with a financial abuse. When the divided interest groups and the multiple public policy solutions balanced out and failed to yield a clear winner, the public's fear of concentrated private economic power often tipped the decisional balance toward whichever interest group, or whichever public policy rationale, supported greater fragmentation of the financial intermediary.

American political organization has been important. Our federal system favored smaller, local interests over concentrated private economic power. An American antigovernment bias tended to suppress the alternative of allowing concentrated private economic power, and building a countervailing national political power in Washington: the public would have more easily accepted powerful private financial structures had there been a stronger central government. Populist fears, interest group maneuvering, and American political structure all had a cumulative effect that repeatedly led Congress and the states to fragment financial institutions, their portfolios, and their ability to network together. These political decisions gave rise to the distinctive form of the modern American corporation: scattered shareholders, with managers in control.

I show that politics—democracy in general, and American democracy in particular—affected the organization of the large firm. The interaction between firms and financiers was, and still is, mediated partly by politicians, and that mediation in a democratic society is a central—and neglected—explanation for the organizational forms we observe. Were the title not already taken, a good one for this book would have been *The Visible Hand*, because the visible hand of politics affected the structures of financial intermediaries, which in turn affected the structure of the large public firm.

In Part I, I review the economic paradigm as explaining the structure at the top of the large public firm and briefly look at the weaknesses and strengths of distant ownership. In Part II, I briefly set up the political paradigm: that American politics deliberately fragmented financial institutions and their strength inside the public firm. In Part III, I assemble the historical evidence for that political thesis. In Part IV, I look at current evidence in the United States—the 1980s takeover wave and ownership trends in the largest firms—and abroad to see how it supports the political thesis and the historical contingency of the American firm. In Part V, I see whether the thesis yields policy recommendations.

This book lies across four disciplines: law, American history, economics, and political science. Although I do not pretend to be expert in all four, to demonstrate my thesis here I must draw upon them all. The cross-cutting nature of the task partly explains why the political underpinnings of the shape of the large firm have been unexamined and the purely economic model remained unchallenged for so many decades. While the politics of some financial rules, particularly the Glass-Steagall Act, which separated commercial from investment banking, has attracted attention, most key rules have not. Lacking these inquiries, I have consulted the original sources (legislative debates, contemporary statements by opinion leaders, news reports, and financial industry trade papers). While more could be done, there's now enough evidence from these four disciplines and from the research I've added here to see that the rules are not unrelated dots in American history; rather, they fit a general political picture. I begin here the job of synthesis.

I have a focus for this book—the interaction between politics and corporate governance—and people with a focus can exaggerate their subject's importance. While corporate governance is one of the matters on the list of what determines economic success or failure, it is only one, and it is probably a good ways down the list in its importance. Similarly, while politics is one of the determinants of corporate governance, it is only one, although, as it turns out, an important one.

The book moves on two levels, one academic and one practical. On the academic level—the main one for this book—I ask how we came to have the corporate boardrooms and the ownership structure that we have. Was it economics alone, or did politics help choose among relatively equal, but different structures? On the practical level I ask: could we do better? On this second level, the evidence is mixed and uncertain, so much so that there's little basis to use law to *encourage* and certainly none to *require* alternative forms of governance. The evidence only warrants *permitting* a few more ways than there now are for American shareholders, financial institutions, and senior managers to interact, to allow greater competition between different organizational forms.

I began thinking about this project in the academic year 1987–1988, when three business problems occupied my attention, one from bankruptcy, one from corporate law, and one from antitrust. For an article on bankruptcy, I came across a speech that William O. Douglas gave when he chaired the

Securities and Exchange Commission, a speech that stunned a 1937 audience of nearly every important Wall Street investment banker. Douglas told the investment bankers:

> [T]he banker [should and will be] restricted to . . . underwriting or selling. Insofar as management [and] formulation of industrial policies . . . the banker will be superseded. The financial power which he has exercised in the past over such processes will pass into other hands.[1]

That year I was teaching courses in bankruptcy, corporations, and antitrust at the University of Pennsylvania Law School. In the bankruptcy course I taught theories of secured debt, one of which explains secured credit as a monitoring device that improves the efficiency of the firm. That theory makes one ask why debt is the best vantage point for monitoring, since a creditor is generally not concerned with total firm value. Stockholders in public firms ought to be the best monitors; indeed, a good part of the corporations course in law school is an inquiry into the relationship between managers and stockholders. The combination of these two problems—explaining secured debt and inquiring into managers and stockholders in large public corporations—led me to the hypothesis that regulation, particularly securities regulation as trumpeted by the 1930s chair of the SEC, kept stockholders from activity.

Later I shifted the emphasis to what seems the deeper cause: the historical inability of major financial institutions to own big blocks of stock and to be active in the boardroom. The role of securities regulation here is to deter coordination among fragmented stockholders; but only once ownership is greatly fragmented do securities regulation's coordination rules become important. The more profound question is why stockholding was fragmented. The principal explanations were then economic, based on the corporate need for size and the shareholders' need for liquidity and diversification. Antitrust's role in forming the hypotheses for a political theory is obvious: some antitrust rules resulted from populist goals of cutting big business down to size, of fragmenting private concentrations of power. Personal and professional obligations kept me from immediately pursuing the thesis fulltime, but by the summer of 1989 I had a working paper, "Political Origins of American Corporate Finance," parts of which were published in 1990 in the *Journal of Financial Economics* as "Political and Legal Restraints on Corporate Control" and in January 1991 in *Columbia Law Review* as "A Political Theory of American Corporate Finance." This book expands and completes that work.

---

[1] William O. Douglas, Democracy and Finance 32, 41 (1940) (collection of Douglas's 1930s speeches).

Introduction

IN 1990, two of General Motors' largest institutional shareholders, unhappy with GM's declining market share, declining employment, and declining profits during the 1980s, sought to talk to GM's leaders about how to choose the successor to the retiring CEO. GM's management rebuffed the shareholders, two of the company's largest; it could get away with that rebuff because each owned *less* than 1 percent of GM's stock.

GM's ownership structure was not inevitable. One could imagine a half-dozen shareholders, each owning 5 to 10 percent of GM's stock and sitting in GM's boardroom. For GM's managers to rebuff such powerful shareholders who expressed concern over GM's declining market share in the 1980s and its enormous losses ($7 billion lost in North American operations in 1991) would have been unimaginable. While a half-dozen individuals with the wealth to hold that big a block of stock would require that a nation have an unusual distribution of wealth, it is easier to imagine that financial institutions could have held those blocks.

GM's ownership structure, which is typical of the large American firm—fragmented shareholders with small holdings and, until recently, no voice in the governance of the large firm—might seem to be the end result of a natural economic evolution. The dominant paradigm explaining the emergence and success of the large public corporation in the United States, articulated more than half a century ago by Adolf Berle and Gardiner Means,[1] sees economies of scale and technology as producing a fragmentation of shareholding and a shift in power from shareholders to senior managers with specialized skills. Technology required firms to be so huge that their enormous capital needs could be satisfied eventually only by selling stock to many dispersed investors. Dispersion shifted power in the firm from shareholders to managers and ownership separated from control, creating an unwieldy organizational structure. But in a Darwinian evolution, the large public firm survived because it best balanced the problems of managerial control, risk-sharing, and capital needs, solving many of the problems created by the new large and unwieldy structures.

I mean here to change that paradigm. The evolution of the firm did not have to turn out as it did in the United States. I argue in Part II that economics alone cannot explain the shape at the top of the large public firm, that a political paradigm is needed to supplement or replace the economic one, because there are organizational alternatives to fragmented ownership,

[1]Adolf Berle and Gardiner Means, The Modern Corporation and Private Property (1933).

the most prominent of which is concentrated institutional voting, a pattern prevalent abroad. The politics that contributed to this evolution did not originate solely in the New Deal; rather, I argue in Part III that its origins lie deeper in the American past. At the very beginning of the twentieth century, the fragmented financial and legal structures were already in place; the New Deal confirmed them.

Engineering technologies made mass production cheaper than craft production at the end of the nineteenth century. Mass production factories had huge capital needs, requiring that the big firms eventually gather the savings of many disparate investors through securities markets, often when the largest firms were formed in industrywide mergers. But there is more than one way to move savings from households to the large enterprises that technology and economies of scale demanded. Savings could also have moved through large-scale financial intermediaries—the banks, insurers, mutual funds, and pension funds that gather people's savings and invest them. *They* could have taken big blocks of stock in the big industrial enterprises. In the United States, the securities markets moved capital from households to big industry; large intermediaries were not viable. The question is why they were not.

American politics repeatedly prevented financial intermediaries from becoming big enough to take influential big blocks of stock in the largest enterprises. Had a tradition of large-block stockholding arisen, corporate authority would differ from what it is now, because owners with big blocks of stock can influence managers. But U.S. law fragmented intermediaries, their portfolios, and their ability to coordinate among themselves, a process that began as early as the nineteenth century with the destruction of the Second Bank of the United States. Thereafter, each state created its own separate banking system, making the U.S. banking system the most unusual in the developed world. When other financial institutions arose with big-block potential—the insurers in particular, and to some extent, the mutual and pension funds— laws sometimes restricted them, too. Law isn't all of the story, but it is part of it. Law inhibited the intermediaries from operating in unison inside the same financial institution, inhibited them from forming financial alliances, and fragmented either them or their portfolios or both, often stopping them from entering the boardrooms of industry. The modern American firm had to adapt to the political terrain.

Deep-seated political forces explain these laws. Although many restraints had public-spirited backers and some rules would be those that wise regulators, unburdened by politics, would reach to deal with financial abuses, many key rules fail to fit this public-spirited mold. Politics repeatedly foreclosed alternatives, largely because of American discomfort with concentrations of private economic power. Politics sought stability in large firms, to prevent technological change from disrupting employees' lives too fast. And narrower interest groups—small-town bankers in particular—helped fragment finance so that few institutions could focus investments effectively.

By focusing on political and historical factors in this book, I do not argue that these were the only determinants of the large public firm. Although economic features are more important, I emphasize the historical and the political to redress the imbalance, not to convey the balance I think appropriate. The economic story has been set out before; the political and historical foundation of the large public firm has not yet been adequately investigated.

Institutional investors became more active in the 1990s—the inquiries to GM were only one instance of institutional activism. This activism casts doubt on the standard paradigm and makes us wonder why institutions were not active and effective long ago. Interpreted in the light of the political paradigm I offer here, institutions' new activity is the delayed result of repeated historical suppression of large institutional stockholders. Right now that activism is weak; if it expands, the history I offer here suggests that decisionmaking would then move from the economic arena into the political arena. There is no guarantee that politics' past results—fragmentation and deconcentration—will repeat, but the key point is that the ultimate decisions on how to frame American corporate governance have thus far been political as well as economic.

Moreover, it's not just that corporate governance decisions are explicitly and consciously made by politicians. It's also that when policymakers in Washington organize the American financial system they profoundly affect the structure of the large firm. True, the organization of intermediaries is too important to be guided by subtle—and debatable—improvements to the corporate boardroom (although governance should be kept in mind). Corporate governance is partly just the tail to the larger kite of the organization of savings. Political decisions about regulating financial intermediaries come to shape, sometimes unintentionally, the large public firm.

The new paradigm I offer does not produce simple prescriptions for reform, because we must see corporate governance in the large firm as deeply embedded in the organization of financial intermediaries. Changing them quickly and radically is not only hard, but risky. Vast financial reform to produce corporate governance changes of debatable benefit could have unintended, costly consequences, because intermediaries have other, more vital functions. Moreover, the alternative corporate systems only yield us *possibilities* for corporate improvement, not *certainties*. This, combined with the ease with which political decisions can have unintended effects for governing the large public firm, should make us better appreciate the value of modest, incremental reform from Washington that slowly gives firms, managers, financiers, and shareholders room to build new relationships. Still, the policy prescription here is secondary to the political story; the recommendation is only to allow a little more corporate diversity, not to push or promote profound new corporate structures. The primary story here is the academic one, to understand how we came to have the corporate structures and to understand that politics is a key determinant of corporate evolution.

Part I

THE ECONOMIC PARADIGM

CHAPTER 1

Diffuse Ownership as
Natural Economic Evolution

THE PUBLIC CORPORATION—with its distant shareholders buying and selling on the stock exchange—is the dominant form of enterprise in the United States. Why? Technology dictated large enterprises as an engineering matter. The large throughput technologies that developed at the end of the nineteenth century—doubling the diameter of the pipe quadrupled the pipe's throughput—meant that cheaper production accrued to the firm with the largest scale. Only the United States had a continent-wide economy with low internal trade barriers, providing a market to those who could achieve the technologically feasible large-scale efficiencies. But getting the tremendous outputs from the new economies of scale eventually required large capital inputs to build the facilities and distribution system. Where could that capital come from?

Some of it came from internal growth as the firm retained its earnings; some of it came from investors. But individuals, even a small group of them, lacked enough capital. Alfred Chandler describes the railroads as the first of the modern business enterprises:

> Ownership and management soon separated. The capital required to build a railroad was far more than that required to purchase a plantation, a textile mill, or even a fleet of ships. Therefore, a single ent[re]preneur, family, or small group of associates was rarely able to own a railroad. Nor could the many stockholders or their representatives manage it. The administrative tasks were too numerous, too varied, and too complex. They required special skills and training which could only be commanded by a full-time salaried manager. Only in the raising and allocating of capital, in the setting of financial policies, and in the selection of top managers did the owners or their representatives have a real say in railroad management.[1]

Even John Rockefeller in his heyday—the richest man in the country—held only a fraction of Standard Oil. New technologies allowed for vertical integration of several steps in production and distribution; transactions that once occurred across markets—making raw materials in one firm, manufacturing

---

[1] Alfred D. Chandler, Jr., The Visible Hand—the Managerial Revolution in American Business 87 (1977).

them into a final product in another, and distributing them in yet another—
were brought inside a single firm, with managers visibly coordinating the
steps of production. Managers had to avoid shortages at each stage of production and ensure a smooth flow from raw material to final sale; *management* became as important to production as marketplace trading.

Eventually these new large-scale enterprises had to draw capital from
many dispersed shareholders, who demanded diversification. Although the
early growth was financed by the firm's own earnings, eventually either the
founders passed from the scene and their heirs sold their stock into the
securities market, or large firms merged and needed a securities market to
finance the merger, or the growing firm's capital needs outstripped its ability
to finance itself from its own earnings. In any case, eventually not investors,
but salaried managers with specialized, often technological, skills took over
day-to-day control of the operations. This combination of a huge enterprise,
concentrated management, and dispersed diversified stockholders shifted
corporate control from shareholders to managers. Dispersed shareholders
and concentrated management became the quintessential characteristics of
the large American firm.

This then became the pattern for constructing America's large enterprises
in the twentieth century. Entrepreneurs would found a business, succeed,
and make the business grow. Frequently banks would lend capital. Eventually the successful firm would go public, issuing new stock (or selling the
founders' stock) to the public. For some firms, the stock market's role was to
raise new capital; for many others, its role was to provide the founders and
their heirs an exit when they wanted to diversify and cash out, often via
mergers. Although descendants sometimes took over running the firm from
the founders, more frequently hired managers did, and stock dissipated into
fragmented holdings as the heirs sold off the inheritance and the managers
raised new capital in public markets. For many other firms, the stock market's initial role was neither to raise new capital nor to directly allow for exit
when the founders diversified, but to finance the massive mergers at the end
of the nineteenth century.[2]

Although the defects of separation are today in the spotlight—without
their own money on the line, managers can pursue their own agendas, sometimes to the detriment of the enterprise[3]—separation of ownership and control was historically often functional (and still is), because it allows skilled
managers without capital to run the firm and separates unskilled descendants from control of a firm they could not run well. Sometimes successful
founders became poor managers, because their accumulated wealth allowed
them to slack off but still live well, as historically was a problem in Britain.

---

[2] Id. at 373.
[3] Adolf Berle and Gardiner Means, The Modern Corporation and Private Property (1933).

They held on to control, but failed to infuse dynamism into the enterprise, whereas in the United States, separation may have created some agency costs, but it put newer, ambitious managers in place.[4] Competitive and organizational mechanisms made the separated firms run, overall, as well as they could. Dispersed individuals would hold the stock, frequently in hundred-share lots. And "[w]hen people observe that firms are very large in relation to single investors, they observe the product of success in satisfying investors and customers."[5]

As the new class of professional managers rose to take over the American firm, in a business evolution sketched here and well-chronicled elsewhere,[6] they faced no counterweight of powerful financial institutions with big blocks of stock. That most managers did well means that the lack of a stock-holding counterweight was not, and probably still is not, a first-order economic problem. There was, for a time, a debt-holding counterweight, which returns every now and then, as lenders played some role at the top, but they disappeared when the firms' need for new capital slackened. Financial institutions tended to cede authority to senior managers.[7] Had there back then been larger, stronger national financial institutions with the financial power to take their own big blocks of stock they could have shared power with the newly emerging managers and taken stockholders' seats in the boardrooms of newly emerging large firms. Ownership would still have separated from control, because the ultimate owners would have been still distant—the engineering technologies demanded that—but the shape of authority in the firm after separation could well have differed; the distant ultimate owners could have held their interests through powerful intermediaries. Both the families that sold out and their buyers in the securities market might have preferred having the managers share power with the institutions to having most ownership become scattered and distant from the firm; truly national financial institutions might have developed more people with the skills to be a positive force inside the boardroom.

As it turned out, as a formal matter shareholders elected the board of directors, and the board appointed the CEO. But everyone knew that in the public firm the flow of power was the reverse. The CEO recommended nominees to the board. Board members were often insider-employees or other CEOs, who have had little reason to invest time and energy in second-guessing the incumbent CEO. The CEO's recommendations for the board went out to shareholders, whose small shareholding gave them little incen-

---

[4] Alfred D. Chandler, Jr., Scale and Scope: The Dynamics of Industrial Capitalism (1990).

[5] Frank H. Easterbrook and Daniel R. Fischel, The Economic Structure of Corporate Law 4 (1991), which is the leading economic analysis of the corporate law.

[6] See Chandler, supra note 1; Chandler, supra note 4.

[7] Chandler, supra note 1, at 491–92.

tive—or means—to find alternatives; they checked off the proxy card and returned it to the incumbents. The CEO dominated the election and the firm. Even today, many directors "feel they are serving at the pleasure of the CEO-Chairman."[8]

THE BERLE-MEANS ANALYSIS; ATOMIZATION

This fragmentation and shift in power were analyzed in the 1930s, in Berle and Means's *The Modern Corporation and Private Property*, which became the classic analysis of the large American firm. Berle and Means announced what came to be the dominant paradigm: "[T]he central mass of the twenti-eth century American economic revolution [is a] massive collectivization of property devoted to production, with [an] accompanying decline of individ-ual decision-making and control, [and a] massive dissociation of wealth from active management." This restructuring turns corporate law on its head: stockholders, the owners, become powerless. The "[s]tockholder [vote] is of diminishing importance as the number of shareholders in each corporation increases—diminishing in fact to negligible importance as the corporations become giants. As the number of stockholders increases, the capacity of each to express opinions is extremely limited." As a result, corporate wealth is held by shareholders as a "passive" investment, and managers control the corporation.[9]

The paradigm is not solely that shareholders and managers separate, or as Berle and Means put it, that there is a "massive dissociation of wealth from active management." The paradigm depends on atomization. Most public companies are held by many shareholders owning only small stakes. In the Berle-Means era, shareholders were mostly individuals; even today, individ-uals directly own half of all stock in U.S. companies, and even though inter-mediaries own the other half, rarely does a single intermediary own more than 1 percent of any individual stock of the nation's very large firms. Be-cause of atomization, an active shareholder cannot capture all of the gain from becoming involved, studying the enterprise, or sitting on the board of directors, thereby taking the risks of enhanced liability. Such a shareholder would incur the costs but split the gains, causing most fragmented share-holders to rationally forgo involvement. In the language of modern econom-ics, we have a collective action problem among shareholders—despite the potential gains to shareholders as a group, it's rational for each stockholder when acting alone to do nothing, because each would get only a fraction of the gain, which accrues to the firm and to all of the stockholders. This share-

[8] Jay Lorsch and Elizabeth MacIver, Pawns or Potentates: The Reality of America's Corpo-rate Boards 17 (1989).

[9] Berle and Means, supra note 3, at xix, xxv, 4–7.

holder collective action problem is then layered on top of a principal-agent problem—agents, in this case the managers, sometimes don't do the principal's, in this case the stockholder's, bidding perfectly.

ADAPTATIONS

The problems of fragmented ownership, a shift in power to the CEO, and suppression of large owners did not threaten the public firm as an organizational form because of several economic features. First, even if the structure had some bad features, its strengths were overwhelming. It facilitated economies of scale and professionalized management—advantages large enough to offset weakened incentives and weakened coordination between managers and shareholders. Managerial discretion, when it was less than absolute, was functional: for managers to build large complex organizations capable of coordinating nationwide production and distribution, they needed day-to-day discretion. The advantages from economies of scale and complex organizational capabilities dwarfed the organizational costs. When the United States had the only continent-wide economy in the world, nowhere else could economies of scale and a geographically big distribution system be attained smoothly. Since nowhere else could firms easily achieve such economies of scale, the smaller organizational costs were hidden.

Second, competition—in product markets, managerial labor markets, and capital markets—reduced the severity of occasional managerial derelictions. In the 1930s, 1940s, and 1950s, the United States was the world's only continent-wide open market, allowing several firms to reach economies of scale. Nowhere else in the world could firms reach comparable economies of scale *and* have workable competition *and* political stability. Markets abroad were closed, other nations were too small, transportation and communication costs were too high, and political upheaval was common.

In prior decades American oligopolistic competition allowed large American firms to show good returns to shareholders. Product market competition is, in the long run, a severe constraint on managers and their firms. If a manager cannot sell product, the firm will not last. Workable even if oligopolistic competition prevented serious productive lapses, while oligopolistic slack gave shareholders a cushion of extra profits.

Third, in a Darwinian evolution, the large public firm survived because it reduced the severity of its weaknesses, balancing off the problems of managerial control, risk-sharing, and capital needs. It mitigated managerial agency problems with outside directors, with a managerial headquarters of strategic planners overseeing the operating divisions, and with managerial incentive compensation. Hostile takeovers, proxy contests, and the threat of each further disciplined managers. Corporate law developed conflict of interest rules and duties of care and loyalty for corporate officers and directors; these rules deterred some managerial derelictions.

Firms with dispersed ownership survived because organizations adapted, solving enough of the governance problems of the large unwieldy structures that technology and capital needs created. No solution was complete and perfect; takeovers and proxy fights, for example, are blunt, confrontational, and costly. But each adaptation tended to help improve the firm's organizational abilities. In the conventional story, the large public firm is an efficient response to the economics of organization; and that part of the conventional story—at least when one assumes American financial laws and politics to be fixed and immutable—is surely correct.

CHAPTER 2

Fragmentation's Costs

GENERAL MOTORS lost billions in the 1980s and early 1990s, laid off tens of thousands of employees, and saw a big part of its once huge share of the American automotive market go to foreign competitors. Its managers were said to be out of touch and its board inattentive until GM lost an awesome *$7 billion* in 1991 in core North American automotive operations. Although ownership structure could not explain all of GM's problems, it might explain some of them, particularly its decade-long slowness in reacting to crisis. Could the costs of some of the problems afflicting firms with dispersed ownership have been reduced by concentrated ownership? While I'll save the inquiry into potential costs and benefits for Part V, I outline here the basic costs of organizing our large firms as we do.

The costs fall into three categories: problems with managers, problems with securities markets, and problems with organizing industry. Problems with managers are obvious. Dispersion in small holdings creates a collective action problem for shareholders, making managers less accountable in a way that can hurt performance, particularly when the firm faces unusual problems. Senior managers in the large public firm are among the least *directly* accountable in American society. While other groups also have low direct accountability—tenured faculty at solvent universities come to mind—few of them have tasks as important as those of senior managers at leading firms.

Problems with securities markets arise from the difficulty of transmitting complex, proprietary, and technological information from inside the firm to the American securities market. If scattered shareholders cannot understand complexity, and if managers cannot be rewarded for what shareholders cannot understand, firms may abandon some long-term, technologically complex projects.

Overlapping ownership—a financial institution that owns a big block in both a supplier and its customer—can sometimes improve the organization of industry. Firms, suppliers, and customers all need to coordinate their activities, and in the United States often do so in big, vertical firms. Overlapping ownership could allow them to stay separate. It could help keep firms smaller and nimbler, reducing the number of slow-moving vertically integrated behemoths. Flat organization at the top might work better when technological change quickly makes many managers' training obsolete. Psychological and sociological theories indicate that nonhierarchical forms may function better in some new industries in today's world.

My point is not that we have theory or data to prove the superiority of other organizational forms, but that there is just enough data, and just enough theory, to tantalize. Had there been a contest between organizational forms, concentrated ownership might have had enough going for it to have been *one* of the survivors. Alternative forms—such as those prevailing in Germany and Japan—seem, despite their own distinctive defects, able to do just about as well as the American forms.

UNWATCHED MANAGERS AS THE PROBLEM?

Complaints are heard that shareholders fail to monitor managers. Managers build empires and pursue bad strategies without shareholder intervention until matters are so out of hand that the ultimate outcome is the violence of the hostile takeover or the bloodshed of a fired CEO or the instability of the leveraged buyout or the waste of a bankruptcy. Many 1980s takeovers targeted firms grown too large, which the takeover entrepreneurs then broke up. In other 1980s takeovers, empire-building firms sought to extend their grasp. Either way, persistent shareholder involvement could have led to intervention before bloodshed.

It is not just that with stockholders scattered, a few managers could pursue their own agendas: building bigger empires, pursuing quieter lives, or persisting in failed strategies because they were familiar. It is also that in trying to do well, some managers did not adopt the best technologies and strategies for the future. That most managers do well is both a tribute to their being professionals and a sign of the other constraints on managers' doing badly, of the adequacy of existing structures. The question is whether different ownership structures in *some* firms could have induced even better performance.

Weak boards have historically been a debility of the large American firm. Board membership has come via invitation from the CEO, who typically invited insiders and CEOs from other firms. CEOs as directors have disadvantages: their time is constrained, they lack the financial incentive to be inquisitive, and, psychologically, they do not want the board to intrude on the CEO's authority any more than they want their own boards to intrude on their own authority. Board members are typically neither large stockholders with an independent base and interest in the firm nor representatives of large stockholders, owning, say, 5 or 10 percent of the firm, because such stockholders rarely exist in American firms.

Weak monitoring and low shareholder involvement depend partly on Berle-Means fragmentation. It's just not worthwhile for a shareholder with a small block to incur the expenses of involvement. It's easier to sit the crisis out, or sell off the stockholding. To implore an owner of $10 million of the stock of a $10 billion industrial firm to be active may do no good. Such a shareholder can capture only one-thousandth of the corporation's gain. The shareholder should rationally decline to invest $100,000 of his or her time and wealth, even if that $100,000 would yield a $100 million gain for the corporation.

The blocks must be big enough to give the shareholder both the incentive and the means for action. The large shareholder, able to capture a bigger part of the gains than can fragmented shareholders, would have a greater incentive to act. A $100 million shareholder would spend more than a $10 million blockholder, because it could capture a tenfold greater part of any gains. And incentives are not enough. Although even a $10 million stockholder has some incentive, it may lack the means to bring about change. Managers can, and often do, deflect the activist, who needs a large holding as a percentage of the firm's stock either by itself or in alliance with other large holders to get the power to be effective.

But, one must ask, since most intermediaries are themselves Berle-Means corporations, why should they not succumb to the same agency problems that affect the Berle-Means corporation? While I'll deal with this in more detail in Part V (and there's no sure answer to this), let me sketch out a few possibilities. As long as the intermediaries' debilities are not the same debilities afflicting the industrial firms in which they own stock, as long as the industrial firm's and the financial firm's weaknesses lie in different dimensions, then there might be improvements. For instance, outside auditors search for managerial fraud in a firm; at times they do succumb to temptation and become part of the fraud. But the outside auditor without daily operational involvement is independent often enough to provide a valuable although not foolproof check. Specialization among agents is a common organizational improvement for principals. A rudimentary management technique is to divide a task: one person does the job, another person checks the work; this can improve results over only assigning the job to the doer *even if* the checker is no better than the doer. She only has to catch a few of the doer's mistakes, and not reverse the doer when he does the job right. Here, I can categorize three potentially beneficial forms of monitoring: hierarchal, collegial, and crisis.

Hierarchal monitoring is specialization. Financiers specialize in getting a financial return; operating executives run firms. Both have their defects, but if we combine the two in the boardroom, but not in the same person, we could hope to reduce their defects, keep their strengths, and improve performance.

Collegial monitoring depends on directors' having the financial incentive to be involved and well informed. No financial institution *commands* the operating managers, but the two groups seek consensus. The operating managers are better informed about the firm and its business prospects; the collegial monitors from financial institutions should have a broader financial picture. Between the two, they might make better decisions at the top than either would alone. Operating managers would take the lead, but have even better financial colleagues in the boardroom than they have now.

Crisis monitoring, the third type, requires neither that the monitors manage day to day nor that they even understand the industry well; they must only be able to identify poor results and evaluate whether these results were due to poor management. If they were, the crisis monitors motivate the responsible executives, or replace them. Even if outsiders with big stock positions were usually passive, they would think about intervening earlier, when results first turn down; managers, aware of that potential, might get better results.

It would be foolish to think that institutions could *run* firms better than managers. Institutions will not be *systematically* better than operating managers, and they need not be. As long as the institutions knew to defer to operating managers, as long as they did little when results were good, they would do little harm and be ready to make a contribution when results were poor. That some institutions, like some managers, may not be savvy enough to know their limits is not a trivial problem; but ex ante we cannot tell whether institutions would systematically intrude too much to waste away whatever gains they might make.

Institutions would also not be entrepreneurial enough for many firms. But firms and monitors should sort themselves out: firms that would benefit from institutional monitoring would tend to have it; firms needing entrepreneurial leaders should tend not to be institutionally controlled.[1] The two forms would then compete.

THE DIFFICULTY OF BUILDING
LONG-TERM FINANCIAL RELATIONSHIPS:
SHORT-TERM SECURITIES MARKETS AS THE PROBLEM?

Maybe managers are not the problem, but shareholders are. Managers complain that shareholders are transients, uninterested in the firm's long-run health. Institutions' trading mentality means that when managers need steadfast investors, the traders are gone. And with small blocks the norm among institutional investors, if they discover a problem early, they have an incentive to dump the stock and run, rather than hanging in to help fix the problem. Big blocks should up the incentives for fixing the problem rather than running. Managers could better depend on the institutions' being there

---

[1] See Harold Demsetz and Kenneth Lehn, The Structure of Corporate Ownership: Causes and Consequences, 93 Journal of Political Economy 1155 (1985).

when managers needed them, which at least in the managerial rhetoric is what managers want.

Maybe there's no systemic problem with managers at all. Some succeed, some fail, and in a competitive market that's just what one would expect. But perhaps there's another problem to be remedied, a systemic defect that *undercuts* managers. Perhaps securities markets are the weak link, transmitting their debilities into operating firms, weakening them by pushing managers into simple short-run strategies, because operating managers cannot transmit proprietary, complex, and technological information well to distant, atomized shareholders. If this happens, senior managers who expect to retire in a few years and cash in their stock options by then could shun long-term investment, and industry would underinvest in research and development as well as human capital, because these investments are too difficult for distant shareholders to understand.[2]

These informational problems are highly speculative, cut against the usual belief that American securities markets are informationally efficient, and so far lack strong empirical backup. For these reasons, *mandated* change to end a speculative, unproven problem isn't sensible. But there is just enough suspicion in the business world that securities markets induce short-term behavior, and just enough plausibility to link this to the American scattered ownership structure, that there is a basis for inquiry here.

INDUSTRIAL ORGANIZATION AS THE PROBLEM?

Organizing industry is complex and subtle. When separate business firms invest in factories that relate to one another—the engine company makes auto engines for the auto assembler and the auto assembler makes auto bodies into which the engine will fit—the relationships governing these separate steps in production cannot all be written down in a perfect contract, because too many unexpected things can happen over the lifetime of the contract. To reduce the conflicts that can arise here, American industry has often brought these different steps in production into a single, vertically integrated firm.

[2] See, e.g., Louis Lowenstein, What's Wrong With Wall Street—Short-Term Gain and the Absentee Shareholder 1, 5, 9, 56–63, 76 (1988); Robert H. Hayes and William J. Abernathy, Managing Our Way to Economic Decline, Harvard Business Review, July–Aug. 1980, at 67, 68–70; Martin Lipton, Corporate Governance in the Age of Finance Corporatism, 136 University of Pennsylvania Law Review 1, 9, 23 (1987); Peter Drucker, A Crisis of Capitalism, Wall Street Journal, Sept. 30, 1986, at 32, col. 3; Judith Dobrzynski, More Than Ever, It's Management for the Short Term, Business Week, Nov. 24, 1986, at 82; Roger Altman and Melissa Brown, A Competitive Liability, Ridding Wall Street of a Short-Term Bias, N.Y. Times, June 1, 1986, § 3, at 3, col. 1 ("professional money managers [push] corporate management to focus on short-term results").

Vertical integration in a single firm has costs, sometimes creating a stultifying bureaucracy and a sluggishness in responding to market signals. Separate firms could avoid bureaucracy and be fast, but the arms'-length contract they would need to govern their relationship over a number of years could be too hard to figure out and write down. A loose ownership relationship between the supplier and customer might work better than either contract or vertical integration alone. Instead of one firm's being a division or subsidiary of the other, each would be partially owned by an overlapping group of financial institutions. Neither would be a controlled subsidiary, but there would be connections, information exchange, and, if there were disputes, a financial "escrow agent," a mediator, to settle those disputes.[3] When financial institutions cannot take big blocks and help to coordinate these relationships, the likely result seems to be more vertical integration and bigger, perhaps slower firms.

PRODUCTIVITY AND FRAGMENTATION

These three costs of fragmentation—less accountable managers, short-term securities markets, and weaker industrial organization—would show up in lost productivity in American history. A debater might observe here (correctly) that U.S. productivity is generally the highest in the world, and then urge us (mistakenly) to ignore fragmentation's costs. The debater would observe (also correctly) that American ownership is fragmented, and the voting blocks of the largest firms in Germany and Japan are not fragmented. Since the United States is generally more productive, big blocks do not induce greater productivity. So ignore them.

That kind of analysis would help us little. Improving U.S. corporate governance would still be worth pursuing if it could be done cost-effectively. Even if it is the best there is on the planet, improving it further would make Americans better off; it does not matter whether an improvement would let the United States "catch" up with, or pull further ahead of, foreign firms. Either way, the United States would be better off. Foreign successes and foreign differences alert us that there are other possibilities for corporate ownership, but a productivity gap disfavoring the United States doesn't tell us if governance produced the gap (there are too many other factors), nor does a productivity gap favoring the United States end the inquiry just because the United States is "ahead." We should not, then, be content to rest on our productive laurels, but ask whether we can improve what is basically a sound system.

[3] See infra chapter 19; Ronald J. Gilson and Mark J. Roe, Understanding the Japanese Keiretsu: Overlaps between Corporate Governance and Industrial Organization, 102 Yale Law Journal 871 (1993).

The evidence from abroad comes in two packages, one clear, one not. The clear one is that ownership structures that contrast starkly with American fragmentation can exist and survive. *None* of the fifteen largest American firms has an institution or group holding 20 percent of the firm's stock—not GM, not Exxon, not IBM. None. In Japan, *every* large firm has a financial group holding an aggregate of 20 percent of the company's stock: Toyota, Fujitsu, Mitsubishi—*every* one. Germany is more complicated, as we shall see in chapter 11, but closer to Japan than to the United States.

The differences and persistence of the different structures (and, as we'll see in chapter 14, the political origins of these ownership differences) are clear, but it's unclear whether the different corporate governance structures overall helped or hurt the foreign firms. The weaknesses that arise when lenders are major stockholders—conflicts of interest, institutions *protecting* errant managers who "buy" them off—are not trivial. Moreover, key tests of foreign governance are only now beginning. Whether those at the top of foreign firms will be *better* than U.S. boards at reacting to crisis and avoiding misspending on capital projects when the firm's franchise deteriorates is yet to be seen, because the industrial crises that hit a mature competitive economy are only now coming to afflict Germany and Japan. The early evidence—from the problems at Volkswagen, Daimler-Benz, and Metallgesellschaft—indicate that boards dominated by institutions are far from perfect. The task of seeing whether they are better—that is, institutional voice only had to cut two years off of GM's ten-year delayed reaction to crisis to have made an improvement, even an imperfect one—is still ahead.

There is another debater's point here. Governance cannot explain some shortfalls in American industry, because the United States more or less had the same corporate governance system fifty years ago, and was then the world's dominant economy. Changes in governance cannot explain the relative decline. Does the fact that the United States had the same corporate governance system decades ago, when it led in productivity by a mile, and in the 1990s, when it leads by less, mean that governance is irrelevant?

Governance is only one contributor to productivity and profitability. Until recently, American industry had two big advantages over much industry abroad: economies of scale and competitive structure. The American market was (and still is today) so large that it could support two or three firms, and hence workable competition, at the highest economies of scale in even the heaviest of industries; no other market in the world could do both. Economies of scale in a small nation meant monopoly, but competition often meant inefficient scale. American industry had both scale and competition, so if some details of organization at the top and in the boardroom were not perfect, no matter, because scale and competition were so important and might allow for profits that would hide a few defects in organization.

Thus the United States' huge lead was at least partly based on these advantages (and perhaps not on any corporate governance advantages); and these advantages of scale and competition are no longer exclusive to the United States. A common market in Europe and a globalized marketplace allow foreign firms both economies of scale and a competitive market. Competition is fiercer, and it is at least possible that competition between corporate governance systems and methods of organization are one dimension of international competition, with each system having a distinctive set of advantages and disadvantages.

COSTS AND BENEFITS

To assert that there are costs to fragmentation is neither to assert that these costs outweigh benefits nor that policymakers can eliminate those costs without creating other problems. The benefits of the Berle-Means corporation in managerial specialization, capital-raising ability, and organizational flexibility—especially in raising capital for new entry into many industries—are quite high. Those benefits may exceed any of the costs.

Moreover, managers work in several markets and social structures. The internal organization of the boardroom and its relationship with institutional shareholders is only one. Professional pride makes managers and directors try hard even if the organizational constraints acting on them are weak. The embarrassment of media attention (or fear of it) will help correct egregious errors. Product markets, capital markets, managerial labor markets, employee labor markets, and corporate takeover markets constrain managers. This is all another way of saying that corporate governance is only one dimension of competition.

The question then is whether fragmentation *sometimes* has enough costs whose elimination could pay for the costs of concentration. Had a GM board with representatives from five or six institutional owners of GM reacted strongly in 1982, instead of 1992 (when the board did react strongly), the gains might have been measured in billions of dollars, paying for more than a few institutional errors. Even if most firms are better off the way they are (and I think most probably are, and the costs of change for many would be too high), *some* firms might be better run if they had concentrated owners. Other nations have them sometimes; the United States, rarely. While our prescriptions will, when we get to Part V, not be to remake the American system, we now have several reasons to want to know why the American firm turned out as it did. First, we would like to know as a matter of academic curiosity whether it was inevitable. Second, we'd like to know if law and history played a big role. And third, if they did play a big role, then the prescriptive question becomes more urgent. That is, to say that one wastes energy from the heat of a lightbulb does not tell us much. We have a cost, but if it's a technological requirement, it's a *necessary* cost of getting light. But if we learn that we can use alternative technologies to make light, and that the choice of technologies depends on nonengineering factors (such as a nation's politics) then the possibility of avoiding waste becomes a real one.

While disadvantages would afflict heavy institutional ownership—the restrictions were reactions to conflicts of interest, financial abuses, cartelization, banking instability, politically intolerable accumulations of power—we shall hold off until Part V a fuller evaluation of whether to let organizational forms compete. Rather than prescription, we want first to understand how politics helped to determine corporate structure.

Part II

THE POLITICAL PARADIGM

CHAPTER 3

Diffuse Ownership as Political Product

AN ALTERNATIVE EVOLUTIONARY PATH
AND ANOTHER PARADIGM

The size and technology story fails to explain the fragmented ownership patterns of American corporations fully. Think about it. Fragmented securities markets are not the only way to move savings from households to the large firm. There is at least one clear contender with the securities markets, namely, the powerful financial intermediary, which would move savings from people to firms and could take big blocks of stock, sit in boardrooms, and balance power with the CEO. Enterprises could have obtained economies of scale and investors could have obtained diversification *through* large intermediaries that brought small investors and large firms together. But American law and politics deliberately diminished the power of financial institutions in general, and often their power to hold the large equity blocks, inducing the adaptations I discussed in chapter 2. The origin of the modern corporation lies in technology, economics, *and* politics.

Although individuals rarely have enough money to hold a big, influential block of stock, institutions do. The four dominant institutions are banks, insurance companies, mutual funds, and pension funds. Respectively, they hold assets of $4.9 trillion, $2.3 trillion, $1.2 trillion, and $3.4 trillion.

These four types of institutions, which hold nearly all of the corporate assets held by U.S. financial intermediaries,[1] clearly could influence big firms. But portfolio rules, antinetworking rules, and other fragmenting rules disable them from systematically having influential blocks. The following chapters show the detail, but these rules can be summarized: Banks, the institution with the most money, have been barred from owning stock or operating nationally. Mutual funds generally cannot own control blocks. Insurers can put only a fragment of their investment portfolios into any one company's stock, and for most of this century the big insurers were banned from owning any stock at all. Pension funds are less restricted, but they are fragmented; securities rules have made it hard for them to operate jointly to assert influence. Private pension funds are under management control; they are not yet ready for a palace revolution in which they would assert control over their managerial bosses.

[1] Board of Governors of the Federal Reserve System, Flow of Funds Accounts—First Quarter 1993, at 86, 92, 96, 98.

And we have just exhausted the major financial institutions in the United States; none can readily and without legal restraint control industrial companies. That is the first step of my argument: law has prohibited or raised the cost of institutional influence in industrial companies.

The second step is to examine the politics of corporate financial structure. Many legal restraints had public-spirited backers; wise regulators, unburdened by politics, would adopt some of those rules. But many key rules do not fit into this public-spirited mold, and even for those that do, wise regulators could have chosen alternatives, but politics helped lead them to choose as they did. Examining financial regulation through the lens of the public choice literature reveals a complex and new political story, of law repeatedly foreclosing alternatives to the Berle-Means corporation. We shall examine the affected groups' interests, popular ideology, and the preexisting pattern of political institutions. We shall see how American politics deliberately fragmented financial institutions so that few institutions could focus their investments into powerful inside blocks of stock. Different ways to develop corporate institutions are imaginable, but American politics cut their development paths off.

Opinion polls show a popular mistrust of large financial institutions with accumulated power, a wariness of Wall Street's controlling industrial America. Politicians responded to that distrust by restricting private accumulations of power by financial institutions. Various interest groups also benefited from fragmentation; Congress and the administrative agencies also responded to them.

An inquiry into political ideology and financial institutions follows. The ideas of opinion leaders and political actors, and the content of major political investigations, lead us to speculate on a political explanation for corporate structure: Main Street did not want to be controlled by Wall Street. Laws discouraging and prohibiting control resulted.

Do not be deceived by the regulatory micro-detail in Part III: A pattern is there. Legislative history, popular ideology, the power of interest groups, and the views of opinion leaders reveal a consistent political story—and hence one part of the foundation of the modern American corporation. Politics never allowed financial institutions to become powerful enough to control operating firms; American politics preferred Berle-Means corporations to the alternative of concentrated institutional ownership, which it precluded.

AMENDING THE ECONOMIC THEORIES

Two economic theories are relevant, agency theory and the contractarian view of the corporation. Under the first theory, the unwieldy structure of the large public firm produced agency costs, as managers, the agents of shareholders, failed to do shareholders' bidding perfectly. In the modern formulation of the problem, managers have been seen as agents of stockholders, and whenever an agent does someone else's work, there are costs: the sum of (1) bonding costs, which managers incurred in trying to "prove" to shareholders that they would do a good job, (2) monitoring costs, which shareholders incurred in trying to oversee managers to make them more faithful agents, and (3) a residual loss from the frictions when agents and principals deal, a residue that could not be eliminated.[2] In its pure and theoretical form, agency theory posited an equilibrium that minimized costs. Managers might make errors, but the cost of correcting the errors by better monitoring would be more than the loss from the errors. Those observed costs were either the residual loss, whose elimination would, again in equilibrium, cost more in offsetting bonding or monitoring costs, or the bonding or monitoring costs, whose elimination would cost more in increased residual loss.[3]

Contractarian thought, which is closely related, comes in two forms: descriptive and prescriptive. The descriptive form says corporate law in fact is a standard contract that shareholders and managers can vary at will. Behind the mystification of the corporation are contracts among shareholders, managers, and employees. State corporate law sets up standard-form contracts that most shareholders and managers want, so that the costs of contracting will be cheap. If the standard terms—describing, for example, who votes, when they vote, and on what they vote—do not suit a firm's managers and shareholders, they revise them. Contractarian thought also has a prescriptive form; its adherents (and I am not wholly excepting myself here) seek to sweep away the remaining mandated terms inconsistent with a contractarian framework, arguing that corporate law *should* be no more than a set of contracts.

Although state law roughly corresponds with the contractarian prescription, the laws governing the relationships between financial institutions and large firms do not, because American law prohibits key aggregations of stockholding, those that go through financial institutions. If law did this deliberately for political reasons, not primarily to foster financial safety or reflect the contract that the parties would want, then contract theory fails to explain the American result adequately. Only once America's financial rules are assumed as immutable (or irrelevant) would the contractarian framework come into play. But if the financial rules were really up for grabs, then other corporate contracts could have been adopted.

[2] The 1970s state of the art analysis of agency costs is Michael C. Jensen and William H. Meckling, Theory of the Firm: Managerial Behavior, Agency Costs and Ownership Structure, 3 Journal of Financial Economics 305, 308 (1976).

[3] Id. See also Symposium, Corporations and Private Property, 26 Journal of Law and Economics 237 (1983).

This political amendment of agency theory and contractarian thought should be clear. American firms may have found the right balance, *given* that some ways to adapt were barred. Or, to view the question as a matter of form rather than cost, American scholarship has focused on the agency costs of managers because of American politics. Had American financial intermediaries been organized differently, the focus would have been on the organizational problems of powerful financial intermediaries with industrial influence. Politics chose where the problems would be.

There is another contractarian argument here: markets will adjust to the restrictions. If government bans institutional ownership, firms will find organizational alternatives. There are two problems with this contractarian rebuttal. First, it fails to rebut the analytic point. If our goal is to understand why one form survived and another form did not, politics may have made the choice, even if in contractarian terms the two choices were equal. The second problem with this contractarian rebuttal is that the substitutes need not be always as good as what was banned. Thus a contractarian prediction would be only that restricting institutional blockholding and voice will lead to more of the alternatives. It cannot predict that firms, or society, will be as well off. A ban on, say, automobiles, would raise demand for trains, airplanes, and ships; it would lead people to travel less, because the substitutes would be more costly and less flexible. A contractarian adjustment will occur; the policy question is how costly the substitutes would be. Or, to use the agency cost analysis, an equilibrium among bonding, monitoring, and mismanagement losses only tells us that adjustments *under the current menu of alternatives* will not improve performance. But an expansion of the menu might lead to another equilibrium with higher productivity. In the short run (of a few decades), viewing financial rules as immutable makes sense; markets adjust faster than government does, but in the long run, if the financial substitutes are imperfect, what the rules are may matter.

We could build a political model. In a broad-based democracy, not all contracts will survive. Even some efficient contracts will be banned, if enough people dislike them. Thus if the average voter dislikes powerful private financial institutions, politics will, all else being equal, ban them. Interest groups might overcome the popular view, but often competing interest groups cancel one another out. One group wants powerful financial institutions and another, such as small-town bankers, does not. The small-town bankers have a leg up in the political infighting, because popular opinion is on their side, leading to a ban on some arrangements that a less regulated economy might produce. Or, to recast the problem in agency cost terms, managers would like to be free from the oversight that powerful financial intermediaries might provide, and in the modern era, politicians might side with managers when the managers' goals of thwarting takeovers align with a public wary of too many hostile takeovers. The politician can satisfy the managerial interest group and be popular at the same time. Agency costs move into the political arena; some contracts are banned, and whether the substitutes that arise are always perfect ones, without additional costs, is an open question.

CHAPTER 4

A Political Theory

THE FIRST STEP in the political paradigm is to show that law restricted the dominant financial institutions from the end of the nineteenth century onward. American banks were fragmented geographically, lacking the size to take big slices of capital of the large American firms emerging at the end of the nineteenth century. Banks' products and portfolios have been further restricted: they were barred from the securities business and from owning stock. Their affiliates were also restricted in the stock they could own. Insurers could not buy stock for most of this century. Mutual funds cannot easily devote their portfolios to big blocks and face legal problems if they go into the boardroom. Pensions cannot take very big blocks without legal and structural problems; the big private pensions are under managerial control, not the other way around.

The second step is to show that these rules were neither random nor economically inevitable. While public interest goals of keeping financial intermediaries prudent and stable explain some of the rules, they do not explain all of them. Two dominant themes lay behind many of the rules: American public opinion, which mistrusted private large accumulations of power, and interest group politics. There were winners in fragmenting financial institutions. These winners had a large voice in Congress, and their goals matched public opinion. For example, small banks wanted to shackle large ones and succeeded in getting and keeping branching limits, bans on banks in the securities business, bans on bank affiliates' moving outside of banking, and deposit insurance (which, by guaranteeing depositors that they will be paid if the bank fails, helps smaller, weaker banks more than it helps more solid, often bigger banks).[1] Investment bankers later sought to thwart commercial bankers' effort to enter the securities business.[2] Public interest rationales were invoked, but cannot explain the results fully. Foreign banks have so far survived without Glass-Steagall (in Germany, for example), without branching limits (in most of the world), and without American banks'

---

[1] Donald Langevoort, Statutory Obsolescence and the Judicial Process: The Revisionist Role of the Courts in Federal Banking Regulation, 85 Michigan Law Review 672, 694 (1987). Other interest groups could have been in play. See infra chapter 7.

[2] Cf. Jonathan Macey, Special Interest Group Legislation and the Judicial Function: The Dilemma of Glass-Steagall, 33 Emory Law Journal 1 (1984); Investment Co. Institute v. Camp, 401 U.S. 617 (1971); Securities Industry Ass'n v. Federal Reserve Board, 807 F.2d 1052 (1986).

deep deposit insurance (until recently, Germany and Japan had none; even now it is narrower).

The simplified political picture I shall use is of politics as the interplay between selfish economic interests and ideology on the playing field of the nation's institutions. Policy choices depend on ideology and interest group power, each of which is impeded or enhanced by existing political institutions. Federalism magnified the power of smaller, local financial institutions that did not want to compete with large, powerful financial institutions; political pressure and a wider American dislike of private economic power helped these small financial institutions maintain themselves as winners. Neither interest group power nor ideology alone appears strong enough to have fragmented ownership patterns, but together they achieved financial fragmentation.

Public choice is about politicians making decisions. Politicians advance their careers, their ideologies, their chance to win the next election by the decisions they make. Popular ideology made it easy for politicians to fragment financial institutions; if the politician believed that was the best result, the voters would impose no penalty. Interest groups also pressured politicians to fragment financial institutions. And once fragmentation became the norm, inertia and the power of interests maintained it.

Ideology is not central in public choice stories about financial rules. This is understandable, but incorrect. Ideology—the opinions of average people without a direct economic stake in the outcome—*is* often irrelevant in politics. People are confused and uninterested; those with opinions have differing, weakly held opinions that often cancel one another out. Although politicians want votes and ideologies can influence votes, when the political issue at hand evokes cross-cutting ideological preferences, confusion, and indifference, politicians can safely ignore ideology. For these reasons, the implicit public choice assumption that ideology does not count much is usually correct. But when the broad mass of people have *even a weak preference, and that preference is the same* for most people, then ideology matters. For fragmenting financial institutions, broad public preferences mattered.

I shall tell the story in this chapter abstractly, not chronologically, separately discussing each element of financial politics, and then, in Part III, we shall go through the rules and politics institution by institution, more or less chronologically. To understand why we have fragmented finance, legislative history is not enough. We must also understand why the laws once passed have remained stable, for a half-century in many cases, for a century in others. Again, ideology and interest group power help explain some of the stability. Even if populist ideology fully explains passage of a financial law, interest group power (that is, for the most part, the preferences of Main Street's small financial institutions) is necessary to explain its stability. Odd as it may at first seem, "history" occurs after passage.

Several rules are public-spirited. Surely, we want some diversification for financial institutions in which average citizens deposit their money. But even that does not eliminate the interest group explanation. If other means were found to effectuate the public interest and to allow for greater institutional influence in industry, opposition would arise. Nor does Congress always adopt and maintain public-spirited rules; we need interest group support and popular opinion to explain even the soundest of the fragmenting rules. An effort to reverse the fragmenting rules could induce the opposition of managers and financial institutions with a stake in the status quo.

Moreover, some generalizations can be made. Intermediaries' governance role is most crucial when firms need to downsize or change strategic direction in a way that will make many incumbent employees superfluous. But when these economic needs are widespread, across many firms, a political conflict becomes likely. Losers would appeal to the legislature to re-do the results, and, anticipating this, institutions have reasons to avoid the conflict.

These political and historical elements, some of which are familiar, have not yet been brought to bear on our understanding of the Berle-Means corporation. We cannot understand corporate finance through deductive economics alone; it is the result of multiple historical forces, of interest groups and populism colliding to restrict the terrain on which the corporation could evolve.

THE POLITICAL PARADIGM: IDEOLOGY

Populism

Americans prefer that no institution acquire significant power. Polls show Americans have an abiding distrust of concentrations of power, inside or outside of government.[3]

Anger at large institutions that seem to control the average person's life is one element of the story. In recent years this anger at large institutions was directed at government, particularly Washington. Earlier it was directed at financiers, particularly those on Wall Street, and big business. At the end of the nineteenth century the populist movement, which had farmers and small businesspeople at its core, gave the impetus to pass the Sherman Antitrust Act, formed its own political party, and then was co-opted by the Democratic Party. The populists reflected deep, widespread sentiments.

Some people want small institutions, even if that small size does not benefit them other than to satisfy their sense that institutional scale should be small. Obviously some populists—small-town bankers, for example—

[3] Seymour Lipset and William Schneider, The Confidence Gap: Business, Labor, and Government in the Public Mind 5–6 (revised edition 1987).

directly benefited from fragmentation. For them, their populist ideology masked self-interest.

By populism, I mean more than the 1890s agrarian political movement. I mean to refer to a widespread attitude that large institutions and accumulations of centralized economic power are inherently undesirable and should be reduced, even if concentration is productive. It is familiar to students of antitrust, and has been part of American ideology since the Jeffersonians through the populists to today, finding modern expression in public choice theories that concentrated private groups can capture government if both are allowed to be powerful. The desirability of limiting private power and government can be both a gut feeling and the conclusion of a sophisticated political theory.

Part of the political story will be familiar to many readers. But I suspect that its familiarity comes from antitrust, which has always had a large dose of politics and populism. Antitrust policy historically sought to reduce the scale of economic organization, to give small firms a comparative advantage, and to promote consumer choice and autonomy. Whether such political goals were always primary and whether they should be submerged to new economic understandings of efficiency have been debated.[4] But no one denies that historically antitrust has had a political component. Less well understood is that populism was also a basis for rules governing the range and size of financial institutions, and their influence in corporate governance.[5]

The populist image has become ingrained in our democratic tradition. In Frederick Jackson Turner's well-known "frontier thesis," American democracy was formed on the frontier. As others put it, "Democracy, in our traditions, has rich connections with the yeoman farmer, involving . . . freedom from the urban banker. . . ."[6] While later scholarship questioned just how democratic the frontier really was, the image and its role in American ideology continued. Politicians evoked similar images: William Jennings Bryan stated, in his Cross of Gold speech: "[O]n the one side stand the . . . moneyed interests, aggregated wealth and capital, imperious, arrogant, compassionless. . . . On the other side stand an unnumbered throng."[7]

---

[4] See Robert Bork, The Antitrust Paradox 15–71 (1978); Hans Thorelli, The Federal Antitrust Policy 164–232 (1954); Robert Pitofsky, The Political Content of Antitrust, 127 University of Pennsylvania Law Review 1051 (1979); Harlan Blake and William Kenneth Jones, In Defense of Antitrust, 65 Columbia Law Review 377 (1965).

[5] Several brief but important exceptions, which do see law as influencing financial structure and corporate governance, can be found in Michael C. Jensen, Eclipse of the Public Corporation, Harvard Business Review, Sept.–Oct. 1989, at 61, 65; William G. Ouchi, The M-Form Society 82, 89 (1984); Lester C. Thurow, The Zero-Sum Solution 164 (1985).

[6] Stanley Elkins and Eric McKitrick, A Meaning for Turner's Frontier, Part I: Democracy in the Old Northwest, 69 Political Science Quarterly 321, 324 (1954) (discussing Frederick Jackson Turner, The Frontier in American History [1920]).

[7] Richard Hofstadter, The Age of Reform—From Bryan to F.D.R. 65 (1955); see also Alan Dawley, Struggles for Justice—Social Responsibility and the Liberal State 60 (1991).

The 1890s populists were not alone in loathing Wall Street, which the Progressives loathed as well. Businesspeople preferred to be uncontrolled. Elites who were not associated with Wall Street feared a Wall Street that would displace their own power and status. Henry Ford's hatred of Wall Street was exaggerated but typical. Senator Robert La Follette, in a prominent speech, argued that a market for capital was needed, but centralized banking concentrations had to be opposed so that small business would have its chance. In 1911, Congress launched a widely followed investigation into the financial workings of Wall Street. The Pujo investigation, as it was called, seemed to confirm the popular judgment that the Morgan interests had their fingers everywhere in corporate America.[8]

At the core of the Progressive movement was the sense that individuals must be protected against the large institutions then forming in business and government; "the Progressive movement was the complaint of the unorganized against the consequences of organization."[9] The populist and Progressive movements, different in most respects, had in common a mistrust of the Eastern seaboard's economic capital, Wall Street. Neither the heroic yeoman farmer, cultivating the land without economic complexities, nor the self-reliant small businessperson or white-collar reformer had any use for a Wall Street stretching its tentacles out from the urban Eastern seaboard into the hinterland. An organized corporate/financial nexus exploited a divided and helpless citizenry of small farmers and businesspeople.[10] Such sentiments made it easy for politicians to pass laws to fragment the ownership interests of Wall Street.

The attitude persisted. Floor debates during the securities legislation of the 1930s show the House of Representatives applauding calls to limit the power of bankers:

> [T]he failure of many of our great industrial corporations is due to investment-banker management. [B]anker directors living remote from the properties operated have no understanding of the . . . industry they direct. . . . The deplorable situation of many of our great industrial corporations is directly due to their banker management. . . . Congress must make it unlawful for any person to act as a director . . . who shall also be [an] investment banking partner. . . .[11]

---

[8] 42 Cong. Rec., 60th Cong., 1st Sess. 3434, 3450 (1908) (remarks of Sen. La Follette); Hofstadter, supra note 7, at 81, 93 (Ford and elites); James Weinstein, The Corporate Ideal in the Liberal State: 1900–1918, 157–58 (1968); Money Trust Investigation: Hearings Before Subcomm. of the House Comm. on Banking and Currency, 62d Cong., 3d Sess. 1019–20 (1913) [Money Trust Investigation].

[9] Hofstadter, supra note 7, at 6–7, 11, 216.

[10] Id. at 20–21, 24, 65 & n.8; Martin J. Sklar, The Corporate Reconstruction of American Capitalism, 1890–1916, at 181 et seq. (1988); Robert H. Wiebe, The Search For Order 52–53 (1967).

[11] 77 Cong. Rec. 2933–34 (1933) (remarks of Rep. Marland).

The Pecora hearings of the early 1930s showed that bankers often were dominating directors of industry. Control of business wealth was concentrated in too few hands.[12]

One major historian, Richard Hofstadter, summarized these ideologies: "[T]he ordinary American's ideas of what . . . economic life ought to be like had long since taken form under the conditions of a preponderantly rural society with a broad diffusion of property and power. In that [rural] society large aggregates had played a minor role. . . ."[13] The average citizen expected to participate in both political and economic decisions.

Anchoring—a psychological term referring to people's tendency to form beliefs based on concrete experience—may have played a role.[14] Local economic groups, such as farmers, dairypeople, or local bankers, can achieve large political influence. Each member may be small and local; and although they can be politically powerful if they are organized, the popular mind disbelieves that many farmers are more powerful politically than one large bank or insurance company. The money center bank *looks* large, inhuman, inaccessible, not amenable to persuasion. It is concrete and huge; small-town bankers, despite their powerful lobbying alliance, seem relatively innocuous. Political restraints on the inhuman and inaccessible institution are therefore necessary.

"The great monopoly in this country," Woodrow Wilson said in a phrase that reverberates in financial populism, is "the money monopoly," whose control over capital had destroyed the "old variety and freedom and individual energy of development." This phrase was the opening passage of Brandeis's *Other People's Money*; it reappeared in newspaper rhetoric; members of Congress quoted it two decades later, when the reformation of financial institutions began. Although evidence indicated that by the 1920s commercial power had already shifted to managers, who by then had many sources of capital, popular belief in Wilson's attitude against a money trust apparently continued.[15]

The legislative history of the laws governing mutual funds reveals hostility to "the concentration of control of the public's money" that the mutual funds facilitated. Such control "serv[ed] no productive function[, served] merely to pervert the use of controlled companies [and was] detrimental to the public

[12] Comm. On Banking and Currency, Stock Exchange Practices, S. Rep. No. 1455, 73d Cong., 2d Sess. 385–91 (1934) [Pecora Report, in reference to its final chief counsel].

[13] Hofstadter, supra note 7, at 215; see Wiebe, supra note 10, at 52, 54–55; Elkins and McKitrick, supra note 6, at 321.

[14] See Judgment under Uncertainty: Heuristics and Biases (Daniel Kahneman, Paul Slovic and Amos Tversky eds. 1982).

[15] Dawley, supra note 7, at 141; Ellis Hawley, The New Deal and the Problem of Monopoly 304–05 (1966) (quoting Wilson); 77 Cong. Rec. 2929 (1933) (remarks of Rep. Pettengill); id. at 2932 (remarks of Rep. Marland).

welfare."[16] The SEC's statement of purpose "declared that the national public interest . . . is adversely affected . . . when investment companies [attain] great size."[17]

Nor should this populist opinion be thought of as a solely historical phenomenon. During the 1955 bank holding company hearings, witnesses and senators discussed concentration of economic power as a justification for regulation.[18] A decade later, the Patman Report began by reciting the Wilson money monopoly quotation and warned that banks, through their trust fund investments, have an "enormous potential power, for good or evil, over important parts of the nation's corporate structure."[19]

In the 1960s, the SEC staff cited classical antitrust rhetoric against size when attacking mutual fund control of portfolio companies: "It is possible, because of its indirect social or moral effect, to prefer a system of small producers . . . to one in which the great mass of those engaged must accept the direction of a few. [G]reat industrial consolidations are inherently undesirable, regardless of their economic results."[20] Antitrust was partly founded on the presumption that big is bad, that there is a curse in bigness in business; the antiinstitutional impulse is similar. In the 1980s, the chair of the Senate's Banking Committee, Senator William Proxmire, in a comment that could have been populist, public-regarding, reflective of the power of small bankers, or some combination of all three, said: "The genius of American banking is competition. And the more competition, the better. You look at every other major country, and they only have a handful of banks that account for most of the business."[21] Populist sentiment helped fuel the antitakeover legislation at the end of the 1980s; managers are the happy beneficiaries of a public opinion that helps insulate them from takeovers.[22]

[16] Pecora Report, supra note 12, at 339, 363, 394.

[17] Hearings on S. 3580 Before a Subcomm. of the Senate Comm. on Banking and Currency, 76th Cong., 3d Sess. 434, 500–01 (1940) [1940 Act Hearings].

[18] Control of Bank Holding Companies: Hearings Before a Subcomm. of the Senate Comm. on Banking and Currency, 84th Cong., 1st Sess. 98 (1955) [Senate Bank Holding Company Hearings] (statement of Ray Gidney, Comptroller of the Currency); id. (comments of Sen. Douglas).

[19] 1 Staff of House Subcomm. on Domestic Finance, Comm. on Banking and Currency, 90th Cong., 2d Sess., Commercial Banks and Their Trust Activities: Emerging Influence on the American Economy iv, 3, 9 (Comm. Print 1968) [Patman Report, in reference to subcommittee's chairman].

[20] Guy Maseritz, The Investment Company: A Study of Influence and Control in the Major Industrial Corporations, 11 Boston College Industry and Commerce Law Review 1, 15 (1969) (quoting United States v. Aluminum Co. of America, 148 F.2d 416, 427–28 [2d Cir. 1945]).

[21] Bartlett Naylor, Proxmire to Seek Bank Size Limits, American Banker, Dec. 10, 1986, at 1.

[22] See infra chapter 10.

Political Investigations: Pujo and Pecora

The congressional investigations of financial institutions and the thought of several opinion leaders show an ideology that ebbs and flows but has always been part of the American scene.

In 1912, Congress's eight-month Pujo investigation (named after the head of the congressional committee) of Wall Street was said to have "frightened the nation with its awesome, if inconclusive statistics on the power of Wall Street over the nation's economy. . . . [T]he nation was suitably frightened into realizing that reform of the banking system was urgent—presumably to bring Wall Street under control."[23] Counsel to the committee attacked J. P. Morgan for his bank's representation on corporate boards and for its hand in selecting managers.[24]

The New Deal began with a seventeen-month investigation of Wall Street practices. The bankers' defensive tone was set early. The next-generation J. P. Morgan testified: "I consider the private banker a national asset *and not a national danger.* [Despite accusations to the contrary, the Wall Street banker has not] become too powerful."[25] But Ferdinand Pecora, counsel to the Senate Banking Committee for the hearings, better reflected the national mood: "[T]he terrific concentration of power in [bankers'] hands from many sources [*was*] *threatening.* . . . The bankers were neither [just] a national asset nor [just] a national danger—*they were both.*"[26] Investment bankers' control over industrial companies was again denounced; representation of banking interests on the boards of industrial companies perniciously magnified banker power.[27]

The Pecora hearings were a conduit through which American populist sentiment could punish Wall Street, presumably with such legislation as the Glass-Steagall Act and the Investment Company Act of 1940:

> The financial skullduggery so often translated to rural voters by Bryan and the Populists as "Wall Street's grip on the farmer" impelled many demands for punitive measures by Congressmen from agrarian districts. Western and southern Representatives were particularly insistent after the Pecora revelations that the transgressors be dealt with harshly.[28]

[23] Gabriel Kolko, The Triumph of Conservatism 220 (1963).

[24] Money Trust Investigation, supra note 8, at 1019–20.

[25] Stock Exchange Practices: Hearings Before the Senate Comm. on Banking and Currency, 73d Cong., 1st Sess. 5–6 (1934) (emphasis added).

[26] Id. at 6 (emphasis added).

[27] Id. at 3836 (testimony of Harley Clarke, Chase Securities Corp.); Pecora Report, supra note 12, at 37, 59, 208.

[28] Ralph F. DeBedts, The New Deal's SEC—The Formative Years 196 (1964).

IDEOLOGICAL LEADERS AND
A CONCEPTUAL FRAMEWORK FOR POLITICAL RESTRAINTS:
BRANDEIS, WILSON, AND DOUGLAS

The Pujo investigators said early in the twentieth century that a Wall Street money trust dominated industrial America. Louis Brandeis then picked through their data to quickly publish popular magazine articles and a book that provided both an ideology and a plan for action; his rhetoric was still being invoked twenty years later during the New Deal.[29] He wrote: "The dominant element in our financial oligarchy is the investment banker. Associated banks, trust companies and life insurance companies are his tools." Return bankers to their proper role as middlemen and eliminate the interlocking of financial institutions; that would end the evils of the oligarchy.[30] Pujo's money trust investigation induced Citibank's predecessor to abandon its fledgling interstate bank holding company network. Historians say that the bankers' desire to avoid more criticism (and presumably regulation) was a reason why they reduced their governance role even without formal regulation.[31]

Woodrow Wilson believed that small groups of people in large firms made autocratic decisions, concentrating in their own hands the "resources, the choices, the opportunities, in brief, the power of thousands."[32] A balance had to be struck. Not all big business was bad, but the trusts were: "I am for big business," said Wilson, "and I am against the trusts," which were combining and growing in size and power. Behind the trusts were the investment bankers, who could or would organize a "combination of the combinations," which might act covertly and, because of their "community of interest," become "more formidable than any conceivable single combination that dare appear in the open." Such a combination of combinations could buy up the

[29] Vincent Carosso, The Morgans—Private International Bankers 1854–1913, 639–40 (1987); Pecora Report, supra note 12, at 39 (favorable senatorial thoughts about *Other People's Money* during the Pecora hearings); see generally Thomas K. McCraw, Prophets of Regulations 80–114 (1984) (detailed inquiry into Brandeis's ideology and notation that phrase "other people's money" appears in FDR's 1933 message to Congress); Richard P. Adelstein, "Islands of Conscious Power": Louis D. Brandeis and the Modern Corporation, 63 Business History Review 614 (1989).

[30] Louis Brandeis, Other People's Money—And How the Bankers Use It 3, 5, 47 (1914).

[31] George David Smith and Richard Sylla, The Transformation of Financial Capitalism: An Essay on the History of American Capital Markets, 2 Financial Markets, Institutions and Instruments 1, 27 (1993); Harold Cleveland and Thomas F. Huertas, Citibank, 1812–1970, at 66–67 (1985).

[32] Woodrow Wilson, The Lawyer and the Community, 192 North American Review 612, 617–18 (1910); see also William Diamond, The Economic Thought of Woodrow Wilson 67 (1943) (financiers, argued Wilson, controlled railroads and industry to the detriment of the nation).

political process, ending democracy. "If there are men in this country big enough to own the government of the United States, they are going to own it."[33] Since investment bankers could organize the truly dangerous combination that could subvert democracy, the conclusion was inexorable—democracy must strike first and end banker domination of the trusts. The idea of a preemptive strike was echoed by Brandeis: "We must," he said, "break the money trust or the money trust will break us."[34]

Several decades later, key actors had similar views. William O. Douglas had a pivotal role in the regulation of financial institutions, as commissioner and chair of the SEC in the 1930s. During his days as commissioner, the SEC proposed the Investment Company Act and formulated rules limiting joint action.

Reflecting the concepts and prejudices of many during the New Deal, Douglas *wanted* to destroy any Wall Street control of Main Street, asserting that the investment and commercial bankers would and should be confined to selling securities and superseded as an influence in management. Banker power in "formulat[ing] industrial policies," said Douglas, "will pass into other hands." Why? "Remote control by an inside few of these fundamental economic and human matters is fatal. There can be in our form of corporate and industrial organization no royalism which can long dictate or control these basic matters," he said. The power of Wall Street must be held at bay: "[F]inance moves into the zone of exploitation whenever it becomes the *master* rather than the faithful and loyal *servant* of investors and business. To make finance such a *servant* rather than a *master* becomes a central plank in any platform for reform."[35] Investigators of the 1930s SEC concluded that the SEC, "[i]nstead of wreaking vengeance [for a discredited securities market], set out to restore legitimacy to Wall Street's *essential* function of channeling investment capital into enterprise."[36]

Moreover, Douglas thought that people who dominate financial markets have "tremendous power. . . . Such [people] become virtual governments in the power at their disposal. [Sometimes it is] the dut[y] of government to police them, at times to break them up, to deter their further growth. . . . "The needs of a small Middle Western community are apt to be better served by a banker at the head of a small local bank than by the same banker at the head of the nation's biggest bank."[37]

[33] Woodrow Wilson, The New Freedom 187, 286 (1913); Dawley, supra note 7, at 145.

[34] Brandeis, supra note 30, at 137.

[35] William O. Douglas, Democracy and Finance 21, 41, 44 (1940) (emphasis added).

[36] Thomas K. McCraw, The Public and Private Spheres in Historical Perspective, in Public-Private Partnership 31, 81–82 (Harvey Brooks, Lance Liebman, and Corinne Schelling eds. 1984) (emphasis added).

[37] Douglas, supra note 35, at 11, 14, 15. Senator Carter Glass had similar thoughts. Bank involvement in securities diverted funds away from local businesses in need of credit. Langevoort, supra note 1, at 694.

In short, bankers should provide and direct the flow of capital, but not control the enterprise after the capital has flowed to it.[38] Douglas was not alone in this view among the key players at the 1930s' SEC; its first chair, Joseph Kennedy—like Douglas, a man who thought he should be president—agreed.[39] And this view is not just historical. In 1980, the Senate Government Affairs Committee staff examined corporate ownership and reported that "Congress [has been] concerned that the tremendous growth in securities held . . . by the larger banks, insurance companies, pension funds, and investment advisors might result in a concentration of economic power by a few institutional traders . . . *over the managements of the companies whose stock they held, and indeed over American industry itself.*"[40]

IDEOLOGY: PUBLIC-REGARDING GOALS

Neither populist ideology nor interest group power explains everything: fragmentation had public-regarding justifications; that is, there were good reasons to believe it would be good for American society. The first key point here is that law helped determine corporate structure. The next step is to note that popular opinion made it easy for politicians to fragment financial institutions, regardless of whether politicians' actions were public-regarding or due to interest group pressures.

What were the public-regarding rationales? Certainly some of the ideological goals—protecting democracy from the potential of governing plutocracy—were public-regarding. Other public-regarding goals were more technical.

Protecting Depositors, Policyholders and Mutual Fund Shareholders

In the nineteenth century, some states found the mixture of banking and commerce too risky for their banks.[41] Similarly, bank affiliates' speculative stock activities, said Senator Glass, had led to "unprecedented disaster

---

[38] Douglas, supra note 35, at 44–45.

[39] Joseph Kennedy, Big Business, What Now? Saturday Evening Post, Jan. 16, 1937, at 10, 11; Vincent Carosso, Washington and Wall Street: The New Deal and Investment Bankers, 1933–1940, 44 Business History Review 425, 444–45 (1970).

[40] Staff of Senate Comm. on Governmental Affairs, 96th Cong., 2d Sess., Structure of Corporate Concentration: Institutional Shareholders and Interlocking Directorates among Major U.S. Corporations 2 (Comm. Print 1980) (emphasis added).

[41] Bray Hammond, Banks and Politics in America from the Revolution to the Civil War 149–55 (1957); Edward L. Symons and James J. White, Teaching Materials on Banking Law 8–11, 33–34 (2d ed. 1984).

which has caused this almost incurable depression."[42] After 1933, a bank failure drained the government's insurance fund, which guarantees repayment to depositors even if the bank runs out of money. Keeping banks out of risky assets such as common stocks seemed to reduce the chance of bank failure. Similar considerations of policyholder protection and ease of government supervision justified limiting insurance company investment in stocks.

As for mutual funds, Congress feared that unsophisticated investors would invest in them expecting diversification, but be unable to evaluate the portfolio. The SEC testified that a mutual fund's *only* positive function was to sell diversification; any extension risked thievery.[43] Keeping mutual fund managers out of controlling positions kept them free of conflicts of interest. A mutual fund's investment adviser, which made the actual decisions of where to invest the fund's assets, was often an investment bank, which it was feared would use the mutual fund to control a firm and force that controlled firm to give the investment bank its securities-underwriting business.[44]

Conflicts of Interest; Tying

Eliminating conflicts of interest was another public-spirited basis for fragmentation. Banks with nonbanking affiliates would be difficult to examine, and money-losing assets could be shunted between bank and operating company.[45] Banks that owned industrial firms might tie their loans to purchases of stock from the industrial company, as sometimes occurs in Germany, where banks own stock and often expect their portfolio firms to be borrowers. Such economic dictates had to be stopped. And since prohibiting the practice might not stop implicit understandings, bank ownership of the firm had to end.[46] Reducing such conflicts is not wrong-headed; it's not a

[42]S. Rep. No. 77, 73d Cong., 1st Sess. 1, 8–12 (1933); 75 cong. Rec. 9904–06 (1932) (remarks of Sen. Walcott); id. at 9910–11 (remarks of Sen. Bulkley); id. at 9882–89, 9915 (remarks of Sen. Glass).

[43] 1940 Act Hearings, supra note 17, at 131, 132 (statement of George Mathews, Commissioner of the SEC), 807 (reiteration by David Schenker, Chief Counsel, SEC Investment Trust Study).

[44] Pecora Report, supra note 12, at 333; 1940 Act Hearings, supra note 17, at 36, 206, 207 (statement of I.M.C. Smith, Associate Counsel, SEC Investment Trust Study).

[45] Senate Bank Holding Company Hearings, supra note 18, at 360.

[46] Id. at 64 (testimony of J. L. Robertson, Governor of the Federal Reserve Board), 66 (comments of Sen. Douglas) ("if there are not alternative sources of credit the [bank] could use [its] control of credit to get control over manufacturing, too"), 106 (statement of W. J. Bryan, Independent Bankers Ass'n of America) ("What chance does free enterprise have if people with ideas and ability cannot obtain capital with which to implement them?").

The Assistant Attorney General for Antitrust argued that restricting banks' nonbanking affiliations was necessary because banks had local monopolies (due to the government's chartering

selfish or narrow-minded goal. But conflicts arise in other settings, for example, when corporate officers deal with their company. Modern law moved away from banning the relationship (of corporate officers that had such conflicts); abuses are resolved in case-by-case lawsuits. Politics needs more than a conflict of interest to prohibit a conflicted relationship across-the-board; for financial institutional conflicts, populism and interest group power provided that something more. And as we shall see in later chapters, when managers benefited from financial conflicts—particularly in the construction of private pension plans—there was little political energy to control those conflicts. Politics meant that financial conflicts merited prohibition; managerial conflicts did not.

The point here is not to argue naively that financial intermediaries have always been paragons of virtue, afflicted by misguided regulators. Rather, the point is that it's at least plausible that those who aspired to control financial abuses could have used other means, such as disclosure, case-by-case attack, and prohibition of dangerous transactions between the intermediary and the firm, instead of a ban on large ownership itself. Given the anti-finance rhetoric, it's plausible that part of the reason well-meaning regulators often opted for across-the-board bans went beyond the severity of the financial abuses, but depended on the political rhetoric they heard in the background.

Big banks might deny loans to small business because the big banks and big business would link up. A policy of fragmenting banks for this reason resembles antitrust's classical hostility to vertical restraints, such as a supplier's restraining how a customer could re-sell the good. At first, antitrust authorities saw few benefits, so they condemned the restraints as foreclosing market entry or threatening autonomy. Later, the restraints were seen as more complicated, because efficiency explained some of them. Rules that ban links between finance and industry resemble antitrust's hostility to vertical restraints. The authorities see little chance of good coming out of them and some risks, so lawmakers ban the relationship.

Antitrust

The policy reason for separating finance from industry could have been that the best way to open the bottlenecks in the financing of new ventures was to

---

restrictions) that would expand when affiliates entered nonbanking markets. With vast financial resources banks could "become the centers of much larger industrial-commercial groups, [as they are in] Japan and other countries." Bank Holding Company Act Amendments: Hearings Before the House Comm. on Banking and Currency, 91st Cong., 1st Sess. 91, 93 (1969) (testimony of Richard McLaren, Esq., Assistant Attorney-General for Antitrust). Accordingly, their nonbanking activities had to be restricted.

stop the few investment bankers that controlled the spigots of finance and coordinated industrial cartels that raised to monopoly levels the prices that consumers paid. The market access problems could have been solved with other mechanisms, for example, by banning financial ties not with *all* industry but just with *concentrated* industry. But the objection that concentrated finance blocked access to financing, when combined with the preexisting animus against financial institutions, could have been powerful.

Historical evidence suggests that capital sources were concentrated at the turn of the century;[47] thereafter they dissipated, partly because of the natural competition that arises to upset a monopoly and partly because of the regulation discussed above. We can view antitrust, labor protection, and financial fragmentation as part of one large movement in American society to tame capital: industrial monopolies would be shattered through antitrust; cartelization by banker coordination would be stymied through bans on interlocking directors; the range of profitable actions of capital would be limited through labor law; and the ties between those who gather capital and those who use capital in industry would be frayed through financial regulation.

Political Stability

Savvy social engineers had a strategic rationale for fragmenting finance. The social turmoil induced by pitting populist antibank sentiment against financial institutions that owned industry could have been too much for American politics to handle. By fragmenting finance, politicians moved issues of public ownership and class divisions off the political agenda. FDR himself said:

> It is time to . . . reverse [the] concentration of power which has made most American citizens, once traditionally independent owners of their own businesses, helplessly dependent for their daily bread upon the favor of a very few, *who by devices such as holding companies*, have taken for themselves unwarranted economic power. I am against private socialism of concentrated economic power as thoroughly as I am against government socialism. The one is equally as dangerous as the other; *and destruction of private socialism is utterly essential to avoid government socialism.*[48]

A prominent historical view is that at crucial times in American history business interests became so powerful that a political counterweight had to arise. Before business could crush others in the economy, politicians saved

---

[47] J. Bradford De Long, Did J. P. Morgan's Men Add Value?—An Economist's Perspective on Financial Capitalism, in Inside the Business Enterprise: Historical Perspectives on the Use of Information 205, 207 (Peter Temin ed., 1991).

[48] Quoted in Hawley, supra note 15, at 281 (emphasis added).

the nation from injustice by checking the business interests. The genius of American politics, in this view, was that business interests were checked, but not destroyed. Arthur Schlesinger's work stands at the center of this perspective. First, it is said, Andrew Jackson rose to destroy the Second Bank of the United States, checking the crushing weight of eastern finance on the average American.[49] Then Woodrow Wilson created the Federal Reserve System, taking power away from Morgan, whose bank had become the nation's de facto central bank.[50] And then in the Great Depression, Franklin Roosevelt built an administrative structure as a counterweight to financial interests that were said to have brought on the Depression.[51] (While later historical interpretations have questioned the business-versus-the-people view—often rival business interests were on both sides of the battle—this historical view, if updated and amended, still tells something about the country's past.)

These views seem at odds with one another. In one, politicians are populists or puppets of interest groups; in the other, politicians are heroes saving the United States from powerful business interests. These two views can be reconciled for our purposes. In the social justice vision, right-hearted politicians save farmers and workers from the onslaught of capital. In the other vision, cynical politicians check capital to benefit favored groups, such as small-town bankers. The *factual* story for each historical vision is roughly similar. It's the spin, the connotation, the sense of rightness that are at odds.

Leading politicians believed they were fighting for the country's soul against a Wall Street conspiracy. Said FDR:

> The real truth . . . is, as you and I know, that a financial element in the larger centers has owned the Government ever since the days of Andrew Jackson— and I am not wholly excepting the administration of W[oodrow] W[ilson]. The country is going through a repetition of Jackson's fight with the Bank of the United States—*only on a far bigger and broader basis.*[52]

In the 1936 campaign, about when the tax code that first prevented mutual funds from exercising corporate control was passed, Roosevelt denounced "economic royalists" who gathered "other people's money"—that phrase again—to impose a "new industrial dictatorship." Roosevelt closed the campaign with a powerful emotional speech: "[O]rganized money . . . hate[s] me. . . . I should like to have it said of my first Administration that [the forces

---

[49] Arthur Schlesinger, Jr., The Age of Jackson 97–114, 334–39, 505 (1945). But see Hammond, supra note 41.

[50] Arthur Stanley Link, Woodrow Wilson and the Progressive Era, 1900–1917 (1954).

[51] Arthur Schlesinger, Jr., The Crisis of the Old Order, 1919–1933 (1957); id., The Coming of the New Deal (1959).

[52] Quoted in William E. Leuchtenburg, Franklin D. Roosevelt and the New Deal 80, 160 (1963) (emphasis added).

of organized money] met their match. . . . [And] I should like to have it said of my second Administration that in it these forces met their master."[53]

Thus one can see the historical bargain between the polity and financial institutions as this: unleashed capital that might create a disciplined firm had to have a political counterweight. Either government would ultimately own the firm or there would be public controls on the firm. Relations with workers, customers, and competitors would be regulated. The American choice was to reject intense regulation, and instead to fragment the market.[54] There is a pattern here in American corporate and financial history: to prefer, at least in the rhetoric of antitrust, industrial monopolies of local producers to large central producers, such as Standard Oil or Alcoa; to prefer a series of local banking monopolies to concentrated banking; and to prefer to deny power over industrial operations to financiers and leave that power in the hands of scattered managers.

Fragmentation of finance can thus be seen not as a stray piece of history but as a necessary part of American government and society. Fragmentation may go hand in hand with weak regulation elsewhere in the American economy, which tends to be less regulated and rigid than it could have been; certainly the American economy is a less regulated economy than the economies of other industrialized nations, such as Germany and Japan. Regulation can take multiple forms. It can dictate the details of what can and cannot be done in the workplace under a labor regulation or a union rule. It can specify general governance mechanisms, such as German codetermination, in which employee directors sit on the supervisory board right next to the bankers who vote a large part of the firm's stock. It can operate through informal understandings, such as those in large Japanese firms, in which financial institutions have influence but powerful norms have in recent decades thus far required lifetime employment for employees. Whether or not these arrangements—fragmented finance and weak employee protection, or strong finance and strong employee protection—*must be* package deals we need not decide; suffice it to say that key actors—none could have been more key in the 1930s than FDR—said they were necessary protections for the stability of American politics.

Once again, I emphasize that I am not in this part arguing that the American fragmentation result is necessarily wrong-headed; my point is that through politics the United States chose to fragment financial institutions. That fragmentation induced, partly unintentionally, a shift in operating power from financial institutions to the managers of the largest corporations. Other countries chose (or accidentally evolved) to have power shared in the boardroom or to have severe restrictions on the range of acceptable

---

[53] Quoted in id. at 183–84.
[54] Cf. Blake and Jones, supra note 4 (similar theme applied to antitrust).

actions by managers. The essential point is that the Berle-Means corporation is in important part a product of American politics, not just economic necessity.

THE POLITICAL PARADIGM:
INTEREST GROUPS

I first sketched populist antibank sentiment for a reason. It is the backdrop to the interest group pressures for fragmentation. Popular opinion alone might not have been strong enough to pass and preserve fragmenting rules, but policymakers could see that fragmentation would foster plausibly public-spirited goals, and at the same time interest groups could press their private advantage. A politician who sought fragmentation, whether to implement public goals or to deliver to an interest group, would not meet public resistance.[55]

Interest group pressures were critical. Small banks wanted to fragment large money center institutions. Small businesses also wanted fragmentation, believing that small banks served them better than did money center banks. Popular theory in the 1930s had it that bank involvement in stock channeled credit away from small business: "If any special interest group was instrumental in [passage of the Glass-Steagall separation of commercial and investment banking] it was probably the smaller businesses and farmers (not surprisingly, [Senator] Glass' Virginia constituents) who considered the unavailability of credit at least partially responsible for their [Depression] woes."[56] These groups have had great weight in the Senate and in congressional committees.

Modern eyes search for managers and labor behind the passage of fragmenting legislation, as they can be found behind modern antitakeover legislation. While we see them here and there, I do not think they played a critical role in *passing* fragmenting financial rules. True, their interest is clear: managers do not want a financial boss. Managers forced to go to Wall Street for equity could be expected to prefer not to have institutional overseers. Sociologists say local business elites deeply resented their relative loss of economic power and status to outsiders.[57] New Deal legislation as a combination of attacks on Wall Street and pressures of organized industry is the picture one leading historian paints of the era.[58]

Perhaps historians will one day find plausible loose 1930s support for

---

[55] See Arthur T. Denzau and Michael C. Munger, Legislators and Interest Groups: How Unorganized Interests Get Represented, 80 American Political Science Review 89 (1986).

[56] Langevoort, supra note 1, at 697.

[57] Seymour Martin Lipset and Reinhard Bendix, Social Status and Social Structure, 2 British Journal of Sociology 233 (1951).

[58] Hawley, supra note 15, at 16.

fragmentation from managers, local controlling stockholders who wanted to get equity capital without losing control to Wall Street, and labor, although no evidence of such a grouping now seems convincing. But whether or not such a coalition *produced* fragmentation—and there is little evidence that it did—once the fragmenting laws passed, the *subsequent* stability of fragmentation probably has been due to managers as an interest group.

Decades after passage of the fragmenting legislation, managers would throw their weight in the way of change. When large financial institutions clashed with managers, managers called upon politicians for aid, as they did when proxy contests heated up in the 1950s and 1960s.[59] Once they got Senator Sparkman to bully mutual funds into supporting incumbent management in a proxy fight. Managers appealed to politicians to raise the costs of proxy contests during the 1950s fights, whereupon the Senate held hearings, politicians sympathized with some managers' complaints,[60] and ultimately the SEC promulgated rules that pulled informal joint discussions among institutions into the proxy ambit. In the 1980s, managers, sometimes allied with labor, were the moving force behind many antitakeover statutes.[61] And when the SEC proposed a mild rollback of these proxy rules in the 1990s, the Business Roundtable, a lobbying arm of managers, attacked this effort.

A similar process can apply to financial intermediaries. The Glass-Steagall Act, by separating investment from commercial banking *might* have been sought by either type of bank to prevent competition between them. It could also have been passed as an aspiration to stabilize finance, or to punish banks thought to have hurt the economy. Still, even if the market division motivations had little influence on passing the law, intermediaries that had not sought the rule have later tried to thwart repeal and rollback, because they benefited from the rule. Investment bankers lobbied to slow the erosion of Glass-Steagall's ban on commercial bank involvement in securities underwriting. Even if bank market division does not explain the *passage* of the legislation, interest politics contributed to its *preservation*.

One might also suppose that labor played a role in the passage of some fragmenting laws, as it did in the passage of some modern antitakeover laws. As news reports said when one takeover law was under consideration:

---

[59] Forbes, Mar. 15, 1967, at 25; The Senators, the Funds, and the Law, Fortune, May 1967, at 152, 153; Wall Street Journal, Jan. 19, 1967, at 3, cols. 2–3.

[60] John Pound, Proxy Voting and the SEC: Investor Protection versus Market Efficiency, 29 Journal of Financial Economics 241, 263 (1991); The Raiders—Challenge to Management, Time, July 25, 1955; Tris Coffin, Proxy Warfare May Provoke Tighter Government Rules, Nation's Business, July 1955, at 32; Edwin F. Dakin, Battle by Proxy—Henceforth New Ground Rules Will Govern These Contests, Barron's Feb. 20, 1956, at 5 ("stormy fights in the past two years [and] bruised contestants [have provoked a] Senate inquiry"); Stock Market Study (Corporate Proxy Contests): Hearings on S.879 Before the Senate Comm. on Banking and Currency, 84th Cong., 1st Sess. (1955).

[61] See infra chapter 10.

"[B]usiness groups supporting the bill *are aligned with unions seeking to protect . . . their members* and local politicians worried about the impact of corporate takeovers on communities."[62] But for labor also, the modern interest group story is present but weak at the original fragmentation. First, how does labor benefit from weakening the ties that bind managers to shareholders? Once workers are inside the system, once they have something akin to tenure, their interest, like that of managers, is *also* to loosen managers' ties to capital. Capital could seek profits by getting highly motivated managers who sweat the labor force. When law creates gaps in the responsiveness of managers to capital, then managers have less incentive to squeeze every penny of production out of labor.

Labor's principal representative in the 1930s Senate made that point: "In order that the strong may not take advantage of the weak," said Senator Robert Wagner, "every group must be equally strong."[63] Since finance was strong and labor weak, law must fragment finance (via Glass-Steagall and the 1940 Act) and strengthen labor (via collective bargaining). Labor's representatives sought institutional financial fragmentation, although their role seems smaller then than it has been for modern antitakeover laws.[64]

One can see a larger historical sweep here. Once a group has a benefit, whether gained by the group's own effort or gained without their own effort but incidental to the operation of other forces, the group subsequently uses politics to maintain and extend that position. Thus one could expect managers and labor to want to loosen the disciplinary restraints that capital would impose upon them. Or, more subtly and more realistically, laws that would loosen the control that capital would have on managers and labor have survival properties. Even if other forces explain the laws' passage, their repeal would be unpopular, and would lose politicians votes. Those laws are stable, shielding managers and workers from the raw and unpleasant consequences of an unrestrained market.

Small businesspeople, like managers, are politically influential. They have money and status and are spread among the states; dispersion with local power makes Congress responsive to their needs. Wall Street is geographically concentrated, less likely to have the ear of many members of Congress. A well-known analogue is the power of savings and loan associations and the real estate lobby; they obtained favorable laws for decades.

Small business representatives wanted to limit bank holding company control of business. The National Federation of Independent Business (one hundred thousand small and medium businesses) wished to "compel bank

---

[62] Leslie Wayne, Pennsylvania Lends Force to Antitakeover Trend, N.Y. Times, Apr. 19, 1990, at A1, col. 3 (emphasis added).

[63] Cf. Leuchtenburg, supra note 52, at 89, 109.

[64] 86 Cong. Rec. 1478 (1940) (remarks of Sen. Wagner); 1940 Act Hearings, supra note 17, at 333–37 (comments of Sen. Wagner).

holding companies to get rid of nonbanking interests," believing that "independent business prospers best when sources of financing are free, independent, local and many."[65] Retailers told the Senate: "Bank holding companies, operated out of New York, cannot possibly know local conditions similar to the hometown independent banker."[66] Small bankers opposed allowing bank holding companies to control industry; the Independent Bankers Association lobbied hard for limits on bank control of industry and even harder for limiting bank holding company expansion. Holding companies said the independent bankers were only fighting to keep their own local monopolies by destroying the holding companies.[67]

This interest group effect need not always reflect *conflict* between *operating* managers and *financial* managers. Some financial managers might have been happy to accept limits, because monitoring is hard work and laws that preclude them all from the task could make their job easier. Once laws that block intermediaries from owning influential blocks of stock are in place, the regulated themselves could resist a rollback, because deregulation would allow competition on bases for which the incumbents lack an advantage.

THE POLITICAL STORY:
THE PREEXISTING INSTITUTIONS OF FEDERALISM,
CONGRESS, AND THE BUREAUCRACIES

Another feature of American politics unintentionally helped to fragment the country's financial system. Federalism fragmented banks; and federalism and the structure of Congress enhanced the political power of those that would further fragment finance. The ideological forces—both public-spirited and self-serving—and the interest group pressures played out in a political system that unintentionally began with fragmented, local banks.

Federalism

The American political system is a federal one, and its federal organization helped to produce a fragmented banking system. State governments and the national government exist side by side. Each state regulates its own state banks; national banks are regulated under the National Bank Acts of 1863

---

[65] Senate Bank Holding Company Hearings, supra note 18, at 279–80 (letter of George Burger, Vice-President, Nat'l Federation of Independent Businesses).

[66] Id. at 280 (George H. Frates, Nat'l Ass'n of Retail Druggists).

[67] For small bankers, see Senate Bank Holding Company Hearings, supra note 18, at 104, 109, 259–60, 280. For holding companies, see id. at 236, 238, 317.

and 1864. Until the 1980s, most states protected local bankers from entry by out-of-state banks. So, when large-scale enterprise emerged in the late nineteenth century, few banks had the resources to finance it. Thus fragmented politics induced fragmented banking, making far-flung stockholders and not banks the best source of risk capital at the turn of the century. In turn, the fragmented banking system created interest groups—local bankers with money in their pockets and political influence—who wanted to maintain the status quo.

The federal structure also favored the forces of fragmentation. Farmers and small-town bankers, whose economic interests and ideology made them favor fragmentation, have been overrepresented in the Senate. For decades the congressional committee structure made southern politicians inordinately powerful. Many combined a conservative ideology of mistrust of central power in Washington with a populist ideology of mistrust of concentrated private financial power. Senator Carter Glass of Virginia and Representative Wright Patman of Texas ended up with a large voice in the fragmentation of finance because of the structure of American politics.

Bureaucracy

A political elite in Washington, of agency bureaucrats and some members of Congress, might have wished to fragment business elites. If Wall Street could not control industrial firms, political elites in Washington would have more room to maneuver. Politicians probably recognized the potential power of a financial-industrial complex. If political actors at key moments could sever finance capital from industry by making financial control difficult, financial-industrial coalitions would be weaker and a less formidable challenge to politicians.[68] William O. Douglas, a key bureaucratic actor during the SEC's formative years, later wrote: "[S]ize is the measure of the power of a handful of men over our economy. . . . *[It] should not exist. . . . Power that controls the economy should be in the hands of elected representatives* [and] not in the hands of an industrial oligarchy."[69] FDR had similar sentiments.[70]

Ferdinand Pecora, counsel to the Senate Banking Committee for the 1933–1934 hearings, concluded:

---

[68] Cf. William Niskanen, Bureaucracy and Representative Government (1971) (bureaucracies with discretion will seek their own ends); Thomas S. Ulen, The Market for Regulation: The ICC from 1887 to 1920, 70 American Economic Review 306, 310 (1980) (Papers and Proceedings) (after 1920, none of the originally dominant interest groups still "had a clear interest in [regulation]. The only group [with] sustained interest . . . was the ICC itself").

[69] United States v. Columbia Steel Co., 334 U.S. 495, 536 (1948) (emphasis added).

[70] Leuchtenburg, supra note 52, at 89–90 and n.76.

Defeated at the polls, big business and finance still have their own crushing economic weapons of pressure and retaliation. In Europe, one may observe the process with the utmost clearness. The manner in which the Labor Government of Great Britain, for example, or the "Popular Front" administration in France was allegedly driven from office by the financial operation of the money powers of those countries, has attracted frequent comment. In the United States, fortunately, matters have not been carried to such an extreme.[71]

Inertia

Social phenomena can occur without an apparent *intentional* causative agent. A rule must be chosen, so a rule is chosen and history is thereafter shaped by the choice as grooves are dug into the path taken. Yet the contrary could sometimes also have been chosen. For example, Senator Carter Glass changed his mind a few years after the Glass-Steagall Act severed investment from commercial banking. Investment banks, he then thought, could not satisfy industry's capital needs without an affiliated commercial bank. Other evidence shows that some of his allies supported severence in the hope of heading off deposit insurance.[72] What if he had changed his mind before Glass-Steagall passed; or what if his allies had taken a different initial negotiating position? And then, as a consequence, what if commercial and investment banking had not been separated? Or to imagine a result more at odds with American political history, what if Carter Glass's vision for solving the banking crisis had been to promote larger, national banks? The financial world was in flux, and it's not impossible that the results in 1933 and 1935 could have been to build stronger intermediaries, and not to prop up the weaker ones.

There's another "finance at a crossroads" example that's relevant, although from much earlier. Glass-Steagall addressed the securities activities of affiliates of banks. Many state laws had already banned the banks from direct involvement in commerce. The root, many argue, lay in American lawmakers' copying, without much thought, of English precedent. When banking legislation was first adopted in the United States, lawmakers copied the 1694 charter of the Bank of England, a royal institution that was prohibited by Parliament from engaging in the wider commercial activity that was allowed private English banks.[73] Legal elites lack the imagination to create

[71] Ferdinand Pecora, Wall Street Under Oath—The Story of Our Modern Money Changers 290–91 (1939).

[72] Langevoort, supra note 1, at 696, 698 n.93.

[73] Hammond, supra note 41, at 128–29; Stephen K. Halpert, The Separation of Banking and Commerce Reconsidered, 13 Journal of Corporate Law 481, 491 (1988); Robert Litan, What Should Banks Do? 13–14 (1987); Bernard Shull, The Separation of Banking and Commerce:

new legal frameworks and prefer to borrow them, say some.[74] In the nineteenth century, England was the obvious place to look for commercial law. But the long-run consequence of separating banks from commerce was apparent neither in 1694 nor when copied and recopied in America, because the large firm had yet to emerge.

THE POLITICAL PARADIGM SUMMARIZED

Thus we have several different but not inconsistent elements of the political story. No single political element alone determined any single regulation, yet not every element was present at the creation of each restriction. Like fragments in a kaleidoscope, they combined and recombined in various patterns to affect the outcome.

First, American public opinion has always mistrusted large institutions. That populist story is well known as part of antitrust attacks on big business that endured beyond the populist politics of the 1890s. Less well known is that a similar sentiment militated in favor of fragmenting financial institutions. Progressive ideology addressed legitimate concerns, and whether the Progressives' goals were right or wrong, the ideology favoring fragmentation and local control influenced lawmakers. We should not see the regulatory-political actors who emerged with an ideology of responsible fragmentation as out of touch with politics or economic reality, but as people who reflected a deeper American ideology; natural selection of a political variety made them influential.

Second, interest group politics were important. There were winners in confining the big institutions; those winners were usually small financial institutions, small business, and eventually managers. Once banking interests were fragmented, there was a powerful, influential interest group that would resist financial concentration, namely the already fragmented bankers. Plausible public-spirited reasons to keep financial institutions out of stock were also in play: to reduce the risk of institutional insolvency, to avoid conflicts of interest, and to break up perceived financial monopolies.

Third, the structure of the American federal system and of Congress gave these local interests a loud voice. And political elites, wary of Wall Street,

---

Origin, Development, and Implications for Antitrust, 28 Antitrust Bull. 255, 274 (1983); see Andreas Michael Andreades, History of the Bank of England 65 (1909); 3 Ephraim Lipson, The Economic History of England 240–41 (2d ed. 1934).

[74] Alan Watson, Sources of Law, Legal Change and Ambiguity (1984); see William Samuelson and Richard Zeckhauser, Status Quo Bias in Decision Making, 1 Journal of Risk and Uncertainty 7 (1988). Even lawmakers with great imagination looked to England. Alexander Hamilton based the charter of the Bank of the United States on English precedent, copying the English prohibition on commercial activity. Hammond, supra note 41, at 128–29.

and bureaucracies seeking to preserve power each had incentives to fragment financial institutions.

To restate: populists might well have wished to destroy all banks, both local and money center ones, perhaps by setting up farmer-worker bank collectives. But politics would not let them; the forces arrayed against them were too strong. Small-town bankers might have wished to destroy the money center banks. But politics would not let them. Agile politicians might have seen that fragmenting the money center banks' ability to control industrial corporations would both appease populist ideology and satisfy small-town bankers. And the structure of Congress put these politicians in important positions.

Popular animus against large financial institutions can take many forms: it can prohibit them in their entirety—as happened to the Second Bank of the United States; prohibit their control of industrial corporations—as banks are prohibited; limit their size or range of operations—as occurred in unit-banking states, and as the SEC proposed in 1940 for mutual funds; or restrict the range of their control activities. Populist sentiment against concentrations of economic power seems to have been continuous, but for that sentiment to succeed in making law, politics also required a catalyst, such as, as we shall see, the insurance company scandals of 1906 or interest group demands or the Great Depression or the bureaucratic incentives of the Federal Reserve in 1956.

Nor can we be sure that the mix of *articulated* reasons is the real mix of reasons. Blatant appeal by an interest group to its self-interest and recitation to senators of the interest group's political clout is unfashionable. Crude articulations of power will attract attention, generating a countervailing coalition. The appeal must be clad in the garb of public interest; if no plausible public interest rationale is available, interest group legislation could fail.[75] Conversely, genuinely public-minded senators still would mobilize the support of benefited interest groups.

The result is that federalism created fragmented banks and gave them a strong voice in Congress, populism made concentrated power in or out of government unpopular, and interest groups—bankers or managers seeking to preserve their favored setting—did not have to fight popular opinion or the political structure. These forces, some weak, some strong, all marched in the direction of fragmenting finance. Once they succeeded—and only once they succeeded—did the Berle-Means corporation become inevitable.

[75] Cf. Macey, supra note 2, at 18 (judicial disbelief that Glass-Steagall Act was special interest legislation); Roger G. Noll and Bruce M. Owen, The Predictability of Interest Group Arguments, in The Political Economy of Deregulation 53 (Roger G. Noll and Bruce M. Owen eds., 1983); Gordon Tullock, Future Directions for Rent-Seeking Research, *in* The Political Economy of Rent-Seeking 465, 473 (Charles K. Rowley, Robert D. Tollison, and Gordon Tullock eds., 1988) ("[most citizens] realize that the government can be expected to do things in their personal interest only if it at least superficially fits the public image").

Part III

THE HISTORICAL EVIDENCE

THE POLITICAL PARADIGM has two parts: First, powerful laws barred or restricted intermediaries in governance roles during most of this century, the century of growth for large firms. Second, there is enough similarity in the pattern behind some of these laws to challenge whether economic evolution alone explains the shape of the large public firm. That pattern gives rise to the political theory here: if a political system fragments intermediaries—and American populism, federalism, and interest group infighting did fragment them—then the Berle-Means corporation is inevitable. In this part, I deepen the argument by examining the history and laws affecting each of the four main types of intermediaries shown in Table 1. If we find that political elements fragmented them, we will have gone a long way toward supporting the political paradigm.

TABLE 1
Aggregate Assets of U.S. Financial Institutions, 1993

Banks	$4.9 trillion
Insurers	2.3 trillion
Mutual funds	1.2 trillion
Pension funds	3.4 trillion

Source: Board of Governors of the Federal Reserve System, Flow of Funds Accounts—First Quarter 1993, at 86, 92, 96, 98.

Notes: Banks include commercial banks and thrifts; pension funds include both public and private pension plans; and mutual funds include money market mutual funds. The division among these institutions is in practice imprecise: advisers to mutual fund complexes also manage pension funds; banks advise pension funds, manage trust funds, and have begun to sponsor mutual funds; life insurers are also affiliated with mutual funds and manage pension funds.

CHAPTER 5

Banks

WHEN FINANCIAL RESTRICTIONS are mentioned, the New Deal laws of the 1930s come to mind, and the Glass-Steagall Act, which separated commercial banks from investment banks, comes to the forefront. But the most serious restrictions on financial institutions *predated* the New Deal and were in place at the end of the nineteenth century for banks and shortly after the beginning of the twentieth century for insurers. Until the rise of mutual funds and pensions in recent decades, banks and insurers were the key financial institutions.

At the end of the nineteenth century, when large-scale industry became technologically feasible, the key financial intermediary was the bank. Where would the new national industries go for financing? They had economies of scale, a continent-wide market, and political stability. But they needed financing. While some large-scale industries were financed internally from retained earnings, others, the railroads in particular, needed outside capital. Even those industries that grew by retaining earnings needed external financing to cement the consolidations during the end-of-the-century merger wave.[1] Banks, however, were incapable of easily financing the new large-scale industry because "[f]or much of its history, the United States has had a banking system like no other in the industrialized world. Since the early 1800s, the U.S. banking system has been highly fragmented, consisting of numerous small banks without extensive branch systems."[2] American federalism fostered fragmented banking, as each state chartered and protected its own banks, excluding branches from other states' banks and often preventing their own single-location banks from branching. Although during the Civil War, the United States did set up what were *called* national banks, the National Bank Act of 1864 was interpreted as confining each to a single location. In 1895, President Cleveland endorsed proposals to allow national banks to branch, but the well-organized unit bankers, which each operated from a single location, killed the proposals. Instead, capital requirements were lowered for rural national banks; many were established, enlarging the antibranching banker constituency of small, weak local banks

[1] Alfred D. Chandler, Jr., The Visible Hand—The Managerial Revolution in American Business 373 (1977).

[2] Robert T. Clair and Paula K. Tucker, Interstate Banking and the Federal Reserve: A Historical Perspective, Federal Reserve Bank of Dallas, Economic Review, Nov. 1989, at 1.

that feared and opposed strong national branching operations. In 1915, the Federal Reserve wanted national banks to branch, but the unit bankers won again. Congress kept banks small and local, largely because its own federal organization tied its members to localities, where small-town bankers were powerful.[3]

Those financing the new large enterprises ninety or a hundred years ago could not go to a big bank for one-stop shopping. No single bank was capable of providing the necessary financing. Although geographic restrictions were crucial, product restrictions were already in play. The important National Bank Act of 1863 and National Bank Act of 1864 gave national banks only limited powers.[4] Control of an industrial company was out of the question. Controversy arose over whether banks could own stocks. The Supreme Court resolved that question against the banks: the power to own stock was not listed in the act; accordingly it was not granted.[5]

In nineteenth-century New England, entrepreneurs bound their operating firms to banks. Yet, these banks did not grow into national financial institutions, and the ties between the entrepreneurs and their local banks withered. Why? As economic opportunities shifted from New England to the national economy, the New England banks could not get good information about distant firms, and the bankers could participate in the national economy only as passive buyers of short-term commercial paper. "[F]irms could issue their IOUs through note brokers, who would market them to *banks and financial intermediaries across the country.* . . . [B]anks lost their ability to assess a customer's total indebtedness."[6] Since information gathering is a banker's advantage, one wonders why they ceded the profits to these note brokers.

The banks probably did not cede the profits voluntarily. Rather, because banks in regions with a capital surplus could not branch into capital-importing areas, the money could not move inside a single organization. (The country's size also impeded such movement.) Investment bankers could market notes and commercial paper throughout the country; the banks could not move nationally. "[T]he legal prohibitions against branch banking and the

[3] Federal Reserve Committee on Branch, Group, and Chain Banking, Branch Banking in the United States 174 (1937); Eugene N. White, The Political Economy of Banking Regulation, 1864–1933, 42 Journal of Economic History 33, 35 (1982); Eugene N. White, The Regulation and Reform of the American Banking System, 1900–1929, at 65, 161 (1983).

[4] National Bank Act of 1864, ch. 106, 13 Stat. 99 (1864) (codified as amended at 12 U.S.C. § 38 [1988]).

[5] California Bank v. Kennedy, 167 U.S. 362 (1892); National Bank Act of Feb. 25, 1863, ch. 58, § 11, 12 Stat. 665; 12 U.S.C. § 24 (Seventh) (1988). State member banks of the Federal Reserve System were later similarly restricted. 12 U.S.C. § 335 (1988).

[6] Naomi R. Lamoreaux, Information Problems and Banks' Specialization in Short-Term Commercial Lending: New England in the Nineteenth Century, in Inside the Business Enterprise: Historical Perspectives on the Use of Information 161, 180 (Peter Temin ed., 1991).

distance between economic cent[er]s produced . . . relatively small, not very closely connected, short-term markets. . . . Because of the prohibition on interstate branching, a national market had to await the development of a . . . commercial paper [market]."[7] Entrepreneurs affiliated with banks could go national, and economic opportunities certainly did go national, but the bankers, because of branching restrictions, could not.[8] The commercial paper market—short-term IOUs from a debtor—was the way financiers and industry "contracted around" the geographic restrictions.

Did the lack of modern telecommunications preclude truly national intermediaries in the nineteenth century? Geography then might explain America's fragmented finance, which explains the structure at the top of the large firm. Although the technology of financial services and America's vast, continental space would have kept many banks local at the end of the nineteenth century, some banks would have become national institutions, just as some industrial firms and some insurers had. The telegraph could coordinate the movement of money in a national financial organization, as it could coordinate the movement of railroad cars in a national railroad. Federalism prevented true national banks that might have developed alongside the early national industrial firms.

National intermediaries were viable. Alfred Chandler described the rise of managerial capitalism as entailing the systematic coordination within a firm of a national production and distribution system and showed that the Second Bank of the United States was the first American national enterprise, coordinating the flow of money across the nation parallel to the flow of trade. It coordinated complex financial transactions running through its many branches, making "it the first prototype of modern business enterprise in American commerce."[9] As is well known, Andrew Jackson killed this first national financial intermediary with his famous veto message, refusing to recharter the Bank.

Ideological and chance factors reinforced the nineteenth-century trend of small, local banks with weak connections to commerce. Although some early American banking charters expected banks to be in commerce—the Manhattan Bank was also a waterworks and some manufacturers had corporate charters that allowed them a bank—many chartering authorities just copied English charters, which separated banks from commerce. By the mid-nine-

---

[7] Lance Davis, The Capital Markets and Industrial Concentration: The U.S. and U.K., A Comparative Study, 19 Economic History Review (2d Ser.) 255, 260 (1966).

[8] Massachusetts (like other states) also *prohibited* its savings banks, some of which were actively engaged in financing industry, from lending to out-of-state firms. Lance E. Davis, Capital Immobilities and Finance Capitalism: A Study of Economic Evolution in the United States 1820–1920, 1 Explorations in Entrepreneurial History 88, 99 (1963).

[9] Chandler, supra note 1, at 30–31, 42–43. Temin analyzes it as an interregional financier and an incomplete crypto–central bank. Peter Temin, The Jacksonian Economy 28–58 (1969).

teenth century separation was the norm, although it could have been other-wise.[10] Some antibranching rules were only designed to stop banks from issuing difficult-to-cash bank notes from remote branches. The words in the National Bank Act that banned branching were ambiguous; regulatory inter-pretation cemented the ban, leading to the many single-location banks that became an antibranching banking constituency. Had early regulatory inter-pretation been to the contrary, the developmental path might have differed.

The role of a central bank was important in two ways. Fractional reserve banking is unstable, with real assets behind bank-"created" currency only a fraction of the bank's obligations.[11] With short-term deposits and long-term loans, banks could suffer from liquidity crises. The modern economy's solu-tion has been a central bank, which creates an elastic currency on the macro-level, and can lend to illiquid banks on the micro-level.

After the destruction of the Second Bank of the United States, the nation had no central bank. Even when one was created, in 1913, it was allowed only to discount short-term obligations, making it inept at facilitating banks with long-term investments. (Nor was it, in 1913, a powerful institution. Agrarians wanted government to dominate the banks; New York bankers wanted to revive a private Bank of the United States. Carter Glass, the key player in Congress, would not defer to the New York banks, and a decentral-ized Federal Reserve System—neither a powerful government central bank nor a powerful truly national private bank—emerged.)[12] Economic his-torians say that the nineteenth-century German central bank's willingness to support private long-term lending facilitated German banks as long-term financiers with a big corporate governance role, while English banks played no long-term role in the nineteenth century, not because they lacked a cen-tral bank, but because law and practice stopped the Bank of England from the long-term lending to banks that would have helped English banks take liquidity risks.[13]

Andrew Jackson's veto of the rechartering of the Second Bank of the United States had, I believe, a second, more important effect on banking. The Second Bank was not only a crypto–central bank necessary for a strong

[10] Bray Hammond, Banks and Politics in America from the Revolution to the Civil War 149–55 (1957).

[11] Fractional reserve banking arises when a bank lends money it does not have, but expects only a fraction of its customers to seek to cash in at any time. To accommodate that fraction, the bank keeps a reserve of funds available. If more customers seek more cash than the bank anticipated, the bank faces a liquidity crisis.

[12] James Livingston, Origins of the Federal Reserve System (1986) (struggle between New York bankers, country bankers, and midwestern big-city bankers); Alan Dawley, Struggles for Justice—Social Responsibility and the Liberal State 146–47 (1991).

[13] Richard H. Tilly, Banking Institutions in Historical and Comparative Perspective—Ger-many, Great Britain and the United States in the 19th and 20th Century, 145 Zeitschrift für die gesamte Staatswissenschaft 189–209 (1989).

banking industry, but was a semi-public, semi-private institution with an interstate branching network. Had it survived, its national branch network could have been a model for future private banking charters. It, or more private but truly national banks, might have played a central financial role in the construction and merger of large national firms at the end of the nineteenth century.

The American timing was both too early and too late for that scenario to succeed. Alexander Hamilton and his successors had built a national financial intermediary at the *beginning* of the nineteenth century, before its usefulness was high, but technology made nationwide railroads and large-scale industry possible at the *end* of the nineteenth century. Had the United States built its first national intermediary when it had a better use, perhaps American politics would have learned how to reconcile national finance with national politics and national industry.

Jackson's veto was a product of two of the key forces that would determine the future structure of financial intermediaries and, hence, the structure of the public corporation: interest group infighting and American populism. State banks disliked the Second Bank, which competed with them and could control them. This dislike was an early reflection of the local bank power that American federalism fostered and that tended to keep America's financial institutions small.[14]

Jackson's veto message attacked the Second Bank as an elitist institution owned "by foreigners . . . and a few hundred of our own citizens, chiefly of the richest class." The Bank, he said, had the potential to be run—and exploited—by a small group of people: "It is easy to conceive that great evils to our country and its institutions might flow from such a concentration of power in the hands of a few men irresponsible to the people. . . ."[15] Although Jackson did not explicitly attack the Second Bank's branching, its branches were implicitly objectionable, because they contributed to its size and power. The veto's rhetoric helped etch on the political psyche stock images of an unwanted elitist concentration of private economic power for future politics; the veto message was for decades assigned reading for schoolchildren.

The background of the veto also shows chance elements behind the fragmentation of finance. The question of whether the United States should have a crypto–central bank was then touch and go. The first Congress chartered one; a later Congress chartered a second one. A majority of the 1832 Congress voted for a new charter for the Second Bank. Had Henry Clay and Nicholas Biddle not decided as a political tactic to force the issue in 1832, or

[14] Bray Hammond, Jackson, Biddle, and the Bank of the United States, 7 Journal of Economic History 1 (1947).

[15] Reprinted in Edward L. Symons, Jr., and James J. White, Banking Law—Teaching Materials 13–16 (3d ed. 1991).

had Biddle not shown the poor judgment to claim that he had stupendous power over the nation's well-being, the Second Bank might well have been rechartered in 1836. Jackson had not opposed the Bank's continuation until Congress rechartered it. Some of Jackson's objections—partial foreign ownership and the delegation of governmental functions to private citizens—could have been handled by reshaping the institution instead of destroying it. A reshaping, however, would have required a stronger national government to absorb the governmental functions of the Second Bank, which would have been difficult for America's weak national government of the early nineteenth century.

In the 1790s, Hamilton had opposed branches for the First Bank, because he thought they would evoke political opposition and could not be well managed centrally; despite some serious management mistakes at Bank branches, Hamilton was eventually proven wrong on the management issue, but eventually correct on the political one. Had he been heeded, a reason for opposition might have been missing and a national Bank might have survived, to branch later in the century. After 1832, had the American people become more comfortable with what by then was an increasingly competently run Bank, popular opinion might have become reconciled to a national financial institution.

Small changes in original conditions can vastly affect later outcomes. The destruction of the Second Bank was for American finance a cataclysmic event—the financial counterpart of the negotiation of a constitution, or the Civil War, or the New Deal. The United States, which for most of the twentieth century has had the most backward and badly-organized banking system of the developed world, had in the early nineteenth century the most advanced. The end of the Second Bank would determine how the country's large-scale industry would be financed in the late nineteenth century.

Thus the key pieces of American banking were in place at the end of the nineteenth century: a fragmented banking system that did not branch across state lines (or often within state lines) and the absence of a central bank that could make the money supply elastic and discount illiquid bank assets. When large-scale industry emerged, the key financial institution of the time was incapable of readily and directly providing financial resources.

CHAPTER 6

Insurers

AT THE BEGINNING of the twentieth century, several of the largest American financial institutions were insurers, not banks. Banks were confined to a single state, and often to a single location; insurers were not. The largest New York insurers were twice as large as the largest banks and were moving into adjacent financial areas. They were underwriting securities. They were buying bank stock and controlling large banks. They were assembling securities portfolios with control potential. Some had already put as much as 12 percent of their assets into stock. The three largest insurers were growing rapidly and seemed to be developing not into the passive institution they eventually became but into an institution that might dimly resemble the powerful German universal banks or the main bank system in Japan.

But in 1905, the industry was rocked by scandal, revealing nepotism, insider financial chicanery, and bribery of legislatures. The New York legislature responded with a political inquiry, called the Armstrong investigation after the state legislator who chaired the investigative committee. By 1906, the law prohibited insurers from owning stock, from controlling banks, and from underwriting securities. Politics fragmented and pulverized the insurance industry, limiting it to its core business of writing insurance and investing in debt.

When the Armstrong investigation began, its chief, Charles Evans Hughes, was an unknown New York lawyer with some experience in public investigations. When it was over, Hughes began a political career that took him to within a handshake of the presidency. A few years later, the investigation's themes of reform to curb financial power were echoed in the congressional Pujo investigation. For half a century, insurers were banned from owning any stock at all; serious deregulation of the ban on stock ownership by insurance companies really did not occur until the 1980s.

Today, institutional investors are criticized for avoiding an active role in corporate boardrooms. Although insurance companies, for most of the century the second-largest institution in aggregate assets, would be plausible players as active investors with boardroom presence, they have been inactive investors. Despite their size, they lag behind other institutions—private and public pension funds, mutual funds, and bank trust funds—in aggregate stock holdings. Moreover, while their holdings are not small in absolute size—they own over 5 percent of the stock market outright, and as pension managers they control yet more stock—insurers are invisible in corporate governance. Thirty years ago, a history of the insurance industry said:

> [Insurance companies are] at the highest level of the nation's business structure. If size counts, and money talks, they should be among the most potent institutions of this society. Yet the large life insurance companies play a curiously limited role in American life. [After fifty years of prohibition on stock ownership, they finally] control increasing amounts of corporate stock, but they do not systematically and purposefully use their voting strength. . . . In many ways, they are giants without power.[1]

In this chapter I explore the Armstrong story and its aftermath to see if they shed light on the current role of insurers as passive institutional investors and to see if they can help illuminate the construction of the Berle-Means corporation in the United States. Armstrong is one corner of the foundation of American corporate finance. In Germany and Japan (and Britain also), insurers play a role in the governance linkage between finance and industry. In Germany, insurers own *more* stock than do the vaunted German banks (the bankers have a stronger voice as shareholders, though, because they control the German proxy system and the insurers own some of the stock as pension manager); in Japan, insurers own nearly as much stock as do the Japanese bankers. In Germany today, insurers are at the center of newly forming linkages of cross-ownership between finance and industry.[2]

When large-scale financial intermediaries emerged at the end of the nineteenth century, American government sought to suppress them. A common misconception is that financial fragmentation began in the 1930s, during the New Deal. True, Glass-Steagall and other financial laws of the 1930s reinforced the fragmentation of banks. But the pacification of the American financial intermediary is in fact deeply rooted in the country's more distant past. As we've seen, at the turn of the century, there were two key financial institutions—banks and insurers. Both were neutralized. First, the battle over rechartering the Second Bank early in the nineteenth century led to the national government's abandoning a role in building a large nationwide financial intermediary; indeed, through antibranching laws it suppressed one. Thereafter "natural" fragmentation of banks arose from American federalism, which created a separate banking system for each state and territory. Second, "intentional" fragmentation of insurers occurred at the beginning of the twentieth century, when three insurance companies, which were developing into truly national American financial institutions, were left shattered in the wake of the Armstrong investigation.

[1] Morton Keller, The Life Insurance Enterprise, 1885–1910—A Study in the Limits of Corporate Power ix (1963).

[2] Hans Eglau, Allianz/Dresdner Bank—Vermachtet und Verschachtelt, Die Zeit, Aug. 16, 1991, at 19.

In this chapter, we first focus on the fact that for most of this century, major American insurers were barred from owning any stock. Second, we see that the 1906 restrictions, arising at a time of economic dislocation, can be traced strongly to popular distrust of concentrated economic power and weakly to interest group warfare. Third, we see that the prohibitions have a continuing influence. Powerful regulation helped to shape the insurers; repeal will not automatically alter the insurer's conduct quickly, or perhaps even at all, if the insurance companies have been molded into passive institutions instead of active, stock-wielding institutions with a serious role in corporate governance of the country's largest firms. Beaten into passivity in a way that few current insurance executives may even be aware of, the insurance industry developed a corporate culture of investment passivity that to this day persists.

OVERVIEW OF INSURERS

Today, insurers have $2.3 trillion in aggregate assets, rivaling banks and pensions in aggregate size,[3] yet in the 1990s they lag behind most of the other intermediaries in stock ownership and corporate governance activity. The point here is not that institutional activity is an unalloyed good. Nor can it be said that insurers would be paragons of virtue without conflicts of interest. They would, as purveyors of insurance products, pension plans, and other financial services to corporations, have reason to mute their corporate governance activities and be bought off. And as mutuals, owned by their policyholders, not by profit-seeking stockholders, some of the big life insurers may not be adept (morally or structurally) at corporate governance action. The point is that the life insurers' corporate governance conflicts and problems are not, prima facie, much greater than those of the other big four financial institutions, and those other financial institutions did become more active in the 1990s, albeit only slightly. Hence one wonders where the insurers are, and finds that for the most part they are silent, inert, and passive.

The Prohibition

During the early growth of large American firms at the beginning of this century, could financial institutions own big blocks of stock in those firms? Even if big blocks yield no efficiency, and are only differences of form, we

---

[3] This chapter is about the big players in the insurance industry, life insurance companies. Property and casualty insurers are of secondary but not trivial importance. The $2.3 trillion in total insurer assets breaks out as $1.7 trillion for life insurance companies and $600 billion for property and casualty, which despite their smaller size hold nearly as much equity as the life insurers.

should still want to know why the fragmented ownership of the American public firm developed as it did. The argument that law had a key historical role would lose plausibility if insurers had always been allowed to grow big and to buy big blocks of stock, but never did. In that case one would presume they found it unprofitable to own those big blocks. But if law had prohibited insurers from owning big blocks, then the efficiency and descriptive questions would be open.

Even if there were no historical bans, changing economic conditions might make big blocks efficient in the future. Moreover, even if a historical ban on big blocks were dropped, it might have created conditions and institutional structures that would stop big blocks from developing, ban or no ban. For example, substitutes for big blocks—better boards of directors or takeovers, say—might have developed, making big blocks less profitable than they otherwise would be. Indeed, the recent legal and economic pressure to professionalize the American board of directors—a partly successful development—is one of those substitutes.

THE ARMSTRONG INVESTIGATION

What happened to the insurance industry in 1905 and 1906? The explosive scandal began peculiarly enough with a lavish party hosted by a young heir, who was the beneficiary of a trust that controlled the Equitable Life Assurance Society, one of the nation's three largest insurers. Equitable paid for the party, the newspapers learned of its opulence, and the matter became a public cause célèbre. Hearst's and Pulitzer's papers followed up on this spark of scandal with reports of corruption and mismanagement in the insurance industry.[4] Soon the New York legislature felt compelled to convene a committee, dubbed the Armstrong committee, after its chair, to investigate.

The scandal had several elements: the political influence of the insurers; public outrage, which aroused an already organized reform movement; a media campaign; and a muted public choice story. This was a time of economic dislocation. Large economic organizations were erupting throughout American society, and the new insurers were among the biggest. In reaction, a wave of populism washed over parts of the American political system. Reformers sought to clean up corruption in government, including the corruption of insurance lobbyists' bribing of officials for favorable rate regulation. The yellow press latched onto the issue and fomented the Armstrong investigation. Interest groups were also in play; bankers enjoyed seeing rival insurers nearly drowned under the investigatory waves. After all, from a banker's perspective, a family buying a life policy was pulling money away

---

[4] Don R. Stelzer, The Armstrong Investigation, Journal of the American Society of C.L.U and ChFC, Nov. 1989, at 74, 74–75.

from a bank savings account. Life insurance premiums were bank deposits that went to the wrong institution, as far as the banker was concerned, and a life insurance mortgage was a substitute for a bank loan.

The Armstrong investigation was an explosive public political event. While one might think the dry stuff of insurers' sales practices and investment portfolios would not command the public's attention, it did. The scandal and investigation were the 1980s takeover wars, the junk bond boom, and the insider-trading scandals rolled into one sustained event; according to a contemporary observer, there was, excepting presidential campaigns, no parallel in popular national interest.[5]

Although the investigation was named for Senator Armstrong, its real protagonist was Charles Evans Hughes, who, when offered the chief counsel's job in August 1905, privately said it was "the most tremendous job in the United States." He immediately took the position; the hearings started in September and lasted only three months. Within six weeks after their completion, Hughes had written his report on how to restructure the life insurance industry. During the hearings, without the accusatory demagogic demeanor or the hectoring air of a bad prosecutor, Hughes methodically extracted admissions from insurance executives of financial slovenliness, bribery, and self-dealing. His skill in explaining complex financial transactions to the general public through the media made him a favorite of the press. His tenacity and the media's attention led several insurance executives to retire early for health reasons, leave the area, or, in one instance, enter a sanitarium. He became the charismatic center of the investigation; when the legislators on the Armstrong committee wanted to slow him down, they backed off when he threatened to resign and announce his reasons.

Hughes carefully uncovered one problem after another at the insurance companies, some small, some not: irregularities in internal voting procedures, window-dressing transactions to keep some assets off the official annual reports, hidden disbursements to the insurers' lobbyists, hidden political contributions, self-dealing by some insurance executives, bribery, and nepotism. These revelations came intermittently during the three-month investigation, regularly putting Hughes and the insurers in the headlines. While many of the revelations were only weakly relevant to the restrictions ultimately enacted, the media attention conditioned the public to support regulation of the big insurers.[6]

[5] Beerits Memorandum, at 14–15, microfilmed on Paper of Charles Evans Hughes (1985) Reel 140 (Lib. of Cong. Photo-duplication Serv.). For extended narratives of Armstrong, see Shepard B. Clough, A Century of American Life Insurance 220 et seq. (1946); Keller, supra note 1, at 245–64; Burton J. Hendrick, Governor Hughes, McClure's Magazine, March 1908, at 521, 531–35.

[6] Autobiographical Notes of Charles Evans Hughes 15, 19, 122 (David J. Danelski and Joseph S. Tulchin eds., 1973); Beerits Memorandum, supra note 5, at 15, 18; 1 Merlo Pusey,

THE ECONOMIC ENVIRONMENT

The scandal must be seen in its economic context. At the turn of the century, the size and growth of the largest American insurance companies were awesome. They had become the largest financial institutions in the country. Today, insurers are smaller than banks with similar industry rankings (that is, the largest bank is larger than the largest insurer, the second-largest bank is larger than the second-largest insurer, and so on).[7] But back then, the insurance industry was growing faster than the banking industry (see Table 2), and the very largest insurers were growing even faster than the average insurer.[8]

TABLE 2
Growth of Largest U.S. Banks, Industrials,
Insurers, and Railroads, 1891–1919
(percent change)

		1905 to	
	1891 to 1905	1912	1919
Banks	192	43	99
Industrials	425	31	139
Insurers	245	55	131
Railroads	90	37	66

Source: Adapted from David Bunting, The Rise of Large American Corporations, 1889–1919, at 28, 44 (1987).

Note: Percentages are for the ten largest insurers, the twenty largest banks, the twenty-five largest railroads, and the hundred largest industrials.

The disparate growth was due not only to insurers' economic advantages, but to their relative freedom from regulation before 1906. Banks faced (and up to the 1990s still faced) heavy interstate and branch restrictions, which accounted for a great deal of the disparity between bank size and insurer size. Insurers could sell outside their home state, although they then became subject to the regulatory authority of another state insurance commissioner.

Table 3 shows the size of the three largest insurers and six largest national

---

Charles Evans Hughes 148 (1951); 1 Robert T. Swaine, The Cravath Firm and Its Predecessors, 1819–1947, at 758 (1946).

[7] 2 Moody's Bank and Finance Manual a5, a15 (1989).

[8] David Bunting, The Rise of Large American Corporations, 1889–1919, at 28, 44 (1987). From 1891 to 1905, insurers increased their asset size 245 percent, while banks increased their assets less, by 192 percent. Industrials were growing rapidly, outstripping them both. Table 2 reflects these trends for the largest institutions.

TABLE 3

Assets of Largest Insurers and Largest Commercial
Banks in New York State, 1900

Insurers	
Mutual	$326 million
Equitable	304 million
New York Life	262 million
Banks	
National City Bank	155 million
National Bank of Commerce	89 million
Hanover National Bank	71 million
National Park Bank	70 million
Chase National Bank	57 million
First National Bank	57 million

Source: Superintendent of Ins. of the State of N.Y.,
Forty-Second Ann. Rep., pt. II, Life, Casualty, Title,
Credit and Mortgage Guarantee Ins. xxxi (1901); Moody's
Manual of Industrial and Misc. Securities 100, 118, 123,
137, 145, 146 (1900) (national banks only).

banks in New York at the turn of the century.[9] The largest New York bank, National City, had assets of $155 million. The two largest insurers each had assets approximately *twice* as great. The *sum* of the assets of the next four largest New York national banks was less than the assets of either of the two largest insurers and not very much more than those of the third-largest. Moreover, the second-largest bank was owned and dominated by insurance companies.[10]

THE POLITICAL ENVIRONMENT

The scandal must also be seen in its political context. This was an era of reform and distrust of big business. Theodore Roosevelt was trustbusting; Upton Sinclair was muckraking. Armstrong was one corner of the scene. The Progressive movement—a reaction to the disruption, corruption, and dehumanizing scale of industrialization and urbanization—was in full swing. The disruptive growth of industry triggered a political reaction—the Sherman Act in 1890 and the antitrust prosecutions of the Roosevelt and Taft

[9] State-chartered banks in some other states, such as California, which did not have statewide branching restrictions, might have rivaled some of the New York banks in size.

[10] 7 Joint Comm. of the Senate and Assembly of the State of New York to Investigate and Examine into the Business and Affairs of Life Insurance Companies Doing Business in the State of New York, Exhibits, Report and Index 25, 96 (1906) [Hughes Report]; 1 R. Carlyle Buley, The Equitable Life Assurance Society of the United States—1859–1964, at 580 (1967).

administrations to break up parts of large-scale industry. The disruptive growth of the insurers also triggered a political reaction—the Armstrong investigation.

Political Corruption and the Insurance Companies

Before 1905, insurers contributed to political bosses to get favorable laws. Who had the upper hand was unclear. Sometimes politicians proposed regulation just so the insurers would bribe them not to pass it. Yet E. H. Harriman, an executive with ties to the insurance industry, could proclaim during the Armstrong investigation: "I should think [the Republican party boss] had political influence because of his relation to me [rather than vice versa]."[11] Influence-peddling and corruption, more widespread than in just the insurance industry, helped breed a New York reform movement, which sought to eliminate the corrupt relationships between politics and business.[12]

Managerial Corruption: Stealing from the Insurers and Their Policyholders

Insurance company officers lined their pockets with policyholder funds through bank ownership. The bank became a conduit for low-interest loans of policyholder funds to the officers. The officers would have the insurance company deposit funds with a bank at low interest; the bank would then make loans to the officers at low interest. A controlled bank was not necessary for the theft, but helped to obscure the transaction. More directly, insurance company executives sold stock to the insurance company at inflated prices. They used portfolio stock of the insurance company to get themselves elected as officers of the portfolio company; as officers they would receive a good salary for little work.[13]

The Press

The press pressured politicians. Newspapers reported that the "whole country was in a state of hysteria over insurance matters, and was clamorous for

---

[11] 1 Pusey, supra note 6, at 161–62; Hughes Report, supra note 10, at 15–21, 85–86, 104–06, 300–04; Robert Wesser, Charles Evans Hughes: Politics and Reform in New York 1905–1910, at 44 (1967).

[12] See Wesser, supra note 11, at 18–20.

[13] Plans for Insurance Betterments Approved, N.Y. Times, Jan. 6, 1906, at 5, col. 3 (president of Chase Manhattan Bank criticizing insurer ownership of banks as a means to enrich insurer officers and insiders); 1 George Kennan, E. H. Harriman: A Biography 407–08 (1922).

victims."[14] Pulitzer's paper, *The World*, ran more than one hundred editorials demanding an investigation.[15] Hughes felt the heat. "There was no time for adequate preparation," he said. "The World was hammering away and the Committee was impatient to have the public hearings begin."[16] Hughes knew he needed to respond to the outcry from *The World*: a more conservative committee counsel had been passed over for Hughes, partly because of the paper's and Pulitzer's opposition.[17] As *The World* analyzed the insurers:

> The insurance companies have now become the great agencies in high finance and trust exploitation. . . . [T]he premiums paid by policyholders . . . provide the money for these colossal schemes of financial centralization. The savings of the people in the form of insurance premiums are turned over to the captains of industry . . . to control gas companies, electric-light companies, telephone companies, street-car companies, railway companies and various other forms of corporation activity. Wherever there is a consolidation of great public-service corporations to stifle competition and squeeze the public it will generally be found that the money of a great life-insurance company is behind it.[18]

Public Opinion and the Reform Movement

The large insurers faced a hostile public. Populist opinion in the prior decade had conditioned the political debate toward antifinance, anti–Wall Street sentiments.

American distrust of concentrations of financial power was the general attitude; dislike of the power accumulating in the large insurance companies by 1905 was its concrete manifestation. The emerging Progressive movement sought to shield individuals against the emerging large institutions of business and government.[19] This sense was not confined to western populists. "The great monopoly in this country [is] the money monopoly," said Woodrow Wilson, who, about to become governor of New Jersey, announced that the money monopoly's control over capital had destroyed the "old variety and freedom and individual energy of development."[20] New York Progressives undoubtedly felt the same.

---

[14] Miscellaneous Life News, The Spectator, Mar. 29, 1906, at 178.

[15] 1 Pusey, supra note 6, at 141.

[16] Autobiographical Notes of Charles Evans Hughes, supra note 6, at 122. See also Wesser, supra note 11, at 35–36.

[17] Keller, supra note 1, at 251.

[18] Life Insurance and High Finance, The World, Feb. 17, 1905, at 6.

[19] Richard Hofstadter, The Age of Reform—From Bryan to F.D.R. 5, 9–11, 93 (1955). "[T]he Progressive movement was the complaint of the unorganized against the consequences of organization." Id. at 214.

[20] Ellis W. Hawley, The New Deal and the Problem of Monopoly: A Study in Economic Ambivalence 304 (1966).

The insurance companies were just too big and too frightening to the public. Although the insurers had many friends, often purchased, in the New York legislature, the *New York Times* reported that "[t]he force of public opinion behind the [insurance] bills is so strong and insistent that the objecting Senators may see that it would not be good politics to be too persistent."[21]

While the insurers' internal practices and political contributions triggered the inquiry, the companies were also condemned because their executives "thought of themselves more as financiers than as insurance [people]."[22] Seen in this context of corruption, Hughes's recommendations make sense. Eliminating the insurers' authority to make political contributions would reduce their political power, and eliminating their authority to own stock would reduce their economic influence by confining them to insurance and keeping them away from finance. The law prohibiting stock ownership was adopted when half of the nation's insurance assets were in New York–regulated insurers. It was then widely copied.[23]

The New York prohibition on insurers' owning stock "was not imposed because of the feeling that stocks were [too risky for] life insurance companies but rather [because of fear] that life insurance companies would control other corporations."[24] Moreover, Hughes reported his fears that the tentacles might spread:

> [Insurance companies might extend their control of] ancillary banks and trust companies [to] control of railroads and industrial enterprises. No tendency in modern financial conditions has created more widespread apprehension than the tendency to vast combinations of capital and assets. . . . [T]he officers and members of finance committees of life insurance companies [are] in positions of conspicuous financial power. . . . [There is a] necessity of guarding against abuses by the requirement of conservative and durable investments. [Accordingly, i]nvestments in stocks should be prohibited.[25]

Other popular opinions were more radical. Insurers were said to have "resources . . . so vast [that] their magnitude, if permitted to grow unrestricted, will soon become a serious menace to the community." Insurance commissioners were told at their annual convention that "[l]ife [insurance c]ompanies are becoming vast financial corporations, and may become a source of danger to the commonwealth by reason of the vast money power

---

[21] Grady Fails to Block the 6 Insurance Bills, N.Y. Times, Apr. 6, 1906, at 9; Hughes Report, supra note 10, at 294, 297–98.

[22] Keller, supra note 1, at 253.

[23] Act of Apr. 27, 1906, ch. 326, sec. 36, 1906 N.Y. Laws 763, 797; Keller, supra note 1, at 254–59; 1 Pusey, supra note 6, at 166–68; Hughes Report, supra note 10, at 289–97, 300–01.

[24] Buist Anderson, The Armstrong Investigation in Retrospect 259 (1952), citing Hughes Report, supra note 10, at 389–90.

[25] Hughes Report, supra note 10, at 294–95.

lodged in the hands of a few men." The Massachusetts commissioner feared that some bold manipulator would gain control of a life insurer's assets and use that control to "financ[e] large enterprise and promot[e] all kinds of corporate consolidations."[26] Hughes concluded that "[t]he business of the [three biggest life insurers] has grown beyond reasonable limits." The public needed not only a ban on stock investments, but a lid on the big insurers' growth, a lid that New York State created in 1906 by capping the dollar amount of new insurance that a single insurer could write.[27]

Fear of Non–New York Regulation

The public's disgust with the big insurers motivated an investigation and, ultimately, the shackling of the insurers. The whole story is more complex, however, involving forays by other states, particularly in rate regulation, and the looming threat of preemptive federal regulation.

For many insurers, portfolio rules were a sideshow. The main event was, and probably still is, rate and other regulation. New York insurers wanted to deter "over"regulation by the states in which they sold insurance. For a time, the big insurers sought federal regulation to preempt the states. A 1905 opinion of counsel to several insurers stated: "Insurance companies have a strong *prima facie* reason for wishing to substitute for the complex state system, the simpler system of federal regulation [if this substitution can] be lawfully accomplished. . . ."[28] They wanted uniformity, both for its own sake and to end the political tax that insurers paid to capture state regulators. When the scandal hit, the insurers feared further restrictive regulation by the states; at the federal level they hoped to have more influence. These hopes were buttressed by President Roosevelt, who called for federal regulation in his State of the Union Address.[29]

[26] Keller, supra note 1, at 136. Ironically, in the aggregate insurers did not own much common stock; they mostly made mortgages, lent money and bought corporate bonds. Two of the large insurers had 12 percent of their investments in stock. Id. at 158–60. Life insurers held less than 0.5 percent of all outstanding stock, and 6 percent of their total assets were in stock at the time of the Armstrong prohibition. By 1922 this percentage was slashed nationwide to 1 percent. Raymond W. Goldsmith, The Historical Background: Financial Institutions as Investors in Corporate Stock before 1952, in National Bureau of Economic Research, Institutional Investors and Corporate Stock—A Background Study 56–58 (Raymond W. Goldsmith ed., 1973).

[27] Hughes Report, supra note 10, at 297–98; Keller, supra note 1, at 136, 253–54; Act of Apr. 27, 1906, ch. 326, 1906 N.Y. Laws 763, 794 (limitation on life insurers writing new insurance).

[28] Carman F. Randolph, Federal Supervision of Insurance, 5 Columbia Law Review 500, 510 (1905); Philip L. Merkel, Going National: The Life Insurance Industry's Campaign for Federal Regulation after the Civil War, 65 Business History Review 528 (1991). See also Richard Sylla, The Progressive Era and the Political Economy of Big Government, 5 Critical Review 531 (1992).

[29] Keller, supra note 1, at 198, 213, 238; Gabriel Kolko, The Triumph of Conservatism: A

Some New York regulation grew out of the insurers' drive for uniformity and preemption of other states. The insurers' early drive for federal preemption collapsed, in part because the public was wary of expanding national power. The big insurers at first hoped to capture the national regulator—as small southern and western insurers feared they would,[30] with the national regulator displacing local regulators, who as friends of the local insurers had made rules advantaging the locals at the expense of the large eastern insurers. Presumably these small insurers in the South and West would influence the votes of southern and western politicians. Thus, the big insurers had to know that the national battle would not be easily won. They had also sought uniform laws, and the New York superintendent was a leader in getting the state regulators to hold a convention.[31] The drive for federal rules also collapsed because key actors came to believe that federal preemption was unconstitutional, and irreversibly so. The Supreme Court had held insurance not to be interstate "commerce," which Congress can constitutionally regulate, and therefore it was not reachable by Congress.[32]

Eventually, the large insurers themselves became wary of federal rules, which they came to fear would only come as part of a general centralization of government power, accompanied by either industry capture or excessive federal regulation, which would cumulate with state rules, not replace them.[33] Insurers wanted only a preemptive regulator, not an additional, powerful one. Moreover, federal preemption would weaken the insurers' antitrust exemption; if insurance were not interstate commerce—as the Supreme Court had held it not to be—the Sherman Act, which regulated "interstate commerce," could not reach it.[34] For federal regulation preempting the states to be constitutional, insurance had to be commerce. Insurers

---

Reinterpretation of American History, 1900–1916, at 93 (1963); Douglass North, Capital Accumulation in Life Insurance between the Civil War and the Investigation of 1905, in Men in Business 238, 251 (William Miller ed., 1952); The President and Insurance, The Spectator, Dec. 7, 1905, at 340. Roosevelt had called for federal regulation of insurers in 1904.

[30] Keller, supra note 1, at 240, 242.

[31] Merkel, supra note 28, at 550–51.

[32] Paul v. Virginia, 75 U.S. (8 Wall.) 168, 183 (1868) (upholding a state's tax on interstate insurance transactions); Randolph, supra note 28, at 510–15, 518; Keller, supra note 1, at 240–41; The Spectator, Sept. 28, 1905, at 181 (address of Frederick Nash, Ass't Att'y Gen'l Mass. to the National Convention of Insurance Commissioners). That view of congressional power was a nineteenth-century or early twentieth-century view, not a modern one.

[33] Randolph, supra note 28, at 526–27; The Spectator, Nov. 2, 1905, at 268 (many "think [federal regulation] would be adding one more department for the companies to report to, which would certainly be undesirable"); The Spectator, Sept. 28, 1905, at 181. State rules would cover the insurers' domestic, in-state activities; federal rules would cover interstate activities.

[34] The Spectator, Oct. 19, 1905, at 227, 238 (report to the Board of Casualty and Surety Underwriters); Randolph, supra note 28, at 509, 518–19. Even if insurance were commerce, Congress could preempt the states with general regulation, and then exempt insurers from the Sherman Act; insurers probably did not think such a bifurcation would be likely.

could not easily have it both ways—commerce for preemption and noncommerce for the antitrust exemption.

The insurers stopped seeking federal preemption—and eventually opposed it—because to get it they would have had to accept federal antitrust regulation. Thus, the insurers came to challenge the constitutionality of federal action because of a sincerely held constitutional view, a fear that a finding of constitutionality would unleash antitrust regulation, and a fear that federal regulation would be cumulative, not preemptive.

I believe this possibility of federal regulation of the insurers was more than a sideshow. A credible national regulator would have allayed populist fears of powerful private concentrations of power and mooted the public interest risks of stock portfolios. However, the public's unwillingness to construct a national regulator left Hughes and the other political actors with little choice but to fragment the private power. Thus, these two American fears of concentration—one of concentrated governmental power, the other of concentrated private economic power—combined to destroy insurer boardroom power and unwittingly to help shift power in the emerging large firms from stockholders to managers.

But insurers did not stop seeking to preempt state regulation when the federal foray failed. The insurers' post-Armstrong acquiescence should be seen as an attempt to find a practical substitute for federal preemption. Insurers could well have asked themselves whether the appetites of the other states, salivating to attack the insurers, might be slaked if the New York legislature built a powerful and respected (but, as far as the insurers were concerned, sensible) New York regulator.

Consider the issue of insurer control of industry. At first, one might think that New York would have welcomed the prospect of having its financial institutions control industry outside of New York. True, the regulation resulted partly from New York–based populism. But consider also the possibility, albeit highly speculative, that the New York regulation eventually had the effect of *benefiting* the New York insurers. New York had something to protect: New York–domiciled insurers wrote policies accounting for 60 percent of the premiums paid in the entire United States; as late as 1940, that percentage was 40 percent, and it was still at 21 percent in 1979.[35] New York became the de facto preemptive regulator, co-opting the widespread call in many other states to regulate the insurers stringently in 1905,[36] and the insurers might thereafter have acquiesced.

The popular revolt—said by the Louisiana insurance commissioner to be "a popular movement to invoke the . . . State to check the unequal and constantly increasing advantage of concentrated corporate power over indi-

---

[35] State of New York Report of the Executive Advisory Commission on Insurance Industry Regulatory Reform 1 (1982) [Governor's Advisory Report].

[36] Keller, supra note 1, at 255–56.

vidual effort"[37]—could not be contained without legislative action. The insurers' weekly journal reported the threat:

> [O]ther State legislatures [are] in session, and . . . it is probable that all of them will attempt to regulate and reform the business of life insurance. The Armstrong investigating committee has set the pace, but it is to be anticipated that other jealous legislators will endeavor to out-Armstrong Armstrong. Already some drastic measures have been proposed, and others are known to be in the incubator.[38]

To defeat non–New York regulation, rational insurers might have formed a cartel and agreed in their collective interest not to interfere in non–New York industry. More realistically, since the insurers at first opposed New York's bill generally (although they accepted that they should not control other firms), they eventually acquiesced to it,[39] and perhaps came to see that New York State regulation could in the collective interest of New York insurers prohibit them from activities likely to trigger other state or federal regulation. In fact, the insurers regrouped after the Armstrong bill passed, formed a new industry association, and announced that they agreed that the law should prohibit insurers from buying stock.[40]

Decades later, New York government officials were clearly conscious of the general preemptive principle. "New York insurers and the New York Insurance Department for many years led the nation in building the public confidence upon which the business of insurance depends," said the 1982 Governor's Advisory Report on insurance regulation, and the report's first words referred to the many jobs that the insurance industry gave to New Yorkers.[41]

If insurers regularly intervened in local industry, if they made financially aggressive concentrated investments, they would become publicly visible

---

[37] Id. at 256.

[38] The Spectator, Apr. 19, 1906, at 217; see id., Mar. 8, 1906, at 129 (other states are investigating the giant New York insurers); Want Uniform Code of Insurance Laws, N.Y. Times, Jan. 20, 1906, at 4 (ten states plan uniform insurance code, but await New York's action); George Henderson, History of the Insurance Investigation 6 (undated pamphlet, circa 1906) (prior to Armstrong, several insurance commissioners discussed a joint investigation by several state insurance departments).

[39] Cf. Swaine, supra note 6, at 762–63 (Equitable publicly supports the Armstrong bill, although motive—to seek practical preemption or to succumb to political reality—unstated); Limiting Investments Discussed by Morton, N.Y. Times, Mar. 10, 1906, at 2, col. 5 (Equitable president says remedial laws are needed and New York should take care to pass a nearly perfect bill, because other states will look to New York for leadership); The Spectator, June 29, 1905, at 356 (in insurers' interest to have an investigation to restore public's shaken confidence in the insurers).

[40] Proceedings of the First Annual Meeting of The Association of Life Insurance Presidents 128–29 (1907).

[41] Governor's Advisory Report, supra note 35, at 1, 7.

and draw political attention. In 1906, "[t]he feeling against life insurance companies was running rather high in some states, and much legislation of a punitive nature was offered." Once the regulators got started, they might get to rate setting or other measures dangerous to insurers. In other areas, the Armstrong committee explicitly recommended, and the legislature quickly adopted, regulatory changes to aid New York insurers doing business in other states.[42]

A "Narrow" Public Choice Story?

To modern eyes, the interest group benefited by the New York regulation first appears to be managers of public companies, because the rules weakened the potential controls on managers. In 1905, contemporary observers saw the insurers' growing role in corporate finance and governance. Hughes recognized that insurers were slowly gaining power vis-à-vis portfolio companies and their management:

> [Securities underwriting and purchase] have brought insurance companies into close relations with railroads, banks, trust companies, banking houses and the flotation of new enterprises, thus involving [insurance companies] in the manifold transactions of the financial world, not in their *normal relation as creditors* through suitable investments, *but as co-owners of the corporations* . . . to which they have thus become allied.[43]

Hughes feared financiers with big blocks of stock. "If the stock investment be a large one," he argued, "it is frequently found advisable to increase it until a substantial control is effected, and the insurance corporation is not only engaged in a different enterprise, but directly undertakes its management."[44]

Yet while managers could have been expected to resist expansion of the role of institutions in corporate governance (as they did in the 1980s, when state antitakeover legislation was being debated), industrial company managers did not lobby back then. With the exception of bankers, no affected group visibly approved of keeping insurers weak. Incipient insurer power was more a factor in shaping public opinion than in shaping interest group pressure.

Bankers did applaud the legislation that kept insurers from owning bank stock. Prior to the New York regulation, insurers controlled several large

[42] Anderson, supra note 24, at 267–68.

[43] Hughes Report, supra note 10, at 293–94 (emphasis supplied).

[44] Id. at 389. Foreign experience suggests, contrary to Hughes, that the usual result is not full control, but mid-sized blocks big enough to make the holder effective in crises, without the holders micromanaging the firm outside of crisis situations. See infra chapter 11.

banks. In a retrospective on the role of financial institutions in owning stock, one commentator observed that the

> influence of financial institutions through acquisition of stock . . . [was] small with few exceptions. One of these [exceptions was] the purchase of bank stocks by . . . insurance companies . . . during the second half of the nineteenth century. . . . [I]n 1880 fully 5 percent, and in 1900 about 8 percent, of all bank stock was held by financial institutions. . . .[45]

If financial supermarkets were going to develop at the turn of the century, they were going to revolve around the three large life insurers emerging in New York, which were already becoming interstate bank holding companies.

Banking journals were outraged at insurers' poaching on the bankers' rightful turf. During the Armstrong investigation, the *American Banker*, in a 1905 article entitled "How the Insurance Companies Injure the Banks," cheered Hughes and the Armstrong investigation and protested the insurers' inroads into the bankers' business:

> The way in which the insurance companies injure the business of the banks is set forth by a morning contemporary: "The modern life insurance company, or nearly all of the big ones, not only have lured investors with promises of savings bank interest, but with hints and pledges that grossly excessive premiums would yield returns far beyond what the money would earn in savings banks. . . . [T]he companies beat down all the barriers preventing them from doing a general banking . . . business through trust companies. . . . Then they swelled the premium payments to several times the amount necessary to buy the simple insurance, and put pressure on their agents to write this class of policies, with dividends deferred as long as possible [so that life insurance came to have the function of personal savings]."[46]

Among bankers, "[t]here was *particularly a disposition to indorse heartily* the committee's ideas on the subject of a greater restriction of life insurance investment and a separation of the life insurance companies from trust companies and kindred institutions."[47] The *American Banker* reported that "bankers received . . . the abolition of stock investment [among other things] with uniform commendation."[48] The bankers' trade paper reprinted Bran-

---

[45] Goldsmith, supra note 26, at 87.

[46] How the Insurance Companies Injure the Banks, 70 American Banker, Nov. 4, 1905, at 2701, col. 1.

[47] Plans for Insurance Betterments Approved, N.Y. Times, Jan. 6, 1906, at 5, col. 3 (emphasis added).

[48] Banker's Opinion of Insurance Bill, 71 American Banker, Feb. 24, 1906, at 479; see also What Insurance Men Think of the Report, N.Y. Times, Feb. 24, 1906, at 2, col. 2 (similar statement).

deis's criticisms of the insurers' financial power.[49] The president of Chase National Bank said that "when the [Armstrong] committee takes up the restricting of investments it ought to prohibit investment in stocks of any kind."[50] Bankers complained that "it would not be long before practically the United States would be owned by three or four life insurance companies."[51] The Hughes Report criticized insurance companies' stock ownership because "[i]n their dealings in securities some have sought, as one of the witnesses frankly expressed it, to approach as closely as possible to the business of bankers."[52]

Moreover, the Armstrong legislation restricted sale of key insurance products, holding back the insurers' growth, and capped the amount of new insurance that a company could write annually. The banks' advantage here is obvious: since life insurance is a form of savings, restricting insurers' products, their investment portfolio, and the amount of insurance they can write would redirect some savings from insurers to banks.

Banker support for restricting insurers could also be a *managerial* interest group story. Insurers already had enough muscle to get into adjacent financial services; they controlled the second-largest bank in New York. Managers of one industry—banking—wanted to get insurers off their backs, although they needed favorable public opinion to do so.

Second, the banking pressure could also be government cartelization, through which banks and insurers used government to divide up financial markets. Banks wanted other financial institutions out of their markets. Roughly contemporaneously with the insurance reform movement, for example, country banks sought blue sky laws that would raise the costs that securities firms would pay when selling stock, thereby impeding them when competing with the banks as places for savers to put their money.[53] Investment banks, one suspects, would have applauded the legislature's prohibition on life insurers' underwriting of securities, because insurers were trying to come closer to the source of securities issuance—to eliminate the middle-

---

[49] Insurance Funds and Banking Capital, 70 American Banker, Nov. 4, 1905, at 2694.

[50] Plans for Insurance Betterments Approved, supra note 47, at 5. The Chase president, himself a former Comptroller of the Currency, could have been offering a public-spirited view of how policyholders should be protected by reducing the risk of insurers' portfolios.

[51] Review and Outlook, Wall Street Journal, Sept. 25, 1905, § 1, at 1.

[52] Hughes Report, supra note 10, at 292.

[53] Jonathan R. Macey and Geoffrey P. Miller, Origin of the Blue Sky Laws, 70 Texas Law Review 347, 364–67 (1991) (strong bank pressure to limit securities sales contributing to enactment of blue sky laws). Perhaps the blue sky laws grew out of the competition between out-of-state investment bankers and in-state small-town bankers. The former did not wield as much political power inside the state as did the local bankers. In New York, on the other hand, the local bankers' raw political power might have been offset by the local insurers' raw power; interest group pressures neutralized each other, making public opinion the dominant legislative force.

man by joining in underwriting syndicates. Some investment bankers owned insurers' equity, so that the bankers could control the insurer's investment portfolio. Those that could not control insurers could have been expected to favor the Armstrong committee's call to eliminate insurer authority to underwrite securities because the prohibited insurers would have had to buy securities for their portfolios from the investment bankers. Commercial banks could have been expected to support the prohibition on insurers purchasing debt instruments that were close substitutes for bank loans.[54]

Integration of an insurance company with a banking firm could produce economies of scale or scope, enabling better delivery of financial services. Stand-alone banks unaffiliated with insurers would not share in any efficiency gains, and would become less competitive. Hence, stand-alone banks would favor legal separation of insurance from banking. Federal and state branching and chartering restrictions effectively gave local monopolies to local banks, which the insurers impinged upon. The point here is not that bankers acting alone pulled the strings to get the New York restrictions passed, but rather that bankers and insurers were in conflict, and public opinion threw the contest to the bankers.

Bankers later played a special interest role, influencing the New York legislature to preserve the separation between banks and insurers. Since 1984, insurers have been allowed to allocate some of their assets to subsidiaries, but no subsidiary can be in the business of banking, because bank lobbying stopped a proposal that would have allowed insurers to own bank subsidiaries.[55] Public opinion alone might have restricted the insurers in 1906 and, when the public furor quieted, rival financial institutions sometimes blocked insurers from obtaining repeal.

Public Interest Explanations

The prohibitions stemming from the Armstrong investigation reflected plausible public goals. I spend little time here on the public interest explanations not because they are unimportant, but because they are obvious.

[54] Vincent P. Carosso, The Morgans: Private International Bankers 1854–1913, at 533 (1987) (insurers eliminating the middleman); Hughes Report, supra note 10, at 31 (insurers in underwriting syndicates); Louis D. Brandeis, Other People's Money—And How the Bankers Use It 5, 13–17 (1914) (bankers owned stock in insurers to control the insurer's portfolio). But cf. Douglass C. North, Life Insurance and Investment Banking at the Time of the Armstrong Investigation of 1905–1906, 14 Journal of Economic History 209, 215–26 (1954) (describing dependence of insurers on investment bankers for securities).

[55] N.Y. Ins. Law § 1701(a) (McKinney 1985 and Supp. 1993); Insurance Reform Restricts Activity: NYS Bill Would Liberalize Industry, Carves Out Banking, American Banker, May 10, 1983, at 2. Banking laws also keep insurers and banks apart.

Because insurance was a form of middle-class savings, a public policy of ensuring insurer solvency was worth pursuing. But, although stock was then probably seen as too risky, the large insurers to which the restrictions were directed were solvent,[56] meaning that any public-regarding impulses were not directed at then-pressing problems. Moreover, stability was not the only issue—there was a valid fear that controlling stockholders would engage in self-interested transactions. The self-interested managerial actions that institutional blocks tend to offset were less vivid.

Although these public interest explanations are plausible, public-regarding rules frequently are not passed. Even when a legislature passes a public-regarding law, it can choose among several rules, each of which would implement the public interest. Which rule passes and persists is determined by some combination of public choice, accident, interest group pressure, and popular opinion. Consider safety in insurers' portfolios, a secondary rationale for the 1906 stock ban. Stock has a role to play in most portfolios. And insurance products could pass the risk of stock investments (and the benefits of their historically higher returns) to insurance beneficiaries. The variable annuity does just that: a beneficiary's investment rises or falls with the underlying stock market portfolio, until converted to a fixed annuity at retirement. While these alternatives were not well understood in 1906, they were understood thereafter, but ignored by revisers of insurance laws.[57]

Federalism

American federalism is probably the leading original reason for the general fragmentation of American finance, because federalism accounts for the fragmentation of *banks* at the turn of the century. Each state chartered and protected its own banks. Congress created national banks, which in fact were national in name and local in operation. This was federalism's primary fragmenting role.

Bankers, although weak economically, were strong politically, with the local ones often becoming powerful figures in their hometowns. When insurers emerged at the turn of the century as financial institutions that could challenge and eclipse the bankers, bankers seem to have wanted to flex their political muscle to suppress an incipient challenge from the three large New York insurers that were rapidly becoming the first truly national American financial institutions.[58]

[56] Henderson, supra note 38, at 1.

[57] Dwight C. Rose, Should Life Insurance Companies Be Permitted to Invest in Common Stocks? (mimeo prepared for New York Joint Legislative Committee Hearings on Life Insurance) (Oct. 21, 1941).

[58] Here, I only project back the recurring power of organized small-town bankers to get their

Precisely how, if at all, the banks influenced the passage of legislation may forever be lost after a near-century of inattention to such public choice stories. Popular opinion seems to have been the motivating political force and no united phalanx of financiers resisted the populist side of the Armstrong investigation. The process by which banker fragmentation could have helped induce or preserve insurer fragmentation after 1905, stripped of real-world complexity (and ignoring the more powerful popular impulse to tie down the galloping insurers), can be seen as follows: (1) banks were fragmented because of federalism and popular opinion; (2) the fragmented banks, particularly in an era of expensive telecommunications, had *local* monopolies; (3) they sought to protect these local monopolies from the insurers, who were increasingly able to compete that monopoly away; (4) local banks not only had the incentive to protect their local monopolies, but also the political muscle to fragment the emerging financial institution, since bankers, particularly local bankers, could affect local politicians more than nonlocal financiers could; and (5) legislatures, influenced in part by the applauding bankers, fragmented the emerging financial institution, by pulverizing its portfolio and severing it from other financial institutions. I suspect that variations of this story can be told not just for insurers, but also for the Glass-Steagall Act's separation of investment and commercial banking, the Investment Company Act's fragmentation of mutual fund portfolios, and the Bank Holding Company Act's restriction of holding-company links with industry.

Still, no clear, visible interest-group story entirely explains the insurance portfolio rules. Rather, federalism explains the primary fragmentation of the American financial system—that of banks at the end of the nineteenth century—and, through its effect on the interests of the banks, federalism might be a secondary cause of the fragmentation of the insurers' portfolios. The primary cause of the latter fragmentation, however, seems to have been popular dislike of the powerful insurers.

THE CONTINUING INFLUENCE OF THE ARMSTRONG INVESTIGATION

My argument thus far in this chapter is that insurers' passivity in corporate governance can be partly traced to a statute and a political history. Populism, preemption, and interest group pressure help explain not only passage but also preservation of these restrictions. In this section, I further argue that

---

way, see infra chapter 7; I do not report findings of small-bank power at the turn of the century. To test this, we would need to see whether small-town bankers outside New York pressed their legislatures to restrict insurers, and link this to the New York legislature's actions responding to pressure from non–New York legislatures. See supra notes 36–40.

the Armstrong legacy of passivity was reinforced several times during the twentieth century. The 1905 rules, preserved intact until 1951, and modified only slightly before 1984, helped channel life insurers into passivity in corporate governance as stockholders, unable and unwilling to play a stockholder's role in the boardrooms of the largest American firms. Only occasionally, usually when the insurer made a big loan, did the insurer's senior people go into a firm's boardroom. And I understand they usually left when the insurer ceased being a big lender.

Today's limits on insurers' influential blocks of stock are real, although not absolute. We should not be surprised that when the rules did permit some activity in 1984, life insurers did not take complete advantage of the permission to own the large, sometimes active, equity positions common among British, German, and Japanese insurers.

The 1941 Proposals and the 1951 Amendments

Whether insurers should have been allowed to invest in stock became a live issue three decades after Armstrong, when in 1940 the SEC proposed that insurers be allowed to invest in stocks. It saw bans on institutional common stock investment as weakening equity markets; industrial companies were using too much debt.[59] "[O]veremphasis upon debt financing," said an SEC commissioner, "would bring about financial chaos in many leading industries. . . . [Although other governmental bodies want insurers confined to investing in debt, they] failed to mention the very important fact that British life insurance companies have successfully invested their funds in stock over a period of many years."[60]

In response, New York convened a legislative committee to hear views. It first called the state's superintendent of insurance, who attacked the SEC proposal as a reversal of the Armstrong understanding. If lawmakers allowed a little stock investment, the superintendent argued, they would not stop there: eventually insurance companies would control industry. But "[w]e do not want to see that control [of industry]," he said. "All that we want is that life insurance companies should make safe and sound investments."[61] He

[59] Commissioner Pike of SEC Wants Life Companies to Buy Common Stocks, The Eastern Underwriter, Oct. 24, 1941, at 7; Temporary National Economic Committee, 76th Cong., 3d Sess., Investigation of Concentration of Economic Power: Statement on Life Insurance, 25, 26 (Comm. Print 1950) (Monograph No. 28-A) [TNEC Investigation] (letter from Sumner T. Pike, SEC Commissioner).

[60] Id. at 26 (the commissioner was referring to the TNEC hearings, which worried about insurance and concentrated economic power, not equity financing for industry).

[61] N.Y. Dep't Warning Regarding Life Companies Buying of Stocks, The Eastern Underwriter, Oct. 24, 1941, at 1, 6; E. M. Ackerman, Discuss Common Stock Investment Plan, 145 Weekly Underwriter 961 (1941).

cited federal hearings—entitled *An Investigation of Concentration of Economic Power*[62]—that had "expressed a fear of the great concentration of funds of life insurance companies which might lead to control of certain industries, or of considerable influence in those industries."[63] The superintendent also said that insurers would inevitably control industrial firms once they began buying stock, which would mean that his department would have to regulate industry, and this was a task that the department wished not to have.[64]

The SEC reformulated its proposals: enable insurers to buy some stocks, but bar them from owning large blocks of a portfolio company.[65] This was the same as the SEC's prescription for mutual funds in the late 1930s: gather funds and invest them, but be passive in corporate governance.[66] Politicians reinforced the Armstrong passivity prescriptions with their rhetoric, and nothing was enacted in 1941.

Insurers were not clamoring for extended power in 1941. They had internalized the Armstrong prescriptions: some declined to join the SEC's proposal; others opposed it.[67] Prudential's managers testified that "they were shy of becoming 'partners in enterprise' lest they be accused of extending their economic power."[68] During a similar revival of the issue in the 1920s, the New York superintendent of insurance and the president of Metropolitan Life opposed expanded authority, and the press reprinted Armstrong's critique of stock ownership.[69]

The insurers' lack of interest could also be seen as an implicit cartelization among the insurers, to keep one arena for competition among them closed off. After a half-century of not owning stock, they were ill equipped even for passive stock investing, much less for an active stockholding role in corporate governance. If law continued to ban those activities, the insurers would

[62] TNEC Investigation, supra note 59.

[63] N.Y. Dep't Warning Regarding Life Companies Buying of Stocks, supra note 61, at 1, 6.

[64] Life Insurance Investments in Industrial Stocks Opposed, N.Y. Times, Oct. 22, 1941, at 33.

[65] Ackerman, supra note 61, at 986. The safety-enhancing effect of the ban was questionable. In 1941, the New York legislative committee commissioned a financial study, which told the committee that diversification *required* that the insurers *buy* some stock for their portfolios. Id. Others stated that safety fears would deter them from owning stock, as long as insurers' obligations were fixed. Kenneth Field, Sees Common Stocks Unsuited for Life Companies, 146 The Weekly Underwriter 152 (1942).

[66] See infra chapter 8. When war required the government to sell its debt, the federal government grew less interested in widening the insurers' investment options.

[67] Ecker against Change of Law to Permit Companies to Buy Stocks, The Eastern Underwriter, Oct. 24, 1941, at 7 (chairman of MetLife states that "[i]t would be a sin to utilize funds of life insurance companies to make such investments, . . . It would be speculation").

[68] Life Insurance Investments in Industrial Stocks Opposed, N.Y. Times, Oct. 22, 1941, at 33, 38.

[69] Life Insurance Law Upheld by Leaders, N.Y. Times, Sept. 29, 1929, at 7.

not have to gear up to learn something new. Moreover, savvy insurers feared that a prominent profile could lead to unwanted regulation. A Prudential senior representative testified that if insurers owned stock, corporate crises or gross mismanagement would induce them to reorganize the company or "join with other stockholders . . . [to] select . . . new officers. . . . [That] action . . . [by] the larger insurance companies . . . would be . . . a heavy . . . responsibility and would be further suspect of seeking economic power and influence."[70] Although the 1905 mobilization of public opinion during the Armstrong investigation was unsustainable over the long term, this Prudential statement suggests that the latent *risk* of mobilizing public hostility was enough to deter some insurers from seeking legal authority to wield power in corporate governance.

The issue of stock ownership came alive again after World War II, with congressional hearings propelling eventual regulatory action in New York. Those hearings made clear that liberalization should "prevent domination by the life insurance companies of individual companies or industries. . . . [Insurer ownership of] common stock of a business enterprise [should] be limited to one percent of the outstanding voting shares or $1,000,000, whichever is larger."[71] Because the proposed 1 percent lid was on buying a *portfolio* firm's stock, not on deploying the *insurer's* assets, Congress primarily feared insurer economic power, not insurer instability.

At this time, after World War II, the insurers pressed to loosen the investment restrictions, mostly to allow them to invest in stocks even if they were barred from buying influential blocks.[72] Some non–New York insurers had greater investment flexibility and greater income, they pled, but their pleas fell upon unsympathetic legislative ears until 1951, when the New York legislature eased the absolute ban, but prohibited an insurer from holding more than 2 percent of the voting stock of any portfolio company.[73] That the legislature limited the voting power that the insurers could amass in the portfolio company's stock—not just the portion of the insurer's assets that it

[70] New York Joint Committee for Revision of Insurance Law, Public Hearings, Oct. 21, 1941, at 149–50. Other insurers also mentioned the obvious safety concerns.

[71] Hearings Before Subcomm. of the Senate Comm. on Banking and Currency (1949) (statement of Thomas McCabe, former Chairman of the Board of Governors of the Federal Reserve System), quoted in Andrew F. Brimmer, Life Insurance Companies in the Capital Market 358 (1962).

[72] State of New York, Report of the Joint Legislative Comm. on Insurance Rates and Regulations, Leg. Doc. No. 55, at 59, 62 (1951) (life insurance industry petitions legislature to loosen restrictions on stock investment); Caution Keynotes Company Feeling on Common Stock Bill, Nat'l Underwriter, Mar. 30, 1951, at 1; New Life Company Investments Proposed, Weekly Underwriter, Jan. 27, 1951, at 253.

[73] N.Y. Ins. Law §§ 46-a, 78.2, 81.13(b) and 227.1(b), discussed in Governor's Advisory Report, supra note 35, at 21–22, 27.

could devote to the investment—shows that its fear was not so much that insurers would take on too much risk, but that they would become too powerful. Even in 1951, a fear of private concentrations of power better explains the laws than does a fear of risky investments. (The legislature's fear could have been that insurers as big controlling stockholders would steal from others in the portfolio firm. But as a full explanation this, too, is dubious: elsewhere corporate law was moving toward case-by-case analysis of such transactions, and away from wholesale bans on large stockholding or on large stockholders' activities. The fear could alternatively have been that insurers with big blocks in what became a failing portfolio firm would throw good money after bad and risk their own solvency by propping up the failing firm. Although possible, this evinces a lack of financial confidence in the insurer; moreover, the problem would be best dealt with by portfolio rules barring the insurer from investing more than a specified percentage of *its own* assets in any one firm.)

Afterward, the New York legislature tinkered with its 1951 rules from time to time, slightly expanding the portion of the insurer's portfolio that it could devote to stocks and the percentage of a portfolio firm's equity that it could take. Not until 1984 did it significantly expand insurers' authority to take big stock positions.

The 1984 Amendments:
Internalization of Passivity

The Armstrong legacy is not just a quaint scandal from nearly a century ago. It has had three lasting effects: first, in the residue of statutory limits; second, in the residue of industry inactivity, since insurance executives are now ill equipped to wield big blocks and insurers have developed as organizations not attuned to active stock investments and corporate governance; and third, in Armstrong's lasting psychological effects on industry executives, who shy from challenging its legacy. In the 1940s, New York's deputy superintendent of insurance wrote that although Wall Street had forgotten Armstrong, "[i]t is safe to say that every life insurance company [person] has this in the back of his mind whenever investment in common stocks by life insurance companies is discussed. . . . [T]he Armstrong Report is still a working Bible."[74] A retired insurance lawyer told me that when he went to work at the New York insurance superintendent's office in the 1950s, his first assign-

[74] Shelby Davis, Common Stock Investments by Life Insurance Companies, Financial Analysts' Journal, July 1945, at 3–13. Davis, the deputy superintendent of the New York Insurance Department, may also have meant that Armstrong was a working Bible for the superintendent's office.

ment was to read Hughes' report, so that he could understand the regulator's mission. In the 1960s, one observer of life insurers said:

> [G]iven the acute sensitivity of life insurance managements to public opinion (and the constant recognition of the possibilities of more intensive regulation), the companies would probably never allow themselves [even if allowed] to get into a situation where their ownership of common stocks in a given corporation could provide influence, real or imagined, over a corporation's affairs. . . . [L]ife insurance companies have generally preferred to sell their stock holdings when corporate performance fell short of expectations rather than engage in extensive efforts to reform or replace existing management. . . . There seems to be no reason to anticipate a substantial change in their attitudes and behavior, so one need not devote much thought to the possibility.[75]

In the 1990s, I interviewed another senior insurance company executive who keeps the Armstrong Report handy and sees it as a reason for insurers to stay passive. The "Wall Street rule" tells institutional investors to sell when unhappy with management. Peel away the surface of the rule, the layers of investigation, scandal, and restriction, and the rule can and should be seen for insurers as the partial internalization of the Armstrong investigation.

How can *past* passivity rules have continuing effect? The 1984 amendments give insurers some leeway in their investment discretion. Although that leeway is not enormous,[76] why don't they use it? Cultural limits elsewhere in finance were strong but eventually gave way; for takeovers, culture constrained the first-tier investment bankers from assisting a hostile acquirer in the 1960s and early 1970s, until Morgan Stanley broke ranks in the mid-1970s. Similarly, large firms in the 1960s and 1970s first felt constrained not to be the hostile offeror, but eventually by the 1980s some changed their mind and many only felt constrained not to be the first bidder. Why do the cultural limits on insurance investments persist, particularly when the informal historical limits are themselves remembered only by some insurance executives?

Could a liquidity preference be a compelling explanation? Some institutional investors prefer liquidity to influential big blocks.[77] Although liquidity is not irrelevant, insurers' liquidity needs do not compel them to keep most of their portfolios liquid; indeed, about half of an insurer's portfolio is usually illiquid.[78] Because their obligations are long-term claims, insurers have not

---

[75] Brimmer, supra note 71, at 363.

[76] See infra notes 87–95 and accompanying text.

[77] See John C. Coffee, Liquidity Versus Control: The Institutional Investor as Corporate Monitor, 91 Columbia Law Review 1277, 1288 and n.29 (1991).

[78] Arthur Snyder, Dispelling the Seeds of Doubt, 92 Best's Review, Nov. 1991, at 14, 120. True, an illiquid private placement is not precisely equivalent to an illiquid block of stock, because the private placement will have interest payments, sinking fund payments, and a ma-

been desperate for liquidity, and have historically invested in big illiquid mortgages and private placements. These investments indicate that illiquidity cannot be a total barrier to big blocks; it is just a secondary cost. Big blocks of stock, although illiquid, may still be more liquid than either the private placements or the real estate that underlies much of the life insurers' portfolios. Foreign life insurers take big illiquid blocks of stock.

If an intermediary's beneficiaries can exit quickly—as can owners of mutual funds—the intermediary needs liquidity. Holders of life insurance policies cannot conveniently control the timing of their own exit. A classic study of the investment behavior of insurance companies begins its discussion of the insurers' framework dismissively, perhaps too much so: "They have little need for liquidity."[79]

Life insurers do need liquidity to back some new products, such as pension management. Moreover, to say that liquidity is secondary does not mean that liquidity is of no concern. Volatile markets or the risk of increased loan demand from policyholders causes insurers to reevaluate their need for liquidity. But for liquidity to be a *critical* bar to insurers' ownership of big blocks, liquidity needs would have to dominate nearly all of an insurer's portfolio, as opposed to being a consideration for just part of it.

What then are the reasons for the insurers' continued reluctance to take big blocks? First, the ongoing formal limits have some bite: they prohibit a New York–regulated insurer from investing more than 5 percent of its assets in non–New York control blocks; they charge debt investments in the controlled company against that 5 percent; and they are probably used by insurers for strategic investments close to the insurance industry (investment banking, for example). Legal barriers have only been lowered, not withdrawn.

Second, perhaps we are seeing cultural lag. Although in 1984 New York loosened insurers' portfolio restrictions, takeovers then addressed many problems that institutional control of large blocks might otherwise have handled. Before 1984, large blockholding was prohibited to insurers; it was superfluous for most of the rest of the 1980s. The one big-block institution that has emerged in recent years is a property and casualty insurer, Berkshire Hathaway. Perhaps it is the first, not the last.[80] Moreover, the recent

---

turity that could correspond with the insurer's expected payment obligations. Moreover, volatility in stock is a constraint; since stock is more volatile than debt, and insurers are leveraged institutions, they cannot absorb too much volatility. Even aversion to volatility is not a showstopper, since insurers invest heavily in real estate markets, which have been highly volatile, affecting them even when their initial investment was as a secured lender, and there are financial instruments that mitigate the volatility of investing in stock.

[79] Brimmer, supra note 71, at 89 (Brimmer subsequently became a Federal Reserve governor). Policyholders can, however, cash out with a loan on some types of policies.

[80] Berkshire Hathaway also illustrates how New York's portfolio rules still bite. It is governed

years have not been good ones for the big life insurers; they do not have the wherewithal to start up a stock investment business. Indeed, as their financial condition weakened in the 1990s, their overall ownership share of the stock market dropped below 5 percent.

Third, insurers grew up in an era when the formal limits were severe. The complete ban on stock investment during the first half of this century precluded insurers from evolving along with large firms; they never developed the necessary organizational skills. Insurance regulation channeled insurers away from stock-based activity in public firms, and into the areas where activity was allowed—real estate mortgages and private placements with tight terms. There the insurers were active and strong. There is some irony here. Insurers have been active in influencing firms through loan documents for private placements and big real estate mortgages and through ancillary governance mechanisms (such as occasional board seats as the firm's big lender). The biggest gains from corporate governance, though, accrue to a firm's stockholders, a category that has not included the big life insurers for most of this century. Owning stock does not always fit well with the insurer's debt-like long-term obligations. But if insurers could easily have owned stock, they might have taken the stock and the associated governance rights not as a pure equity investment, but to protect their big loans (as happens at times in other nations). Unable to take stock for most of this century, the insurers learned other ways to protect their big loan investments. Unable to use big blocks of stock to protect their loans, the insurers learned how to use tightly covenanted debt for self-protection.

Fourth, the gains from changing the way they've learned how to do business may be too small in two respects. The overall social gains of boardroom stockholding activity might be meager. Or, the total gains might make involvement socially valuable, but a single insurer would be able to capture only a fraction of them. Gains will be shared by all shareholders, but the insurer with 5 percent of a company's stock gets only 5 percent. The cost/benefit calculation for the insurer might make involvement privately unprofitable. The private costs—creating a new organizational form, changing executive style, upsetting traditional customers, and possibly inciting a challenge from insurance regulators—are borne solely by the insurer. Even mild restraints can be enough to deter.

Fifth, to be effective in a crisis, even an active 5 percent stockholder must turn to *multiple* large block owners for allies;[81] but with other institutions

---

primarily by Nebraska's property and casualty rules, in contrast to most large life insurers, which are governed by life insurer rules, and often by New York's version of those rules. Berkshire Hathaway could not take ownership positions as large as it does if it were governed by New York's life insurer rules.

[81] This is the pattern in Germany and Japan. See infra chapter 11.

only now beginning to acquire sizable blocks, the critical mass of big-block investors has been missing. Insurers can adequately protect themselves when enforcing a debt, but cannot easily do so when wielding a big block of stock, because big-block allies are scarce. Also, multiple monitors can keep an eye on one another, as well as on managers. Managers are usually best left alone to run their own show, with institutions intervening only when results are poor. For multiple monitoring to be effective, the ownership structure must involve several large institutions with large, but not domineering, blocks.

Sixth, life insurers hold stock for pension management, which puts other structural and legal obstacles in the way of their becoming big-block investors. The most basic obstacle is the crude fact that operating managers control the deployment of pension funds and have not yet found it in their interest to encourage pensions to be big block investors.[82]

Finally, insurance executives know they face one big private cost: additional regulation. A high profile in corporate governance can trigger unfavorable regulation. When the public outcry died down after Armstrong, the insurers came back, not to get investment restrictions removed, but to remove restrictions closer to their pocketbook, such as requirements that they use legislatively mandated forms for writing life insurance contracts,[83] limits on renewal commissions, limits on expenses, and limits on the amount of insurance they could sell.[84] History thus suggests that insurers use their political resources primarily to reverse or to keep off the law books limits directly related to writing insurance; portfolio limits have historically been low on their political agenda. Perhaps even today they understand that a high profile ups the risk of renewed regulation in the "pocketbook" areas.

The 1980s Reminder

New York replayed the Armstrong themes in the 1980s, even as it liberalized the investment rules. The state advisory panel explained that while the insurers would get more latitude in investing, the New York government did not want them to become active investors. The advisory panel said that the then current "limitation[s are] unnecessarily low, . . . [but the panel's] recommendation would not change the traditional role of the insurance industry as a *passive* investor, *which we endorse.*"[85]

The Governor's Advisory Report recommended that insurers be allowed

[82] See infra chapter 9.

[83] William H. Price, Life Insurance Reform in New York, 10 American Economic Association Quarterly 26–33 (1909).

[84] Keller, supra note 1, at 259–60.

[85] Governor's Advisory Report, supra note 35, at 27 (emphasis added).

into the banking field, but the proposal raised the hackles of the banking industry, which lobbied to prohibit insurer ownership of banks. Banks disliked the potential for competition, and some bankers preferred not to have some banks (perhaps their own) become subsidiaries of life insurers.

TODAY'S RULES

Statutory Constraints

Until 1951, New York prohibited life insurers from owning *any* common stock. In that year a small wedge opened: 3 percent of the insurer's assets could go into stock. But the insurer's investment in a particular company was limited to 2 percent of that *portfolio company's* stock. In 1951, New York law governed about 85 percent of the insurance industry's assets.[86]

Thereafter, the wedge widened, the portfolio restraints loosened, and by the 1980s 20 percent of a life insurer's assets could go into stock.[87] That widening allows for some activity, although insurers are not completely free from constraints. The 1982 advisory report to the governor of New York endorsed expansion of permissible stock investments, but said the legislature should preserve the Armstrong principle—that insurers be passive.[88]

The statutory web implementing the passivity principle is complex, because New York simultaneously expanded the insurer's permissible investments in stock and limited the insurer's authority to own big blocks. First, no more than 2 percent of a life insurer's assets could be invested in any one firm—obviously a reasonable safety limit. Second, a subsidiary's goodwill was carved out from coverage tests.[89]

The third and most important rule prohibits New York insurers from putting more than 5 percent of their assets into "non–New York subsidiaries," a term that the statute defines broadly and vaguely enough to potentially sweep in most large-block investments. If an insurer owns a majority of the stock of a firm, that firm is a subsidiary; this much is unexceptional. But because the law defines an insurer's subsidiary as any firm for which the insurer has "possession, direct or indirect, of the power to direct or cause the direction of the management and policies of [that firm], whether through

---

[86] Act of Mar. 31, 1951, ch. 400, § 5, 1951 N.Y. Laws 1065, 1071; Haughton Bell and Harold G. Fraine, Legal Framework, Trends, and Developments in Investment Practices of Life Insurance Companies, 17 Law and Contemporary Problems 45, 46 (1952). A 2 percent position does not preclude activity—a few American institutional investors are today a bit active with only 2 percent—but it does cut down on the incentives for action.

[87] N.Y. Ins. Law § 1405(a)(6), (8) (McKinney 1985 & Supp. 1993).

[88] Governor's Advisory Report, supra note 35, at 1.

[89] N.Y. Ins. Law §§ 1302(a)(1), 1405(a)(6)(i), 1414(f), 1705(a)(2) (McKinney 1985 & Supp. 1993).

the ownership of voting securities, by contract or otherwise," even smaller blocks can trigger subsidiary status. Conceivably, even extremely tight loan terms that yield control make the borrower a subsidiary if the loan gives the insurer indirect power to direct a firm's management.[90]

If the insurers became minority stockholders with big blocks, they would probably not *immediately* seek to direct their portfolio firm's management and policies. Indeed, they might never seek tight direction, because activity *without* control would ordinarily be their best policy, since the institution is unlikely to run the firm better than the firm's own managers. And since the insurer would not be "direct[ing] . . . management and policies"—the statutory standard for control that triggers the New York portfolio limit—the insurer would lack *current* control and arguably be outside of the portfolio limit. They might take a few board seats and seek influence and knowledge. Only in a crisis, would they actively take control and reorganize the firm's management. Thus, Berkshire Hathaway, an insurance holding company not bound by these rules, took a minority stock position in Salomon, but did not direct Salomon's management and policies until the Treasury scandal hit Salomon, when Berkshire had the means and incentive to take control, and did. Institutions abroad play a similar role: The Japanese main banks do not direct day-to-day industrial policies, but they assert power in crises.[91]

But then, if an insurer wanted influential blocks, multiple crises could lead it to direct the management and policies of a few firms in its portfolio. If its total investment in such firms exceeded 5 percent of its assets, it would violate the law.[92] And these minority positions, even when not used for control, are in a gray area of the law, which defines control as requiring only that the insurer have the *power* to direct management and policies. That the insurer chooses not to exercise its power does not exempt it.

If the insurer controls or has the power to control a firm, its *total* investment in that firm—debt, mortgage, and stock—is charged against the law's limit of no more than 5 percent of the insurer's assets in subsidiaries.[93] But nonequity investments, such as loans and mortgages, are the bread and butter of a large insurer's investment portfolio. Since insurers often want tight loan covenants to protect their big loans, they should usually prefer to avoid taking any stock, so as not to aggravate the risk that they would be found to control the debtor firm. (A plausible way to protect insurers, if regulators thought insurers would imprudently throw good money after bad, would just be to limit an insurer's total investments, including debt and equity, in

---

[90] Id. § 107(16), 107(40)(A)-(C).

[91] Paul Sheard, The Role of the Japanese Main Bank When Borrowing Firms Are in Financial Distress (Stanford Center for Econ. Policy Res. Pub. No. 330) (Nov. 1992).

[92] N.Y. Ins. Law § 1705(a)(1) (McKinney 1985 & Supp. 1993).

[93] Id. § 1705(c)(1)(iii).

a single portfolio firm to a small, say, 2 percent, percentage of the insurer's total assets.)

Moreover, activity increases the possibility of a regulatory finding of control, because activity implies that the insurer might have the power to control management. Owning 10 percent of a firm's stock might not always be enough to direct management and policies, but the insurer that becomes active, choosing new management through its board seats or through an implicit threat to foreclose on the mortgage, shows that it *can* direct management and policies, triggering the standard that defines a statutory subsidiary.[94]

I understand that insurers use their limited authority for noninsurance subsidiaries to buy firms that advance the insurer's core business, but that are not yet defined for statutory purposes as insurance subsidiaries (which would be exempt from the 5 percent limit). Thus some insurers view themselves as financiers and use up their subsidiary allowances for investment banking subsidiaries. Insurers and portfolio firms also shrink from triggering subsidiary status, because that status would pull the portfolio firm into the regulators' orbit.[95]

Indirect Constraints

An insurer could control a portfolio firm as its creditor, without owning a stock interest. But this kind of control is often not optimal for the *portfolio* firm, because the creditor that owns *no* stock will tend to be excessively risk averse; it is hurt if the firm deteriorates, but isn't rewarded enough if the firm does unusually well. The creditor who does not own stock wants to assure itself of repayment; it does not want to be an entrepreneurial risk-taker. Stock can support a big loan by muting the extreme risk aversion of the big creditor. (Similarly, adding a loan to a stock investment helps to align the stockholder with the preferences of those employees, managers, suppliers, and customers who make big investments of their human or rela-

---

[94] To be precise, the finding of control due to activity would not in itself trigger a statutory violation, because the statute prohibits new investments if the 5 percent threshold has been (or would thereby be) breached. In finance jargon, the statute uses an incurrence test, not a maintenance test. Id. § 1705(a)(1).

[95] See Carol J. Loomis, The New J. P. Morgans, Time, Feb. 29, 1988, at 44. There are two 5 percent tests here, which could cause confusion. One limits the firm's control blocks by restricting the insurer to investing only 5 percent of its own assets in non–New York subsidiaries; the other is a rebuttable presumption of noncontrol if the insurer owns less than 5 percent of a portfolio firm's stock. New risk-based capital rules for insurers disallow 30 percent of the value of stock they own for their own accounts from assets when testing the adequacy of an insurer's capital.

tional capital in the firm. Not all firms are served by this alignment of interests, but some would be.) Moreover, not only is the big influential creditor frequently too risk averse, but the creditor's control might *still* trigger the portfolio rules, because a finding that the insurer is in control, even as a creditor, activates the restrictions.

The statute's control-based portfolio limits parallel bankruptcy-related doctrinal limits. Lender control of the portfolio firm, coupled with overreaching behavior, triggers lender liability and equitable subordination of the lender. When lender liability applies, the controlling lender becomes liable for losses it causes the portfolio firm; when equitable subordination is in play, the lender's loans are subordinated to the loans of other creditors if the portfolio firm goes bankrupt.[96]

Even if law did not restrict the investments of life insurers, they frequently prefer debt to equity anyway. When insurers' payment obligations are actuarially fixed, insurers prefer investment returns to track their obligations. Debt would track their obligations better than equity would, and the insurers' profits would come from the spread between their debtlike obligations and their debt investments. Still, this potential mismatch between obligations and investments is not a showstopper: insurers have already owned over 5 percent of the American stock market, and insurance vehicles could pass on some equity risks to the beneficiary, as does the variable annuity or pension plan. And stock's role could be, as we have already seen, to support big debt investments, not to be an independent part of the portfolio.

These rules *help* to explain why insurers have historically been passive, and why even today portfolio limits have continuing bite. But since it is now *possible* for them to become influential, insurers could yet emerge from their historical passivity. (This chapter is about the big insurance players, life insurers, not property and casualty insurers, about which a word might be said, because investors affiliated with them—Laurence Tisch, Saul Steinberg, and Warren Buffett—*are* active, often with influential stock positions. Tisch and Steinberg do not make these investments through their property and casualty firms, but through holding companies not subject to the insurance regulators' portfolio rules. Buffett's Nebraska-based property and casualty insurance companies take big blocks in portfolio firms in ways that I understand were not allowed until the 1980s, when Nebraska's insurers got Nebraska to change its portfolio rules to allow concentrated investments.)[97]

---

[96] Taylor v. Standard Gas and Elec. Co., 306 U.S. 307, 323–24 (1939); State National Bank of El Paso v. Farah Mfg. Co., Inc., 678 S.W.2d 661 (Tex. Ct. App. 1984).

[97] Neb. Rev. Stat. § 44–311.04 (1988). Buffett might be the first, with followers to come later.

Lack of State Competition in Providing
Insurance Regulation

State law sets the basic rules for corporations, and competition among states has explained why many corporate law rules emerge. Why don't states compete in the same way to make insurance law?

The state of incorporation—Delaware for most large firms—sets the major rules in corporate law, but the state where the policy is sold sets insurance law. This helps explain why state competition to provide insurance rules cannot occur in the way it can for corporate rules. A corporation dissatisfied with its state's corporate rules can usually reincorporate in a small state that offers more favorable rules. But although an insurer could also reincorporate in a small state with more favorable rules, the small state's rules do the insurer little good, since the small state has few buyers of the insurance. Because insurers usually wish to sell policies in more than one state, they are often subject to the insurance laws of several states. New York requires out-of-state insurers that sell in New York to comply "in substance" with New York's rules, including its investment limitations.[98] New York law still governs 58 percent of the life insurance industry's assets—most insurers want to sell to New Yorkers and must substantially comply with New York portfolio rules to do so.[99] And other states have similar rules.[100]

SUMMARY AND CONCLUSIONS

The major insurance company regulation wrought by the Armstrong investigation is not explicable as a pure interest group story. A scandal hit in 1905 and change came in 1906, but the change was not solely or even primarily due to the rise of another interest group. The media created public interest in the scandal. Politicians then responded to an aroused public. If any group motivated the investigation, it probably was the middle-class reform movement in New York. Media and public opinion were the central causal agents of reform and regulation.

A "narrow" interest group story is there, but muted. Banks applauded the

[98] See N.Y. Ins. Law § 1413(a) (McKinney 1985 & Supp. 1993). New York also became the model state for insurance company investment regulation.

[99] The New York–governed statistic came from the Bureau of Research of the New York Insurance Department in the early 1990s. Aggregate assets came from A. M. Best's information department.

[100] If they did no business in New York, insurers from states with fewer restrictions could invest readily in common stocks. Yet, smaller, local insurers have historically not invested in stocks even if permitted, because of the expense of assembling a staff to do so. See Brimmer, supra note 71, at 349–50.

regulation of insurers, in particular the ban on insurers' owning common stock, which at that time mainly meant bank stock. Banks could have been cheering the crippling of a competitor; in some cases, bank managers might have been cheering on the elimination of a boss. But these elements do not seem to be crucial motivating forces.

The regular prohibition on financial institutions' taking large stock positions was crucial to the development of the Berle-Means corporation, with its fragmented share ownership. In 1932 Berle and Means analyzed what has come to be known as the Berle-Means corporation, in which fragmented ownership shifts power in the firm to managers. What they discovered had partly been created twenty-five years before by Charles Evans Hughes and the New York legislature. As enterprises grew, only powerful financial institutions could counterbalance managerial power in the large public firm. American banks were already fragmented. Insurers emerged in their place and were about to become national financial enterprises, but then the Armstrong investigation shattered their incipient power. Thereafter, the insurers grew with no reason to develop the capacity to own stock (for their own accounts or for their customers) or to develop the ability to operate as big stockholders. There was no point in doing any of this, because not until 1951 could they own *any* stock at all, and not until the 1980s could they operate with significant freedom to buy big blocks of stock.

Managers eventually benefited from this fragmentation. In the case of a few other financial laws—antitakeover laws and efforts to roll back some modern limits on institutional investors—managers have been active in seeking self-protection. But for the fragmentation of insurer portfolios, this "narrow" interest group story is weak. It can be discerned only in the banks' vocal support for the elimination of insurance companies' power to own stocks. The public and the legislature intended to pacify the insurers; they did not intend to build the Berle-Means corporation and to centralize corporate authority in managers. As an unintended consequence of the reformist goal, a media campaign, and a public opinion that distrusted powerful financial institutions, one corner of the foundation of the modern American corporation was laid down in 1906.

CHAPTER 7

Banks Again

In 1932, when Berle and Means "discovered" the modern corporation, with its distant shareholders and centralized managers, they were discovering a business organization partly produced by weaknesses in the organization of the early twentieth century's principal intermediaries, banks and insurers. While one might attribute the splintered American financial system to the New Deal, the origins of fragmentation lie deeper in the country's past.

THE NEW DEAL

The New Deal law's importance is in *confirming*, and not so much in creating, a fragmented banking structure by (1) keeping bank branching restrictions; (2) severing commercial from investment banking, thereby creating two deep but separate financing channels; and (3) adopting deposit insurance, which propped up small banks by stopping deposits from running off to large banks and encouraged all banks to weaken their own equity (to the point that they could not safely hold much stock). A chief propellant behind the laws was the preexisting strength of small-town banks, which got many of the benefits, and the public's predisposition both to protect them and to punish money center banks.[1]

The McFadden Act

Congress confirmed the state-by-state, separate banking systems first in 1927 by passing the McFadden Act, which allowed national banks to branch, but only as state law permitted, and again in 1933, when the New Deal Congress revisited the issue. The 1927 act allowed national banks to branch within a city or town, if state law permitted branching; the 1933 act allowed them to branch within the entire state, if state law permitted it.[2]

---

[1] Donald Langevoort, Statutory Obsolescence and the Judicial Process: The Revisionist Role of the Courts in Federal Banking Regulation, 85 Michigan Law Review 672, 694, 697, 720–23 (1987); Jonathan Macey, Special Interest Group Legislation and the Judicial Function: The Dilemma of Glass-Steagall, 33 Emory Law Journal 1 (1984); George Benston, The Separation of Commercial and Investment Banking (1990).

[2] McFadden Act, ch. 191, 44 Stat. 1224; Banking Act of 1933, ch. 89, § 23, 48 Stat. 162 (1933) (codified at 12 U.S.C. § 36 [1988]).

Today, regional banking pacts allow some interstate banking, and permission for nationwide branching does seem right around the corner. But as I write in 1994, the United States, unlike most countries, lacks a true national banking system; this was the key historical bar to powerful American banks in corporate governance.

The Glass-Steagall Act

Glass-Steagall did not sever national banks from direct stock ownership as is sometimes said; the National Bank Act, as interpreted, had already done that. To avoid these interpretive problems for stock *dealing*, commercial banks dealt in securities indirectly, through affiliates, and by 1930 nearly half of the new offerings went through them. Securities dealing figured in a prominent Depression-era bank failure that captured the public's attention.[3]

Congress then believed that the failure of stock affiliates damaged banks and that the resulting bank failures had caused, not reflected, the Depression. Fears were expressed that a bank whose affiliate sold securities had a severe conflict of interest that could only be remedied by severing the securities-selling affiliate from the bank. In 1933, with the passage of the Glass-Steagall Act, Congress barred bank affiliates from owning and dealing in securities, thereby severing commercial banks from investment banks.[4] Today, prohibitions on commercial banks' underwriting and affiliation with companies dealing in securities are breaking down[5] and the problems and abuses once seen to afflict banks with securities affiliates no longer seem credible to many observers. Banks with securities affiliates may really be *more* stable than those without the added income stream; and the ability to make a profit from a customer by either taking a deposit or selling a security often may reduce a banker's conflicts in giving advice, since it can make some profit either way. These changing perceptions have helped to undermine the strictness by which courts and regulators have enforced Glass-Steagall.[6]

---

[3] California Bank v. Kennedy, 167 U.S. 362 (1897); George David Smith and Richard Sylla, The Transformation of Financial Capitalism: An Essay on the History of American Capital Markets, 2 Financial Markets, Institutions and Instruments 1, 28 (1993).

[4] Act of June 16, 1933, ch. 89, 48 Stat. 162 (codified as amended in scattered sections of 12 U.S.C.).

[5] Securities Industry Ass'n v. Board of Governors of the Federal Reserve System, 468 U.S. 207 (1984) (upholding Fed's authorization of Bank of America to acquire Schwab, a securities dealer); see also In re J. P. Morgan and Co., Fed. Banking Law Rep. (CCH) ¶ 87,554 (Sept. 21, 1990) (Fed approves application of a commercial bank to establish underwriting affiliate); Bankers Trust New York Corp., 75 Federal Reserve Bulletin 829 (1989) (Fed approves application of commercial banks to engage in some brokerage activities).

[6] Langevoort, supra note 1.

Bank safety and punishing money center banks were not the only motivations for Glass-Steagall's separation of investment from commercial banking. Its architects hoped to channel savings to local uses, and the law's passage and preservation has been seen by different analysts as resulting from the power of either small-town bankers, who wanted to thwart money center bankers, commercial bankers, who wanted to thwart investment bankers, or investment bankers, who wanted to thwart commercial bankers.[7]

Because stock dealing was under a legal cloud even before Glass-Steagall, and because without nationwide branches the banks lacked a retail brokerage network, we can never know how vigorously they would have developed as investment bankers. Their persistent efforts to enter stock-based financial services and the fact that despite the handicaps they accounted for half of the new securities placements in the late 1920s suggest vigor.

Deposit Insurance

Banking's preexisting fragmented framework, produced by federalism's forty-eight state banking systems in 1933, helped to pass McFadden's branching limits, Glass-Steagall's separation, and deposit insurance. During the Depression, thousands of banks failed. Their local deposit base was too small; if the local economy went bad, their loans became uncollectible, their deposits declined, and there was not enough new business. Risky small banks had trouble holding onto their deposits, which could flee to stronger banks; these small banks wanted deposit insurance to stem the outflow.[8] They got it enacted,[9] extended it, and then beat back later attempts to get it under control.[10]

[7] On small-town bankers, see Langevoort, supra note 1, at 697. On money center bankers, see id.; William Shughart, A Public Choice Perspective of the Banking Act of 1933, in The Financial Services Revolution 87 (Catherine England and Thomas F. Huertas eds., 1988); Thomas Ferguson, From Normalcy to New Deal: Industrial Structure, Party Competition, and American Public Policy in the Great Depression, 38 International Organization 41, 70–72, 83 (1984). On investment bankers, see Macey, supra note 1, at 15–21.

[8] Some of the strength of large money center banks came from being "too big to fail," meaning that the government would ignore the insurance limits and see that all depositors were paid off, to stop the failure of any really big bank.

[9] Carter H. Golembe, The Deposit Insurance Legislation of 1933: An Examination of Its Antecedents and Its Purposes, 76 Political Science Quarterly 181 (1960); see also Gerald P. O'Driscoll, Jr., Deposit Insurance in Theory and Practice, in The Financial Services Revolution: Policy Directions for the Future 165 (Catherine England and Thomas Huertas eds. 1988) and sources cited therein; cf. Langevoort, supra note 1, at 695–97.

[10] Kenneth H. Bacon, White House Bill on Bank Law Reform Faces Hurdles as It Goes to House Panel, Wall Street Journal, May 14, 1991, at A24 (reporting Independent Bankers Association's attempts to head off Treasury effort to limit deposit insurance coverage). Some deposit insurance for the poor and middle class is socially desirable and could explain a downsized system, but cannot explain the extensive system the United States has. See generally Robert C. Clark, The Soundness of Financial Intermediaries, 86 Yale Law Journal 1 (1976).

The federal, small-bank politics of deposit insurance also helped induce Congress to pass Glass-Steagall, which was originally not high on the New Deal agenda.[11] Although small banks wanted Glass-Steagall, since they were not big enough to profitably participate in the securities business, they wanted deposit insurance even more. The failure, due to its securities activities, of the frighteningly named Bank of United States, which was really a minor bank, primed the public for separation to promote the safety and soundness of the banking system and to punish the money center banks. (The perceived conflicts of interest arising from banks' selling securities also primed some policymakers for separation.) Meanwhile, Senator Carter Glass, a key player in Congress, thought that letting banks engage in the securities business took them away from their true function—lending to local farmers and small businesses. New York banks desperately wanted to avoid deposit insurance, because they expected deposits running off from small, weak country banks to come to them. Not making money in the securities business anyway—it was the middle of the Depression—they offered Glass-Steagall separation as a sop to the public and to the small banks, hoping to lessen Congress's and the small banks' interest in deposit insurance. They got Glass-Steagall, but they also got deposit insurance.

This series of laws—McFadden, confirming the branching restrictions to a single state; Glass-Steagall, keeping banks out of the securities business; and federal deposit insurance, preserving small-town banks—should all be seen as resulting from two primary forces, popular dislike of large money center banks and the political power of the small country banks.

The federal organization of fragmented banking thus allowed for powerful *political* networks that further fostered fragmentation. Bankers were powerful local figures. With some minimal organizational effort, they became powerful political forces, as the repeated successes of the savings and loan industry demonstrate and McFadden, Glass-Steagall, and federal deposit insurance reflect.

POSTWAR STRUCTURES

Bank Trust Funds

Bank trust departments, commercial banks' last direct link to equity, had their activity with stock chilled intentionally by postwar politics and unintentionally by (sometimes sound) fiduciary rules, which foster a hyperfragmentation of the portfolio, beyond what financial economists say is needed to diversify. (The origin of trustee laws had little to do with the typical fears of private power or interest group maneuvering, although their effects link up with such fears, as we see in chapter 9.) No more than 10

[11] Langevoort, supra note 1, at 695 and n.81.

percent of a bank's trust funds may be invested in the stock of any single corporation,[12] although banks would rarely go above 10 percent anyway. In the 1960s, Wright Patman, head of the House Banking Committee, investigated big banks' ownership of stock as trustee, resulting in the Patman Report, which warned against the growing power of bank trust departments,[13] inducing lawyers to warn banks against being active with their trustee stock.

The Bank Holding Company Act

The bank holding company, a commercial bank's last indirect link to equity, is regulated by the Bank Holding Company Act of 1956. Banks in the 1950s evaded the bar on branching by reincorporating as holding companies and chaining banks together as separately incorporated subsidiaries. The holding company was not as stringently regulated as its bank subsidiaries; it could engage in commerce and own stock. In response, Congress enacted the Bank Holding Company Act of 1956, which restricted a holding company's activities to those closely related to banking, banning it from owning more than 5 percent of the voting stock of a nonbanking firm.[14] By the 1950s, American banks were too small and weak to own big blocks of stock in large public firms, prohibited from doing so anyway, and after 1956 allowed only to own smallish blocks (5 percent or less) of voting stock through affiliates.

Today, other rules reinforce these past results. Equitable subordination rules, which can put loans of an influential creditor at the end of the line in a bankruptcy of the borrower, would make banks justifiably wary of owning big blocks of stock even if they could take them. A bank might try to combine its holding company's directly held stock with its trustee stock and thereby wield an influential block, but trustee laws tend to punish that kind of activity and the Fed has usually interpreted the 1956 Act's permission to own stock as allowing only passive investments in stock (see chapter 12).

The Bank Holding Company Act of 1956 was an important, and I believe, underrated influence on corporate structure. It, like Glass-Steagall and Mc-Fadden, did not *break* up a system of powerful intermediaries, but it blocked one from developing. Absent its passage in 1956, a nationwide banking system might have emerged late in the 1950s. Once one was in place, the walls

---

[12] 12 C.F.R. § 9.18(b)(9)(ii) (1990); I.R.C. § 584(a)(2)–(b).

[13] 1 Staff of House Subcomm. on Domestic Finance, Comm. on Banking and Currency, 90th Cong., 2d Sess., Commercial Banks and Their Trust Activities: Emerging Influence on the American Economy (Comm. Print 1968).

[14] Robert T. Clair and Paula K. Tucker, Interstate Banking and the Federal Reserve: A Historical Perspective, Federal Reserve Bank of Dallas, Economic Review, November 1989, at 6–12. Bank Holding Company Act of 1956, § 4(c)(6)–(7), 12 U.S.C. § 1843(c)(6)–(7) (1988).

separating finance and the nation's biggest firms might then have been breached as there then could have been powerful institutions able to own or control big blocks in industrial firms.

A Small Theory for the Bank Holding Company Act

Bureaucratic incentives could have played a role in maintaining the small-bank status quo when the Bank Holding Company Act was passed in 1956 and from time to time thereafter. If banks had securities portfolios and big blocks of stock, the Fed's authority in the current system, which makes bank regulators important people, running important institutions, might have diminished. Regulating institutions that each controlled a few industrial firms would differ from regulating banks. Change in the regulated institutions might have changed the identity or power of the regulating institution.[15] And in a reconstituted banking system, the Fed might have been unable to mobilize politically powerful small bankers, as it has done to its own bureaucratic advantage.

In 1954, when Wright Patman introduced a serious bill to audit the Federal Reserve, bank holding company legislation began to wind through Congress.[16] Patman's audit and budget bill would have compromised the Fed's autonomy, a matter of no small institutional significance to those running the Fed.[17] To defeat it, the Fed mobilized the small banks, which wanted holding company restrictions, and then lobbied for the holding company law, becoming the responsible regulator (although one "capture" theory would indicate that it would want large banks free to do more). The Fed chose *who* would capture the agency (small banks with a diffuse but *politically* powerful congressional constituency instead of large economically powerful banks), in an implicit trade-off with Wright Patman.

[15] See generally Milton Friedman, Monetary Policy: Theory and Practice, in Central Bankers, Bureaucratic Incentives, and Monetary Policy 11, 28 (Eugenie Froedge Toma and Mark Toma eds. 1986) (Federal Reserve wants more banks in Federal Reserve System not for Fed's monetary function but because of "the prestige, sense of importance, power, and effective lobby that the system gains by supervising many thousands of banks and other financial institutions").

[16] H.R. 7602, 83d Cong., 2d Sess. (1954); Federal Reserve Act Amendments: Hearings Before the House Comm. on Banking and Currency, 83d Cong., 2d Sess. 8–11 (1954) (testimony of William McC. Martin, Chairman of Board of Governors); Neil Skaggs and Cheryl Wasserkrug, Banking Sector Influence on the Relationship of Congress to the Federal Reserve System, in Central Bankers, Bureaucratic Incentives, and Monetary Policy 169, 175 (Eugenie Froedge Toma and Mark Toma eds. 1986).

[17] The Federal Reserve makes money in its open-market operations. Because, unlike other federal agencies, it has not been subject to the budget and appropriations process, it has had more autonomy, which it has vigorously sought to keep. In the mid-1950s the Federal Reserve had just freed itself from a political accord that had made it an adjunct to the Treasury Department.

Seen slightly differently, Wright Patman's populists wanted the Fed under direct congressional control *and* wanted a fragmented banking system with banks unable to control industrial companies. Then a politically agile Federal Reserve defeated the populist sentiment that threatened it, by capitulating to the populist desire to fragment financial control.

(The converse could happen if banks decline in economic importance, as they indeed had by the 1990s. The bureaucratic incentive might shift, to expand the power of banks to help them survive and also to be sure there was something to regulate.)

The Story Continues

In 1991, the Treasury Department tried and failed to get Congress to repeal McFadden, Glass-Steagall, and part of the Bank Holding Company Act.[18] While times had changed and anti–big-bank populism was not as strong as it once was, fears of concentration, although weak, were still in play. *Business Week* reported that "the recent wave of big-bank mergers fed lawmakers' fears that allowing interstate branching would create a handful of monopolistic megabanks."[19] Interest groups—particularly the small-town bankers and, since the bill would have allowed banks to sell insurance, independent insurance agents—were instrumental in killing the reform.[20]

Although Congress did not repeal the rules right away, they are breaking down via regulatory interpretation, some will probably be repealed soon anyway, and banks are pressing the rules' limits. Banks now give investment advice to mutual funds, despite the contrary ruling in the last U.S. Supreme Court decision on point. (Later decisions create enough ambiguities so that the banks' aggressive interpretations are not flouting the courts.)[21] I understand that some banks pushed the rules to their limit in 1980s leveraged buyouts, taking the 5 percent voting block that the law allows, the additional 20 percent *non*voting block it allows, and then, perhaps in conflict with the

---

[18] U.S. Department of the Treasury, Modernizing the Financial System: Recommendations for Safer, More Competitive Banks xviii–26 (1991).

[19] Mike McNamee, Just When Bank Reform Seemed Almost in the Bag, Business Week, Sept. 9, 1991, at 51.

[20] Jerry Knight, A Banking Bill That Suits No One: Special Interests All Want the Law Tailored Their Way, Washington Post, Nov. 13, 1991, at G1.

[21] In Investment Company Institute v. Camp, 401 U.S. 617 (1971), the Supreme Court barred banks from running mutual funds. Later, in Board of Governors of the Federal Reserve System v. Investment Company Institute, 450 U.S. 46 (1981), it held that a bank may advise a different kind of fund, a closed-end fund, and banks have interpreted the latest holding as allowing them to advise any kind of investment company, although the 1971 decision has not been reversed. E.g., Prospectus for Vista Capital Growth Fund, at 8 (Feb. 28, 1992) (Chase Manhattan admits cloudy legality in acting as adviser to equity mutual fund).

Fed's passivity interpretations[22] (but not in conflict with the formal words of the statute) became fairly active. Perhaps they believed that when the Fed revisits the issue, it will conclude differently. Even the branching rules are being eroded, by interstate compacts, and it is hard to see how they can continue.

SUMMARY

When the banking laws were strong, they determined much of the development of financial and corporate history. Now they are breaking down, but they still help to explain today's corporate structures, because the breakdown is incomplete and previously built organizations adapt slowly.

The modern banking laws—McFadden, Glass-Steagall, the Federal Deposit Insurance Corporation Act, and the Bank Holding Company Act— should not be seen as fragmenting the banking system. Fragmentation arose in the nineteenth century; the modern laws cemented it. There is no history of powerful bank financiers that the New Deal shattered; they always were fragmented. Even J. P. Morgan, powerful as he was, never controlled a national network of capital-gathering commercial banks; nineteenth-century laws prohibited it, and the legislation enacted in the wake of the Armstrong investigation stopped the first finesse of these laws when the insurers were on the verge of becoming interstate bank holding companies. Glass-Steagall stopped another finesse of the rules, but it should not be seen as shattering a truly powerful, stockholding intermediary, because no such intermediary then existed. It should be seen as the United States' declining to build and refine a system of powerful intermediaries that could have come to counterbalance managerial power in large public firms. The banking laws of the 1930s and the important Bank Holding Company Act of the 1950s only refined the American system by adjusting the preexisting topography of the country's fragmented and dispersed intermediaries, not by building something really new.

[22] See infra chapter 12.

CHAPTER 8

Mutual Funds

MUTUAL FUNDS, despite huge financial resources of $1.2 trillion—half in stock—rarely participate in corporate governance. They channel funds from distant individuals to industry, gather information about industrial investments that their owners cannot easily get and evaluate, and do the paperwork that individuals begrudge. They are not intermediaries that get funds from disparate investors, combine them into concentrated holdings, and then enter the corporate boardroom to represent their shareholder beneficiaries and, if need be, check management.

In the 1930s some funds began to act as monitoring intermediaries. They underwrote securities, were active in bankruptcy reorganizations, and participated in management.[1] The 1936 tax act, followed by the 1940 Investment Company Act, helped induce them to stop.

The cutoff's timing is ironic, because Berle and Means had just published their finding that the atomization of shareholdings had shifted power from shareholders to managers. Key political players then *wanted* to ban mutual fund (and other banker) control of industrial firms. Explanations for their preference for passivity include popular mistrust of large financial institutions, public-spirited rules to foster stable, honest mutual funds for the average investor, the accidents of tax doctrine, and a faint interest group story as some political actors favored local managers over Wall Street.

THE INVESTMENT COMPANY ACT OF 1940

Mutual funds pool investments from many investors, who get diversification and buy expert management from the fund's managers. Even when the Investment Company Act of 1940 was passed, cognoscenti recognized that mutual funds offered a third function: "[The investor] may be able to join in

---

[1] See SEC, Report on the Study of Investment Trusts and Investment Companies 370–71 (1939–1942) [SEC Investment Company Study]; SEC, Abuses and Deficiencies in the Organization and Operation of Investment Trusts and Investment Companies, pt. III, H.R. Doc. No. 270, 76th Cong., 1st Sess. 2501 (1939); Investment Dilemma—Trusts Forced to Choose between Drastic Reorganization and High Tax, under New Law, Business Week, July 11, 1936, at 45, 46.

the purchase of control of one or more other corporations."[2] Mutual funds could have evolved into the missing link between dispersed investors and large operating firms.

Power of Control

Congress disliked funds that controlled industry; passivity was best. Unscrupulous financiers and industrialists sometimes used investment companies to get control "of the wealth and industries of the country." To stop concentrated control, Congress had to "prevent the diversion of these [investment] trusts from their normal channels of diversified investment to the *abnormal* avenues of control of industry," perhaps by "completely divorc[ing] investment trusts from investment banking."[3] Congress then directed the SEC to draft legislation regulating mutual funds.

The SEC declared in its proposed bill that "the national public interest . . . is adversely affected . . . when investment companies [have] great size [and] excessive influence on the national economy."[4] In 1935, 56 investment companies controlled 187 portfolio companies. Little good could come out of control over portfolio firms. The investment company could lack diversification and fail. It might pump money into the portfolio firm to protect its large position. It might unwisely change the financial policy or capital structure of the portfolio firm, or unwisely force out high dividends. Finally, it might force a merger on terms disadvantageous to minority interest in the controlled company.[5]

The SEC conceded that fund control could reduce the informational and organizational problems of scattered shareholders; with its specialized personnel, the fund would have expertise, the motivation to improve managerial performance, and the clout to do so. But the downside of powerful funds

[2] See Alfred Jaretzki, Jr., The Investment Company Act of 1940, 26 Washington University Law Quarterly 303, 305 (1941) (Jaretzki represented a group of investment companies at congressional 1940 Act hearings).

[3] Stock Exchange Practices: Report of the Comm. on Banking and Currency, S. Rep. No. 1455, 73d Cong., 2d Sess. 393 (1934) (emphasis supplied) [the Pecora Report, in reference to its final chief counsel]. See also id. at 333–34, 363; Investment Trusts and Investment Companies, Pt. I: Hearings on S. 3580 Before a Subcomm. of the Senate Comm. on Banking and Currency, 76th Cong., 3d Sess. 36 (1940) [1940 Act Hearings] (similar statement); cf. Adolf Berle and Gardiner Means, The Modern Corporation and Private Property 183–85 (1933).

[4] 1940 Act Hearings, supra note 3, at 434. The statement of purpose also showed concern for efficient investment management and protection of investors. Id.

[5] SEC Investment Company Study, supra note 1, at 8, 22; Wharton School of Finance and Commerce, A Study Prepared for the SEC, H.R. Rep. No. 2274, 87th Cong., 2d Sess. 399–400 and 400 n.9 (1962) [Wharton Investment Company Study].

offset the upside. The SEC wanted mutual fund directors and employees off the boards of all portfolio firms; they wanted a Glass-Steagall type of severance. They also wanted to cap fund size at $150 million in assets.[6] Eventually the SEC compromised with the mutual fund industry, but it achieved substantial severance.

Diversification

First, a mutual fund cannot advertise itself as diversified if it owns in the regulated part of its portfolio more than 10 percent of the stock of any company. Three-quarters of the portfolio is subject to this fragmentation rule, *even if* that influential block of stock is a small portion of the fund's portfolio. (Several states have had more severe rules, banning a fund from selling its shares to state residents if the fund owned more than 10 percent of any firm; many mutual funds conformed to the most severe restrictions.)[7] The SEC wanted that restriction to disable control.[8]

To be sure, these portfolio limits allow for some, perhaps even substantial, corporate governance activity, particularly for the very large mutual funds that have arisen in recent years. But the smaller funds that prevailed until recently could not build large blocks without devoting a big part of the fund's portfolio to a few firms in a way that the 1940 Act made harder than it had to be. Even today the very biggest funds cannot take big blocks in the largest firms without bumping into these portfolio rules. (And the portfolio rules cumulate with other restraints to raise the cost of activity.) Whether mutual funds should be able to offer undiversified portfolios to investors is a question about which policy-makers may disagree. But the point here is that the portfolio rules make that kind of a big-block fund difficult, or illegal.

Second, a fund calling itself diversified has 75 percent of its portfolio restricted; for that portion, it can have no more than 5 percent of its assets in the securities of any one issuer. As a diversification standard, this provision is crude but understandable. Many mutual funds are designed for unsophisticated investors who cannot assemble a diversified portfolio or evaluate the

[6] SEC Investment Company Study, supra note 1, at 371; Wharton Investment Company Study, supra note 5, at 400; 1940 Act Hearings, supra note 3, at 188 (statement of David Schenker, Chief Counsel, SEC Investment Trust Study), 216–20, 375, 400–01, and 412. The SEC also refused requests that it recommend to the IRS that the IRS allow mutual funds with control blocks to have untaxed, pass-through status.

[7] Wharton Investment Company Study, supra note 5, at 403 (Ohio, California, and a few others).

[8] Id. at 188, 192 (statement of David Schenker). See also 1 Tamar Frankel, The Regulation of Money Managers § 33.1, at 343 (1978); Pecora Report, supra note 3, at 348–51.

mutual fund's portfolio.[9] By requiring some standard of fragmentation if the fund chooses to call itself diversified, the 1940 Act helps make sure that investors get what they were promised.

But this crude standard justifies only the 5 percent restriction (no more than 5 percent of the mutual fund's assets in any single company). The 10 percent restriction (no more than 10 percent of the *portfolio* firm's stock) adds nothing to diversification. Obviously, an investment company could have a small portion of its assets in a single firm, but if the firm were middling-sized, the investment company could have an influential block of stock. The goal seems to have been to disable control, not to promote diversification.

Networks and Affiliates

Although the 1940 Act exempts a quarter of the "diversified" fund's portfolio from the fragmentation rules, and theoretically the fund could choose not to call itself diversified and then be free of the portfolio rules entirely, it could not escape the similar tax portfolio rules I discuss below.

Other restrictions apply. True, as enacted, the act does not stop a fund or its employees from sitting on the board of a portfolio firm. But if a fund either owned 5 percent of a portfolio firm's stock or sat on its board, the portfolio firm would become a statutory affiliate of the fund *and* of the mutual fund's principal underwriter.[10] This would trigger transactional prohibitions, many of which *are* quite sensible safeguards against the risks of insider self-dealing, and these prohibitions would deter the relationship. A buyout, exchange of shares, conversion of shares from one class to another, and sale of shares by the portfolio firm to the fund all seem to be covered and to require special SEC exemption. (The SEC has issued some blanket exemptions, but their application to transactions when the fund has a director on the portfolio firm's board is uncertain.)[11] And without SEC exemption, the fund cannot act jointly with another financial institution to go onto a

---

[9] Id. § 5(b)(1), 15 U.S.C. § 80a–5(b)(1) (1988); 86 Cong. Rec. 1478 (1940) (remarks of Sen. Wagner); Pecora Report, supra note 3, at 348–51 (congressional criticism of mutual fund that put 9 percent of its assets into a railroad's stock).

[10] Investment Company Act of 1940 § 2(a)(3), 15 U.S.C. § 80a–2(a)(2) (1988); 17 C.F.R. § 17a-6 (1990).

[11] The statute and SEC rules here are unusually opaque. Conceivably new rules allow some joint undertakings but not those where there is incentive compensation. Compensating a fund officer on performance probably loses the exemption. 17 C.F.R. § 270.17d–1(d)(5)(i). See R. James Gormley, On the Same Side of the Table: Is Investment Company Act Rule 17d-1 Partly Invalid? 20 Securities Regulation Law Journal 115, 117–18 (1992) (section 17d rules are "a morass of unascertainable depth," SEC acknowledges 17d as "uncertain"); Ronald Gilson and Reinier Kraakman, Investment Companies as Guardian Shareholders: The Place of the MSIC

portfolio firm's board of directors, or otherwise exert control.[12] Until recent years, banking law was interpreted to bar banks from close affiliation with a mutual fund, further reducing the prospect of joint influence.

The 1940 Act bars cross-ownership between a portfolio firm and its mutual fund, meaning that a portfolio firm's managers could oust an active mutual fund by buying up enough of the mutual fund's stock. No fund may buy a firm's voting stock if both would own more than 3 percent of the voting stock of the other.[13] I understand that target firms have neutralized mutual fund ownership in a hostile takeover via the cross-ownership ban.

If the fund wanted to act jointly with an affiliate to exercise control, it would need prior SEC approval.[14] Imagine an incipient network of institutional investors: An investment bank, an insurance company, or a commercial bank could become the investment adviser to a mutual fund. The adviser might take 4.9 percent of the portfolio firm's stock, as does the mutual fund, and combine it with a holding of the investment bank, the insurer or the commercial bank's trust department. That block would be big enough to be influential, to get a representative into the boardroom. Perhaps SEC approval of activities, control actions, and control changes would be easy for the mutual fund and the other institutions to obtain, but in the absence of a blanket SEC authorization more expansive than that now given, the rules are at least another cost to joint activity.

ORIGINS IN THE 1936 REVENUE ACT

Subchapter M of the Internal Revenue Code

A mutual fund controlling portfolio firms would risk being taxed on its *entire* portfolio, since tax law allows only *diversified* funds to pass income up to shareholders, untaxed to the conduit fund. The 1936 Revenue Act notion of diversification, like that of the Investment Company Act, was not a notion found in a modern textbook on corporate finance: no investment in a firm constituting either more than 5 percent of the portfolio *or* more than 10

---

in the Corporate Governance Debate, 45 Stanford Law Review 985, 993 n.72 (1993) (incentive compensation to fund director may make exemption unavailable).

[12] See SEC v. Talley Indus., Inc., 399 F.2d 396 (2d Cir. 1968), cert. denied, 393 U.S. 1015 (1969).

[13] Investment Company Act of 1940 § 20(c), 15 U.S.C. § 80a–20(c) (1988); Hugh Bullock, The Story of Investment Companies 90 (1959).

[14] Investment Company Act of 1940 § 17(a)(1)–(2), 15 U.S.C. § 17(a)(1)–(2) (1988); Wellman v. Dickinson, 475 F. Supp. 783 (S.D.N.Y. 1979), aff'd, 682 F.2d 355 (2d Cir. 1982), cert. denied, 103 S.Ct. 1522 (1983). There are some exceptions, but not when the investment company commits more than 5 percent of its assets to the joint enterprise or puts a director on the board of the affiliate. 17 C.F.R. §§ 270.17d-1, 270.17d-5 (1990).

percent of the *portfolio firm's* stock. Later, in 1942, Congress eased up, allowing half of the portfolio to be more concentrated.[15] Witnesses at the hearings on the 1940 Act said that the diversification rules were not tax policy but regulatory policy, to distinguish "good" mutual funds (those that did not exert control), which were left untaxed, from the others, which would be taxed.[16]

If a mutual fund could not get pass-through status, its income would be taxed, resulting in a triple taxation, which would destroy the fund. The portfolio firm would pay taxes on its earnings, and then the fund would pay taxes on dividends it received from the portfolio firm, at an effective tax rate of about 10 percent on dividends; it would pay capital gains at a higher rate. This income would be taxed again when paid to shareholders of a nondiversified fund, yielding three tax events for the same income, one in the portfolio firm, one in the fund, and one for the owner of the fund. The tax rules, like the 1940 Act rules, don't stymie all mutual fund activity, but they eliminate one important financial product—the big-block fund—and make other kinds of action less likely.

People knowledgeable about the multiple taxation of intercorporate dividends view the rule as merely technical. But it is not. Dig into the legislative history, and one finds that the New Deal Congress taxed dividends to discourage complex corporate structures.[17] It is part of a pattern from antitrust and financial regulation that seeks fragmentation and arm's-length dealing and has continuing effects today. Not only does it help explain the path of mutual fund regulation and taxation—the funds needed some doctrinal hook to free themselves from the intercorporate dividend tax, and the "passive" trust was the handy hook—but it stops nonfinancial interlocks. Suppliers and customers might take blocks of stock in one another, in ways similar to what often occurs in Japan.[18] The intercorporate dividend tax discourages this, not just as a technicality but because Congress used tax rules to discourage the complex structure itself.

Let's see in more detail why taxes deter most ordinary corporations from large long-term ownership blocks, because even if financial intermediaries cannot take big blocks, one might ask why ordinary corporations do not. Part of the answer is that to get pass-through tax treatment, the business probably

---

[15] I.R.C. § 851(b)(4). Venture capital firms, which would provide monitoring for *small* firms, not the large firms that are our subject, are partially exempt from the no-control provision. I.R.C. § 851(e).

[16] 1940 Act Hearings, supra note 3, at 435–36 (statement of Raymond McGrath, Executive Vice President, General American Investors).

[17] Boris Bittker and James Eustice, Federal Income Taxation of Corporations and Shareholders § 5.0, at 5-22 n.61 (5th ed. 1987).

[18] Infra chapter 19; Ronald J. Gilson and Mark J. Roe, Understanding the Japanese Keiretsu: Overlaps Between Corporate Governance and Industrial Organization, 102 Yale Law Journal 871 (1993).

has to qualify as one of these financial institutions. A corporation might accept the unfavorable tax status in the short run, as a prelude to a takeover and restructuring. But a firm asserting long-term influence would need acute skills to make up for the taxes. If it received half of its income in capital gains and half in dividends, it would pay approximately 20 percent of its income in taxes. Nor could it organize itself as a partnership, which usually can pass through its income to owners without itself paying a tax. To get pass-through status, a publicly traded partnership *must* comply with subchapter M's portfolio rules.[19] Private partnerships with under one hundred investors can get pass-through treatment without conforming to the tax law's portfolio rules; these private partnerships in fact exist, suggesting that some public mutual funds, with their wider access to capital, might have developed similar big block portfolios.

Thus if a fund wished to sell services as a monitor, by dividing its portfolio into three or four stocks, it could not get the advantage of pass-through tax treatment. Such organizations do arise elsewhere. In Sweden, for instance, large mutual funds own big blocks of five or ten companies;[20] they would be taxed out of existence here.

TAX DOCTRINE: ARE MUTUAL FUNDS TAXABLE AS CORPORATIONS?

Investment Trusts: Carrying on a Business?

A persistent tax problem is determining which entity has to pay the separate tax levied on a "corporation," a term which, said the Revenue Act of 1926, includes "associations, joint-stock companies and insurance companies."[21] Were trusts and mutual funds taxable as corporate associations, and not as pass-through, untaxed entities?

A trust that did not carry on a business (and met other requirements) did not have to pay the corporate tax.[22] But "common law trusts . . . which act or do business in an organized capacity" did have to pay the corporate tax.[23]

---

[19] The key tax provisions are at I.R.C. §§ 243, 1201, and 7704(c).

[20] Gilson and Kraakman, supra note 11, at 993 n.34, 996 n.45.

[21] 44 Stat. 9 (1926), codified at I.R.C. § 7701(a)(3).

[22] Regulation 69, art. 1504, quoted in Leonard Wallstein, Some Legal Questions in Relation to Investment Trusts 11 (1928) ("the trustees did not 'manage the mills,' i.e., carry on a business"); Hecht v. Malley, 265 U.S. 144 (1924). Case law concluded that the entity was not taxable if "the trustees were, in substance, merely holding property for the collection of the income and its distribution among the beneficiaries and were not engaged, either by themselves or in connection with the beneficiaries, in the carrying on of any business." Wallstein, supra, at 9. The other critical tax distinction was whether the beneficiaries controlled the trustees.

[23] Regulation 69, art. 1502, quoted in Wallstein, supra note 22, at 11.

Whe[n] trustees merely hold property for the collection of the income and its distribution among the beneficiaries of a trust, and *are not engaged . . . in the carrying on of any business* . . . no [taxable] association exists. . . . [W]hen the trustees are not restricted to the mere collection of funds and their payment to the beneficiaries, but are associated together with similar or greater powers than the directors of a corporation for the purpose of carrying on some business enterprise, the trust is [taxable as] an association within the meaning of the statute.[24]

Was controlling an operating firm and affecting its policies a business? Probably. But trusts said that when they assembled a passive portfolio of diversified stocks and did no more, they were not taxable corporations.

Morrissey

The IRS then responded that providing diversified investments was itself a taxable business, making all trusts and mutual funds taxable at corporate rates. In 1935, the Supreme Court decided *Morrissey v. Commissioner of Internal Revenue*, in which it agreed with the IRS.[25]

The *Morrissey* decision left the unit investment trust as the only tax-free fund left.[26] That kind of trust puts together a portfolio, sells interests in it, collects the earnings, and returns them to the beneficiaries. The trust usually does not trade the securities in its portfolio; it is passive.

These passivity doctrines persist in today's tax law. Not only does portfolio fragmentation induce passivity, but pass-through treatment is available only to funds that derive 90 percent of their income from investment in stocks, bonds, and other securities.[27] On the statute's face, it is dubious whether a fund making more than 10 percent of its income from *management*, as opposed to passive investment, would be untaxed.

Liberalization in the 1936 Tax Code

The 1936 tax code "liberalized" tax law for mutual funds by exempting fragmented funds. Yes, such funds were carrying on a business. But it was not a "real" business. It was the business of picking stocks and bonds, not of

---

[24] Regulation 69, art. 1504, quoted in Wallstein, supra note 22, at 11 (emphasis added). See generally Note, Taxation—Taxability of Business Trust as "Association" within Meaning of Income Tax Act, 84 University of Pennsylvania Law Review 666, 667 (1935).

[25] Treasury Dep't, Gen. Couns. Mem. 1881 (1928); Wallstein, supra note 22, at 19–22; Morrissey v. Comm'r of Internal Revenue, 296 U.S. 344 (1935).

[26] See Wallstein, supra note 22, at 23.

[27] I.R.C. § 851(b)(2).

making operating decisions. As the president of a leading mutual fund said: "[The tax code] now recognise[s us] as being, for purposes of taxation, *not a productive agency* in itself which should shoulder a heavier tax burden, but in effect merely a managing agency to collect dividends and gains for distribution to its shareholders."[28]

Proponents said that "another safeguard that the amendment contains . . . is to prevent an investment trust or investment corporation being set up to obtain control of some corporation and to manipulate its affairs."[29] The safeguard could have been against the "evil" of Wall Street control of industry or the deterioration of tax doctrine in not allowing the investment trust to carry on a true business.[30]

WHY? CONSISTENCY WITH THE POLITICAL PARADIGM

The American public mistrusted accumulations of economic power, as we have seen; bankers and the mutual funds they sponsored were not politically popular, especially if they were perceived as out to control industry. As we have also seen, FDR thought that political stability depended on a dispersal of economic power. Whether the issue was rechartering the Second Bank of the United States or interstate banking or insurer ownership of stock or mutual fund control of industry, American politics usually opted for fragmentation of financial power.

A standard move in public choice analysis is to look for interest groups that "bought" legislation at the expense of a diffuse and disorganized citizenry. In financial regulation of banks and takeovers, commentators see strong elements of this public choice, interest group approach. But this approach is less useful for the 1940 Act, because mutual funds just were not important enough then to provoke much interest group intervention. Rather, politicians were operating at the symbolic level, *creating* via regulation and taxation a framework in accord with their concept of what a mutual fund ought to be. *Thereafter* mutual funds had to grow up within that framework.

ANTI–WALL STREET SENTIMENT

In the early 1930s, Congress held widely-publicized hearings into the ways Wall Street affected the Great Depression. These hearings, called the Pe-

[28] Investment Trust Hails New Tax Act, N.Y. Times, July 23, 1936, at 31, col. 1.

[29] Id. at 11 (May 27, 1936) (comments of Mr. Kent, Assistant General Counsel to the Treasury Department).

[30] Id. at 38 (comments of Mr. Kent).

cora hearings, after Ferdinand Pecora, its leading counsel, reflected the public's anti–Wall Street sentiment and, through publicity, heightened that sentiment. These hearings and the popular sentiments they reflected were factors in the New Deal confirmation of a fragmented financial structure generally, and of the mutual fund regulation specifically. As we saw in chapter 4, Wall Street bankers were defensive at these hearings, with Morgan claiming that the bankers were not really the national danger Pecora claimed they were. Popular opinion, such as that also seen in Father Coughlin's widely heard speeches, was virulently antibanker and anti–Wall Street.[31] To understand the sudden rise to national prominence of Huey Long and Father Coughlin, one must, concludes one historian, see that while the two men had their repulsive, demagogic side, they also tapped deep-seated, sensible sentiments of popular protest against distant financial institutions:

> The most troubling feature of modern industrial society, Long and Coughlin maintained, was the steady erosion of the individual's ability to control his own destiny. Large, faceless institutions; wealthy, insulated men; vast networks of national and international influence: all were exercising power and controlling wealth that more properly belongs in the hands of ordinary citizens. These same forces had created the economic crisis of the 1930s and threatened, if left unchecked, to perpetuate it. . . . Power, they argued, should not reside in distant obscure places; the individual should not have to live in a world in which he could not govern or even know the forces determining his destiny. Instead, the nation should aspire to a set of political and economic arrangements in which authority rested securely in the community, where it could be observed and, in some measure, controlled by its citizens. Concentrated wealth and concentrated power had damaged the nation's social fabric; a system of decentralized power, limited ownership, and small-scale capitalism could restore it.[32]

Bankers in general and Wall Street bankers in particular caused the Depression; they had to be punished. Certainly, bankers were too powerful. Both Huey Long and Father Coughlin extolled the virtues of small business and small banks:

> Essential to the survival of the community, therefore, was an economy of small-scale, local enterprise. How important such an economy was to Long and Coughlin was apparent in the frequency with which both men lamented its disappearance. One by one, they complained, the autonomous local institutions that sustained a meaningful community life were vanishing in the face of distant, impersonal forces. . . . Local financial institutions—what Long described as "the little banks in the counties and the parishes" and what Coughlin termed

[31] Alan Brinkley, Voices of Protest: Huey Long, Father Coughlin, and the Great Depression 116–17, 148–53 (1982).
[32] Id. at 144.

the "small bankers outside the great ring of Wall Street"—were in dire peril. So were the "small industrialists," who had, Coughlin claimed, "been bought out or . . . destroyed by questionable competition."[33]

Roosevelt had reason to coopt Long (who had in 1933 led the fight on behalf of the local bankers to prevent widespread bank branching)[34] and Coughlin:

> It was that possibility—that Long and Coughlin would not only continue to gain support, but that their movements would begin to complement each other and to merge—that politicians like Franklin Roosevelt and James Farley found particularly alarming. Separately, Long and Coughlin were formidable foes; together, many feared, they might mobilize a popular following of truly remarkable proportions.[35]

The politics of the "Second" New Deal, begun in 1935, tried to co-opt the less ugly elements of Long's and Coughlin's program. Against that background, the next year's Revenue Act fragmented mutual funds. When the mutual fund provisions of the 1936 Revenue Act were discussed in committee, Senator La Follette argued specifically against mutual funds that facilitated investment banker control of industry and generally against the concentration of control of the public's money in the hands of a few financiers.[36]

William O. Douglas, chairman of the SEC and a key player in New Deal financial legislation, such as the 1940 Act, articulated a general goal of fragmenting economic power. People who dominate financial markets have "tremendous power," he said. "Such [people] become virtual governments in the power at their disposal. [Sometimes it is] the dut[y] of government to police them, at times to break them up, to deter their further growth."[37] Wall Street bankers should provide and direct the flow of capital, but not control the enterprise after the capital has flowed to it, he said.[38]

In 1935 Long seemed likely to seek the presidency the next year; the 1935

[33] Id. at 145 (footnote omitted).

[34] Donald Langevoort, Statutory Obsolescence and the Judicial Process: The Revisionist Role of the Courts in Federal Banking Regulation, 85 Michigan Law Review 672, 722 (1987).

[35] Brinkley, supra note 31, at 209.

[36] Revenue Act of 1936: Confidential Hearings on H.R. 12395 Before the Senate Comm. on Finance, 74th Cong., 2d Sess. 36–37 (1936) (citing the Pecora Report). To view the 1936 law as part of the co-opting of Huey Long and Father Coughlin is precarious. By 1936, Long was dead, and Coughlin was in decline. The reaffirmation in 1940 could not have directly resulted from an early 1930s political movement. And the co-opting, if that is what is was, occurred on an ideological dimension that was widespread in the United States, stretching back to the Jeffersonians and 1890s' populists and forward to today.

[37] William O. Douglas, Democracy and Finance 15 (1940). "The needs of a small Middle Western community are apt to be better served by a banker at the head of a small local bank than by the same banker at the head of the nation's biggest bank." Id. at 11, 14.

[38] Id. at 44–45.

tax proposals, coming before he was assassinated, were said to steal his thunder, and to shock both Congress and the business community.[39] They were "a stick to beat off the storm troops of Senator Long and Father Coughlin."[40] FDR said tax change was needed because the tax code had "done little to prevent an unjust *concentration* of wealth and *economic power.*"[41] The later 1936 provisions that fragmented mutual fund portfolios should be seen as a residue of this populist, anti–Wall Street feeling.

PUBLIC INTEREST PERSPECTIVES

For most of the New Deal financial legislation, looking only at populism, federalism, and interest groups, as we have been doing, distorts the picture. I emphasize them not because they are the only explanations, but because they have been neglected as causes of corporate ownership fragmentation. They are not a full explanation, but they are an important and neglected partial one. Many political players also had public interest goals and these helped motivate the legislation.

Protecting Unsophisticated Investors

Congress feared that unsophisticated investors would expect diversification but be unable to evaluate a portfolio to see whether it really was diversified. And since the SEC thought, as it said, that a fund's *only* positive function was to diversify there was little reason not to require diversification; anything more risked thievery, anything less had no positive purpose.[42] Keeping mutual fund managers out of controlling positions kept them free from conflicts of interests; prohibiting insider transactions kept retail shareholders from being bilked. The serious question here was *where* to draw the line, not *whether* to draw one. The funds' investment adviser, an investment bank, would use the fund's control to get securities underwriting business

---

[39] Arthur Schlesinger, Jr., The Age of Roosevelt: The Politics of Upheaval 325–29 (1960).

[40] Randolph E. Paul, Taxation in the United States 188 (1954) (summarizing views of Charles Beard). I alluded to Beard's work in the first sentences of the preface. In An Economic Interpretation of the Constitution of the United States (1935), Beard claimed that the Constitution, usually seen as a political document, was influenced by the economic position of the framers; in this book I claim that corporate economic structure has been influenced by political forces.

[41] 79 Cong. Rec. 9657 (1935) (message from the president, June 19, 1935) (emphasis added); John F. Witte, The Politics and Development of the Federal Income Tax 100 (1985).

[42] 1940 Act Hearings, supra note 3, at 131, 132 (statement of George Mathews, Commissioner of the SEC), 807 (reiteration by David Schenker, Chief Counsel, SEC Investment Trust Study).

from the portfolio firm.[43] Or the investment bank would unload bad securities onto a gullible public that owned the fund.[44] Or the fund would force a transaction with a portfolio firm that was favorable to the fund, so that the fund could report high earnings to its own shareholders. (The legislative history does not show an equal mistrust of the potential rapacity of corporate managers, and does not weigh whether the greed of the fund and that of the corporate managers could neutralize each other.)

The mutual fund industry did not strongly oppose the restrictions. It was interested in selling its product and felt it needed a code of conduct that would certify it to the general public.[45] Indeed, one type of mutual fund— the Massachusetts trust—preferred that Congress require all mutual funds to use a structure that it had already adopted, which prohibited control over industry.[46] When the 1936 tax act was considered and passed, one key player, the chair of the Senate Finance Committee, was from Massachusetts; he advocated that all mutual funds conform to the Massachusetts trusts' structure. Massachusetts trusts could comply without a change in operation; others would have to bend.

Promoting Political Stability

The political stability perspective also has a public-regarding dimension. As we saw in chapter 4, FDR himself said:

> It is time to . . . reverse that process of concentration of power which has made most American citizens, once traditionally independent owners of their own businesses, helplessly dependent for their daily bread upon the favor of a very few, *who by devices such as holding companies,* have taken for themselves unwarranted economic power. I am against private socialism of concentrated economic power as thoroughly as I am against government socialism. The one is equally as dangerous as the other; *and destruction of private socialism is utterly essential to avoid government socialism.*[47]

If Roosevelt was right, then political stability in the United States—surely a worthwhile objective—was dependent in the 1930s on fragmenting finance.

---

[43] Pecora Report, supra note 3, at 333; 1940 Act Hearings, supra note 3, at 36, 206, 207 (statement of I.M.C. Smith, Associate Counsel, SEC Investment Trust Study).

[44] Pecora Report, supra note 3, at 381–82.

[45] Chelcie C. Bosland, The Investment Company Act of 1940 and Its Background: II, 49 Journal of Political Economy 687 (1941). Certification also has a cartel-like quality of eliminating some rough competition.

[46] Dwight P. Robinson, Massachusetts Investors Trust—Pioneer in Open-End Investment Trusts 10, 14, 16 (1954).

[47] Ellis Hawley, The New Deal and the Problem of Monopoly 281 (1966).

One way to fragment finance—at least symbolically—was to eliminate investment banker control of industry through mutual funds.

The financial reality of the mutual fund industry in the 1930s was that destruction of mutual fund power was symbolic. Sure, the funds had taken some first steps toward influencing industry, and, yes, mutual funds had the *potential* to be big players in finance and industry. But their aggregate assets were then too small to threaten political stability directly; in 1940 there were only sixty-eight mutual funds, with total assets of only $400 million.[48] It was not the *immediate* prospect of "unwarranted economic power," to use Roosevelt's words, but the symbolic potential, or, at best, the prospect that *in alliance* with other financial institutions, the mutual fund would play a serious role.

Fighting Cartels

Blocking control also blocked cartelization. A mutual fund could be the means by which an investment banker controlled several companies in a single industry to promote and police a cartel.[49]

The anticartel theory is still in the tax law. Although Congress liberalized the fragmentation rules in 1942 at the behest of the mutual fund industry,[50] it still restricted control, barring a fund from putting more than a quarter of its portfolio into two or more controlled firms "engaged in the same or similar trades or businesses or related trades or businesses."[51] Owning 20 percent of the stock of a portfolio firm gave the mutual fund control for purposes of this rule. In Germany and Japan, one function of bank ownership is industrial organization, loosely linking vertically related firms.[52] In the United States neither banks nor insurers can help this linkage, and the intercorporate dividend tax makes partial, loose linkage costly. Tax rules help to deter mutual funds from linking vertically related firms.

The antilinkage rule produces odd results. If the fund fragments its entire portfolio, it can put it all into one industry. A few do this—Fidelity's "Select" funds come to mind—giving their investors lots of company but no industry diversification. Because the fund managers are investing in a single industry, they might get the expertise to second-guess some firm managers

---

[48] William J. Baumol, Steven M. Goldfeld, Lilli A. Gordon, and Michael Koehn, The Economics of Mutual Funds Markets: Competition versus Regulation 10 (1990).

[49] Pecora Report, supra note 3, at 360–63, 381.

[50] Revenue Act of 1942, § 170(a), Pub. L. No. 77-753, 56 Stat. 798, 878 (1942), codified at I.R.C. § 851(b)(4)(B).

[51] Id. See Revenue Revision of 1942: Hearings Before the [House] Comm. on Ways and Means, 77th Cong., 2d Sess. 122 (1942).

[52] Gilson and Roe, supra note 18; infra chapter 19.

every now and then. They might feel comfortable with a few influential stock positions. After all, the shareholders are not getting much diversification from the fund anyway: its portfolio is all in one industry. But the fund cannot put more than 25 percent of its assets into control blocks in a single industry; the fund *cannot* make big-block investments in a single industry without tax penalty.

INTEREST GROUPS

The Faint Role of Managers

Did managers support mutual fund fragmentation? Although they bene-fited, the evidence does not show that managers directly lobbied or even testified in 1936 or 1940. Although they probably did not bother to exert their influence in the 1930s because mutual funds were then minor financial players, and the political action was mostly symbolic, we should not dismiss a managerial public choice story completely. Some politicians promoting the 1940 Act appealed to managerial freedom from Wall Street control, and the fragmentation rules of the 1936 Act and 1940 Act had survival strength *be-cause* they did not threaten managers.

During William O. Douglas's days as commissioner, the SEC proposed the Investment Company Act and formulated rules limiting joint action. Douglas's statements show a displeasure with Wall Street, which corre-sponds to our populist principle, and with bankers controlling managers, which corresponds to our managerial interest group story. He surely *wanted* to destroy Wall Street control of Main Street, saying in 1937, as I've noted before, that investment bankers would be "restricted to . . . underwriting or selling" and stripped of "[t]he financial power [they had] exercised in the past over [industrial policy]."[53] The power of Wall Street must be held at bay: "[F]inance moves into the zone of exploitation whenever it becomes the *master* rather than the faithful and loyal *servant* of investors *and business*. To make finance such a *servant* rather than a *master* becomes a central plank in any platform for reform."[54]

Members of Congress applauded calls to limit the power of bankers, who, members said, were responsible for many great industrial failures. Bank di-rectors who lived "remote from the properties operated have no understand-

[53] Douglas, supra note 37, at 41 (emphasis supplied). As noted previously, supra note 37, this speech was made in 1937 before a shocked group of Wall Street investment bankers.

[54] Id. at 21, 44. Cf. Thomas K. McCraw, The Public and Private Spheres in Historical Per-spective, in Public-Private Partnership 31, 81–82 (Harvey Brooks, Lance Liebman, and Corinne Schelling eds., 1984) ("Instead of wreaking vengeance [for a discredited securities market], however, the [SEC] set out to restore legitimacy to Wall Street's essential function of channeling investment capital into enterprise").

ing of the . . . industry they direct. . . . Congress must make it unlawful for any person to act as a director . . . who shall also be [an] investment banking partner.[55]

Survivorship

Even if managers were not crucial to passage of the legislation, one can still see a managerial interest group picture, although a dimly lit one. If the rule had seriously impinged on managers' authority, they would have objected, and the evidence suggests that they could have killed it; a rule threatening management would have been unstable, challenged, and probably reversed.

Contrast the fifty-year persistence of fragmentation in the 1936 Revenue Act—which has been watered down only once, in 1942—with the tax on accumulated corporate income in that same tax act. A firm was taxed, at up to 27 percent of undistributed income, if it failed to distribute its income to its shareholders.[56] That tax made managers more dependent on capital markets than they had been in its absence, because the tax pushed them to distribute all profits, forcing growing firms to go back to capital markets to get back these funds. When the firms went to the capital markets, bankers and securities buyers would scrutinize the managers' results, and penalize them (via higher capital costs) if the results were poor. Firms whose prospects for profit suggested contraction would find it harder to raise funds than to retain earnings. During the Depression, many firms merited contraction; once they dividended out their funds, they would have to shrink. Managers would unhappily find themselves controlling a smaller enterprise.

While this view of capital markets and managers has a modern ring,[57] it was intuitively understood during the 1930s. A representative of management said during the 1936 hearings that the undistributed profits tax will cause conflict "between those engaged in the management of a business and those who are purely investors."[58] Berle and Means recognized and advocated finding ways to subject managers to the capital markets:

> Only one general protection beside the power of active revolt remains to guarantee a measure of equitable treatment to the several classes of security holders. The enterprise may need new capital. The management must, therefore,

[55] 77 Cong. Rec. 2933–34 (1933) (remarks of Rep. Marland).

[56] Revenue Act of 1936, § 14(b), Pub. L. No. 74-740, 49 Stat. 1648, 1656 (repealed 1939).

[57] See Frank Easterbrook, Two Explanations for Dividends, 74 American Economic Review 650 (1984); Saul Levmore, Monitors and Free-riders in Corporate and Commercial Law Settings, 91 Yale Law Journal 49 (1982).

[58] Revenue Act of 1936: Hearings on H.R. 12395 Before the Senate Comm. on Finance, 74th Cong., 2d Sess. 514–15 (1936) (statement of Herman H. Lind, General Manager, National Machine-Tool Builders Ass'n).

maintain a situation in which additional capital is forthcoming. . . . This need for new capital sets a very definite limit on the extent to which those in control can abuse the suppliers of capital. . . .[59]

Rexford Tugwell, the Roosevelt administration's principal proponent of an undistributed profits tax, and at times an academic and administrative colleague of Berle, offered managerial discipline as a rationale. Although his principal goal was to reduce excessive corporate savings, a reduction he thought would increase consumer spending, he and others in the administration also thought the tax "would give the stockholders more influence in the formulation of corporation dividend and corporation saving policies."[60]

"Few taxes," one analyst has written, "have evoked such a storm of passionate and partisan controversy. . . . Spokesmen for corporations objected strenuously on the ground that the tax made for economic instability [and] interfered with corporate policies. . . ."[61] In 1938, the Chamber of Commerce, the National Association of Manufacturers, the American Mining Congress, and the New York Board of Trade all opposed the tax.[62] First they got Congress to cut its rate.[63] The next year they got Congress to repeal it.[64] The corporate tax would no longer be affected by managers' decisions on how much of the profit to pay out to shareholders; managers could retain earnings, freeing themselves from the discipline of the capital markets.

The survivorship argument should now be clear. Proposals can originate in the Treasury Department without any interest group pressure, based on what the Treasury thinks would be best for the country. But to survive, a proposal must not gore the ox of a powerful interest group. The tax on undistributed profits threatened managers; within a few years the tax was dead. The Treasury's simultaneous proposal to tax mutual funds with only fragmented portfolios did not incur the ire of managers; it survived.

[59] Berle and Means, supra note 3, at 280–81.

[60] Sidney Ratner, Taxation and Democracy in America 474 (1967); see Daniel Fusfeld, The Economic Thought of Franklin D. Roosevelt and the Origins of the New Deal 211–12 (1956); Schlesinger, supra note 39, at 506–07.

[61] Ratner, supra note 60, at 474. See also Roy G. Blakey and Gladys M. Blakey, The Federal Income Tax 410, 411 (1940) (citing 80 Cong. Rec. 6317) ("Reed [N.Y.] attacked the bill because he considered the tax on undistributed earnings a plan of industrial control, and a 'hasty superficial undigested substitute for the present corporation method of taxation, which with all of its defects, is nevertheless something to which the business of this country has become adjusted and which is providing steadily increasing revenue'"); Enright, Business Opposes Tax on Surplus, N.Y. Times, Mar. 8, 1936, § 3, at 9, col. 4 (reporting managerial displeasure with undistributed profits tax).

[62] Hearings Before the [House] Comm. on Ways and Means on the Revenue Revision—1939, 76th Cong., 1st Sess. 102, 104, 133, 135, 145, 150–51, 174, 177 (1939).

[63] Revenue Act of 1938 § 13(c), Pub. L. No. 75-554, 52 Stat. 447, 455 (1938).

[64] Revenue Act of 1939, Pub. L. No. 76-155, 53 Stat. 862 (1939).

Managers were not the moving force behind the mutual fund tax bill in the same way that they were the moving force behind some modern anti-takeover legislation. This story suggests that managers might have killed mutual fund fragmentation if it threatened them. They did nothing about it either because they liked it or because they were indifferent to it. Since mutual funds were small players in the 1930s, managers may have cared little about the structure of mutual fund portfolios back then.

CURRENT PROSPECTS

Mutual funds may yet emerge as viable corporate governance players. In the early 1990s, Vanguard, one of the biggest mutual fund complexes, found itself with enough stock in Chrysler that the senior manager of its stock portfolio, John Neff, became interested in the succession and retirement of Lee Iacocca.[65] Indeed, Neff led an unusually active mutual fund complex, "shipp[ing] a set of two-sentence 'pointed but not hostile' faxes to the . . . Chrysler directors, who were gathering for a special meeting."[66] Unlike most big stockholders of a public firm, neither Vanguard nor Neff went into the Chrysler boardroom, perhaps because of some of the considerations outlined here. They spoke through a fax machine, not from a boardroom seat.

For our purposes, investment companies can be seen as coming in two main varieties: the open-end mutual fund, which stands ready to turn its shares into cash overnight; and the closed-end investment company, which never redeems its shares. The two types have different business characteristics that bear on how well each can act in corporate governance.

The open-end mutual fund has liquidity problems, which will deter it from active involvement in corporate governance. Big blocks are illiquid, but if the fund must be ready to redeem overnight it cannot afford to be illiquid.

Law compounds this problem, because for an open-end mutual fund to raise cash if it is hit with heavy redemptions, it must sell some of its portfolio of investments. But section 16(b) of the Securities Exchange Act of 1934 requires that a shareholder with 10 percent or more of stock *or* any director *must* return any short-swing profits *even* if the trading was done without inside information. Stockholders that buy a big block and hold it will not find this rule more than a nuisance. But mutual funds, which *must* trade, will find section 16(b) a serious impediment, putting lots of big blocks out of the question.

[65] Floyd Norris, Power behind the Windsor Fund, N.Y. Times, Mar. 6, 1992, at D1, col. 3.

[66] Kevin G. Salwen and Joann S. Lublin, Giant Investors Flex Their Muscles More at U.S. Corporations, Wall Street Journal, Apr. 27, 1992, at A1, col. 6, A6, col. 6.

The rule, which applies to a company's 10 percent–plus shareholders *and* to its directors, tends to keep a mutual fund from sending one of its people in to be a director of a portfolio firm; the rule also frays the fund's potential ties with other directors. If a court sees a portfolio firm's director as having been "deputized" by the mutual fund, then the fund's trading could be subject to 16(b) limitations, even if the fund never had inside information and never itself owned more than 10 percent of the firm's stock. Thus while the 1940 Act restricts each fund's portfolio, it does not directly restrict a group of affiliated mutual funds run by the same firm from taking stock positions that aggregate to a big, influential block. One fund might take 5 percent, a second one might take another 5 percent, and a third another 5 percent. But I understand that some mutual fund complexes have restricted themselves from taking a cumulative block of 10 percent, fearing that regulators might treat the stock in their different funds as a single block.

When Peter Lynch, the star manager of Fidelity's Magellan fund, joined the board of W. R. Grace in the early 1990s (just before he retired from Magellan), Magellan sold its Grace stock. Fidelity's general counsel said: "[W]e do not [think] that institutional investors should be represented on boards. . . . It causes a lot of legal problems."[67]

Open-end funds must be liquid; regulations require that 85 percent of the fund's assets be liquid,[68] a ratio most might approach anyway without the rule. The combination of 16(b) liability with a block of 10 percent or more or with a deputized director would render the influential portion of the portfolio illiquid, because then the only way to avoid 16(b) liability would be to avoid trading. But mutual funds must be ready to redeem out their investors quickly, and their resulting need for liquidity precludes carrying many big, difficult-to-sell blocks.

Keep in mind that section 16(b) would hit funds *even* if they did not trade on inside information; it applies if the big investor or the investor with a boardroom deputy trades in a short period. More general insider trading laws would deter some mutual funds; I do not analyze this problem here, because these rules against true insider trading are sound. Big blockholders should not be able to dump their stock when they learn of negative information. Indeed one might argue that in return for being permitted to take big blocks, the new big blockholders might be required to make even greater commitments to a long-term relationship than laws now require.

The closed-end fund does not have the liquidity problem that open-end funds have; indeed, there is at least one nation where closed-end funds are involved in corporate governance. In Sweden, where the portfolio rules do

---

[67] Allison Cowan, A Savvy Outsider Ventures Inside, N.Y. Times, Aug. 3, 1989, at D8, col. 3.

[68] Investment Company Act of 1940 § 22(e), 15 U.S.C. § 80a-22(e) (1988); Revisions of Guidelines to Form N-1A (Mar. 12, 1992), 57 Fed. Reg. 9828 (Mar. 20, 1992), 17 C.F.R. § 274.11A (1993).

not bind as tightly as do the subchapter M and 1940 Act rules, a noticeable governance institution is the closed-end fund with big blocks of stock and boardroom influence.[69] But they would have a different structural problem here in the United States, because they do not discipline *fund* managers as well as the open-end funds do. The nature of a closed-end fund is that the shareholders cannot redeem their shares and move their assets out easily. Persistent discounts—the American closed-end *fund's* shares often sell for less than the value of the fund's assets—in their share price also make the structure unpopular here.[70]

Current U.S. regulation forces an extreme trade-off for investors, a trade-off that makes "big-block" funds cumbersome. Either the investor must buy a liquid open-end fund or the investor must buy a closed-end fund. Liquid open-end funds that redeem overnight provide excellent discipline to mutual fund managers: if the fund managers err badly, they will find themselves managing funds with no assets, because investors can cash out overnight. But liquidity needs mean the fund cannot take big blocks easily. Closed-end funds do not stand ready to redeem overnight, but they provide poor discipline to their managers and have been unpopular. The statute and the rules do not contemplate hybrids.

Business entails trade-offs, trade-offs that the American rules here do not yet allow. An investor cannot yet buy a fund that takes big illiquid blocks with the investor allowed to redeem on only, say, three months' advance notice.[71] Such vehicles would be particularly useful for retirement money, for which the investor has a long horizon, not expecting to withdraw it for decades.

———

Even though neither fund managers nor corporate managers were critical in getting the 1940 Act and the related tax rules passed, incumbent institutions might in the 1990s oppose even permission to change. They understand the current financial world in which they have succeeded, and often see no reason to change it. People's sense of the right way to do things is often shaped by the way things have usually been done in their lifetime. The general counsel to the largest American mutual fund complex recently examined the possibility of big-block mutual funds and concluded that "[t]o

---

[69] Gilson and Kraakman, supra note 11, at 993 n.34, 996 n.45 (Swedish funds invest in five to ten companies, which would run afoul of American tax rules for mutual funds).

[70] Reinier Kraakman, Taking Discounts Seriously: The Implications of "Discounted" Share Prices as an Acquisition Motive, 88 Columbia Law Review 891, 902–05 (1988).

[71] Division of Investment Management, Securities and Exchange Commission, Protecting Investors: A Half Century of Investment Company Regulation 425, 442 (May 1992) (SEC staff proposal to allow such funds).

implement their ideas on a broad scale, [those seeking big blocks] would have to persuade Congress to relax the current limits on institutional investors substantially." But although institutions and managers would then remain free to reject the big blocks if they found them inefficient, the mutual fund counsel predicted that "[c]orporate executives would undoubtedly oppose such a relaxation as a threat to management control, *and they would find allies in most institutional investors,*" whom he said are repelled by a German or Japanese model.[72]

CONCLUSION

Just when Berle and Means were announcing the emergence of the public corporation with uncontrolled managers at the helm, Congress raised the cost of mutual fund influence. The restrictions in the 1936 tax code and the 1940 Act make it impossible to deploy a majority of the fund's portfolio in control blocks. The 1940 Act raised the cost of control even with the unregulated portion of the portfolio, but for genuinely public-regarding reasons. Still, the rules may cut wide, because stymieing any and all influence was then seen as valuable, not as a cost.

Each rule is a cost to big blockholding, not a complete show-stopper. But their sum is considerable, and can tip open-end mutual funds, which are not financially well-suited to take big long-term blocks anyway, into passivity. To avoid the corporate tax, an activist fund must build an odd portfolio. It could divide the portfolio in half, with one half in two firms and the other half in ten. None of the ten could have more than 10 percent of a portfolio firm's stock. And the two 25 percent blocks (if they yield 20 percent of the portfolio firms' stock) could not be in the same industry, or even in related industries. Even if a mutual fund used the most concentrated portfolio it could, it would usually have had to form alliances with other investors to be effective, especially because until recently equity mutual funds have been small. Those alliances are hard to bring off in any case, and the securities laws have historically discouraged them.

The fund could avoid these rules by holding very big blocks and then accept taxation that is high enough to wipe out the private gains from activity. And mutual funds, which must redeem stock regularly, cannot take too many illiquid big blocks; short-swing trading rules stymie funds from trading in big blocks, inducing greater illiquidity. And putting a director onto the portfolio firm board, or owning 10 percent of the portfolio firm also triggers 16(b), requiring disgorgement of any trading gains and embarrassing a finan-

---

[72] Robert C. Pozen, Institutional Investors as Corporate Activists: The Reluctant Activists, Harvard Business Review, Jan.–Feb. 1994, at 140, 149 (emphasis supplied).

cial business that needs to cultivate probity and avoid headlines of violations of even "technical" SEC rules.

And then there are the transactional rules, which prohibit joint transactions with affiliates (which two 5 percent owners of a portfolio firm would be), and prohibit (unless they got a SEC exemption) transactions with the portfolio firm. Intended to deal with transactions that hurt minority shareholders or fund beneficiaries, the rules also stymie innocuous financings and recapitalizations. The blanket SEC exemptions help, but may not work well when the mutual fund has a director in the boardroom.

Elements of a basic public choice story—of interest groups buying favorable laws—are present. And elements of a basic public-oriented, good regulation story are also present. But the interest group scenario did not drive the legislation, and some of the good regulation goals could have been accomplished through other means. Rather, the ideology of fragmentation seems paramount in tipping the balance. Key actors—FDR and Douglas—thought that Wall Street control of industry was bad. The interest group story lies less in visible lobbying than in the appeals some political players made, sometimes favoring managers over bankers, and in the survival properties of the fragmenting legislation. Simultaneous with passage of the fragmenting tax legislation, Congress passed an undistributed profits tax, which threatened managerial independence. That tax was unstable, challenged, and eventually repealed.

Rather than an interest group story, we should think of the politics of mutual funds in the 1930s as *creating* mutual funds. Without tax exemption, the funds could not readily prosper. Politicians allowed tax exemption consistent with their conception of what a mutual fund should be and should not be. It should not control industry; it should not have concentrated investments; it should not be entangled in financial alliances that could create conflicts of interest. Politicians created a framework for mutual funds to grow, a framework that made it difficult or impossible for mutual funds to actively enter the governance structure of their portfolio firms.

CHAPTER 9

Pension Funds

WITH BANKS and insurers out of the picture, and mutual funds nearly so, pension funds—the fastest-growing stock market player in recent decades—are the final frontier for finding powerful intermediaries. From 1970 to 1993, pension funds grew from owning only $81 billion in equity, less than 9 percent of the stock market, to owning over $1.5 trillion, nearly *one-third* of the market (see Table 4), more than mutual funds, insurers, and bank trusts combined.[1] If aggregated, today's pension funds have a control block in most major American firms.

Social change induced the rise of huge pension funds: rising wealth after World War II, increasing life spans, increasing preference for earlier retirement, and changing mores—adult children cared for their elderly parents with decreasing alacrity—made retirement savings important. Demand for pensions increased, and employers were a natural vehicle to satisfy it. Accidentally, corporate managers at those employers ended up controlling huge pools of equity capital, and they tended to induce the private pension funds to be passive in corporate governance.

In this chapter I trace the history of the rise of private pension funds. The social change story is central, but incomplete. Pension funds became important partly by default; their relative importance today resulted in no small part from the earlier suppression of banks and insurers as powerful intermediaries.

Managers also came to control pension funds partly because of labor-management politics and antitrust issues. After a brutal, headline-grabbing series of strikes in 1946 and 1947, Congress *barred* unions from completely controlling new pension funds. Simultaneously, General Motors, threatened by an antitrust attack, barred its pension fund from taking big blocks of other companies' stock. These two institutional features, rooted in American politics, helped to produce pension fund patterns that persist to this day.

In 1974, Congress passed ERISA, the Employee Retirement Income Security Act, which, with no discernible governance-related motive, confirmed the preexisting structure of corporate governance by encouraging pension

[1] Board of Governors of the Federal Reserve System, Flow of Funds Accounts—First Quarter 1993, at 112 (1993 data); Board of Governors of the Federal Reserve System, Flow of Funds Accounts, Assets and Liabilities Outstanding, 1957–1980, at 39 (corporate equities–line 1) ($906.2 billion in corporate equities outstanding in 1970); Federal Financial Institutions Examination Council, Trust Assets of Financial Institutions: 1991, at 11 (1989).

TABLE 4

Equity Holdings of U.S. Pension Funds,
Mutual Funds, and Insurers, 1993

	Equity Holdings	Share of Total Equity Market
Pension Funds		
Private	$1,094 billion	22.0%
State/local	462 billion	9.3
Total	1,556 billion	31.3
Mutual funds	511 billion	10.3
Insurers	263 billion	5.3

Source: Board of Governors of the Federal Reserve System, Flow of Funds Accounts—First Quarter 1993, at 112.

Note: Households (which for Federal Reserve reporting purposes include bank trusts) account for nearly all of the rest of the stock market.

funds to adopt the fragmented, passive stockholding structure that the other big institutions—banks, insurers, and mutual funds—usually adopt. For these others, a public choice story can be told, based on a combination of public discomfort with powerful private financial institutions and the maneuvering of benefited interest groups to pacify such institutions and limit large-block stockholdings.

The fact that managers control their own firms' pension funds is basic to understanding pension passivity. Few managers want their pension fund to be more active in the corporate governance of other firms than they want their own stockholders to be in their firm. Yet, while managers might want mutual protection, coordinating such a preference is difficult. ERISA's doctrines, although they did not arise from managerial preferences, reinforce them by heightening the legal risks facing a pension manager who is active or takes the big blocks of stock necessary for activity.

Institutional investors' increased activism during the early 1990s makes analysis of ERISA important. Boardroom coups at General Motors, IBM, and American Express make us wonder whether the structure of authority in the American public firm is about to change. Former SEC Chairman Breeden said that some of ERISA's standards, "may have the inadvertent [and unnecessary] effect of making it impractical for institutional investors to play a meaningful role in a smaller number of companies."[2]

However, a change in ERISA's doctrines may not alone affect corporate governance. Pension fund activism comes more from public plans, such as

[2] Joel Chernoff, Breeden: Act Like Owners—SEC Chief Backs Larger Stakes, Larger Role for Institutions, Pensions and Investments, June 8, 1992, at 3.

CalPERS, the California Public Employee Retirement System, than from private ones, who are usually followers not leaders. However, it is the private plans that own most pension-owned stock, and a core structural problem afflicts them: they are not distant gatherers of disparate savings, impeded only by a few ERISA rules from big blocks and a boardroom presence, but are corporate pension funds that managers direct. The alternative model—intermediaries with a boardroom presence that would balance power with managers—does not fit pensions well, because managers direct *them*. Managerial dominance does not preclude finding any useful relationship, but it makes for complications.

THE PROBLEM AS SEEN IN 1974 AND
THE ERISA SOLUTION

ERISA responded to two public interest problems: unfunded pensions and unvested pensions. Unfunded and unvested pensions left some workers without security for their old age. Many plans had no vesting until retirement, creating insecurity—lose your job and you lose the pension. The General Motors plan, a prototype for others, had ten-year "cliff" vesting—nothing unless the employee had worked ten years for GM. Cliff vesting made workers overly dependent on the firm in the few years before vesting; if they quit or were fired, they lost the pension. Half of the employees covered by plans never got a pension because it never vested. Even if the pension did vest, the firm could disappear, along with the pension, if the firm's obligations were unfunded. Although most pensions were funded—money was set aside to pay the pension, largely because of pre-ERISA tax rules—some were not. Of the 12.5 million employees with pension plans in 1956, 1 million were in unfunded plans. Employees presumably lacked the skills to negotiate details about funding or financial guarantees.[3]

ERISA was the solution to these problems.[4] To get a tax deduction under the new law, the firm had to shorten the cliff or vest employees in steps, so that loss of the job would not lead to total loss of the pension. To aid employees who risked losing a pension if their employer failed to fund the plan and then went bankrupt, ERISA strengthened funding rules, and set up an insurance fund to cover most unfunded pension plans.[5]

[3] William Graebner, A History of Retirement 134 (1980); Paul Harbrecht, Pension Funds and Economic Power 39, 63, 254, 291–92 (1959) (art. II, §§ 1(a) and 2(a) of The General Motors Hourly-Rate Employees Pension Plan); Employee Retirement Income Security Act of 1974, H.R. Rep. No. 533, 93d Cong., 2d Sess. 6 (1974); cf. Peter F. Drucker, The Unseen Revolution: How Pension Fund Socialism Came to America 17 (1976).

[4] Underfunded plans could also be relational contracts that increased employees' dependence on the firm's success. Richard A. Ippolito, Pensions, Economics and Public Policy 167–86 (1986).

[5] H.R. Rep. No. 807, 93d Cong., 2d Sess. 3–5 (1974); Jeffrey D. Mamorsky, 1 Employee

These then were the institutions that created ERISA's distinctive features: funding with managerial direction of the funds, and underfunding with government guarantees of payment. If plans were unfunded, managers would not control a big asset pool; firms might have bought guarantees from private insurers to ensure payment to employees. That path was not taken. Instead, funding with managerial direction of the resulting funds unintentionally insulated managers from corporate accountability.

THE MODERN CORPORATION AND PRIVATE PENSIONS: STRUCTURAL MANAGERIAL CONTROL

Funding made pensions central to modern corporate governance, by creating a huge investment pool—about $3 trillion as of 1993, half of which was in equity, amounting to one-third of the stock market. Were pensions unfunded promises, as they have been in some foreign nations, they would be bit players in corporate governance. Yet, although the current arrangements seem natural—managers invest their employees' retirement savings and appoint pension managers—the path to funding and managerial direction of the funds was not inevitable.

Glimmers of an Interest Group Story

It is not inevitable that managers control pensions. Employees could do so, either individually—as they now do through Individual Retirement Accounts and Keogh plans—or collectively, for example, through a union or a government-controlled fund. When unions sought improved pensions after World War II, policy proposals arose to expand the social security system, by allowing voluntary worker contributions into it or by requiring larger employer contributions. Some unions instead wanted industry-wide, union-managed pension plans, which accounted for about one-third of then-existing plans, expanded.[6]

Benefits Law—ERISA and Beyond § 5.03, at 5-8, § 9.01[3], at 9-4 (1992); Michael J. Graetz, The Troubled Marriage of Retirement Security and Tax Policies, 135 University of Pennsylvania Law Review 851, 884–85 (1987). Tax law induced funding before ERISA, because deductibility depended on the pension's being seen as a charitable contribution, which required a set-aside of funds. ERISA adopted the doctrine, to protect the employee. Graebner, supra note 3, at 134; J. S. Seidman, Seidman's Legislative History of Federal Income Tax Laws: 1938–1861, at 516–17, 604–05 (1938).

[6] See 93 Cong. Rec. 4745, 4747 (1947) (remarks of Sen. Taft rejecting government administration); Harry A. Millis and Emily Clark Brown, From the Wagner Act to Taft-Hartley 567 (1950) (expanded social security beaten back, so private alternatives needed); H.R. Rep. No. 245, 80th Cong., 1st Sess. 64, 79 (1947).

Managers attacked these alternatives on two fronts. They got Congress to pass the Taft-Hartley Act, a conservative reaction to the New Deal, to require that managers and unions jointly direct collectively bargained pension plans, banning unions from sole control of pensions. (Managers can solely control; unions cannot.) Fear of labor racketeering, and of the power that union officials would wield over their membership if they fully controlled pension funds, and a more general fear of big unions' controlling serious capital, induced Congress to end employee collective control over the retirement fund. The aggressive House version would have banned *all* union influence over pensions, because "it is not in the national interest for union leaders to control these great, unregulated, untaxed funds."[7]

An interest group story is visible.[8] The 1946 coal strike, during which the United Mine Workers demanded that employers fund a pension that the union would administer, commanded the nation's attention and became the "crux of the dispute which led to seizure of the coal mines [by the United States.]"[9] Headlines proclaimed democracy to be in danger, and conservative Democrats saw the stakes as fundamental. Senator Byrd said that "if John L. Lewis were to get his way and a precedent for labor control over these funds was to be firmly established, it would mean a complete destruction of the private enterprise system of the U.S."[10] Congressional witnesses from the coal industry said UMW-type funds "are now on the agenda of

[7] [House] Comm. on Education and Labor, Labor-Management Relations Act, 1947, H. Rep. No. 245, 80th Cong., 1st Sess. 29–30 (1947); House Set to Compromise on Labor Bill in Order to Obtain Measure on Which Veto Could Be Beaten, Wall Street Journal, May 10, 1947, at 3, col. 1; Labor Management Relations (Taft-Hartley) Act, 1947, ch. 120, § 302(c)(5)(B), 61 Stat. 136, 157–58 (1947), codified as amended at 29 U.S.C. § 186(c)(5)(B) (Supp. III 1991); 93 Cong. Rec. 4751–54 (1947). To the extent employees understood and preferred full control of their own pensions, presumably corporate stockholders paid for this control.

[8] Jeremy Rifkin and Randy Barber, The North Will Rise Again: Pensions, Politics and Power in the 1980s, at 101–02 (1978), see management wresting control of pension money from the authors' friends, organized labor: "Senator Claude Pepper of Florida . . . suggest[ed] that Taft and his business friends, when they fretted over possible union abuses of the funds, were really fretting over the possibility that they might lose control of the potential pool of capital that pension funds represented. Pepper was right, but despite the fact, or probably because of it, the vote went against labor. [Truman vetoed the bill, but Congress overrode] President Truman's veto."

[9] Anthony Leviero, Millions Paid Out by Welfare Funds, N.Y. Times, May 23, 1946, at 12.

[10] Rifkin and Barber, supra note 8, at 100; William S. White, Senate Votes 48-40 to Curb Union Rule of Welfare Funds, N.Y. Times, May 9, 1947, at 1, col. 1, 12, col. 6 (Sen. Taft implies that rule aimed to set back the United Mine Workers demand that it administer the workers' fund). See also Supplemental Views of Senators Taft, Ball, Donnell, and Jenner, in [Sen.] Comm. on Labor and Public Welfare, Federal Labor Relations Act of 1947, S. Rep. No. 105, 80th Cong., 1st Sess. 52–54 (1947) ("[union welfare funds] may well become a mere tool to increase the power of the union leaders over their men"), as cited in Millis, supra note 6, at 565. Byrd's aim may have been to support the mine owners; his rhetoric might have been what he thought necessary to convince others to help the owners.

every central union in a program of sweeping encroachment on the earnings and on the functions of ownership and management, with no limitation whatever except the conscience of the union dynasty."[11]

Despite the hot rhetoric, pension funds were small then and unlikely to be big for decades. Corporate governance was not an issue for 1946; managers probably wanted to control pension plans to control the level and timing of their funding as much as for any other reason. Moreover, for managers to attack union control on governance grounds in 1946 required both prescience and a discount rate inconsistent with the short-term horizons usually said to afflict them. Rather, the managerial control provision arose from the mine owners' influence with key senators and a public wary of union power and very hostile to the UMW's John L. Lewis, who had defied public opinion with strikes during World War II. Truman vetoed the first effort to end union sole control; a year later, a new Congress passed it again. Truman vetoed it again, but Congress overrode the veto.

Even if unions had had the legal authority to control pension plans completely, they were unlikely to have become key corporate players, because union membership declined in the ensuing decades, explaining weak union pensions better than does Taft-Hartley.[12] And I understand that management usually defers to unions in administering the joint plans (although were union plans capable of strong influence, perhaps that deference would recede). I am unaware of important foreign union-dominated pensions, suggesting that either the organizational form is inept or that where unions can win political victories they try for other results, such as better government pensions or socialized large firms. Still, one could imagine a different, although perhaps inferior, corporate governance balance of power. If only 5 percent of equity were in union-dominated pension plans, manager-dominated plans would decline because of the shift, and union plans might target their investments to take some big blocks in specific firms or form alliances with public pension plans on issues of common interest.

The second managerial front that encouraged passive pensions was contractual. General Motors, hoping to head off expanded social security or bigger union plans, set up a private, long-vesting pension plan, and GM's

---

[11] Louis Stark, New Strike Looms, Coal Official Says, N.Y. Times, Feb. 12, 1947, at 5, col. 3; Louis Stark, Lewis Sees U.S. Powerless to Prevent Coal Strikes Unless It Goes Totalitarian, N.Y. Times, Mar. 8, 1947, at 1, ("'the government [is using] a blackjack in favor of the . . . coal operators'") (quoting John L. Lewis). See also C. P. Trussell, Pepper Plan Upset, N.Y. Times, May 23, 1946, at 1; Rifkin and Barber, supra note 8, at 99.

[12] Unionization in recent decades has been weak for many reasons, including an unfriendly regulatory apparatus and economic shifts from previously unionized sectors, such as manufacturing, to new, nonunionized sectors, such as services. Paul Weiler, Promises To Keep: Securing Workers' Rights to Self-Organization under the NLRA, 96 Harvard Law Review 1769 (1983); Robert J. Lalonde and Bernard D. Meltzer, Hard Times for Unions: Another Look at the Significance of Employer Illegalities, 58 University of Chicago Law Review 953, 956–58 (1991).

plan quickly became the model for large firm pensions. The autoworkers' union was wary, preferring union- or publicly controlled pensions, but went along. GM's senior managers wanted a pension plan that would have a small number of large holdings, and their bankers, J. P. Morgan and Morgan, Stanley, advised them not to fragment the pension plan's portfolio.[13] But eventually they forced fragmentation. When the GM plan was adopted, GM's managers told their pension managers not to meddle in corporate governance, instructing the pension managers to "avoid any possible charge that control or management responsibility is being acquired" and directed them not to acquire over 0.0075 of a *portfolio* firm's stock. Because GM instructed its pension managers to keep the percentage of the portfolio firm low, not just to keep the percentage of the plan devoted to any single investment low, GM obviously expected the plan to be inert in corporate governance, as it explicitly said.[14]

Why did GM insist that its own pension fund be fragmented? Small blocks enhanced salability, and perhaps that idea reversed GM's initial inclination to take big blocks. But more seems to have been at work. True, although fragmentation's *effect* would be to insulate managers when GM became a model, I think GM was seeking not managerial insulation, but something more basic. GM's senior managers feared that the United Auto Workers could end up controlling its pension fund.[15] By disabling the pension from taking corporate control positions *before* the UAW got control of the pension fund, GM made it less likely that the UAW would take control blocks anywhere, including in GM. The UAW would have had to change investment direction once it got control of the fund, and if the fund already lacked control blocks, the UAW would have had to justify a change in policy. This anti-UAW scenario fits well with a "political" theory; GM, I understand, internally debated the trade-offs of taking big blocks versus taking small, salable blocks. Fearful of union power and pension plan control, it preferred salability of stock and an inert, powerless pension plan to a powerful one. This scenario also fits nicely with the conflicts prevailing in U.S. labor relations in the later 1940s, such as the Taft-Hartley reaction to John L. Lewis and the UMW strikes.

GM had another reason to prefer that its pension fund be weak, even if the UAW never got to control it. At the time GM had reason to fear an

[13] Drucker, supra note 3, at 4–7, 169; Letter from Peter F. Drucker (Dec. 9, 1993) (re GM's initial preference for big positions, decision to keep small, salable blocks, and fear that the UAW would eventually control the GM pension).

[14] Drucker, supra note 3, at 4–7, 169; Harbrecht, supra note 3, at 8. Wilson, GM's CEO, rejected investment in GM stock as too risky for workers; the UAW, however, was attracted to ownership of GM. William M. O'Barr and John M. Conley, Fortune and Folly: The Wealth and Power Of Institutional Investing 18–19 (1992).

[15] Drucker, supra note 3, at 4–7, 169; Drucker, supra note 13.

antitrust structural attack that could break it up into several smaller auto companies. The Justice Department in 1946 began an inquiry into dissolution of GM; and, as an outgrowth of that inquiry, in 1948 the United States brought suit to dissolve GM's relationship with DuPont.[16] GM's motive for fragmenting its pension fund (and for keeping it fragmented, once its fear of UAW control subsided) may have been to show that GM was inert in the governance of other firms, to deflect big-is-bad attacks from antitrust authorities.

Thus, it is plausible that labor-management conflict and antitrust—in the 1940s and 1950s often a discomfort with concentrated industrial power and a preference for a nation of small producers, even at economic cost[17]—were weakly behind pension fragmentation. GM's pension fund could have taken big blocks in other firms and become involved in their governance. In that era GM was a powerhouse firm that could have become the hub of cross-ownership of customers and suppliers. DuPont, a principal supplier to GM of fabrics and finishes, was already connected. Others could have joined through their pension funds in a mechanism that dimly paralleled features of the Japanese keiretsu, where customers and suppliers own some of one another's stock (see chapter 19).

This was not just an aberrational event. While I sympathize with the idea that slight variations in original conditions can profoundly affect later developments,[18] this is not one of those instances, because GM's policy—fragmenting its portfolio, apparently either to deflect antitrust attack or to weaken the UAW's potential control—is widespread in rules for financial institutions. American discomfort with concentrated private economic power helps explain many bank laws, insurance portfolio rules, and mutual fund rules. Although the antitrust and antiunion impetus came indirectly, and was implemented privately, it still came from the same public force.

Managers sought to avoid expanded social security and union control of active, big-block pension funds; managers of large firms needed to deflect

---

[16] United States v. E. I. DuPont de Nemours and Co., 353 U.S. 586 (1957); Alfred P. Sloan, Jr., My Years with General Motors 361–62 (1963); Theodore P. Kovaleff, Divorce American-Style: The DuPont—General Motors Case, Delaware History, Spring–Summer 1978, at 28. The Justice Department's chief antitrust lawyer said in 1949 that the big problem was the "concentration of economic power in industries controlled by a few large companies—the big threes and the big fours. . . . [T]he Antitrust Division is now directing its main enforcement activites [against them]." Neil Fligstein, The Transformation of Corporate Control 176–77 (1990).

[17] United States v. Aluminum Co. of America, 148 F.2d 416 (2d Cir. 1945) (antitrust's purpose "was to perpetuate and preserve, for its own sake and in spite of possible cost, an organization of industry in small units"; "great industrial consolidations are inherently undesirable, regardless of their economic results"); Brown Shoe Co. v. United States, 370 U.S. 294 (1962), United States v. E. I. DuPont de Nemours and Co., 353 U.S. 586 (1957).

[18] See James Gleick, Chaos—Making a New Science (1987).

antitrust attack. Other firms had the same goals, because if big, they had antitrust fears, and if small, they lacked the financial strength to take big blocks. To implement these goals, firms and managers set up managerially controlled fragmented funds; again, the purpose was not to keep managers from corporate governance oversight, but that was the effect. The corruption of the most visible union fund in the 1950s—the Teamsters' pension fund—surely solidified managerial control of pensions.[19]

Alternative Structures

This short history suggests several alternatives. Pension funds could have flowed into collective investment vehicles for employees—union-controlled plans, for example, or separate trusts, such as TIAA-CREF, the acronym for the huge pension plan for university employees. This was the salient alternative to managerial control, and Congress prohibited the solely union-controlled version in 1947.[20]

Another alternative could have been to cut out both managers and unions with a fiduciary rule aimed at both union and managerial conflicts of interest, banning both managers and unions from pension fund management. With such bans in place, employees would control and direct their own pension monies, as they now do for IRA or Keogh accounts. Employees would send funds to large financial institutions, such as mutual fund complexes or insurers, and choose their investment vehicle, such as a particular fund or annuity contract; managers would not be part of the command structure of these pension plans.

The third alternative would have been to enhance publicly funded pensions, that is, social security. In other industrialized nations, social security plays a much larger role in old age pensions than it does in the United States;[21] American aversion to public programs made big private pensions possible.

[19] The second interest group story: In 1974, the steel industry was in desperate shape. The government guarantee of the unfunded pensions helped the steel industry, then particularly politically influential. The United Steelworkers and the United Auto Workers were key lobbyists for ERISA and the guarantees. David Langer, Protector Becomes the Threat to Pensions, Pensions and Investments, Sept. 14, 1992, at 15, col. 3.

[20] Employee-controlled plans have divergent histories. The Teachers' Insurance and Annuity Association–College Retirement Equities Fund (or TIAA-CREF, as it is nearly always called) is often viewed as one of the best. It is the biggest institutional investor in the United States, and has no taint of corruption. The other famous employee-driven plans are the Teamsters' pension plans, which have been corrupt. (I am not offering this alternative as economically superior, but only as a plausible alternative that was cut off.)

[21] Teresa Ghilarducci, Labor's Capital: The Economics and Politics of Private Pensions 135, 142 (1992).

These alternatives would not be without problems. A bigger government system would have had costs. Cutting managers out is not as easy for defined-benefit plans as it would be for defined-contribution plans. (Defined-benefit plans promise the employee a specific retirement benefit; the firm takes the investment risk if the funds it sets aside do not earn enough to provide that benefit. In defined-contribution plans, the firm contributes to the employee's retirement accounts; the employee's retirement income then depends on how well the investments do.)[22] Defined-contribution plans (such as IRAs and Keoghs) appeal to knowledgeable savers, and not all pension beneficiaries are knowledgeable enough.[23] Because the company takes the primary risk of the pension fund manager's bad performance in defined-benefit plans, there is reason for managers of such pension plans to be accountable to company managers. Moreover, defined-benefit plans provide the firm and its managers with some flexibility to match funding with corporate cash flow, because the actuarial assumptions for funding are malleable.

Nevertheless, with TIAA-CREF, IRAs, Keoghs and the defined-contribution concept in mind, we see alternatives to managerial command of pension funds. These alternatives would have reduced managerial domination in governance of the large firm; they might have given large financial institutions, independent of management, a greater voice in corporate governance.

Managers' Structural Control

To avoid a precedent that could redound to their detriment, managers do not want their pension managers to be active in other firms.[24] Pension funds are usually run from the firm's treasurer's office; senior pension officers are often right at the corporate headquarters.[25] Half of the pensions are managed in house, with company employees investing the funds. ERISA permits the firm's own "officer, employee, agent, or other representative" to run the fund,[26] a critical permission for our purposes. And even when the funds

---

[22] Actually, complex financial instruments could pass this risk on to a financial institution. Guaranteed investment contracts (GICs), usually issued by insurance companies, do this, and would allow an employee to turn a defined-contribution plan into the financial equivalent of a defined-benefit plan.

[23] Pension policy is paternalistic, forcing myopic individuals to save when their immediate preference is to spend; an expansion of *voluntary* IRAs and Keogh plans would have carried out this policy poorly. Deborah Weiss, Paternalistic Pension Policy: Psychological Evidence and Economic Theory, 58 University of Chicago Law Review 1275 (1991).

[24] Usually that preference would be weak. Free-riding among managers could destroy their coordination. See infra text accompanying notes 36–37.

[25] O'Barr and Conley, supra note 14, at 94 n.2.

[26] ERISA § 408(c)(3), 29 U.S.C. § 1108(c)(3) (1988).

are managed outside the firm, the fund managers know that the operating managers are not looking for activist fund managers. In other settings, law sometimes bans such relationships with potential conflicts of interest. The Glass-Steagall Act, for example, barred affiliations between investment and commercial banks, partly because of fears that the conflicted bankers would bilk unwary consumers; the Investment Company Act of 1940 bars many dealings between the mutual funds and portfolio firms because of justified fears that the dealings would benefit those controlling the mutual fund.

The high activism of public pension plans, which are run for state employees, contrasts with the passivity of the private ones. Public pension funds persistently propose charter amendments, prod managers, establish lobbying groups.[27] Some actions may be political posturing, but many are not. They are acting, roughly and imprecisely, the way owners would tend to act. They lack the managerial command structure that private pensions have.

Let me give two examples. A savvy CEO remarked that officers of *public* pension funds often talk to him about stockholders' getting cumulative and confidential voting, suggest staggered boards, and criticize poison pills. These incursions threaten managers. Private pension funds, under the influence of their own managers, do not raise such "delicate" matters with him.[28]

During the 1980s takeover wars, managers were not always subtle in using their power to direct pension plans. One fund manager said, quite explicitly:

> Some guy's company was being taken over and he called his crony at some other company, who's the CEO, and he'd say, "Your pension fund owns 500,000 shares of our stock and I want you to vote . . . to protect management forever." And so the [crony] CEO would [talk] to the pension officer and say, "Does one of our managers own 500,000 shares of Harry's stock?" . . . "[T]ell him that I can't play golf with Harry next Saturday if we don't vote in favor of what Harry wants to do.[29]

At other pensions, outside managers purport to have "total discretion" in voting proxies, "except" that they must tell their corporate bosses if they plan to vote against management. Notice is superfluous, one may say cynically, because, as one fund manager reported: "Voting against management is unusual."[30] Two investigators concluded after interviewing fund managers that pension fund "disengagement . . . [arises from] a pension fund version

---

[27] Kevin G. Salwen and Joann S. Lublin, Giant Investors Flex Their Muscles More at U.S. Corporations, Wall Street Journal, Apr. 27, 1993, at A1.

[28] H. B. Atwater, The Governance System Is Sound, Directors & Boards, Spring 1991, at 17, 19 ("I have never been asked about poison pills by a private pension fund, but I am asked all the time by public pension funds").

[29] O'Barr and Conley, supra note 14, at 182.

[30] Id. at 196–97.

of the Golden Rule: Do unto other companies as you would have their pension funds do unto your company."[31]

When voting on corporate issues that would be bad for corporate managers but good for their stockholding employees, pension managers have ducked, refusing to vote until the Labor Department directed them to do so.[32] Their theory for ducking was that the expense of voting would be borne by beneficiaries, a convincing claim when the pension holds only a sliver of the firm's stock, because the expense is not balanced by a good chance of influence. The more subtle question is whether pension managers avoid the larger blocks that would make informed voting cost effective *because* they want to avoid having to choose between their "operational" bosses, the company managers, and their nominal bosses, the employees to whom the pension managers owe fiduciary duties.

The realpolitik of who now calls the shots—operating managers—is decisive. Whatever may be the doctrinal duties running from pension fiduciaries to beneficiaries, management has the power to hire and fire the pension fiduciary.[33] One might hypothesize that pension managers structure their portfolios to satisfy both their beneficiaries and their managerial bosses; among the plausible portfolio strategies, they choose one that will least damage management and the beneficiaries. Private pension managers rarely are visible in the new institutional investor activism of the 1990s; when they have been visible, the managerial derelictions have been seen as unusually egregious.[34] Only one major private fund has announced that it will pursue an activist corporate governance policy; that announcement of an event counter to the usual passivity was a newsworthy event.[35]

[31] Id. at 197, 200. Confidential voting would increase pension managers' independence, but not as much as might be thought. There would be some prehiring screening of managers. And under ERISA, managers can retain investment or voting authority, reducing the impact of confidential voting. Cf. James A. White, Pension Officers Back Proxy-Rule Shifts, Wall Street Journal, Apr. 1, 1991, at C1 (pension managers guardedly back confidential voting). Confidential voting should be seen as helping to break the loose managerial oversight, similar to antitrust analysis of how and when to control price observation in concentrated markets.

[32] Labor Department Opinion Letter on Proxy Voting, 17 Pens. Rep. (BNA), No. 5 at 244 (Jan. 29, 1990). See also Labor Department Letter on Proxy Voting by Plan Fiduciaries, 15 Pens. Rep. (BNA), No. 9, at 391 (Feb. 29, 1988) (Avon letter) (fund manager cannot accept directions to vote from others; must determine what is good for beneficiaries); O'Barr & Conley, supra note 14, at 181, 183.

[33] James Brickley, Ronald Lease, and Clifford Smith, Ownership Structure and Voting on Antitakeover Amendments, 20 Journal of Financial Economics 267 (1988); James Heard and Howard Sherman, Conflicts of Interest in the Proxy System 40–49 (1987) (Investor Responsibility Research Center, Washington, D.C.); John Pound, Proxy Contests and the Efficiency of Shareholder Oversight, 15 Journal of Financial Economics 237 (1988).

[34] Marlene Givant Star, Managers Lead AmEx Coup—Investment Firms Take Up Corporate Governance Fight, Pensions and Investments, Feb. 8, 1993, at 1.

[35] Nell Minow, Do Your Duty, Retirement Managers, New York Times, Jan. 30, 1994, § 3, at 11, col. 3; Susan Pulliam, Campbell Soup Fund to Take Activist Role, Wall Street Journal, July 15, 1993, at C1.

Managers' Collective Action Problem

I have been looking at managers as if they acted as a group. But at least two problems afflict viewing them as acting as a group. One, they have not agreed to act as a group: to analogize to antitrust, they may act in a consciously parallel fashion—each may decide not to rock the governance boat—but they have not met and agreed to be passive. And, two, their individual incentives are mixed: while each CEO may want not to be overseen, it does not follow that each will protect the other CEOs from oversight. They face a collective action problem: each CEO would like the others to be passive vis-à-vis his or her own firm, but would like to profit by being active himself or herself. Cartels are similar; each cartel member would like the others to keep their prices high, but would like to profit by shaving its own price a bit to gain the extra business. Just as cartels—either formal via explicit agreement or informal via conscious parallelism—break down when their members become numerous and each "cheats" on the collective price, any managerial "cartel"—again, at most an implicit one, because no group of CEOs ever met like a price-fixing cartel to prescribe their pension funds' behavior—should break down.

True, the CEO's incentive for inducing pension activity is weaker than the cartel-breaker's incentive for lowering price. The CEO's firm gets only some of the benefits of governance activity but it incurs the offsetting costs of innovation. The CEO captures an even smaller fraction of these benefits; the antitrust cartel-breaker can often capture greater profits than the CEO can. Still, while the strength of the incentives differs, the parallel is there, and one needs more to explain pension fund passivity than managerial preferences alone.

Ideology can impede people from pursuing selfish financial interest. CEOs would be pained if they had to clash with cultural norms that investors not take big blocks or meddle in corporate governance, norms that arose from American individualism, trading culture, and historical restraints on the other major financial institutions. Banks, insurers, and mutual funds do not often take big blocks and go into boardrooms, so CEOs and pension fund managers find themselves in a corporate culture that denigrates big blocks and boardroom activity. The pension people play by these unwritten rules, which in turn were strengthened by the written rules that govern other financial institutions; there is a feedback loop, feeding back between law and culture, with each reinforcing the other.

Culture often breaks down when money can be made.[36] Analogous norms

---

[36] If each individual actor can only capture a small portion of the gains from change, culture can be stable. While a few big firms' pension funds could change corporate governance for some smaller firms single-handedly, most pension funds need to coordinate change with others—a

in the early takeover days often shackled CEOs from making hostile take-over offers. But raiders put targets in play, releasing culturally constrained CEOs from their shackles; they could become white knights who would protect the target firm, by taking it over. Eventually enough takeovers oc-curred that cultural restraints eroded. Similarly, although private pensions had little interest in fostering hostile takeovers, when a raider acted, the fund managers had little choice but to tender the stock at the high offer price. Anything else risked fiduciary violations of ERISA.

Raiders triggered the takeover action, which in turn triggered the partici-pation of pensions and CEOs—but as yet, few governance analogues to the raiders exist, since few institutions have big blocks of stock, sit in board-rooms, and are active. One potential analogue is the *public* pension funds, which are not beholden to managers directly; if they continue to be active and become strong enough leaders, investment norms could shift.[37] But today, without enough others to break down the perhaps paper-thin barrier of tradition for the private pension funds, the investment culture has some effect.

Another analogy to cartels provides an even stronger explanation of why managerial collective action has not yet broken down. A cartel can fail if one of its member seeks a few more sales below the cartel-fixed price, then an-other does, and then they all do. But as the cartel unravels, its members frequently appeal to government to force the cartel members to continue to fix the price, for government to fix the price directly, or for government to exclude competitors. Government enforces the private cartel arrangement.

And so it is with the collective action problem of managers. ERISA and trustee doctrine help to fragment pension portfolios, to prevent big blocks, and to keep pension managers out of the boardrooms of portfolio companies. I do not for one moment believe that managers *sought* these rules—which are well-intentioned doctrines designed to protect pension beneficiaries—to solve their collective action problem. But the *effects* fit neatly with man-agers' goals. Managers would resist efforts to reconstruct pensions by repeal-ing these governmentally enforced rules, bringing the analogy to govern-ment protection of cartels closer.

The result then is a combination of three weak forces with unintended effects, all pointing in the same direction: (1) Structure puts managers in command. In their collective self-interest, they prefer to limit oversight. So they expect their pension fund managers to be passive and inert. A collective

---

cost. And agency costs arise again, because neither the pension manager nor the CEO of the cultural renegade would capture much of the gain from change.

[37] "'Public funds have legitimized more active involvement by (other) institutional inves-tors. . . . Calpers and others made it safe . . . for investment managers to raise questions about corporate governance,' said James E. Heard, president of Institutional Shareholder Services Inc., Washington." Star, supra note 34, at 43.

action problem would lead a few managers to defect. Defection would be rapid if others, outside of the managerial control structure defected, as happened in takeovers. (2) But this time the outsiders—banks, insurers, and mutual funds—have been stopped from acting. A cultural attitude—institutions should be uninvolved in corporate governance—puts a small barrier between pensions and action.[38] (3) Finally, ERISA and trustee doctrines reinforce that barrier. These are the doctrines we next examine.

ERISA'S DOCTRINES:
EXCESS DIVERSIFICATION AND INSUFFICIENT INNOVATION

ERISA's technical doctrines weakly foster excess diversification, reduce innovation, and discourage big, visible blocks. For a fiduciary to go into the boardroom (or send someone else in), it needs a big percentage of the portfolio firm's stock to absorb the expenses of activity and to overcome managerial aversion to independent sources of power in the boardroom.

This need for a big block interacts with fiduciary duties in four ways. First, ERISA's diversification standard might be interpreted as a hyperdiversification rule, requiring hundreds of stocks, with each position too weak for effective involvement. Second, ERISA tends to make imitation of prevailing practice the safest strategy. Third, traditional trustee law, which is not formally part of ERISA, makes big blocks risky because antinetting rules do not always allow the trustee to defend against a lawsuit by pointing to the overall sound performance of the fund. Fourth, the fiduciary would risk enhanced liability standards when entering the boardroom.

Excess Diversification

ERISA requires the fiduciary to diversify, unless it is *clearly* prudent not to do so. Although diversification is good, it has costs; we can have too much of a good thing.

While ERISA's diversification rule has been held up as a high barrier to pension funds' having big blocks of stock and boardroom presence,[39] its im-

---

[38] Also, there are perhaps few gains from breaking the "cartel" because oversight does not improve the portfolio firm enough, or at all. Or more likely, there is some improvement, but the 10 percent blockholder cannot capture enough of it to be worth the heavy price of being seen as a renegade from the dominant investment culture.

[39] Bernard S. Black, Shareholder Passivity Reexamined, 89 Michigan Law Review 520 (1990); John C. Coffee, Jr., Liquidity Versus Control: The Institutional Investor as Corporate Monitor, 91 Columbia Law Review 1277 (1991); Mark J. Roe, Political and Legal Restraints on Ownership and Control of Public Companies, 27 Journal of Financial Economics 7, 10, 15 (1990).

portance has been exaggerated, since the law does not define diversification, and economists say most diversification comes from the first fifteen or twenty different stocks.[40] While the law's mandate to avoid large losses[41] could be interpreted to require avoiding large losses on any investment,[42] irrespective of the percentage of the fund's total assets, the more plausible interpretation is that it commands the fund to avoid large losses in relation to the size of the portfolio. But without extensive case law support for these interpretations,[43] pension managers might well conclude that the benefits of a restricted portfolio (if any) accrue to the beneficiaries, while the fund managers and their firms bear the risks—even extremely small risks—of a suit for breach of ERISA's fiduciary rules, including the risk that the mandate against large losses will be interpreted against the pension manager.

In the end, the diversification rule, while not without its ambiguities, is not the main barrier to big blocks and activity. Pension managers determined to get over it probably could. Labor Department interpretation would probably gain judicial deference. Hyperdiversification might just be an excuse for validating the managerial command structure.

Prudent Investments: A Prod to Follow the Crowd

Other rules are bigger barriers. ERISA, by requiring "diligence . . . that [would be used] in conduct of an enterprise of a like character and with like aims,"[44] encourages pensions to imitate other institutions' investments, creating another feedback loop. A pension manager who gets out of line with prevailing portfolio practice risks liability. By looking to typical actions—in other words, the prevailing wisdom—the fiduciary rule makes innovation risky.

A recent case reduced that risk by validating actions consistent with a respectable *minority* view in the investment community.[45] Although this doctrine could reduce the impact of the prevailing-wisdom rule, there is obviously still a chicken-or-the-egg problem. Before there can be a respectable minority, someone has to go first. But whoever goes first lacks a respectable minority for doctrinal protection.

Some evolution is now occurring. A few public pensions, such as Cal-PERS, are active in talking to boards and prodding managers. Although pub-

---

[40] James Lorie, Peter Dodd, and Mary Kimpton, The Stock Market: Theories and Evidence 85 (2d ed. 1985). Some financial models show, however, that for very large funds, even the tiny increase in a little more diversification can help beneficiaries.

[41] ERISA § 404(a), 29 U.S.C. § 1104(a) (1988).

[42] Coffee, supra note 39, at 1356–57.

[43] Sandoval v. Simmons, 622 F. Supp. 1174 (C.D. Ill. 1985).

[44] ERISA § 404(a)(1)(B), 29 U.S.C. § 1104(a)(1)(B) (1988).

[45] Jones v. O'Higgins, 11 Employee Benefits Cas. (BNA) 1660, 1666–67 (N.D.N.Y. 1989).

lic pension plans are not under ERISA (but are under state rules, which often resemble ERISA's), they are enterprises "of a like character and with like aims," the phrase ERISA uses to measure private pension funds' prudence. Public pensions are closer kin to the private ones than are other financial institutions, and their activity could become doctrinally important. A few other intermediaries, such as Berkshire Hathaway and some investment partnerships, are also taking big blocks and sitting in boardrooms. If the activities of public pensions and the maverick institutions expand, they will be the "respectable minority" that gives doctrinal cover to activity by private pension funds. Moreover, *if* their activity spreads, ERISA's rule could create a snowball effect, as previously passive institutions come to fear that *inactivity* indicates a *lack* of the "diligence . . . [used by] enterprise[s] of a like character and with like aims," the legal standard.

But these active ones are now few, and what the majority does forms the safest standard of prudence behind ERISA's requirement of "diligence . . . that [would be used] in conduct of an enterprise of a like character and with like aims. . . ."[46] Moreover, were prevailing practice to take big blocks and be active—had banks and insurers not been constrained from doing so—ERISA would then be *encouraging* fiduciaries to enter the boardroom. *Not* taking big blocks would be seen as being irresponsibly weak, leaving the fiduciary unable to protect its beneficiaries from corporate misdirection.

Thus, in my view, ERISA's key fiduciary restraint is not to force passivity but to reinforce whatever the prevailing practice is. ERISA mandates imitation. Were an ERISA-like law to be enacted in Japan or Germany, where big blocks are standard, then a pension fund would worry that *failure* to take big blocks would expose it to liability. Thus, the prudent investor rule is really an imitation rule, is context sensitive, and is amenable to evolution.

Analysis of ERISA's imitation rule reinforces the political theory not because its doctrines have a clear political motivation, but because they have a political fit. What do pension fiduciaries imitate when exercising a "diligence . . . that [would be used] in conduct of an enterprise of a like character and with like aims"? "Enterprises[s] of a like character and with like aims" to private pension plans can be arrayed in concentric circles around that single private pension plan, according to the other enterprises' institutional character and their beneficiaries' aims. Those enterprises entrusted with families' long-term savings, would form circles around the center. Other private pension funds would be in the innermost ring of that circle, public pension funds next, life insurers next, bank trusts on the next ring, and then banks, mutual funds, property and casualty insurers, and other institutions on the outermost ring. Pension funds would be told to imitate one another, but also to imitate insurers, bank trust funds, and mutual funds, for which a

[46] ERISA § 404(a)(1)(B), 29 U.S.C. § 1104(a)(1)(B) (1988).

more direct political story helps explain their passivity. In effect, ERISA unintentionally incorporates—by reference, so to speak—the political story behind these other institutions.

Antinetting

Trust law's antinetting rule bars the fiduciary from offsetting a loss from a breach of trust with a gain from elsewhere. The big loser must be shown to have been an investment made with adequate information and care; the loser cannot be automatically netted against a big winner.[47] The clearest case to justify the antinetting rule would be the fiduciary who steals $1 million on Thursday, and earns $1 million on Friday. Although there is good reason not to net the outcomes there, the value of antinetting for a well-intentioned breach is more debatable.

Say the fiduciary takes three large positions, each big enough to get into the boardroom, amounting to 30 percent of its portfolio; the rest of the portfolio is highly fragmented. Losses from one of the three are huge and trigger a lawsuit in which plaintiffs argue that the trustee badly executed that basic investment policy of taking big positions. The trustee incurred the big loss because it had bad information or inadequately monitored the big investment.

Although the trustee can defend its policy, as a plausible minority view of prudence, it has other troubles. True, the Restatement of Trusts (which is not explicitly applicable to ERISA plans) says:

> If the trustee makes a profit and also incurs a loss through breaches of trust that *are not separate and distinct*, the beneficiaries are entitled . . . to the amount of the profit only after deducting the amount of the loss or to charge the trustee with the loss reduced by the amount of the profit.[48]

But the plaintiff argues that the failure to monitor or get adequate information was *a separate* breach. The big-block policy might be a respectable minority view, but even if the overall portfolio return was satisfactory, the failure of this one particular big block is a separate, actionable breach. The Restatement of Trusts says: "If a trustee is liable for a loss caused by a breach of trust, the amount of the liability is *not reduced* by profits of the trust estate

---

[47] See Restatement (Third) of Trusts (May 18, 1990) (Prudent Investor Rule); cf. Leigh v. Engle, 727 F.2d 113 (7th Cir. 1984), on remand, 669 F. Supp. 1390, 1405 (N.D. Ill. 1987) (damages are difference between amount earned on one poor-performing big block and a prudent alternative), aff'd, 858 F.2d 361 (7th Cir. 1988).

[48] Restatement (Third) of Trusts § 213 cmt. e (May 18, 1990) (Prudent Investor Rule) (emphasis supplied).

resulting from *other actions* of the trustee that do not involve a breach of trust."[49]

Each block decision must be evaluated separately, as a distinct investment requiring the trustee's rigorous review before making the investment. Failure to monitor or to be adequately informed is a *distinct breach of trust*. And big investments require lots of care. The plaintiffs could bolster their case by showing that for the other big bets, the winners, the fund had taken better care. Moreover, in retrospect big mistakes often look like acts taken without adequate information, or the results of inadequate monitoring. Retrospective uncertainty will attach to all big blocks, some of which are bound to fail.

This doctrinal inducement to avoid big blocks also fits with the business pressures on pension managers, who want to avoid public and private, not just legal, responsibility for a mistake. Indexing and other fragmentation strategies help managers to avoid crisp, formal responsibility. A portfolio decline due to a market crash is easier to explain away to those who hired the pension manager than is a big bad performer.[50]

How can fiduciaries protect themselves from liability—whether formal and legal, or informal—for big mistakes? One clean solution for the fiduciary is to avoid making any *big* mistake by hyperfragmenting the portfolio. Institutions thus have an incentive *not* to take large positions that would give them influence inside the boardroom. Little mistakes aren't likely to induce plaintiffs to sue, and the information and care taken might justify the action taken for a little investment. How wrong can one be if the portfolio more or less tracks the performance of the stock market and other institutions? A big loser makes the level of information and care look inadequate in retrospect; a fragmented portfolio that barely trails the market is not a basis for a lawsuit.[51]

ERISA's Prudent Expert Standard versus the Business Judgment Rule

ERISA's prudent expert standard[52] should make pension fiduciaries wary of going into a portfolio firm's boardroom. Fiduciaries have to know their business. When they are passive investors, their business is the business of investing. If ERISA fiduciaries enter the boardrooms of industry, have they thereby made their business the business of directing industrial firms?

[49] Id. cmt. c (emphasis added).

[50] O'Barr and Conley, supra note 14, at 88.

[51] Bevis Longstreth, Modern Investment Management and the Prudent Man Rule (1986).

[52] ERISA § 404(a)(1)(B); DOL Reg. § 404a-1; H.R. Rep. No. 1280, 93d Cong., 2d Sess. 302 (1974).

Pension fiduciaries who sat on the boards of portfolio firms would be sued. As directors, they owe duties to shareholders: They cannot steal, they must be loyal, they must be attentive. But they can defend themselves with a business judgment rule that allows them a wide range for error in making corporate decisions. Disgruntled shareholders must show more than that directors erred; they must show extraordinary abuse.

ERISA's prudent expert rule is a tighter standard. Beneficiaries might sue both the individual fiduciary who sat on the portfolio firm's board and the fiduciary institution for the mistaken corporate decision, arguing that although the directors' actions may have passed muster under the business judgment rule, they failed to satisfy the stricter prudent expert standard.

These problems pose a general principal-agent problem. The risk to the fiduciary-agent is liability for the full amount of the loss. The gains to the fiduciary-agent are the enhanced fees and prestige from innovative action: portfolio loss (times risk of liability) versus gain in fees. The beneficiary-principal balances the risk of loss against portfolio gain. The agent will tend to be more conservative than beneficiaries would desire. There is a mismatch in incentives between the fiduciary and the beneficiaries.

In reaction to these risks, however small, the fiduciary institution could nominate someone not regularly employed by it. That distant nominee would then be so distinct from the fiduciary that he or she would not carry ERISA's prudent expert standard into the boardroom. Although this avoids the prudent expert standard, it loosens bonds between the board and the fiduciary. The board member might no longer feel as bound to the fiduciary as would an employee or full-time agent of the institutional investor. The board member may then be "captured" by management.

THE FIT WITH FINANCIAL THEORY

Efficient capital market theory, indexing strategies, and portfolio theory are well-developed, legitimate financial theories that happen to fit well with managerial goals, because their users are unlikely to play a governance role. Similarly, the practical views of traders, who try to beat the market, also fit well with managerial goals, because traders do not own enough stock for long enough to play a governance role. No equally prominent theory yet extols the virtue of coupling large block investing with boardroom presence.

LIQUIDITY AND CONTROL

Institutions need liquidity; hence, one could argue, they might want small, liquid blocks of stock even if they were freed from restraints on influence.

But in practice the need for liquidity poorly explains pension fund passivity. Pension funds do not need much liquidity, because their obligations to pay are long term and predictable. Thus the need for liquidity does not by itself *cause* pensions to forgo influence.[53]

BEGINNINGS OF A MODERN PUBLIC CHOICE STORY

Thus far, the story for private pensions has been one of indirection, of well-intended efforts that had a side effect of supporting the manager-centered firm, or of interest group jockeying in nonmanagerial dimensions that eventually had a promanagerial effect. But once a structure is in place, incumbent groups benefit and could resist change. Managers could be expected to resist changing private pensions, biasing the corporate structure toward the status quo.

Social change could reorder governance and private pensions, just as social change accidentally put managers in charge of nearly a quarter of the stock market. If pension funds' current trend toward individually managed accounts at financial institutions grows, then managers' command structure will weaken. Today's increasing job mobility and deterioration of long-term employment at a single firm could increase demand for self-directed pensions, which would move pension funds, and hence the stock market, away from managerial control. This is already a small trend.[54] Corporate governance will determine very little about whether that movement to self-directed pensions is powerful, but if it is, corporate governance could be profoundly affected. If employees and not senior managers come to be the ones who decide who will manage employees' pension money, those institutions that employees choose will feel less beholden to corporate managers than do today's pension fund managers. The largest conflict of interest—arising when managers hire the firms that invest pension money—will diminish. (Oversight of the *institutions* would then become more important, because under today's system the corporate managers have some incentive both to choose fund managers who are neither corrupt nor incompetent and to check their work.)

[53] Beneficiaries may want liquidity in a defined-contribution plan. They may want portability to prevent abuse by the manager, or to allow the beneficiary to change investment direction. But these matters could be traded off.

[54] Margaret Price, Defined Contribution Popularity a Concern, Pensions and Investments, May 31, 1993, at 3 ("Defined contribution plans are being started at roughly 4.5 times the rate of defined benefit plans. Their assets will equal those in defined benefit plans by the year 2003."); Allen R. Myerson, I.R.A.'s Surging as More Worry about Pensions, N.Y. Times, Apr. 15, 1993, at 1, col. 5. In late 1993 and early 1994 the modest trend toward defined-contribution plans slowed.

Imagine how hard it would be to *deliberately* restructure pensions for corporate governance purposes. Even if the public benefits are plausible, they have to be small: slightly greater GNP, slightly better-managed firms, slightly longer-term horizons, slightly better industrial organization. But the beneficiaries are diffuse, disorganized, unlikely to even know they might benefit. Diffusion, disorganization, and ignorance do not make for a powerful interest group presence. Nor would the arguments appeal to those prepared to sacrifice for the public interest. Effects are subtle, arguments complex, results uncertain. Eight-second sound bites could never convey the complexity and subtlety of the evidence.

Public choice does not explain how we got here; but it helps explain why we cannot easily get out. If managers disliked governance relationships between private pensions and the corporate boardroom, they would resist facilitating legal change, and they should prevail, since the arguments for change are not overwhelming—governance might not improve, and pensions have other purposes that might be compromised. Pension reconstruction in governance is more likely to come as an unanticipated effect of social change or as a goal *desired* by managers.

Although direct, intentional change is for now unlikely, if *managers* found it in their interest to change the role of pension funds in corporate governance, those funds would restructure their portfolios, and doctrinal barriers would turn out to be weak or easily repealed. This restructuring nearly happened in the 1980s, when managers, odd as it might at first seem, nearly sought ownership structures dimly similar to those prevailing in Germany and Japan. Those foreign structures, which seem so distant and alien to American managers and financiers, were closer than most thought, when takeovers led managers to a crossroads from which one path led to fighting takeovers directly with powerful antitakeover technologies, and the other path led to building the foreign structures. American managers fought takeovers directly and for the most part won, but when they were at risk of losing, they nearly went down that other path, and might do so yet again in the late 1990s, as we will see at the end of Part IV, in chapter 16. But to see these crossroads clearly, we must first reexamine the takeovers of the 1980s and better understand how the German and Japanese structures differ from the American structures.

Part IV

THE CONTEMPORARY AND COMPARATIVE EVIDENCE

THE HISTORICAL evidence is that American ideology favored fragmentation, and politically powerful interest groups—primarily small-town bankers in the past and managers today—benefited from that ideology. Political actors sometimes sincerely sought to implement public interest goals—including at times the goal of fragmentation for its own sake, but frequently the more technical public interest goals could have been obtained through other means.

The political paradigm predicts that if a political system fragments intermediaries, the Berle-Means outcome is inevitable; if a political system does not fragment them, they could be organized differently than they are in the United States. Differently organized intermediaries could then yield different governance structures at the top of the large firm. The ideal experiment would be to rerun American history with changes in popular ideologies and interest group power to see if the large firm turns out differently.

That experiment is not yet possible, making us look to other economies to see if they have differently organized intermediaries and, consequently, differing corporate forms. Although comparative work is full of pitfalls, it helps. Even in Britain, the country most like the United States, we find that different financial histories yield slightly different structures; Britain has had weaker restrictions on some intermediaries, particularly insurers, and they have had a somewhat stronger role in corporate governance than their American counterparts have had. But the strongest contrasts come from examining Germany and Japan. Even a superficial glance at them reveals profound differences, which confirm the political paradigm. After all, if economic evolution best explains how firms are organized, then we would expect the top of the large German or Japanese firm to resemble the top of the large American one. But it does not; the German and Japanese firms have a flatter authority structure at the top. The best explanation seems to lie not in differences of economic task but in differences in the organization of financial intermediaries.

The existence and persistence of the foreign structures casts doubt on the standard paradigm, which tends to see small, liquid holdings in well-developed securities markets as the best and highest, or at least essential, form of financial development and ownership, combining liquidity, diversification, and ownership rights with just the right proportion of trade-offs. Germany and Japan are sometimes seen to be behind the United States in financial structures, but are seen as rapidly securitizing to catch up to the better-developed American financial markets. But the persistence of the foreign ownership structures, and the nature of the forces threatening them—many are political forces—show that there is more than one evolutionary path, and that some features of German and Japanese corporate governance are as likely to be pale images of the American future as American securities markets are likely to be the foreign future.

Contemporary U.S. evidence also supports the political paradigm. There is a weak trend toward concentration of voting stock and increased institutional activity. The trend is weak; the concentration small. But new institutional activity should be seen as the delayed result of suppressing strong intermediaries in the United States.

The political paradigm allows us to reinterpret the 1980s takeover wave, first, as partly the *product* of a century of American financial fragmentation, and, second, as a replay of the political struggles affecting corporate governance, but with new players. That reinterpretation is the first chapter of this part.

CHAPTER 10

Takeovers

ON THE EVE OF THE 1980S

The United States entered the 1980s with ownership of the large public firm fragmented, making managers freer than they otherwise would have been from financial influence. Institutions with big blocks might influence managers; big blockholders might also stymie takeovers. Scattered ownership in small blocks was a benefit and a curse for managers in the 1980s: although it freed them from day-to-day institutional influence, it made takeovers possible; institutions with small blocks were usually thought to tender their stock in the 1980s takeover wars.

A raider would have had trouble mounting a takeover if two or three financial institutions controlled the vote of large blocks of stock in industrial companies (as they do in Germany), or if cross-ownership of the largest industrial companies and the largest financial institutions were common (as it is in Japan). Takeovers coalesce ownership structures. If ownership were already coalesced, takeovers could not readily occur.

Thus takeovers did not originate solely in the changing financial technologies of the 1980s, but were rooted in the American political past of financial fragmentation, stemming from the federal fragmentation of banking, the Armstrong-induced passivity of the insurers, the partial sterilization of mutual funds by tax law and the 1940 Act, and the structural control managers have of private pensions. Do all this and a nation will have fragmented institutional owners unwilling or unable to directly deal with managers in the boardroom. History thus set the stage for takeovers. That is the first political claim I make for takeovers.

This leads into the second political claim. Takeovers are done with *dollar* votes to buy stock. But *ballot* box votes elect the politicians who make takeover laws. State antitakeover laws, which by the early 1990s were in place in more than forty states, raise the cost of a hostile takeover. Some responded to distortions favoring raiders; distortions favoring incumbents went uncorrected, or were increased. The laws were the response of local politicians to local business leaders, to employees, and to public opinion. Tactical success in a takeover need not make for political success. True, views of the "merits"—are takeovers functional or not?—affected legislators. But other factors affect political outcomes, such as public opinion and political strength. Neither need be closely related to the "merits" of takeovers.

Hostile takeovers weakened managers in the 1970s and 1980s, shifting power from managers to shareholders and to the takeover entrepreneurs. Takeovers had losers—target firm managers and employees, primarily. But the losers did not sit idly by; they called for political reinforcements, lobbying legislatures to pass laws that prohibited the takeovers, raised their cost, or delayed them long enough to give target firms room to maneuver. Although managers in the 1980s were losing autonomy, they struck back in the political arena, where they won back the autonomy that they had lost in the transactional economic arena.

These antitakeover laws do little that the corporation's shareholders could not do themselves. The implication of this contractual alternative is that managers did not ask shareholders for protection because they feared that shareholders would not give it to them. Rather than seeing the firm as just a complex contractual mechanism between senior managers and shareholders, we should see the antitakeover laws as imposing political limits on the firms' transactions. (Although one might see the antitakeover laws as contractual—setting terms that shareholders and managers could not easily negotiate among themselves—this is unconvincing, because most of the antitakeover laws' contractual "terms" are easy to draft and implement in a corporate charter. If there is an implicit contract it must be a complicated one involving other parties, such as employees.)

Takeovers disrupt the lives of managers and workers; both groups sought to stabilize the workplace by restricting takeovers. Any efficiency gains from takeovers are diffusely distributed, making gainers less motivated than targets to influence politicians, who respond well to pleas to maintain the status quo. Because public opinion was dubious about the value of takeovers and because managers were lobbying against them, laws restricting hostile takeovers were predictable. In fact, because antitakeover forces in many states had the votes from the very beginning, the real question is why they took so long to win.

VOTERS

Voters were unsympathetic to hostile takeovers. In a Harris poll, 58 percent of those polled thought hostile takeovers did more harm than good; only 8 percent thought hostile takeovers were beneficial.[1] The takeovers dis-

---

[1] Who Likes Takeovers?, Forbes, May 18, 1987, at 12; Roberta Romano, The Future of Hostile Takeovers: Legislation and Public Opinion, 57 University of Cincinnati Law Review 457 (1988).

rupted employees' lives, and the average person mistrusted takeovers and financial maneuverings. In popular novels, movies, and the press, Wall Street's greedy investment bankers were shallow yuppies who served no useful function. In Tom Wolfe's 1987 novel *The Bonfire of the Vanities*, a character explained the protagonist's Wall Street investment banking job (as a bond salesman, to be sure, not a takeover engineer) as slicing and reslicing the cake, hoping to keep the crumbs that fall off with each slicing. While the popular image of dysfunctional money changers and moneylenders is not entirely recent, these popular images helped to define takeover's political terrain.

The public's hostility or indifference to takeovers made political action easier for interest groups seeking to restrict them. Although the losers would have sought legislative protection whatever public opinion was, public opinion made it easier for the lobbying to succeed. Politicians do not always respond to interest groups, because some politicians seek the public interest, or fear association with special interests. But for takeovers, politicians who responded to the losers' interests were not seen as catering to special interests, because the bystanders—other voters—believed that takeovers are unproductive and unfair. And some politicians surely shared the public's wariness about takeovers.

The public sympathized with workers displaced by manipulators from Wall Street. In the public's eye, takeovers were lumped with Ivan Boesky's insider trading, the other insider-trading scandals, and Michael Milken's junk bonds. When the U.S. Supreme Court upheld an important state anti-takeover statute, the *Wall Street Journal* reported that its

> decision came on the heels of Wall Street's insider-trading scandals and amid a national uproar against takeovers. While the justices didn't directly acknowledge that background, their tone indicated that they, too, believed the merger game had gone too far.[2]

Takeovers disrupted the status quo; bust-up takeovers threw managers and employees out of work. Managers and employees at firms that were not yet targets were anxious and fearful (would they be next?) and sympathized with employees at targets. The losers knew they had lost. Winners, other than raiders and some stockholders, were scattered; any efficiency gains were spread through the economy. Diffuse winners did not even know they had won.

Managers seeking political protection did not climb uphill in the political arena; legislators who did managers' bidding did not have to fear reprisal from voters. It was the opposite. Politicians who bashed Wall Street and thwarted takeovers were rewarded by the average voter, not punished.

[2] Wall Street Journal, July 1, 1987, at 1, col. 6.

FEDERALISM: THE DIVISION OF RESPONSIBILITY
BETWEEN THE SEC AND THE STATES

Public opinion and the interests of managers and employees had to influence the tilt of takeover law. How influential they would be depended partly on *where* in the American political system that law was made.

Washington and the state governments both make corporate law. Although Congress has left most matters of corporate governance to the states, Congress *could* exercise more authority—in fact all of corporate law could be federalized. Congress passed the securities laws in the 1930s, mandating disclosure and prohibiting insider trading, and extended them to takeovers in 1968 through the Williams Act, which requires offerors to disclose takeover plans, prohibits fraud and deception in takeovers, and regulates how long bids must be kept open. As first interpreted by the courts, these laws were "exclusive"; the federal government acted, and states had to leave the takeover legal action to the federal government. Only at the end of the 1980s did new interpretations of the balance between state and federal law free states to make their own stringent antitakeover laws. This makes it important to understand how each state is more likely to respond to the goals of targets than of raiders, because when states were allowed to make binding takeover laws, they favored targets over bidders.

CORPORATE POLITICS IN THE STATES
AND CORPORATE POLITICS IN WASHINGTON

The political balance in the states differs from that in Washington, inducing states to oppose takeovers of local businesses more vociferously than Washington would. Imagine a state, say Pennsylvania, with several large public companies that are evenly divided between potential targets and potential offerors. The state will *not* be evenly divided between protakeover and antitakeover laws, but will have an *anti*takeover tilt. To be sure, Delaware, with half of all the large corporations in the United States, is the state that counts, and other factors are important to Delaware's political balance; indeed, the importance of what the other forty-nine states do lies mostly in how they affect Delaware. I argue here that (1) Delaware did not produce binding antitakeover laws in the early 1980s partly because federal law stopped it and other states from doing so; (2) in the early 1980s Delaware also feared that the federal government would preempt Delaware if it acted precipitously; (3) the states felt free to produce antitakeover law at the end of the 1980s, after the Supreme Court limited the SEC's powers and after Congress decided not to pass new federal takeover law; and (4) when states persistently produced antitakeover law at the end of the 1980s, Delaware felt pressured to follow them.

Managers of Pennsylvania targets will invest heavily in political antitakeover action, because if they succeed, they immunize themselves from takeover both by Pennsylvania raiders *and* by out-of-state raiders. Those with something to lose will tend to invest more heavily in protectionist legislation than those facing an equal offsetting gain.[3] And targets were often already organized, in Chambers of Commerce and industry associations, groups that could and did influence legislatures to pass antitakeover laws. Raiders often wanted to streamline the targets; threatened employees want antitakeover law. State politicians had reason to defer to the preferences of threatened employees more than to the preferences of raiders.

True, *out-of-state* raiders and stockholders tried to block the antitakeover law. But they faced organizational problems. Mancur Olson offered the most popular view on the organization of interest groups: focused groups prevail over dispersed, disorganized groups.[4] For raiders and targets, the stakes were different. Raiders look to the other forty-nine states for targets, so they will less intensely oppose their own state's antitakeover law. Out-of-state raiders are more dispersed than in-state targets; they might sit back or do little. And out-of-state institutions are less influential *in* the state; politicians respond first to their constituents, the in-state targets, not to the out-of-staters. (When an offer is launched, the target shareholders do become a discreet group. But they have only a few weeks to organize for political action. By the time they do, they will be too late.)

How about the Pennsylvania raiders? A strong antitakeover statute does not prevent raiding. Pennsylvania law deters *only* raids on Pennsylvania corporations. Raiders can look for targets in the other forty-nine states. In-state raiders will invest less in politics than will in-state targets.

In national politics the organizational disparities between targets and raiders are smaller, because raiders and targets have a symmetrical interest in federal takeover law. In national politics there are no in-state raiders who are only tangentially interested in the legislation. And for national legislation, managers and targets are geographically dispersed, just like raiding companies. The president, unlike state politicians (and members of Congress), is the one nationally elected politician.

Although the picture here of state lawmaking is unattractive, federal lawmaking also has drawbacks. By "monopolizing" law, before the regulated conduct is well understood, it can stunt growth and experimentation, lock-

---

[3] Russell Hardin, Collective Action 82–83 (1982). This is just a corollary of the standard economic concept of diminishing marginal utility: as one gets richer, one buys less crucial goods with one's last $1,000 than with one's first $1,000. All other things being equal, losses are more strongly felt than gains.

[4] Mancur Olson, The Logic of Collective Action (1965).

ing firms in too early. Moreover, I am not saying that state politics was anti-takeover and national politics was protakeover. Public opinion has been moderately antitakeover, tilting even the national balance as reflected in the major national takeover law, the Williams Act of 1968, which was mildly antitakeover. Congress is more likely to preserve the status quo than to take the (questionable) efficiency side of the debate and support a program that might have diffuse gains that too few voters can recognize. And in the 1980s target firms were *already* organized and ready for political action at both political levels—in Chambers of Commerce, in the Business Roundtable, in industry associations. But the new raiders were not politically ready and had to form new lobbying organizations. Finally, because target firm managers had their economic lives on the line, they fought and lobbied more intensely than offerors; targets were defending their "homeland" from invasion.

But national politics, although also antitakeover, was less so than state politics during the 1980s. The 1980s SEC and Federal Trade Commission were protakeover, with the SEC attacking state antitakeover laws as unconstitutional and recommending that Congress overturn them. And Congress does not get to items far down on its agenda, such as takeover policy. This difference in degree between states and nation was lengthened in the 1980s by the free market ideology of the presidency, reflected in presidential appointments to the SEC.[5]

To be sure, the federal result may have been that Congress had many reasons not to act. If it had acted, it might have been antitakeover, and because of its "monopoly" position, state-level experimentation with takeovers would have ended. But I doubt that the difference between federal action and state action was only that the Congress just did not get around to passing major antitakeover laws; the full range of inputs at the federal level would probably have led to laws that differed from the state laws. Federal antitakeover legislation would probably have also limited the targets' tactics by regulating management's defensive tactics, such as poison pills and greenmail, in ways that state laws had not.

In the early 1980s it looked as though takeover law would be national law under the Williams Act, passed in 1968 to regulate takeovers mildly, mostly via disclosure and timing requirements. Although Congress might not have

---

[5] Roberta Karmel reports: "[T]he SEC's tilt has been to foster takeovers. This is because takeovers are perceived as a corporate governance mechanism and also because investors appear to benefit from takeovers, at least in the short term. Also relevant are the fees takeovers generate for the securities industry." Roberta Karmel, Do the Capital Markets Need So Many Regulators? N.Y. Law Journal, Oct. 18, 1990, at 3. Even the SEC's tilt was politically contingent. SEC commissioners prior to the Reagan era were more hostile to takeovers.

To speak of free market ideology here is peculiar. Mergers are highly regulated and subject to large influences from small changes in tax law or antitrust law. Free market ideology is really a hesitancy to add more regulation, or to change existing regulations. And the free market ideology emphasizes the importance of takeover's disciplinary effect on management.

decided to act anew in the 1980s, federal courts and the SEC would interpret and enforce that 1968 act, which as interpreted prohibited states from doing anything important. States, particularly Delaware, were quiet, partly because they had reason to fear new national lawmaking and partly because they could not do anything important under the Supreme Court's interpretation of the Williams Act. Thus, while the political forces in most states were poised to ban or restrict takeovers from the word go, federal courts at first ruled that most state restrictions were unconstitutional.

THE FEDERAL PUNT

National law and state law could conflict in four areas. First, Congress could pass new laws governing takeovers, and the states could be quiet. Second, courts could interpret national laws on the books as explicitly displacing state law. If Congress told firms to "do this" while states said "don't do this," Congress would prevail; its law is "supreme." Third, if Congress and a state pass laws that are in tension, courts decide whether the national law "preempts" the state law. If national law systematically regulates that part of commerce, then states cannot intrude there, even if they do not explicitly contradict the national law. Finally, if states trample too much on interstate commerce—which the Constitution says Congress can regulate—then even if the state law does not yet explicitly conflict with the federal law, courts will strike down their interfering acts.

The High Tide of National Authority:
The Williams Act and Federal Preemption of State Law

Federal courts would strike down state laws that clashed with the Williams Act, which Congress passed in 1968. That federal law required disclosure in takeovers, regulated some takeover procedures, and, its sponsors said, provided a level playing field for takeovers. At first, in 1982, the Supreme Court interpreted the Williams Act as a comprehensive takeover regulatory scheme that "occupied the field," precluding all state takeover law. Thus, when Illinois allowed state regulators to kill an offer even if it complied with the Williams Act, the Court held that the Williams Act balanced the interests of offerors, target companies, and shareholders, preempting state law that upset this balance. The Court also held that the Illinois law's burden on interstate commerce was so great as to be unconstitutional.[6]

This decision, *Edgar v. MITE*, was important. At the time, thirty-seven

[6] Edgar v. MITE Corp., 457 U.S. 624, 643–46 (1982).

states had similar antitakeover laws, probably arising from the protectionist political forces I outlined above. But *MITE* made them all unconstitutional. Moreover, the Williams Act prohibited "fraudulent, deceptive or manipulative acts or practices in connection with any tender offer."[7] This phrase had the potential to make all takeover tactics a matter for federal interpretation by the SEC and the federal judiciary, *not* by the states.

All takeover tactics were really "manipulative," in the broadest sense of the term. And if "manipulative," they were subject to federal regulation, not state regulation. A federal court of appeals, the level just below the Supreme Court, decided that one set of antitakeover tactics was indeed covered by the term "manipulative" in the Williams Act.[8] The decision could have been a wedge toward completion of a policy of making takeover law national.

The Ebbing Assertion of National Takeover Authority

But that decision was superseded in 1985, when the Supreme Court ruled in another case that "manipulative" meant only lying or bid rigging, not most takeover tactics.[9] Moreover, the Court's interpretation would also stop the SEC, whose authority to regulate takeovers comes from the same phrase. After the 1985 Supreme Court decision, states were no longer going to find the SEC or the courts determining the legality of takeover tactics.

There was one more barrier to state regulation of takeovers. Although the Supreme Court ruled in 1985 that the SEC's and the federal courts' power was slight, states might still not be free to enter the vacuum because the Supreme Court had said in 1982 that state antitakeover rules unconstitutionally burdened interstate commerce, which under the Constitution only Congress can regulate. The next question was how far the states could go.

During the mid-1980s managers sought to defend their environment from the repeated takeover attacks throughout corporate America. They and their advisers came up with two primary tactics, one transactional, the other leg-

---

[7] Williams Act § 3, 82 Stat. 454, as amended; Securities Exchange Act § 14(e), as amended, 15 U.S.C. § 78n(e) (1988).

[8] Mobil Corp. v. Marathon Oil Co., 669 F.2d 366 (6th Cir. 1981), cert. denied, 455 U.S. 982 (1982). Ronald Gilson, The Law and Finance of Corporate Acquisitions 1043 (1986 and 1990 Supp.); Elliot Weiss, Defensive Responses to Tender Offers and The Williams Act's Prohibition against Manipulation, 35 Vanderbilt Law Review 1087 (1982).

[9] Schreiber v. Burlington Northern, Inc., 472 U.S. 1 (1985). The story is more complicated, because the Court said that the SEC could prohibit tender offer activities that were not themselves deceptive, if the prohibition stopped steps leading to deceptive tender-offer actions.

Courts later restricted the SEC's range of action, holding that the SEC lacked power to promulgate a one share, one vote rule. Voting rules were a corporate governance matter for the states, a matter that the SEC could not regulate. Business Roundtable v. S.E.C., 905 F.2d 406 (1990).

islative. The transactional tactic was the poison pill, which disrupted the raiders' ability to buy up the target's shares. The buy-up would be uneconomic unless the poison pill—which required that the captured firm make large payments to shareholders who did not sell their stock to the offering firm—was "pulled," and only the target firm's incumbent board could "pull" the pill. The second tactic was to get state legislatures to disrupt the raiders' transactions. Some targets sought "control share" statutes, which required that when a raider got a big block of shares, say, 20 percent, the *other* shareholders would vote to decide if the new control share could vote. Several states passed "control share" statutes, which federal courts at first struck down as unconstitutional.[10]

In March 1986, Indiana passed a "control share" statute. Dynamics Corporation offered to buy the stock of CTS Corporation, an Indiana corporation. CTS management resisted, using the Indiana law against Dynamics, which sued, asking a federal district court to declare the Indiana law unconstitutional. This the court promptly did, because, it said, the state law clashed with the Williams Act by "wholly frustrat[ing] the purpose and objective of Congress in striking a balance between the investor, management, and the takeover bidder in takeover contests." And it clashed with the Commerce Clause because its "substantial interference with interstate commerce . . . outweigh[ed] the articulated local benefits."[11] Either way the statute was dead. CTS appealed, but the federal court of appeals said:

> Even if a corporation's tangible assets are immovable, the efficiency with which they are employed and the proportions in which the earnings they generate are divided between management and shareholders depends on the market for corporate control—an interstate . . . market that the State of Indiana is not authorized to opt out of, as in effect it has done in this statute.[12]

Legal commentators questioned whether state court decisions validating the poison pill could continue to stand in the face of this decision.[13]

CTS then appealed to the Supreme Court, hoping the Court would overturn *MITE*, reverse the lower federal court's ruling, and uphold the Indiana law's constitutionality. The Supreme Court did so: Congress can preempt state takeover laws, said the Court.[14] But Congress did not say it was preempting state law in the Williams Act; in fact, the law has an *anti*preemption clause. It preempted Indiana law only if Indiana had made compliance with the Williams Act impossible. Indeed, Indiana can regulate the internal af-

[10] Gilson, supra note 8, at 529.

[11] Dynamics Corp. v. CTS Corp., 637 F. Supp. 389, 399, 406 (N.D. Ill. 1986).

[12] Dynamics Corp. v. CTS Corp., 794 F.2d 250, 264 (7th Cir. 1986).

[13] John C. Coffee, The Future of Corporate Federalism: State Competition and the New Trend toward De Facto Federal Minimum Standards, 8 Cardozo Law Review 759, 762 (1987).

[14] CTS Corp. v. Dynamics Corp. of America, 481 U.S. 69 (1987).

fairs of corporations having sufficient contact with Indiana. Thus five years after the Supreme Court blocked strong state antitakeover law in *MITE*, it gave states back the constitutional room to maneuver in *CTS*.

An explosion of state antitakeover moves followed,[15] some perhaps overstepping what *CTS* made constitutionally permissible. Delaware did not wait long: *three* days after *CTS* came down, Delaware's secretary of state asked the Delaware bar association whether it should consider new takeover legislation. Later that year, the Delaware bar produced a takeover statute that it believed would be more effective than the Indiana "control share" statute.[16]

Congressional Inaction

But would Congress pass the law that would preempt state regulation of takeover tactics? Congress held hearings in the 1980s on poison pills, greenmail, golden parachutes, and other takeover tactics, but passed no important takeover law. Had *CTS* not shifted the battleground to the states, managers would have pressed Congress to pass antitakeover laws, as they were doing before *CTS*. Perhaps they would have succeeded; business lobbyists won narrow victories in the Senate Banking Committee just after *CTS* came down. (The bill died, though.) But a congressional antitakeover law was likely also to curb managerial defenses, such as poison pills, as the leading bills would have done.[17] Regardless, during the period between 1982, when the Supreme Court in *MITE* struck down a state antitakeover law as unconstitutional, and 1987, when the Supreme Court held in *CTS* that a new state antitakeover formula was constitutional, managerial pressure on Congress failed. After *CTS*, managers shifted their pressure to the states, where they succeeded.[18]

WHAT THE STATES HAVE DONE

States passed antitakeover laws. Few are show-stoppers, but nearly all raise the cost of takeovers, thereby stopping some. Moreover, the key move probably was when states validated the poison pill, which *can* be a show-stopper. Since the key move validating the poison pill was judicial and judges are

[15] Ellen Lieberman and Jeffrey Bartell, The Rise in State Antitakeover Laws, 23 Review of Securities and Commodities Regulation (Standard & Poor's) 149 (1990).

[16] Gilson, supra note 8, at 559 (1990 Supp.).

[17] Vicky Cahan, Dean Foust, and Ellyn Spragins, States vs. Raiders: Will Washington Step In? Business Week, Aug. 31, 1987, at 56.

[18] 20 Sec. Reg. & Law Rep. (BNA) 368 (Mar. 11, 1988); CQ Almanac 351 (1984); CQ Almanac 282 (1985); CQ Almanac 298 (1984).

often seen as above politics, I do not think it is usually seen, as it should be, as part of takeover politics. It is often seen as only a tactic that worked and was not struck down by the courts. But because legislatures could reverse the judicial decisions, there is a public choice structure to the emergence and survival of the poison pill—the takeover show-stopper—as well.

States, Free-Riding Shareholders, and the Corporate Contract

Managers are often behind these state antitakeover laws. When a company becomes a target, its managers ask their state legislature to thwart the takeover. Managers, who could get the same protections via a shareholder vote, lack time to get shareholders to vote or know that shareholders will vote them down. The empirical evidence shows that state antitakeover laws do not affect firms with contractual antitakeover devices,[19] suggesting that antitakeover laws do no more than what charter amendments *could* do. Politics trumps shareholders' preferences.

After *CTS* unleashed the states, state legislative action was swift, often in response to a real takeover. Asher Edelman bid for Burlington Industries, a North Carolina company. On April 23, 1987, two days after the Supreme Court announced its *CTS* decision, the North Carolina legislature passed a law requiring bidders to get a favorable vote from 95 percent of the stockholders; Burlington's managers controlled more than 5 percent of the stock. When Dayton Hudson, a Minnesota corporation, became a target two months later, "Dayton Hudson managers got Minnesota to hold a special legislative session. Within hours, the state had a new antitakeover bill." When Citizens & Southern National Bank, a Georgia bank, became a target, the Georgia legislature was convinced by the bank's representatives that Georgia corporate law should be changed to allow directors to weigh effects on corporate constituencies. Greyhound, an Arizona company, feared a takeover; in July 1987 it got an special session of the Arizona legislature to pass an antitakeover bill. "Greyhound said 'Jump' and we said, 'How high,'" said one state representative.[20]

---

[19] Jonathan Karpoff and Paul Malatesta, The Wealth Effects of Second-Generation State Takeover Legislation, 25 Journal of Financial Economics 291 (1989).

[20] N.C. Sess. Laws c.88, s.1 (April 23, 1987), codified at N.C. Gen. Stat. § 55-9-02 (1990) (North Carolina and Burlington); Expropriation at Home, Wall Street Journal, Oct. 9, 1987, at 24, col. 1 (Minnesota and Dayton); Minn. Stat. Ann. § 80B.01(9) (West 1986 and Supp. West 1990) (law passed June 25, 1987, effective retroactively to June 1, 1987); William Carney, Does Defining Constituencies Matter? 59 University of Cincinnati Law Review 385, 423 n.155 (1990) (Citizens & Southern and Georgia); Ga. L. 1989, p. 946, § 10, codified at Ga. Code Ann. § 14-2-202(b)(5) (1989) (enacted April 10, 1989); Expropriation at Home, supra (Arizona and Greyhound); 1987 Ariz. Sess. Laws 3d. ss. ch. 3 (enacted July 20, 1987, effective July 22, 1987), codified at Ariz. Rev. Stat. Ann. §§ 10-028, 10-1201 to 10-1223 (1990 and Supp. 1990); Los Angeles Times, Sept. 15, 1987, at 1 (Greyhound quote).

I do not want to portray the state statutes as absolute show-stoppers. Some present no more than a paper barrier; others just raise the cost of takeovers, but do not prevent them. Court decisions that validated the poison pill are more important, because the pill can be a show-stopper.[21] The Delaware legislature could have killed the pill—as some congressional bills would have—but did not. (Although the poison pill's justification comes from preventing shareholder coercion by raiders' manipulative tactics, it goes much further, preventing *all* offers until the board "pulls" the pill. The pills could have been written, or enforced, to prevent *only* coercive offers.) State law's impact was as much in the transactional barriers it left standing as in the barriers it created.

The political forces were not hidden in the debate in Pennsylvania before a sweeping antitakeover package passed in 1990. One press report said:

> Behind the debate [on the merits] in Pennsylvania is a power struggle between the shareholders . . . and the directors and managers. . . . Pennsylvania business groups supporting the bill are aligned with unions seeking to protect the jobs of their members. . . . The bill's supporters point to a wave of populist revulsion with the takeover boom of the 1980s. . . .[22]

Labor and Pennsylvania's Chamber of Business and Industry lobbied hard:

> [The] lobbying effort is the product of teamwork between . . . Pennsylvania labor unions and a coalition of over two dozen corporations working for the passage of the bill under the well-organized direction of the Pennsylvania Chamber of Business and Industry. A hard-core group of a dozen manufacturing concerns, including Armstrong, Scott Paper Company, PPG Industries Inc., The Rorer Group Inc., Aluminum Co. of America, and Consolidated Rail Corporation—along with several banks and utilities—have been the most active supporters.[23]

Institutional investors opposed the law; the Pennsylvania statute sapped investors of $4 billion in value according to a recent estimate.[24] But the best these principally out-of-state forces could muster was a short (ninety-day) opt-out provision. And in New York, the governor appointed a business-

---

[21] Moran v. Household Int'l, Inc., 500 A.2d 1346 (Del. 1985), was critical. It might be explained as part of Delaware's zigzagging. The Delaware court had just held, in Smith v. Van Gorkom, 488 A.2d 858 (Del. 1985), directors liable for failure to review merger terms carefully. *Moran* might have been the Delaware court's way of making amends to managers. Then political forces prevented the legislative reversal of *Moran*, but did not prevent the legislative reversal of *Smith*.

[22] Leslie Wayne, Pennsylvania Lends Force to Antitakeover Trend, N.Y. Times, Apr. 19, 1990, at A1, col. 3.

[23] Management and Labor Join Forces to Stiff-Arm Raiders in Pennsylvania, 7 Corporate Control Alert 1, 8 (Jan. 1990).

[24] Samuel Szewczyk and George Tsetsekos, State Intervention in the Market for Corporate

labor task force, which proposed that New York public pension systems be prohibited from financing hostile takeovers.[25] Politics and not just economics determines the weak ties between shareholders and managers.

DELAWARE

Thus we have a political explanation of why states with targets, particularly Rust Belt states, would try to stymie takeovers that would downsize the hometown firms.[26] What we lack is an explanation of why *Delaware*, the home to half the country's large companies, would also be antitakeover. Delaware is a small state, not as susceptible to the pressures of managers, employees and public opinion, as larger Rust Belt states.

Delaware is sandwiched between two forces: it does not want the national government to take a greater role in corporate governance, and it does not want to lose incorporation business to other states. One must understand that Delaware's state treasury gets a big fraction of its revenue from corporate charter fees and that some influential professionals (including its first-rate business law judges) have an important place in American business society. If Delaware lost its corporate business, that loss would hit the state's pocketbooks a bit and would damage professional pride even more. Delaware could lose corporate business in two ways: If the important issues were decided in Washington, then Delaware's importance in producing American corporate law would end. If other states' corporate law became more attractive to corporations than Delaware's law was, then firms might reincorporate out of Delaware. Either way Delaware and its corporate professionals would lose.

Delaware had to fear that heavy-handed moves to favor managers in the early 1980s could have led to federal takeover law. It had little reason to join the antitakeover states when the national government had a high chance of regulating takeovers and when sister states lacked the constitutional authority to make their antitakeover laws stick.

At the beginning of the 1980s these two forces tended to keep Delaware's antitakeover tendencies mild. Its legislature was not strongly antitakeover.[27]

Control—The Case of Pennsylvania Senate Bill 1310, 31 Journal of Financial Economics 3 (1992).

[25] Governor [Cuomo]'s Task Force on Pension Fund Investment, Our Money's Worth, June 1989.

[26] Roberta Romano, The Political Economy of Takeover Statutes, 73 Virginia Law Review 11, 121–22, 138–41 (1987); Lyman Johnson and David Millon, Missing the Point about State Takeover Statutes, 87 Michigan Law Review 846 (1989).

[27] Delaware had a "first" generation antitakeover statute on its books, but it did little more than track the Williams Act. Del. Code Ann. tit. 8, § 203 (repealed 1987).

Some Delaware court decisions blocked takeovers; others facilitated them.[28] Even decisions allowing defensive tactics were "intermediate": managers could not "qualify for the protections of the business judgment rule simply by pointing to a 'danger to corporate policy' based on a carefully orchestrated record. . . . [D]efensive tactics [had to] face a proportionality test: They [had to] be shown to be 'reasonable in relation to the threat posed.'"[29] In 1986, the Delaware courts required target firm management to conduct an auction for the company, once it was clear that the company was going to be sold somehow; target management could not force a sale to its friends.[30]

But by the end of the decade Delaware was appearing to move in an antitakeover direction. Delaware politicians believed that their "market share" was threatened. Its governor affirmed his support for antitakeover legislation, noting the threat of exodus unless Delaware joined the antitakeover bandwagon. He said that the "$188 million annual revenue from corporations—18 percent of the state's total revenues—is in danger because of competition from other states if Delaware does not protect its corporations the way other states have."[31] Soon afterwards, when Delaware court opinions were not sufficiently antitakeover for the taste of targets, prominent antitakeover lawyers sensitive to where Delaware felt vulnerable publicly urged managers to consider reincorporation: "Unless Delaware acts quickly . . . the only avenues open . . . will be [to] leav[e] Delaware for a more hospitable state of incorporation."[32] They publicly advised their clients that "New Jersey, Ohio and Pennsylvania, among others, are far more desirable states for incorporation than Delaware in this takeover era. Perhaps it is time to migrate out of Delaware."[33] Merger and acquisition conferences in 1988 and 1989 were said to abound with dismay with Delaware and threats to move to better corporate law states.[34] Because by 1987 federal law replacing Dela-

[28] Moran v. Household Int'l, Inc., 500 A.2d 1346 (Del. 1985), was a key decision impeding them; it validated the poison pill in 1985. Decisions facilitating offers were: City Capital Associates v. Interco, Inc., 551 A.2d 787 (Del. Ch. 1988); Grand Metropolitan PLC v. Pillsbury Co., [1989 Transfer Binder] Fed. Sec. L. Rep. (CCH) ¶94, 104 (Del. Ch. 1988); Robert M. Bass Group, Inc. v. Evans, 552 A.2d 1227 (Del. Ch. 1988). Inconveniently for the time line I offer, the facilitating decisions were *after* CTS. They were, however, before the Pennsylvania antitakeover law became prominent takeover news.

[29] Gilson, supra note 8, at 203–04, 211 (Supp. 1990); AC Acquisitions Corp. v. Anderson, Clayton and Co., 519 A.2d 103 (Del. 1986).

[30] Revlon, Inc. v. MacAndrews and Forbes Holdings, Inc., 506 A.2d 173 (Del. 1986).

[31] Tom Troy, Gov. Throws Support behind Takeover Bill, United Press International, Jan. 12, 1988 (quotation is UPI's paraphrase of governor's statement).

[32] Wachtell, Lipton, Rosen and Katz memo to clients, You Can't Say No in Delaware No More (Dec. 17, 1988).

[33] Wachtell, Lipton, Rosen and Katz memo to clients (Nov. 3, 1988).

[34] See Jeffrey Gordon, Corporations, Markets, and Courts, 91 Columbia Law Review 1931, 1959 (1991).

ware law was no longer a viable threat and sister states were making anti-takeover law, Delaware had reason to shift from indifference (or more accurately, from zigzagging) to become more clearly antitakeover.

Delaware judges were conscious of the SEC breathing down their necks. In *Moran v. Household International, Inc.*, an opinion validating the issuance of poison pills, the Delaware Supreme Court referred in their first paragraph to the SEC's amicus brief opposing validation, but quickly noted that the SEC split 3-2 on whether to intervene.[35] In a 1987 speech, a Delaware Supreme Court judge quickly noted that Congress was not doing much in the corporate control area, implying that the Delaware judiciary had room to maneuver.[36]

In starkly painting these forces, I do not mean to portray the Delaware legislators, judges, and governor as automatons, crudely calculating their (or their state's) advantages and disadvantages every six months. Some judges may have never thought about keeping the business in Delaware. All I want to say is that by the end of the 1980s, political and economic forces had pressed Delaware in an antitakeover direction. Politicians and judges who were protakeover were swimming against the tide. Whether the new antitakeover legislation and judicial opinions resulted from these forces, or would have occurred without these forces, I cannot say.

We have too few "data points" to confirm this direction: an antitakeover statute, which is not leakproof,[37] and one major Delaware Supreme Court decision, *Paramount Communications v. Time, Inc.*,[38] which, given the Delaware judiciary's previous takeover instability, does not establish a trend. Although legal commentators said there was an antitakeover trend in Delaware,[39] the paucity of "data points" makes me reluctant to believe firmly that Delaware shifted. When the implausibility of migration of Delaware firms to other states becomes clear to Delaware players, they may resume their previous zigzagging. Similarly, if takeover offerors in the 1990s come to be large firms, not the small, junk bond–financed entrepreneurs they had become in the 1980s, then Delaware may respond favorably to big-firm raiders, because big firms have historically been a Delaware constituency.[40]

In *Time*, Time's board refused to allow its shareholders to consider a bid from Paramount, preferring that Time merge with Warner at a lower price,

[35] Moran v. Household Int'l, Inc., 500 A.2d 1346 (Del. 1985).

[36] Justice Andrew Moore, State Competition: Panel Response, 8 Cardozo Law Review 779 (1987).

[37] It is a moratorium rule prohibiting many offerors from merging with the target for three years after buying a stake. Del. Code Ann. tit. 8, § 203(a) (1990).

[38] 571 A.2d 1140 (Del. 1990).

[39] Law Firm View on Impact of Paramount/Time Decision, 4 Insights 34 (May 1990).

[40] Delaware decisions in late 1993 and early 1994 indeed were going in this direction. In re Tri-Star Pictures, Inc., 634 A.2d 319 (Del. 1993); Paramount Communications Inc. v. QVC Network Inc., 637 A.2d 34 (Del. 1994).

probably because Warner would allow clear managerial continuity at Time. One lawyer who often defends management in hostile takeovers hailed Delaware's *Time* decision as the all but "explicit recognition that a [board may] 'just say no.'"[41] The *Wall Street Journal* complained that *Time* "shows how far the law has moved from the notion that corporate boards exist to serve stockholders."[42] With a poison pill in place, target firm management could as a matter of business judgment refuse to "pull" the pill. They needed no more than a business plan for the future that contemplated the company as an independent firm. While other lawyers read the decision differently, and decisions in early 1994 showed Delaware to shift again (when the federal and state competitive pressure was off), *Time* can be seen as part of the reaction to takeovers as the 1980s slipped into the 1990s.

Summary: The Dimensions of State Competition

Delaware law is the product of many forces: ideology about what is the best law, interest group pressures, fear of losing tax revenues, reaction to scandal, and more. When other states systematically provided antitakeover rules, there was little advantage to Delaware in not providing roughly similar rules, at least when Delaware no longer feared federal preemption. Rust Belt states have little reason to keep the cost of capital primary in their takeover lawmaking; their firms were shrinking, not seeking new capital. Legislators look to the next election; if takeovers are unpopular, then no matter what financial economists may say about efficiency effects, state legislators have reason to pass antitakeover laws, especially law that allows capital-seeking companies to opt out, as takeover law usually does. When managers and big labor press for these laws, and only politically weak, primarily out-of-state groups press against them, state legislators, many of whom share the popular mistrust of takeovers anyway, had little reason to resist.

Delaware politicians might have been able to resist the rhetoric of threatened migration out of Delaware. They may have mistakenly overreacted, because migration is really more difficult than it sounds, since shareholders have to approve the migration. But even so, when sister states passed antitakeover laws, Delaware actors had little reason to resist becoming antitakeover. (There is a constant *influx* of firms reincorporating *into* Delaware.

---

[41] Martin Lipton, A Long-Term Cure for Takeover Madness, Manhattan Lawyer, March 1990, at 15. For similar assessments, see also Barbara Franklin, Tough Takeover Statute—Critics Say Pennsylvania's New Law Is Extreme, New York Law Journal, May 3, 1990, at 5; The "Buzz-Off" Defense: A Play on the Time Ruling, M and A Dealmaking, Mar./Apr. 1990, at 7 ("[a]s soon as the ink dried on the Time-Warner decision, companies under siege were using its key provisions to tell hostile buyers to get lost"); Corporate Counsel Weekly (BNA), Oct. 17, 1990, at 6, 8; Insights (1990), at 34. Shamrock Holdings, Inc. v. Polaroid Corp., 559 A.2d 257 (Del. Ch. 1989), also was not a protakeover decision.

[42] Wall Street Journal, March 7, 1990, at 19, col. 3.

Managers can block this in-migration more easily than they can induce an out-migration from Delaware.) Delaware might have thought it too risky to take a principled protakeover position, especially when the basis for such a principled stand seemed disputable. Rather than racing to the bottom ahead of the competitive pack, Delaware in the takeover competition seems to have been a reluctant (perhaps unnecessary) follower. When it realizes that reincorporation is an empty threat (or if the federal or state competitive pressure lifts), it may return to make takeover doctrine without immediate political pressure.

Moreover, I do not want to dismiss the public-regarding dimension to antitakeover legislation. There was public doubt whether takeovers primarily disciplined target firm managers or primarily broke up good companies, built empires, exploited inefficiencies in the securities markets, and exploited tax deductions that target firms left unused. Although financial economists' commentary was less divided about the net benefits of takeovers, legislators respond more to public opinion and local interests than to the concerted opinion of financial economists. To many legislators and judges the disruption to collateral interests—workers, community, suppliers—was not always worth the gains. People want stability in their lives; takeovers disrupted established patterns, making everyone insecure.

Whatever the strength of these forces may be in explaining judicial results, they help explain legislative results. True, the Delaware antitakeover rules even at their 1989 height were weaker than those of other states. But that does not diminish the public choice story. Delaware is poised between two political boundaries: It cannot offend the federal body politic too much or federal lawmakers (which could be the Congress, the SEC, or the courts) will abolish Delaware as the leading center of corporate law; if the important decisions are made in Washington, Delaware has nothing important to offer. And if Washington allows state corporate lawmaking to be important, Delaware cannot be too far out of line with the other states. These pressures changed in the 1980s to push Delaware toward a promanager, antitakeover result. When Delaware courts threatened managers, the Delaware legislature acted swiftly and effectively to overturn the rulings. When Delaware courts protected managers, by validating the poison pill, the Delaware legislature stood by, watched, and then gave the targets further protection.

CONCLUSION

Once again, politics is one of the determinants of corporate governance. Takeover rules at the end of the 1980s arose from popular dislike of takeovers, managerial interest group maneuvering, and federalism, which in the end left states the primary decisionmakers. Laws set the rules for corporate takeovers, and politics influenced what laws were made.

Two political moves deeply influenced the takeover boom of the 1980s. The first arose from the politics of organizing financial institutions. American politics fragmented financial institutions and their portfolios and severed ties that would have allowed them easily to coordinate the stock they held. Financial intermediaries cannot easily assert authority in industrial boardrooms. Explanations for fragmentation lie in American federalism, the political power of small financial institutions, popular opinion that favored fragmenting Wall Street, and the plausible public-spirited view that fragmented financial institutions led to a more stable financial system.

The 1980s' takeovers should be seen as arising partly out of the history of American financial fragmentation. The United States has not had many financial intermediaries powerful enough to take influential positions in industrial companies.

Takeover politics comes in a second, more direct, variety. The takeovers of the early 1980s shifted power from managers to shareholders and the takeover entrepreneurs when a market for corporate control developed. Managers, losing their prior autonomy in the marketplace, then struck back in the political arena. It is not too much of an exaggeration to say that by calling for political reinforcements, managers won in state-by-state political combat what they could not win in contract-making with shareholders. To overstate the result only slightly, they for a time won freedom, nearly complete, from takeover.

The decline in takeovers at the end of the 1980s has additional explanations. The stock market was up at the end of the 1980s, takeover techniques such as junk bonds were less available after the demise of Drexel Burnham, takeover activity worldwide was down, and the best takeover targets were hit during the 1980s, leaving slimmer pickings by the end of the decade. Many takeovers broke up conglomerates of unrelated businesses that senior managers could not run well; others stopped firms, chiefly oil companies, from misusing their cash. Both problems had been reduced by the end of the 1980s. But mass revival of takeovers for these or other reasons will need new takeover technology to overcome the antitakeover laws or a shift in those laws. Public opinion made these antitakeover laws possible, by helping to fragment private financial power in the first place and then by making it easier for managers to get antitakeover legislation.

Federalism makes local politics important. Federalism long ago tilted politics to favor small financial institutions; in the 1980s it tilted politics to favor managers. Federalism enhanced the power of small financial institutions that wanted to fragment Wall Street and enhanced the power of managers who wanted to thwart takeovers. The politics of corporate governance are largely determined by these interest groups and a public of bystander-voters that is sympathetic to fragmenting financial institutions and suspicious of takeovers.

CHAPTER 11

Corporate Ownership in Germany and Japan

IF THE CONSTRUCTION of large firms requires the ownership structures found in the United States, then similar ownership and governance structures should eventually emerge in other countries. If large firms in different countries have persistently different ownership structures, the differences would cast doubt on the prevailing paradigm: there might be several ways to solve the organizational problems of large firms, and politics might help to determine the choice among them. Differences would especially support the political paradigm if they tied in to different political histories. If we found the structures abroad to be identical to those in the United States, our inquiry would be harder. Similarity could undermine the political paradigm, but not if it turned out that similar political forces helped to create the foreign similarities. The complex task then would be to sort out whether politics helped determine corporate structure there too.

Drawing sharp conclusions from corporate dissimilarities also has problems, because the dissimilarities might mean either that the foreign nations lag the United States in financial evolution or that their economic task differed from the American economic task. Different structures might also be cosmetic variations, of little economic significance. Politics might explain the differences in structure and form, but those differences might not affect productivity and firm efficiency.

The complex task of sorting out whether democratic politics everywhere influences firms identically is not yet necessary, because the corporate structures in the world's two recent economic successes, Germany and Japan, differ markedly from those in the United States. Senior managers in Germany and Japan face frequently active intermediaries that, among other things, wield the votes of large blocks of stock. Although the foreign firms' organization *below* the very top resembles that in the United States in similar industries,[1] the structure *at* the top does not. Managers and intermediaries abroad share power, and there are checks, balances, and accountability. No institution or person—neither a single bank, as is sometimes thought, nor the CEO, as is common in the United States—has complete control. In contrast, the American corporate governance structure has until recently usually focused power in management, and especially in the CEO.

---

[1] Alfred D. Chandler, Jr., The Visible Hand—The Managerial Revolution in American Business 500 (1977).

Although others with a deep knowledge of German and Japanese law, language, history, and politics will have to extend and deepen what follows, I have carefully looked at the evidence now available and it supports the view I have presented in this book—that the Berle-Means corporation cannot be fully explained by economics alone. True, to reach economies of scale, American firms had to tap vast pools of capital, and with shareholders diversifying, scattered ownership shifted power to managers. But as should now be clear, this dominant paradigm omits a critical step: shareholders could have diversified through intermediaries; functions could have further specialized, with intermediaries sharing governance functions with managers. That happened in Germany and Japan, but not in the United States. In Parts II and III, I argued that another paradigm is needed (or the old one must be modified) to explain the American result: the politics of financial fragmentation, dominated by federalism, populism, and interest group pressures, pulverized American financial institutions, contributing heavily to the rise of the Berle-Means corporation. German and Japanese structures help confirm this argument.

Each foreign structure would be illegal here. The Japanese firm's five largest stockholders own a fifth of its stock; five German bankers vote nearly half of the largest firms' stock. Banks there are large compared to the largest firms in their nations. Here they are small; an American intermediary trying to control 5 percent or 10 percent of the largest industrial firm's stock would be akin to a pup trying to grab a lion. The foreign banks have a national scope that would violate the McFadden Act, accounting for the size disparity. They are frequently active, in ways that for banks would violate regulatory interpretations of the Bank Holding Company Act, and that for other intermediaries would be hard. In Germany, banks enter boardrooms by combining votes from stock they own directly, stock in bank-controlled investment companies, and stock they hold only as broker but also vote. Combining banks, brokers, and mutual funds in this way would violate the Bank Holding Company Act of 1956, the Glass-Steagall Act, the Investment Company Act of 1940, and the Securities Exchange Act of 1934. If German bankers had to operate under American laws they would run their banks from jail.

Americans, inured to bankers as lenders, would expect bank power to come from credit allocation. In both nations bank power *did* grow out of their control over credit. But in Germany, bank boardroom power no longer depends on controlling credit but on controlling *stock*, including stock that banks do not own, but vote; the banks influence the German *proxy* system in ways similar to the way American managers control the American proxy system.

As in the United States, politics influences corporate structure in Germany and Japan, but the ways and degrees differ. In Japan, transforming credit-based financial power—which is weakening—to stock-based boardroom power will be hard, because laws left by the post–World War II American occupation preclude it, and the resulting interest groups—bankers versus brokers—want to maintain many of those laws. To transform themselves, the Japanese must dismantle the American framework, and, although they are beginning to do so, they may fail. In Germany, persistent popular pressure to reduce banker power induces Parliamentary proposals to reduce their power over industrial stock. These pressures have had an effect. Thus Germany has strong popular pressure, but weak interest group infighting; Japan has weak popular pressure, but bloody interest group infighting. The United States has had both. The extent of the foreign restrictions are parallel: Germany has some (mostly informal and due to popular pressure) and Japan has more (from the legacy of the American occupation), but neither has the complete set that the United States has.

History counts; paths once wide open eventually become narrower. Today, American institutions would have to fight their way into the boardrooms, both politically and transactionally. But private gains from shared authority would probably be modest, making a costly fight often not worthwhile. Power sharing in the United States might come through evolution, as it did in Germany and Japan. Managers there prefer institutional white squires, who shield managers from outside pressures, to takeovers. But American managers have defeated takeovers for now, and need not concede institutional power.

In this chapter we first assemble the basic facts of ownership and governance in the large German and Japanese firms. The stock in German and Japanese large firms is voted in big blocks. Despite large legal differences between Germany and Japan, firms in both nations have an ownership structure of shared power. No institution or person—neither a single bank nor the CEO—has complete control. Although the German and Japanese systems differ from each other in countless ways, they are alike in that corporate power at the top is shared, making both systems in this dimension more like each other than like the American one.

GERMANY

German intermediaries are relatively much larger than those in the United States; the voting blocks in the largest firms are also larger than those in the United States. The three largest American banks have assets equal to 7 percent of GNP; the three largest German banks have assets equal to 36 percent of GNP, making them *five* times "stronger" than the American banks. They have the financial strength to hold large blocks of stock in Germany's largest companies.

Concentrated Voting Blocks

Germany has fewer public firms than does the United States. For the largest German public firms, three or more banks each frequently control a 10 percent voting block; often industrial firms also control big blocks. Bankers as stockholders share authority with other firms that own stock and with families with big blocks of stock. In contrast, CEOs of the ten largest American firms face no such big institutional blocks, and only occasionally face a large family block. Table 5 shows GM's ownership structure and the voting structures for the largest automakers in Germany and Japan.[2] Table 6 shows the bank voting blocks for several large German firms.

Sources of Voting Authority

German bankers' voting power comes from direct ownership of stock, from control over mutual funds, and, most important, from authority to vote stock that the bank's brokerage customers own but deposit with the bank. Although the German banks do not own a large amount of stock directly for their own benefit, when they deploy their capital in stock ownership, they deploy it in big blocks. (While the banks' *voting* in Daimler-Benz [see Table 6] are not unusual, the high bank *direct* ownership in Daimler-Benz is.) In the hundred largest German industrial enterprises, German banks directly own for their own accounts thirty blocks of at least 5 percent of the outstanding stock (see Table 7).

German banks are also big stockbrokers, and they vote the brokerage stock they hold as custodians. Typically, individual investors deposit the stock they own with their banks, and, unless the owner gives the bank special instructions, the bank votes the custodial shares. German banks often hold as custodians and vote more than 10 percent of the stock of a large company.[3] In many firms, private, family ownership is important; indeed, a large minority of firms have big bank voting blocks (with only a few of those blocks directly owned by the banks), a quarter of the firms have other firms

[2] The GM and Toyota data are typical for the very largest American and Japanese firms. Daimler-Benz's largest vote holder is atypically large. For a complete breakdown of institutional ownership for the ten largest American firms, see Carolyn Kay Brancato et al., Institutional Investor Concentration of Economic Power: A Study of Institutional Holdings and Voting Authority in U.S. Publicly Held Corporations app. 2 (Sept. 12, 1991) (unpublished study).

[3] See Detlev F. Vagts, Reforming the "Modern" Corporation: Perspectives from the German, 80 Harvard Law Review 23, 53–58 (1966); Hermann H. Kallfass, The American Corporation and the Institutional Investor: Are There Lessons From Abroad? 3 Columbia Business Law Review 775, 782–83 (1988).

TABLE 5

Top Five Institutional Voting Blocks in GM, Daimler-Benz, and Toyota

Daimler-Benz		Toyota		GM	
Deutsche Bank	41.80%	Sakura Bank	4.9%	Michigan State Treasurer	1.42%
Dresdner Bank	18.78	Sanwa Bank	4.9	Bernstein Sanford	1.28
Commerzbank	12.24	Tokai Bank	4.9	Wells Fargo	1.20
Bayerische Landesbank	4.41	Nippon Life	3.8	College Retirement Eq.	.96
—	1.16	Long-Term Credit Bank	3.1	Bankers Trust, New York	.88
Top five share- holders	73.98		21.6		5.74
Top twenty-five shareholders	N.A.		N.A.		13.93

Source: CDA Investment Technologies, 13(f) Institutional Portfolios, Spectrum Institutional Portfolios (database for year-end 1990 GM data, assembled by Riverside Economic Associates); Arno Gottschalk, Der Stimmrechtseinfluß der Banken in den Aktionärsversammlungen der Großunternehmen, 5 WSI-Mitteilungen 294, 298 (1988) (data for Daimler-Benz's voting blocks at 1986 shareholders' meeting); Japan Company Handbook 790 (Toyo Keizai, Inc., 1992) (data for Toyota's 1992 voting blocks).

TABLE 6

Aggregate Voting Blocks of Three Largest German Banks, 1986

Rank of Company	Company	Percentage of Shares Voted at Meeting	Percentage of Shares Voted by:			
			Deutsche Bank	Dresdner Bank	Commerz-bank	All Big Banks
1	Siemens	60.64	17.64	10.74	4.14	32.52
2	Daimler-Benz	81.02	41.80	18.78	1.07	61.66
3	Volkswagen	50.13	2.94	3.70	1.33	7.98
4	Bayer	53.18	30.82	16.91	6.77	54.50
5	BASF	55.40	28.07	17.43	6.18	51.68
6	Hoechst	57.73	14.97	16.92	31.60	63.48
9	VEBA	50.24	19.99	23.08	5.85	47.92
11	Thyssen	68.48	9.24	11.45	11.93	32.62

Source: Arno Gottschalk, Der Stimmrechtseinfluß der Banken in den Aktionärsversammlungen der Großunternehmen, 5 WSI-Mitteilungen 294, 298 (1988). Although Gottschalk's data, from 1986, is stale, it is the most recent available.

Note: Voting holdings include brokerage stock, directly owned stock, and mutual fund stock.

TABLE 7

Percentage of Stock of Hundred Largest German Corporations Held Directly by
German Banks, 1990

Rank of Company	Company	Bank	Percentage of Stock
1	Daimler Benz	Deutsche Bank	28.3
		Dresdner Bank	1.6
		Commerzbank	1.6
8	Thyssen AG	Commerzbank	5
		Allianz	5
15	BMW AG	Dresdner Bank	5
18	MAN AG	Commerzbank	6.4
		Allianz	11.8
20	Dresdner Bank AG	Allianz	20
22	Preussag AG	Westdeutsche Landesbank	34.1
		Dresdner Bank	3.8
25	Karstadt AG	Deutsche Bank	Over 25
		Commerzbank	Over 25
26	Allianz AG	Deutsche Bank	12.5
		Dresdner Bank	10
		Bayerische Vereinsbank	10
30	Deutsche Unilever GmbH	Deutsche Bank	11.2
		Dresdner Bank	6.2
		Bayerische Vereinsbank	5
33	Zahnradfabrik Friedrichshafen AG	Deutsche Bank	7.5
37	Metallgesellschaft AG	Deutsche Bank	7.3
		Dresdner Bank	13.0
		Allianz	5.9
39	Degussa AG	Dresdner Bank	10
49	Continental AG	Deutsche Bank	5
		Dresdner Bank	Under 5
		Allianz	5
50	Asko Deutsche Kaufhaus AG	Westdeutsche Landesbank	10
52	Bayerische Hypotheken und Wechsel Bank	Allianz	24.7
53	Linde AG	Deutsche Bank	10
		Commerzbank	10
		Allianz	12
54	Philipp Holzmann AG	Deutsche Bank	30
		Commerzbank	5.5
59	Vereinigte Elektrizitätswerke Westfalen AG	Deutsche Bank	Over 6.3
		Westdeutsche Landesbank	Over 7.1
70	Klöckner-Humbold-Deutz AG	Deutsche Bank	Over 25
74	R+V Versicher. und Holding AG	Deutsche Bank	Over 25
81	Beiersdorf AG	Allianz	34.2
95	PWA Papierwerke AG	Bayerische Hypotheken und Wechsel Bank	23
98	Südzucker AG	Deutsche Bank	20

Source: Neuntes Hauptgutachten der Monopolkommission 205 et seq. (1993).

Notes: Allianz is the large German insurer, not a bank. This table shows the stock directly owned by the bank; the percentages do not include stock that the banks vote and hold as broker and custodian.

with big blocks, and another quarter have families with big blocks. In the few large firms that lack a family presence, the banks have a big presence. All totaled, few large German firms lack a big blockholder.[4]

Effects of Voting Authority

Large voting blocks give the German banks influence but not dominance for two reasons. First, German stockholders elect only half of the supervisory board of the biggest companies; employees appoint the other half. The supervisory board appoints a management board and approves major corporate decisions; the management board handles day-to-day decisions. German banks elect their nominees to the supervisory boards to most of the hundred largest German firms. Second, no single bank generally has the votes to control a firm; *together* the three German large banks can, if they act in unison, dominate the shareholding side of many supervisory boards, and in others, a family or another firm also has a big block.

Banks' control over large voting blocks, probably more than their control over credit, is the biggest difference between the German and the American structure. (True, German bankers do sit on some boards where they lack votes, as do American bankers. Because banks are more important there than in the United States, bankers' experience and networks make them valuable; firms would often seek out bankers as board members even if the bankers did not vote a lot of stock. Stock affects the frequency of banker influence; its absence does not bar influence.) Although bank loans helped create close relationships between bankers and managers, the importance of the "house bank" debtor-creditor relationship has faded, and German firms no longer rely on a single bank for credit. German banks control the proxy system, not monopolistic sources of credit.

Structured Interaction

German CEOs regularly interact with large owners. The supervisory board appoints a managerial board to a five-year term and loosely reviews firm and management performance, typically two to four times a year. Although the CEO and the rest of the managerial board handle day-to-day decisions, they must report to the supervisory board, which the CEO may not join,[5]

[4] Julian Franks and Colin Mayer, The Market for Corporate Control in Germany 6 (European Science Foundation Network in Financial Markets Working Paper) (October 1993).

[5] 2 Ernst Geßler et al., Aktiengesetz 138–39 (1974) (commentary on § 105 of German corporations code). The leader, or "speaker," of the managerial board ("Vorstand") is first among equals. Several large firms are private firms (GmbH, for Gesellschaft mit beschränkter Haftung,

much less dominate. Managerial turnover increases when firm performance slackens.[6]

Not only do German managers *not* control the proxy machinery, it is doubtful that they can even lawfully make a proxy solicitation,[7] a process American managers dominate. Instead, German managers must filter proxy solicitations through the bankers, who vote their own stock, their mutual funds' stock, and their customers' custodial stock. The banks get fifteen-month revocable proxies from their brokerage customers, and, prior to voting the custodial stock, inform their customers of their intended votes, giving the customers an opportunity to instruct them to vote differently.[8] Rational apathy leads most shareholders to ignore the solicitations; customers rarely disapprove of their bank's recommendation.[9] One would expect managers to consult their bankers before making a controversial proxy proposal, as I understand happens. Bankers control the proxy machinery and hence elect the stockholding side of many supervisory boards.

It would, however, be easy to exaggerate the power of the German supervisory board. First, translation of the German board's name, *Aufsichtsrat*, as "supervisory board," while linguistically correct, does not quite reflect the board's authority, which is less than that of a supervisor. A better translation might be "advisory board," with "advisory" referring to not just gratuitous consultation but a power similar to the U.S. Senate's power to *advise and consent* to treaties and appointments, which yields consultation and influence but not supervisory control.

For example, the supervisory board cannot formally remove the managerial board at will during its five-year term, although I understand that informally fired managers get no more than the salary for their remaining term. Moreover, the managerial board is said to co-opt some of the supervisory board's formal authority when a vacancy arises on the supervisory board, in a manner similar to, but weaker than, the American CEO's ability to name the board, by suggesting to the supervisory board who should fill the va-

---

or "firm with limited liability"), whose stock is not traded. These firms tend to have founding families, who seek to maintain influence.

[6] Steven N. Kaplan, Top Executives, Turnover and Firm Performance in Germany (February 1993) (unpublished manuscript).

[7] Alfred F. Conard, The Supervision of Corporate Management: A Comparison of Developments in European Community and United States Law, 82 Michigan Law Review 1459, 1470 (1984).

[8] Aktiengesetz (AktG) §§ 135(1)–(2) (1991) (German corporations code) (authorizing revocable general proxy to banks).

[9] Sprachlose Eigentümer: Aktionäre nehmen viel zu selten ihre Rechte als Inhaber von Unternehmen wahr, Die Zeit, June 7, 1991; see also Arno Gottschalk, Der Stimmrechtseinfluß der Banken in den Aktionärsversammlungen der Großunternehmen, 5 WSI-Mitteilungen 294, 296–97 (1988); Wir sind Gerngesehene Berater, Der Spiegel, Sept. 4, 1989, at 45, 48.

cancy.[10] German codetermination at times induces managers to give the supervisory board as little information as possible, because they do not want the board's labor side to be well informed.[11] It sometimes also induces shareholder representatives to want the supervisory board to supervise less than it otherwise would, because a powerful supervisory board would enhance the authority of the employees, who have half of the board's seats. The bankers generally prefer to take their chances with the managerial board. True, were there to be a boardroom confrontation, the banker-shareholders could defeat the employees, because the chair of the supervisory board is elected by the shareholding side and in a tie can cast the deciding vote. Moreover, in some firms, a dominating shareholder group with a supermajority vote can send directions to the managerial board, bypassing the supervisory board.[12] Thus, the supervisory board gives big bank shareholders influence in corporate governance, not control. Managers still have the upper hand, but the tilt is not nearly as promanagerial as it has historically been in the United States.

JAPAN

Concentrated Ownership

The ownership of large firms in Japan is roughly analogous to that in Germany. Large Japanese firms typically belong to a keiretsu, a group of industrial firms and financial intermediaries that own some of one another's stock, usually aggregating to ownership of half of one another's stock.[13] A main bank owns 5 percent of the stock of the keiretsu's industrial firms, which in turn own some stock in the main bank. Generally, four other banks and insurers own blocks of stock in the industrial firms, creating a latent five-holder coalition with 20 percent of the outstanding stock. The 1967–1993 records of Japanese firms show a persistent pattern of concentrated ownership, a pattern of concentration that prevails, not just for small or medium-sized firms, but for Japan's very largest ones—Toyota Motor, Nissan Motor, Matsushita Electric Industrial, and Mitsubishi Heavy Industries (see Table 8). In the United States, in contrast, the five largest holders in the

[10] Paul Windolf, Codetermination and the Market for Corporate Control in the European Community, 22 Economy and Society 137, 140–41 (1993).

[11] Klaus Hopt, Labor Representation on Corporate Boards—Impact and Problems for Corporate Governance and Economic Integration in Europe (Centre d'études juridiques europeannes, University of Geneva, September 1993).

[12] Windolf, supra note 10, at 143.

[13] Michael L. Gerlach, Keiretsu Organization in the Japanese Economy, in Politics and Productivity: The Real Story of Why Japan Works 141, 159 (Chalmers Johnson, Laura D'Andrea Tyson, and John Zysman, eds., 1989).

TABLE 8

Institutional Ownership in Japan's Largest Firms, 1967–1993
(percentage owned by five biggest institutional stockholders)

	Toyota	Matsushita	Mitsubishi	Nissan	Nippon Steel
1967	21	20	15	24	N.A.
1972	23	17	16	26	12
1977	22	18	18	25	12
1982	22	18	17	26	11
1987	22	18	17	24	18
1988	22	18	18	24	18
1989	22	19	19	23	19
1990	22	18	18	22	17
1991	23	17	18	22	15
1992	22	17	17	22	16
1993	22	19	17	22	15

Source: Annual Company Reports to Japanese Ministry of Finance; Japan Company Handbook (various dates); Daiyamondo Kaisha Yoran (various dates); Keiretsu no Kenkyu (various dates).

aggregate rarely own much more than 5 percent of the outstanding stock of the largest firms,[14] the amount the single largest owner typically has in Japan.

The 20 percent five-shareholder block in the largest Japanese firms is bigger than any five-shareholder institutional block in the two dozen largest American firms. In GM, Exxon, and IBM, the largest *twenty-five* shareholders vote *less* stock than the largest *five* stockholders in Japan's largest firms. The aggregate voting levels of these twenty-five institutional investors— typical for the largest American industrial firms—are 13.93 percent (GM), 11.47 percent (Exxon), 13.54 percent (IBM), and 12.89 percent (GE).[15] (Only when we get to smaller American firms, does the voting concentration approach that typically found in Japan; even then, the American concentration is less than that in the very largest Japanese firms.)[16] If shareholder groups with twenty-five members could coordinate as well as groups with five, this difference in ownership concentration would be of little importance, but they cannot.

---

[14] See generally Brancato et al., supra note 2, at app. 2.

[15] Id.

[16] Compare Table 8 with Paul Clyde, The Institutional Shareholder as a Monitor of Management tbl. 2 (June 1991) (unpublished manuscript) (top five financial institutions own 18.4 percent of stock in 511 American companies). As we get to smaller firms, one would expect *more* concentrated ownership, because investors can take a big percentage of stock and still diversify. Yet, these last two sources indicate, the bigger Japanese firms are more concentrated than just about all of the American Fortune 500.

Structured Interaction: The Presidents' Council

Although the German pattern in the boardroom follows what an American corporate law scholar would predict—large stockholders have board seats and influence—the Japanese pattern does not. Despite concentrated voting blocks, the Japanese directors are typically insiders, formally elected by stockholders but usually appointed by the CEO, with the occasional advice and consent of large stockholders, who usually do not themselves appear on the board absent a crisis. Large stockholder influence arises only in crisis, or informally.

There is, however, an informal mechanism for stockholder influence: the Presidents' Council, monthly meetings in which the financial intermediaries' and industrial firms' leaders interact in a forum that resembles a second board, one analogous to the German supervisory board. Although votes are not taken at the meetings and participants do not direct one another, individual presidents feel constrained by the consensus of the council, largely because the council members are capable people who collectively control much of the stock in the CEO's firm. Council members are said to be consulted on major decisions, such as when a CEO chooses a successor.[17]

Public knowledge of the details of the monthly Presidents' Council meetings is vague. Minutes are not leaked, and agendas for council action are not printed in the Japanese press. Some reports indicate that business is discussed,[18] while others say the meetings are purely social,[19] paving the way to do business later. In the following discussion, I take the Presidents' Council as including both the meetings and the information and decisionmaking channels created through social interactions.

No single council member controls enough stock to control the others (although historically bank domination of credit gave the bank control). Since a *group* of these stockholders could exert control, however, no one member can withstand the ire of a coalition of the others; moreover, in a culture that values consensus, no one member should be willing to risk the ire of the others:

> These [council] meetings are not organs of decisionmaking in the sense that a majority vote would carry the day, but they are manifestations of the very dynamic process of consensus. Views are exchanged, opinions heard, and ac-

[17] W. Carl Kester, Japanese Takeovers: The Global Contest for Corporate Control 69 (1991); Charles A. Anderson, Corporate Directors in Japan, Harvard Business Review, May–June 1984, at 30, 32.

[18] Masahiko Aoki, The Economic Analysis of the Japanese Firm 3, 12 (1984).

[19] Michael L. Gerlach, Twilight of the Keiretsu?—A Critical Assessment, 18 Journal of Japanese Studies 79, 80–81 (1992) (reporting this view).

tions reciprocally adjusted, more on an ad hoc basis than in terms of binding policy. . . .[20]

The Presidents' Council is not a hierarchical command structure, but a forum for communication and perhaps a collegial monitoring of near-equals.

The power Japanese banks historically exercised over credit complicates any inquiry into the influence of institutional stockholders. When Japanese firms were rapidly expanding after World War II, they sought new funds from the banks, through which Japan channeled credit. The banks' power to cut firms off from funding for new projects yielded the banks sufficient influence, irrespective of their stockholding.

Both stock and debt are relevant in the prevailing models, which see delegated monitoring among Japanese banks, by which several banks buy stock in, and make loans to, several firms. The banker group assigns each borrowing firm a "main bank," to which the other banks delegate monitoring tasks. In these models, the main bank speaks with the authority of both creditors and stockholders owning 20 percent of the firm's stock.[21]

Joint influence through the two obviously does not make stock irrelevant, and if banks' power over credit allocation continues to weaken, we shall see whether stock alone gives them influence. *Individual* stockholders are powerless, but intermediaries seem to have influence through their stock. Although Japanese culture may often deter large stockholders from formally firing the CEO, mild criticism in a Presidents' Council meeting may shape actions in a culture that values harmony. And bankers do send in directors when serious problems arise and performance weakens.[22] Even when the CEO stays in place, the new director dilutes the CEO's authority; sometimes the CEO may be "promoted" to the less powerful position of chairperson. Moreover, in 1992, the CEOs of 14 percent of all Japan's public companies left, about one-third of them involuntarily.[23] Informality may prevail, but when informality fails and confrontation ensues, stockholding

---

[20] Robert J. Ballon and Iwao Tomita, The Financial Behavior of Japanese Corporations 68 (1988); see also Michael L. Gerlach, Alliance Capitalism: The Social Organization of Japanese Business 108 (1992) (power of Presidents' Council members is an implicit influence that is continually negotiated); Anderson, supra note 17, at 30 (Japanese corporate governance "appears to take place behind the scenes between the senior corporate official and the major institutional shareowners").

[21] Paul Sheard, The Main Bank System and Corporate Monitoring and Control in Japan, 11 Journal of Economic Behavior and Organization 399 (1989).

[22] Steven N. Kaplan and Bernadette Alcamo Minton, "Outside" Intervention in Japanese Companies: Its Determinants and Its Implications for Managers (August 1993) (unpublished manuscript); Randall Morck and Masao Nakamura, Banks and Corporate Control in Japan (Sept. 1, 1992) (unpublished manuscript).

[23]And in Japan, Fortune, Feb. 22, 1993, at 10 (reporting ousters, although not explicitly tying ousters to stockholder initiatives).

banks have taken control of the board and dismissed the CEO. When a scandal in a large department store chain implicated the CEO, who uncharacteristically refused to resign, the Mitsui Presidents' Council decided to replace him, and the banker on the store's board engineered the coup de grace.[24] Formal action is usually unnecessary; in a small group, large shareholders should have only to raise their voice to assert influence.

Other incidents, such as Japanese greenmail—twenty-two instances in the 1980s—and a successful hostile takeover, indirectly suggest shareholder power. Moreover, Japanese managers face fractious annual stockholder meetings, where gangsters threaten disruption; managers nevertheless control the meetings reasonably well because they go to them armed with proxies from their large shareholders. Obviously, if the large stockholders denied managers the proxies, managers would face more difficult annual meetings. Finally, stockholding institutions unhappy with managers can threaten to sell their stock, leaving managers at risk of a takeover. Not only have Japanese commentators described this potential as an important theoretical source of stock-based influence, but financial intermediaries have publicly made such threats.[25]

Although Japanese cross-ownership could insulate presidents from ouster,[26] the turnover and ousters indicate the insulation is incomplete. If cross-holdings were fully protective, they would not allow roughly one out of every twenty CEOs to be involuntarily ousted in a single year. The insulation hypothesis may confuse intent with effect; cross-holdings arose primarily because managers wanted to stave off takeovers and uncertainty, but friendly 5 percent shareholders turn unfriendly when results are poor. Moreover, the latest data suggest that corporate cross-ownership, which comprises about one-third of the total cross-holdings, tends to insulate managers, while intermediaries' ownership, which comprises about two-thirds of the total cross-holdings, tends to discipline managers.[27] Or the insulation hypothesis might have seemed warranted when the Japanese economy was

[24] Gerlach, supra note 20, at 111–13.

[25] Kester, supra note 17, at 17, 247–48; Merton J. Peck, The Large Japanese Corporation, in The U.S. Business Corporation: An Institution in Transition 21, 22 (John R. Meyer and James M. Gustafson eds., 1988); Kunio Ito, M&A to Kabushiki Mochiai no Honshitsu, Kinyu Journal, Dec. 1989, at 11. Insurers have become unhappy with dividend payouts and have threatened to dump the stock of companies that fail to increase their dividends. The observed threats are the tip of an iceberg—of uncertain size—of private influence. See Stephen D. Prowse, The Structure of Corporate Ownership in Japan, 47 Journal of Finance 1121, 1138–40 (1992). The insurers' demands may not arise directly from firms' misuse of cash, but from the insurers' need to receive larger dividends to comply with insurance regulations.

[26] See John C. Coffee, Jr., Liquidity versus Control: The Institutional Investor as Corporate Monitor, 91 Columbia Law Review 1277, 1298–99 and n.82 (1991).

[27] George M. Pushner, Ownership Structure and Corporate Performance in the U.S. and Japan (Ph.D. diss., Columbia University, 1993).

humming along and good results shielded even second-rate managers from inquiry.

In both German and the Japanese large firms, structured interaction between stockholding intermediaries and corporate managers enables bankers to influence managers' actions, but not to control them completely.[28] In Germany, managers can ally with employees, who hold half of the seats on the board. Since the large voting blocks are typically split among a handful of banks, firms, and families, any single big blockholder must form a coalition to challenge an alliance between managers and employees; when they do not form a united front, and the codetermined employee half sides with managers, shareholder power weakens. In Japan, in contrast, banks are not represented on the board, except in crisis. And, since bank-controlled stock is typically split among a handful of banks, a main bank must form a coalition to act. As in Germany, the resulting authority structure in Japan is flatter than that in the United States because the Japanese CEO seems unable to completely dominate decisionmaking. And since no single intermediary can dominate, but must form a coalition to amass a dominating block of stock, the foreign governance structure is not equivalent to replacing an American-style dominating CEO with a dominating institution. Thus structured interaction, without a shift in day-to-day control, is the second major structural difference between the German or Japanese firm and the American one.

SIZE AND SCOPE OF JAPANESE BANKS

The three largest banks in Japan, a country with a GNP about 60 percent that of the United States, are about three times as large as the three largest American banks (see Table 9). Yet the largest Japanese industrial firms are smaller than the largest American firms.

Because the largest American financial intermediaries are much smaller than their Japanese counterparts (see Table 10), the American intermediaries are too weak to take a large block of stock in GM or Exxon or IBM. In Japan, the intermediaries' mass makes large blocks possible. For example, the largest Japanese bank is eight times the size of the largest Japanese automaker; the largest American financial institution is barely larger than the largest American automaker (see Table 11).[29]

[28] There are exceptions, such as Deutsche Bank's dominant 28 percent block in Daimler-Benz.

[29] Table 11 shows the relative ability of a nation's largest banks to take a large piece of the capitalization of its largest industrial company. Fears that American banks could not take a large piece of its largest firms are well founded. Fears that the banks would be poorly diversified are also well founded. By contrast, the German and Japanese banks could take larger pieces of the

TABLE 9
Summary of Bank Size in Germany and the United States

	(1) Assets of Three Biggest Banks	(2) Assests of Three Biggest American Banks	(3) Foreign GNP	(4) American GNP	(5) Relative Size of Foreign Banks [(1)/(3)]	(6) Relative Size of American Banks [(2)/(4)]	(7) Ratio of Foreign Size to American Size [(5)/(6)]
Germany	$600B	$424B	$1.65T	$5.5T	.36	.08	4
Japan	1,345B	424B	3.44T	5.5T	.39	.08	5

Source: Bank assests calculated from Table 10.

TABLE 10
Assets of Ten Largest German, Japanese, and American Intermediaries
(billions of dollars)

German Banks		Japanese Banks		American Institutions	
Deutsche Bank	267	Dai-Ichi Kangyo	435	Citicorp	216
Dresdner Bank	189	Sumitomo	407	Fidelity	164
Commerzbank	144	Fuji	403	Prudential	133
Bayerische V-bank	138	Mitsubishi	392	Bank of America	110
D. Genossen-bank	137	Sanwa	387	Merrill Lynch	107
Westdeutsche L-Bank	137	Industrial (IBJ)	285	MetLife	103
Allianz Insurance	119	Tokai	246	TIAA-CREF	99
Bayerische H & W	117	Bank of Tokyo	228	Chase Manhattan	98
Bayerische L-bank	114	Mitsubishi Trust	226	J.P. Morgan	93
Nord-d Landesbank	83	Norinchukin	224	Vanguard	93
Total	1,445		3,233		1,216

Source: Carolyn Kay Brancato, Institutional Investors: A Widely Diverse Presence in Corporate Governance, tbls. 9, 12 (background paper prepared for Columbia Institutional Investor Project, Center for Law and Economics, Feb. 25, 1933); Top 200 Pension Funds/Sponsors, Pensions and Investments, Jan. 20, 1992, at 20; The Global Service 500, Fortune, Aug. 26, 1991, at 174–75. Assets are at various dates from year-end 1990 to 1992.

TABLE 11
Relative Size of Largest Intermediary and Largest Automaker, in Germany, the United States, and Japan

$$\frac{\text{Assets of largest German intermediary}}{\text{Assets of largest German automaker}} = \frac{\$267 \text{ billion}}{\$ 41 \text{ billion}} = 6.5 \text{ times larger}$$

$$\frac{\text{Assets of largest U.S. intermediary}}{\text{Assets of largest U.S. automaker}} = \frac{216 \text{ billion}}{173 \text{ billion}} = 1.25 \text{ times larger}$$

$$\frac{\text{Assets of largest Japanese intermediary}}{\text{Assets of largest Japanese automaker}} = \frac{435 \text{ billion}}{55 \text{ billion}} = 7.9 \text{ times larger}$$

Sources: Table 10 (for intermediary size); Worldscope (available in Nexis) (for automaker data).

MORE HIERARCHY OR LESS?

A key problem in the American agency cost inquiry is this: Increasing institutional power could reduce managerial agency problems, but at the cost of increasing institutional agency problems. How can one decrease one without increasing the other? Since most intermediaries are themselves large Berle-Means firms, they could have too many scattered shareholders to give their agents the proper incentives. Why should reducing managerial agency costs at the firm not just displace the problems up one level into financial intermediaries, making bankers the source of a new agency problem? Empowering financial institutions may improve the performance of owners' agents in the corporation, but expanding the duties of the owners' agents in the financial institution may create new problems.

This question may make the normative inquiry a dead end. But power *sharing* differs, at least in form, from completely *shifting* authority from managers to bankers, affecting both the quality of collegial decisions and the degree of monitoring. Measuring whether the gains in the firm exceed the losses in the intermediary is hard.

This shared authority lies between market and hierarchy, linking finance and industry in a complex way. "Control" is not the right word to describe these relationships. "Interlock," or "Escher-like overlap," might be more apt.[30] Escher-style, one hand reaches out from the bank to control the firm, but then another hand reaches out from the firm to control the bank.

---

largest industrial company without committing as much (as a percentage) of their assets and equity as would an analogous American bank.

[30] M. C. Escher was a Dutch graphics artist with whose work most readers will be familiar. Escher's drawings show, for example, realistic renditions of staircases that descend to the top of their own ascent and walls that abut ceiling and floor at the same joining point.

Corporate governance structures in Germany and Japan resemble less a hierarchical pyramid—the American picture—than an Escher-like staircase: while always walking downstairs, we wind up on top of the staircase from which we started. Banks own industry, but industry owns banks; managers direct employees; but employees sit on the supervisory board. The model resembles in some ways American political governance, with checks and balances.

EVOLUTION AND THE SECURITIES MARKETS

Although the different German and Japanese structures could merely mean that they lag a more advanced American securities market, there is reason to think that an economic lag is not the primary explanation for the differences. A view that fragmentation and dispersion of stockholding is inevitable to financial evolution faces four problems. First, the cohesive ownership and voting power in Germany's and Japan's public firms face great pressures but they have not yet fragmented. Predictions are not facts. The foreign institutions still vote large blocks of stock. Second, although securitization of debt in Japan may undermine banks' influence as creditors, it has not yet done so on the equity side; moreover, Japanese proposals to amend the Japanese "Glass-Steagall Act" may mean *more* powerful intermediaries; allowing stock to move off the bank's balance sheet and into securities affiliates, where the bank would not be at risk, such as in affiliated mutual funds. Third, some large Japanese firms outside the old-line keiretsu built *new* keiretsu, and German firms now form keiretsu-style relationships. Current data show Japan developing two financing systems: the traditional main bank system and a parallel securities-based system; the first system is not yet breaking down, but the parallel one is arising.[31] Fourth, for Americans to view the American-style firm as the most advanced ownership form risks self-congratulation. And indeed recent concentration trends in the United States suggest that the American firm may be weakly evolving to look a bit more like the foreign firms than it has looked thus far.[32]

SUMMARY

In Part V, we will begin to assess the normative significance of the foreign structures. Certainly the troubles in recent years in Daimler-Benz, Metall-

---

[31] John Y. Campbell and Yasushi Hamao, Changing Patterns of Corporate Financing and the Main Bank System in Japan (June 1993) (World Bank unpublished paper).

[32] Other factors—the absence of funded pension plans in Germany and Japan, for example—might be important. Funding, if it develops, might further loosen the power of the incumbents and change the foreign systems.

gesellschaft, and Volkswagen hardly tell us that different structures are a cure-all for corporate governance problems, or even that they are better; future across-the-board research will tell if they are better or, more plausibly, where they work better and where they work worse than the U.S. structures do. But we must not miss the main point here—that they differ from what now dominates in the United States. Concentrated blocks, shared authority, and big intermediaries are the three key structural differences. German and Japanese senior managers share power for better or worse with large financial intermediaries, which own and vote big blocks of stock and are active in corporate governance, formally through supervisory boards in Germany, and informally through Presidents' Councils in Japan. The survival of these foreign firms over several decades suggests that the classical economic model of the firm must be reinterpreted as a special case in the U.S. setting, because firms can prosper with different governance structures. These differences appear to correlate, not so much with differences in economic task, but with differences in the organization of financial intermediaries. Concentrated blocks, shared authority, and powerful intermediaries are not only uncommon here in America; they have also been, as we see in the next chapter, illegal.

CHAPTER 12

A Small Comparative Test
of the Political Theory

COULD American firms and intermediaries imitate the German or Japanese structures without violating basic financial laws?

The disparity in size is central. The numbers show that large American banks play a role in the American economy equal to only *one-quarter* of the role played by large banks in Germany and Japan.[1] It is not so much that the United States relies less on intermediaries as that its largest intermediaries are not very big. This difference in size correlates with law. American legal restrictions have historically kept American banks small and weak, by banning them from operating nationally; from entering commerce; from affiliating with investment banks, equity mutual funds, or insurers; and from coordinating stockholdings with these other intermediaries.

The National Bank Act of 1863 confined national banks to a single location, and the McFadden Act of 1927 only allowed branches of national banks to the extent state law permitted. Although states may permit out-of-state banks to open local branches (or affiliate with in-state banks via holding companies), until recently they did not. Although federal law could override state law and permit interstate branching, for the country's first two hundred years it has not. The United States still lacks a truly national banking system like that of most other nations.

American banks have also faced product limits. The Glass-Steagall Act historically denied banks a securities business and close affiliation with investment banks and, until recently, mutual funds. The Bank Holding Company Act prohibits affiliation with insurers and fine-tunes Glass-Steagall by prohibiting bank ownership affiliation with nonbanks except passive ownership of no more than 5 percent of a nonbank's stock.

Many of these rules are now eroding: Bank sponsorship of mutual funds, historically banned and only recently accommodated under banking law, is growing, despite its cloudy legality.[2] Congress seems poised in the mid-1990s to allow nationwide bank branching. Even with legal erosion, the

---

[1] See supra chapter 11, tables 9 and 10.

[2] Leslie Wayne, Questions on Bank Sales of Funds, N.Y. Times, Dec. 31, 1992, at C1; Prospectus for Vista Capital Growth Fund 8 (Feb. 28, 1992) (prospectus of equity mutual fund sponsored by Chase Manhattan Bank concedes cloudy legality under Glass-Steagall of bank sponsorship).

intermediaries do not change immediately; the historical bans have continuing effects because they made American intermediaries weak, and the weak intermediaries will need years to evolve into stronger ones.

American deposit insurance encouraged weak bank capitalization, which limited banks' ability to make large equity investments. Bank managers can raise the private value of bank stock by keeping their own equity thin, thereby displacing some risks of bank failure onto the public. By encouraging weak capitalization, extensive deposit insurance has made many banks too weak to own much stock, even if they were permitted to own it. Moreover, while bans on banks' engaging in commerce and owning stock predated deposit insurance (which was added in the 1930s), we could think of the bans conceptually, as protecting the insurer. An insurer wants to control the insureds' level of risk; once Congress set up extensive deposit insurance, it also would have wanted to control the banks' risk-taking, by banning them from owning stock. Although stock is today seen in theory as part of a properly diversified portfolio, it appears risky, and puts risk on the insurer; a banker in a "spread" business, matching its loans' time duration to the duration of its sources of funds, is seen as a low-risk intermediary. If deposit insurance were less extensive, either market forces or new bank regulation would press banks to raise more equity, to attract uninsured deposits, and to avoid bank runs.[3]

GERMAN-STYLE UNIVERSAL BANKS IN THE UNITED STATES?

If U.S. banks tried to imitate German banks, they would smash into nearly every important U.S. financial regulation. German banks not only have a national scope, which would violate McFadden's geographic restrictions, but also hold about thirty large positions in the hundred largest German firms, which would violate both the U.S. ban on bank stock ownership and the Bank Holding Company Act's 5 percent limit on owning nonbank stock. The largest German banks are also Germany's largest brokerage houses, and they control the proxy machinery, which would violate the historical product restrictions of the Glass-Steagall Act. If U.S. banks were to act as brokers, stock exchange rules would prohibit them from voting their customers' stock

---

[3] During the early 1990s, regulatory initiatives to force banks to increase their equity were successful. Whether unregulated banks would increase their own equity to enable them to hold stock in other firms would depend on whether the costs of holding big blocks of equity—such as lost liquidity and increased risk—outweighed the benefits. I outline some of the considerations in Part V. There is, however, one unnerving fact in favor of equity: stock persistently yields a higher return than debt. Andrew Abel, The Equity Premium Puzzle, Federal Reserve Bank of Philadelphia, Monthly Review, Sept. 1991, at 3.

on anything important,[4] while German bankers can vote their customers' stock on anything at all, and they do.

German banks combine modest direct holdings of stock with extensive holdings of custodial stock. American retail brokerage houses have depended on having a nationwide network of local offices, a network that American banks historically could not have. American banks might try to imitate them by combining modest stock holdings in affiliates with their extensive holdings of trust stock. The American banks would face several obstacles, the first of which arises from trust law, which tends to induce the hyperdiversification of portfolios, to reward passivity, and to reinforce dominant investment norms of passivity.

Trust law is an obstacle but not the only one. A formal combination of holding company stock and trust stock via the bank giving a proxy to the holding company would probably violate the Bank Holding Company Act, which prohibits bank affiliates from controlling more than 5 percent of a firm's stock.[5] An informal combination via consciously parallel voting would, by itself and if the banks did nothing more, seem to be within the limits of the act. But its success would still depend on how aggressively the regulators would apply interpretations that required holding companies to hold stock passively. During an earlier manifestation of bank power through trust stock, the House Banking Committee, headed by Wright Patman, held extensive hearings and castigated banker power derived from owning stock in trust accounts, implicitly threatening banks with political costs if they used trust stock to exert influence over corporate governance.[6] Although we can only speculate as to whether these political forces would arise again if banks tried today to assert influence, we know that they did once arise and induced prominent legal practitioners to warn banks not to use trust fund stock to build control blocks.[7]

Had American banks during most of this century tried to imitate the German ones, they would have failed since they have been barred from operat-

---

[4] See, e.g., New York Stock Exchange, Listed Company Manual ¶402.06(D) (looseleaf 1990), *analyzed* in Bernard S. Black, Shareholder Passivity Reexamined, 89 Michigan Law Review 520, 560–61 (1990); see also Alfred F. Conard, The Supervision of Corporate Management: A Comparison of Developments in European Community and United States Law, 82 Michigan Law Review 1459, 1469–70 (1984). Technically, American banks cannot be regulated as brokers, but they nevertheless did not, until very recently, operate brokerage firms, making the "freedom" from broker-dealer regulation moot.

[5] Bank Holding Company Act of 1956, ch. 240, §4(c)(6), 70 Stat. 133 (1956) (codified as amended at 12 U.S.C. § 1843[c][6] [1988]).

[6] Staff of Subcomm. on Domestic Finance of House Comm. on Banking and Currency, 89th Cong., 2d Sess., Report on Bank Stock Ownership and Control 10 (Comm. Print 1966).

[7] Raymond A. Enstam and Harry P. Kamen, Control and the Institutional Investor, 23 Business Lawyer 289, 290–91 and n.14 (1968); A. A. Sommer, Who's "In Control"? 21 Business Lawyer 559, 570 (1966).

ing nationally, from entering the securities business, from using affiliates to take blocks above 5 percent, and perhaps also from combining trust stock with directly held stock to be active. McFadden, Glass-Steagall, the Bank Holding Company Act, and trust law each seem sufficient to have deterred American bankers, who, had they tried to imitate the German bankers, as I said earlier, would have had to run their banks from jail.

JAPANESE-STYLE MAIN BANKS IN THE UNITED STATES?

For most large Japanese firms, a latent bank and insurer group controls 20 percent of its stock. The latent group activates itself to intervene during crises, and the leading bank meets with managers of affiliated firms during monthly Presidents' Council meetings, where, according to some,[8] they reach consensus on direction and operations. Could this system work under U.S. law, given that no single bank in the Japanese groups can own more than 5 percent of a firm's stock, the same amount permitted a bank holding company under U.S. banking law? Can U.S. bank holding companies be active in corporate governance and take control in crisis as long as they limit their stock ownership to 5 percent of a firm's outstanding shares?

American "main" banks would suffer from the geographic and product limitations that make them puny in comparison to Japanese banks. The combined assets of Japan's ten largest banks total $3 trillion, yet the total for the ten largest American intermediaries is only $1.2 trillion[9]—and the American economy is larger than Japan's. No U.S. bank has the financial strength needed to purchase a 5 percent stake in GM easily or to extend a huge loan without heavy syndication. The risk to a small American bank in taking a big slice of a large industrial firm's capital was historically also heightened by geographic restraints, which led to underdiversified assets and deposits. A bigger Japanese bank can purchase a 5 percent stake in Toyota without incurring the same risks. Moreover, since *multiple* blocks might make the system work (we will discuss this in Part V), an American main bank system might need a half-dozen or dozen financial firms with enough strength to take big blocks in multiple industrial firms, and the United States now has nearly none.

Small size is enough to make law a complete barrier to an American main bank system for America's largest firms. The National Bank Act and Glass-Steagall Act reinforce this barrier by blocking the bank from owning stock anyway. And the Bank Holding Company Act adds yet more to this barrier

[8] See supra chapter 11, notes 17–28 and accompanying text.
[9] See supra chapter 11, table 10.

by encouraging banker passivity in wielding stock that affiliated companies own. Thus, although banks in both Japan and the United States face identical 5 percent limits on stock ownership, the McFadden Act's branching restrictions and the Bank Holding Company Act's passivity rules have made the American system different.

The Bank Holding Company Act begins by proscribing not just control of an industrial firm, but (subject to exceptions) by banning ownership *or control* of any voting stock in an industrial firm: "Except as otherwise provided in this chapter, no bank holding company shall—(1) after May 9, 1956, acquire direct or indirect ownership or control of *any voting share* of any company which is not a bank. . . ."[10]

In the most aggressive interpretation of this prohibition, Citicorp would violate it by accepting an irrevocable proxy to vote a single share of GM stock. The Act then carves out an exception: the holding company may own "shares of any company which do not include more than 5 per centum of the outstanding voting shares of such company."[11] But, arguably, a holding company that combined affiliate stock with trust stock by owning 5 percent and taking proxies from the trust for another 15 percent of the outstanding shares would "acquire . . . indirect . . . control of . . . voting share[s] of any company which is not a bank"[12] in excess of the 5 percent exemption, and thereby would violate the Act.

An American banking group could try to overcome the 5 percent barrier by informal, parallel action. Five banks and insurers could each own 5 percent; a main bank would nominate directors; and all would vote their 5 percent for the nominees. This parallel action, even if coordinated with interbank discussion, would comply with the words of the statute but still face two banking law problems, one general and one specific. (It would also face securities law and other problems.) First, as mentioned above, Congress castigated American banks as recently as the 1960s for having more subtle means of influence, leading lawyers to recommend that banks keep away from such boardroom power;[13] even if this castigation were not a risk today, it was surely one in the past. Second, the Federal Reserve Board rejected a roughly similar proposal as banned by the Bank Holding Company Act:

[I]nvestments made in reliance on [the 5% permission in] section 4(c)(6) *must be essentially passive* . . . section 4(c)(6) is not an unqualified grant of permission for a bank holding company to acquire or retain a 5 percent voting interest in

---

[10] Bank Holding Company Act of 1956 § 4(a), 12 U.S.C. § 1843(a)(1) (emphasis added). To be precise, an American *bank* cannot own any stock: the permitted ownership is for a bank *holding company*. This distinction probably increases the costs of certain transactions, but I assume that the effect is not large.

[11] Id. § 4(c)(6), 12 U.S.C. § 1843(c)(6) (1988).

[12] Id. § 4(a), 12 U.S.C. § 1843(a) (1988).

[13] See supra note 7 and accompanying text.

any company. It is the Board's view that the prohibition against bank holding companies' engaging in nonbanking activities extends to joint ventures or *concerted action by a group of bank holding companies* in a nonbanking activity as entrepreneurs.[14]

Congress did not, with the 5 percent rule, unleash banks to use small blocks of stock to gain influence in corporate boardrooms, or at least so ruled the Federal Reserve Board. Later the Board reiterated that it "believe[d] that section 4(c)(6) should properly be interpreted as creating an exemption from the general prohibitions . . . on ownership . . . *only* for passive investments amounting to not more than 5 percent. . . ."[15]

The passivity interpretations would seem to seal the fate of an American bank effort to imitate the Japanese main bank system. Yet, the law does not explicitly require passivity for a 5 percent blockholder and does not explicitly cover the informal relationships used in Japan; the law's formal wording is unclear. In the Federal Reserve Board's interpretation, if the main bank is not passive, it violates the Bank Holding Company Act, but a literalist judge might interpret the statute differently, or the Fed might change its mind. Indeed, these explicit passivity interpretations were somewhat undercut by an earlier Federal Reserve Board interpretation, concerning, ironically enough, keiretsu main bank cross-ownership. For a time the Bank Holding Company Act, if read literally, prohibited Japanese banks operating in the United States from owning stock *in Japanese* firms located *in Japan*. Although the Fed never enforced the extraterritorial reach of the Act (thus undercutting its passivity interpretations), saying it was meant to apply only to U.S., not Japanese, commerce,[16] the Fed asked Congress to amend the Act when many foreign banks entered the United States in the 1970s,[17] and Congress did so.[18]

These passivity rules could break down through regulatory reinterpretation, just as regulatory reinterpretation has expanded banks' securities power in recent years, because the rulings come not from the clear com-

[14] Federal Reserve Regulatory Service 4–338.2, Jan. 22, 1986.

[15] 12 C.F.R. § 225.137 (1990) (emphasis added). See generally Pauline B. Heller, *Federal Bank Holding Company Law* § 4.03[2][a], at 4-60.9 (1992).

[16] And then, since the Act did not exempt foreign banks' foreign operations from the Act's reach, the Fed did not adopt its later passivity interpretations and said that activity, as long as there was no control, passed muster. In re Dai-Ichi Kangyo Bank, 58 Federal Reserve Bulletin 49, 49 (1972) ("[i]n light of the [Act's] purpose . . . to maintain separation of banking from commerce *in the United States*") (emphasis added).

[17] International Banking Act of 1978, S. Rep. No. 1073, 95th Cong., 2d Sess. 1 (1978). Actually, the Federal Reserve Board sought congressional action even before 1972. International Banking Act of 1976: Hearings Before the Subcomm. on Financial Institutions of the Senate Comm. on Banking, Housing and Urban Affairs, 94th Cong., 2d Sess. 21, 30 (1976) (statement of Fed Vice Chairman Gardner, quoting 1970 Senate testimony of Chairman Burns).

[18] International Banking Act of 1978, Pub. L. 95-369, § 8(e), 92 Stat. 623 (1978) (codified at 12 U.S.C. § 1841[h][2] [1988]).

mand of the statute, but from the Fed's plausible interpretation of that statute. Indeed, I understand that in recent years banks participated in leveraged buyouts in a way that might clash with these interpretations, suggesting a partial regulatory erosion similar to that which Glass-Steagall has undergone. (However, the participation was often indirect. Typically, the bank would buy equity of a leveraged-buyout partnership, with the partnership active and the bank inactive, allowing the banks to conform to the formality of the Act and the Fed's interpretations: the banks were not themselves active; only the partnership was active.)

Although the passivity interpretations may seem to be minutiae, they really were not, because they completed the broad historical congressional policy preference exhibited in McFadden's branching restrictions, Glass-Steagall's stock ownership restrictions, and the Bank Holding Company Act's line-of-business restrictions: to keep banks small, to keep private economic power unconcentrated, and to put a fault line between banking and industry.

MAIN BANKS AND UNIVERSAL BANKS—
THE POTENTIAL FOR CONTROL

If American banks tried to imitate either the Japanese main banks or the German universal banks, the Bank Holding Company Act would still deter them even if the Fed revoked its passivity rule and allowed activity short of control, a "compromise" that the Fed seemed to sympathize with in some interpretations.[19] Large investors want the *option* to exert control, even if they rarely exercise it. When Berkshire Hathaway buys a big block of stock and sits on a firm's board, it does not want day-to-day control. It does, however, want the freedom to take control—to replace the CEO in a crisis, as it did in the Salomon Brothers scandal in the early 1990s. Short of crisis, large shareholders with the potential to exert control are more influential if not barred from control. Since crisis intervention is a key function of the foreign systems, a regulatory bar on control is a steep barrier.[20]

U.S. banks can and sometimes do assert control over firms, particularly small firms, as lenders, without violating the Bank Holding Company Act. (Thus, I understand that some banks involved in leveraged buyouts have

[19] When the literal reading of the statute prohibited Japanese banks from acquiring American banks if they were active in commerce in Japan, the Fed interpreted § 4(c)(6) as prohibiting only control, not activity. See supra text accompanying note 16.

[20] Paul Sheard, The Role of the Japanese Main Bank When Borrowing Firms Are in Financial Distress (Stanford Center for Economic Policy Research Working Paper No. 330, 1992).

accepted the risks outlined in this section.) Banks whose holding companies own stock should be shy of doing so, because the source of control—debt or stock—would probably be unclear. Indeed, stock can support the loan, because in a crisis, stock can confer control by enabling the holder to vote in new directors faster than debt can confer control by enabling the creditor to enforce covenants or take the firm over in bankruptcy.

(Moreover, even if U.S. banks can show that their control comes from lending, not owning stock, and therefore does not violate the Bank Holding Company Act, stock ownership and control [whether via the debt or via the stock] heightens the risk that the court will equitably subordinate the banks' loans in bankruptcy or that a debtor could sue the banks on a lender liability theory. Equitable subordination forces controlling banks that behaved badly to wait on line while other creditors are paid first, even though the bank loan had a contractual priority; lender liability makes creditors pay firms if the lender's actions wrongfully damaged the firm. Since the bank often finds it hard to know whether agressive actions would be the bad action that, if combined with control, would justify subordination, they sometimes find the safest action avoidance of control. It's disfavored or barred through stock under the Bank Holding Campany Act, as interpreted, and it can get them into trouble under sensible but difficult-to-apply bankruptcy doctrines. Without control, there will be neither equitable subordination nor a problem under the Bank Holding Company Act. Unlike main banks in Japan, which are subordinated by custom, informal agreement, and Ministry of Finance guidance, U.S. banks can avoid equitable subordination (and lender liability) by being passive.[21] The Japanese main bank, already subordinated, can improve its return on its loan by fixing the firm that is in crisis, not by ignoring the crisis.)

MAIN BANKS AND UNIVERSAL BANKS—
SUPPRESSION AND CAPTURE OF THE SECURITIES MARKET

A society can move savings from households to firms through strong stock-holding intermediaries or through a securities market or through both. In the United States, the Glass-Steagall Act severed the intermediary channel from the securities channel, weakening American intermediaries by creating two channels. In Germany, the banks captured the securities channel, a result that allows for powerful intermediaries, which can provide both banking and securities services to firms and households. (The securities channel is weak, which probably is detrimental to both foreign nations in not promot-

---

[21] See, e.g., Taylor v. Standard Gas and Electric Co., 306 U.S. 307 (1939); State National Bank of El Paso v. Farah Mfg. Co., 678 S.W.2d 661 (Tex. Ct. App. 1984); J. Mark Ramseyer, Japanese Main Banks as a Regulatory Artifact: The Legal Framework (1991) (unpublished manuscript, on file with author).

ing new enterprises.) As we have seen, a large part of the German banks' voting power comes from securities owned by the banks' customers and deposited with the banks.

The Japanese situation is more complex. One might think that because Japan has a "Glass-Steagall Act"—imposed on it during the American postwar occupation—it would resemble the United States in having two channels. One might then mistakenly argue that because Japan has a "Glass-Steagall Act," Glass-Steagall did not restrain the development of powerful U.S. banks.

Such an argument would misunderstand Japan's "Glass-Steagall Act," because until recently Japan has more resembled Germany in having essentially one channel. Like the American version, the Japanese law severed commercial banks from investment banks. But the Japanese system then took a different path: Japanese postwar regulation skewed industrial financing toward banks and away from the securities market by (1) suppressing the bond market through regulation; (2) limiting competing sources of corporate finance, such as public sales of new stock; (3) impeding the development of investment companies; (4) requiring that banks serve as trustees for bondholders when companies were allowed access to the bond market; and (5) holding down the interest rates banks paid on deposits to enable banks to profit even when lending at low rates.[22]

Properly understood, postwar Japan adopted two offsetting sets of regulations. One set *segmented finance* but not as severely as did U.S. regulation— although Japanese banks could not issue securities, sell insurance or own very large blocks of stock, they could become large and be active in corporate governance. The second set *channeled finance through banks* by ensuring that depositors had few options other than banks and that large corporate borrowers had few nonbank financing sources. Thus, Japan effectively "repealed" the American-imposed "Glass-Steagall" separation, not by allowing commercial banking to mix with investment banking, but by stymieing a securities market and channeling savings and corporate financing into the banking system.[23] (This is hardly a recommendation that the United States

---

[22] (1) Frances McCall Rosenbluth, Financial Politics in Contemporary Japan 157–66 (1989); (2) Robert Zielinski and Nigel Holloway, Unequal Equities: Power and Risk in Japan's Stock Market 156 (1991); Ramseyer, supra note 21, at 23–31; Mikuni and Co., Banking 5 (Occasional Paper No. 2, 1987); (3) Hideki Kanda, Politics, Formalism, and the Elusive Goal of Investor Protection: Regulation of Structured Investment Funds in Japan, 12 University of Pennsylvania International Law Review 569 (1991); (4) Masahiko Aoki, The Japanese Firm as a System of Attributes: A Survey and Research Agenda 17–18 (Stanford Center for Economic Policy Research Publication No. 288, 1992); (5) J. Mark Ramseyer, Explicit Reasons for Implicit Contract: The Legal Logic to the Japanese Main Bank System 9 (1993) (unpublished paper). Thus Japan pushed corporate borrowers into commercial banks and limited savers' options.

[23] See Bruce Kasman and Anthony P. Rodrigues, Financial Liberalization and Monetary Control in Japan, Federal Reserve Bank of New York Quarterly Review, Autumn 1991, at 28, 29–31 and n.4.

distort its entire financial system to get some disputable corporate governance benefits; this is an analysis of what Japan did.)

Determining which is the "natural" base—American securities markets or Japanese banks—is difficult because the United States burdened big banks while Japan subsidized them. However, nationwide banking does seem to be a natural baseline, which only the United States eliminated, thereby reducing nonsecurities alternatives for large firms and facilitating the development of a securities market. If large American banks had existed, they might have made the large loans and stock investments that instead had to flow through the securities market.

Hence, although laws in both nations severed investment banking from commercial banking, the results differed, because, unlike the Americans, the Japanese allowed their banks nationwide operations, forced savers to use banks on terms favorable to the banks, and required corporations to seek financing through the banks. In operation, Japan did not have the Glass-Steagall Act that America had. America constructed two big competing financial channels; Japan channeled both savings and finance through the banks. The single channel allowed the Japanese banks to be powerful enough to take a serious role in corporate ownership. Germany also constructed a single channel, not by fully suppressing the securities channel, but by putting it under bank domination. Only the United States has two (or more) vibrant channels for the flow of finance from savers to industry. Neither U.S. channel is filled with large, powerful intermediaries.

The Japanese single channel for finance is now weakening for two reasons. Success has given Japanese firms the luxury to retain earnings, thereby sidestepping the banks' control over the financing channel; this may make bank control over stock more important than it has thus far been. Also, the channeling regulations that once offset the Japanese "Glass-Steagall" separation are disappearing. Regulatory change has opened up the securities channel a bit, thereby weakening the commercial banks, because they have not completely succeeded in getting regulators to allow them full entrance into the newly widening securities channel.

OTHER REGULATORY IMPEDIMENTS

Since my purpose here is not to catalog unending legal impediments but only to show that the German and Japanese banking systems would fail under American law, even one historical show-stopper restriction—McFadden, for example—suffices. In addition, the other major U.S. financial intermediaries—insurers, mutual funds, and pension funds—have historically also been precluded from taking big financial positions in the largest firms, a pattern consistent with the general thesis that the structure of the large firm is highly sensitive to the structure of financial intermediaries, which in turn is highly sensitive to law. For half a century, major American insurers were prohibited from owning *any* stock, and mutual funds have been discouraged from acquiring influential blocks of stock. Private pension funds, while not formally prohibited from buying influential blocks, are controlled by managers of large firms, who discourage such influence, rather than by managers of financial intermediaries, who might encourage it.

Securities laws historically have made communication among stockholders costly. Until 1992, ten stockholders who merely spoke with one another about corporate events and managers risked violating proxy rules.[24] Interbank (and interfinancier) communications among banks with large blocks of stock could have been construed as a proxy solicitation, thus necessitating a public filing with the SEC. Under state antitakeover laws, group votes are generally sterilized, trigger poison pills, or violate "control share" statutes.[25]

Why do U.S. industrial firms not participate directly in one another's governance by holding large blocks of one another's stock? Although there are no explicit prohibitions, operating firms are poorly suited to the holding of large blocks of stock because they usually prefer to deploy their capital for other purposes. Even in Japan, where industrial cross-holdings play a role, financial intermediaries hold two-thirds of the blocks, while industrial firms hold only one-third of them. Moreover, American industrial cross-holdings would be taxed. In the 1930s Congress passed a dividends-received tax explicitly to discourage such corporate complexes.[26]

Why did the United States adopt so many impediments to an institutional voice in corporate governance? American populism—a popular mistrust of powerful institutions, including private financial intermediaries—and American interest group jockeying yielded many of the restrictions. Other restrictions, although not all of them, came about because of a perception— often based on fact—of financial abuse, fraud, and self-dealing. While German and Japanese politics display some similarities to American politics— particularly popular distrust in Germany and interest group infighting in Japan—they have on the whole been historically different. Different political paths yielded different financial institutions, and different financial institutions yielded different corporate structures.

---

[24] See Black, supra note 4, at 537–41. New proxy rules, adopted on October 15, 1992, reduce, but do not eliminate, some of these possibilities.

[25] See, e.g., Cullen v. Milligan, 578 N.E.2d 123 (Ohio 1991) (applying Ohio "control share" statute); Atlantis Group, Inc. v. Alizac Partners, No. 1:90 CV-937, 1991 WL 319384, at *1 (W.D. Mich. Aug. 27, 1991) (applying Michigan "control share" statute).

[26] See supra chapter 9. As of early 1994, the effective tax rate was about 10 percent of the dividend. The tax also discourages bank cross-holdings.

CHAPTER 13

Counterpoint I

SEVERAL ARGUMENTS tend to undermine the thesis that politics was a key determinant of intermediaries and the ownership structure of the large firm. I have addressed several as they have come up. For example, some restrictions were sound and inevitable, and even some of the unsound ones had public-spirited aspirations. But political forces created enough rules, and influenced enough others, that the political theory makes sense. Several arguments, which are worth addressing separately, are variations on the theme that intermediaries would fragment their holdings anyway, despite the American political history of fragmentation. Evidence for this view includes the possibility that financial institutions in Germany and Japan will, or are, fragmenting their holdings; the fact that some of the American rules do not absolutely bar institutional involvement, but just up the cost of involvement without banning it; and financial theories that give some basis for institutional passivity irrespective of the fragmenting rules.

FRAGMENTATION EVEN WITHOUT IMPEDIMENTS?

Perhaps finance fragments anyway as a nation advances economically. This kind of statement is difficult to disprove, since those with this view can always assert that the natural economic fragmentation is just around the corner. There have been recurrent predictions of the end of the Japanese keiretsu and its main bank system, as well as of a massive sell-off of German bank–owned stock. Perhaps, the argument would run, diversification is so important that institutions will voluntarily fragment their portfolios. Perhaps there is a natural scale to intermediaries that precludes large size. Or perhaps institutions' need for liquidity is so important that they will not take large illiquid blocks.

The current facts of institutional ownership in Germany and Japan, although mixed, do not yet support the natural evolution thesis. Although the German and Japanese systems are hardly static, and the Japanese main bank system is weakening, its weaknesses have not yet shown up in big declines in stock ownership. Japanese banks' stock ownership has been stable for twenty-five years; influence via loans may be weakening, but not stock ownership—indeed, one recent study shows an *increased* overall role for bank stockholding in Japan in the 1970s and late 1980s.[1] As of December 31, 1993, the Japanese intermediaries owned the same big blocks in that nation's largest firms as they did on December 31, 1967 (see Table 8 in chapter 11). Other studies suggest that the main bank system continues for most firms, but some new firms are securities based, meaning that rather than a weakening of the old system, a parallel and competing financing system may be arising. Although there is rhetoric in Germany of banker withdrawal from stock ownership, actual ownership changes for the hundred largest firms are small and in the wrong direction for the natural evolution thesis. I examined the German Parliamentary Monopoly Commission reports on stock ownership and found that the number of relatively large blocks (5 percent or over) owned directly by the banks was *increasing*, not decreasing. They *rose* from twenty-three such blocks in 1986 to twenty-six in 1988 and thirty in 1990.[2] The reports of a German bank sell-off must mostly be based on *expectations* of future sales, or on actual sales of bank-owned stock in smaller firms; many smaller German firms tend to have families as influential stockholders, meaning that the German transformation (if there is one at all) may not be to American-style public-firms but to further family dominance.

LIQUIDITY

Institutions want liquidity, and the big blocks that are a prerequisite to boardroom involvement tend to be illiquid. Liquidity is important but it can easily be overrated, because many American intermediaries need not keep their portfolios entirely liquid. Indeed, liquidity transformation—by which an intermediary manages and balances off liquid versus illiquid investments and provides liquidity to its own beneficiaries, whom it knows will not seek to redeem en masse—is a prime function for an intermediary, according to finance theory.

Several financial institutions—life insurers and pension funds in particular—have the very long-term obligations that make liquidity a secondary concern for them. Other institutions, such as mutual funds, have liquidity problems that are compounded, not eased, by regulation. Moreover, American institutions are finding themselves with substantially illiquid stockholdings *despite* the lack of big blocks; as some stockholding institutions have

[1] See supra chapter 11, table 8 (1967–1992 ownership); George Michael Pushner, Ownership Structure and Corporate Performance in the U.S. and Japan 33 (Ph.d. diss., Columbia University, 1993) (increased overall role).

[2] Deutscher Bundestag, Achtes Hauptgutachten der Monopolkommission, Drucksache 11/7582, at 202–06 (1990); Neuntes Hauptgutachten der Monopolkommission 205–08 (1993).

grown large, their investments have also grown so large that they are illiquid (or, in case of indexers, who buy the entire market of stocks, they are potentially liquid but do not trade). The American pattern of increasing concentration yields illiquidity (or untraded portfolios) with meager influence. In any case, liquidity is a cost, not a show-stopper.

Critics of today's institutions say institutions will never use big blocks and boardroom seats responsibly because when the portfolio firm faces problems, they will sell, not fight. This is plausible for many institutions, but not necessarily for all. *Today's* institutions disproportionately have that preference, but institutions can change; even today, some prefer to fight despite having only small stakes. Were law more permissive, at least a few others would find it worthwhile to take bigger blocks and boardroom seats.

This cut-and-run hypothesis is not a pure liquidity argument, but an insider-trading argument, since it assumes that the institution will learn that a firm has problems before they are reflected in the firm's stock price, allowing it to sell before the market learns of the problems and adjusts the firm's stock price. Such sales would usually violate the insider-trading laws, but could be difficult to detect; for this reason a change that led to more insider involvement should lead to a look at the adequacy of the insider-trading rules and enforcement. Still, this scenario is too pessimistic because it projects *today's* small-block intermediaries onto a big-block alternative, without making the necessary adjustments. Insider sales by an institution owning a *small* block might be hard to detect. But once an institution takes a big block or boardroom seats (and especially if it takes both), its trades on inside information will be easy to detect when the firm's problems come out. Big blocks and boardroom seats are too visible to hide.

Lastly, this scenario posits that the only good that big blocks do is to help a firm in trouble. In Part V, we will see that big blocks have other constructive roles, in helping to build better information channels to the firms' top and in helping firms in related industries organize simultaneous investments in complex components. Once in the boardroom for these reasons, institutions may be well placed to help a firm in trouble.

Even if economic factors, such as liquidity, are *more* weighty than politics in explaining why institutions do not take big blocks and become active in corporate governance, the political theory is still important and possibly the crucial, marginal determinant. The natural economic factors might align so that the costs of institutional power for some large minority of firms are, while considerable, just barely outweighed by the benefits. But then a small increment of political restraints tips the balance—historically in the United States toward withdrawal and in Germany and Japan toward entry—and politics, as the marginal, the variable factor, affects the outcome.

GREAT BRITAIN

Comparisons with Germany and Japan show how different politics can produce different financial intermediaries, which can produce different systems of corporate governance. Comparison with Great Britain blurs the sharpness of the other foreign comparisons, because on the surface Britain has fewer financial restrictions than the United States, but still has a financial system tied to securities markets. British banks are unimportant in corporate governance. But although Britain may be the most difficult comparison for substantiating the political paradigm, it fits better with that paradigm than one might at first think.

British insurers never faced the absolute ban on stock ownership that the largest American insurers faced for most of this century. And, consistent with the political paradigm, the British insurers are more active in corporate governance than their American counterparts. More generally, British stock ownership is somewhat more concentrated than in the United States, and British financial institutions are somewhat more active.

Although after the recent "Big Bang" of financial liberalization, British banks could own securities firms, they had faced historical restrictions. The stock exchange barred its members from having a business other than brokering stocks, a restriction roughly parallel to those that American (and Japanese) interest group conflicts had produced or preserved. Moreover, the British historical concept of a bank was as a short-term lender uninvolved in commerce, and in the nineteenth century central banking policy did not provide the banking system with liquidity for long-term bank investments. Social restrictions were also important: British banks did not gather and distribute long-term capital, partly because leading bankers and industrialists at the beginning of the twentieth century had little interest in technology and the construction of vertically integrated firms; they preferred to emulate and join the British landed aristocracy. British banks could own stock in the twentieth century, but needed the Bank of England's permission, which until recent years the Bank would not give. Moreover, during Britain's pre-Thatcher Labour era from the 1950s until 1979, investment managers who took large and visible positions in industry had reason to fear that the British government might nationalize either the industrial firm with visible financial ownership or nationalize the financial institution itself that was too active.[3]

[3] Richard Tilly, Banking Institutions in Historical Perspective: Germany, Great Britain and the United States in the Nineteenth and Early Twentieth Century, 145 Zeitschrift für die Gesamte Staatswissenschaft [Journal of Institutional and Theoretical Economics] 189, 196–98 (1989); O.M.W. Sprague, Branch Banking in the United States, 17 Quarterly Journal of Eco-

Thus the political paradigm fits well with seven of our eight "data points"—banks and insurers in the United States, Germany, and Japan and insurers in Britain—but is ambiguous in explaining the eighth "data point," British banks. To the extent that historical banking restrictions and a fear of nationalization are important, even the eighth "data point" may fit with the political theory.

RETAINED EARNINGS

A firm's managers can retain earnings, freeing themselves from the oversight of capital-providing financiers. The firm may later face problems, but stockholding intermediaries will not be in place to discipline management or help out in a sudden crisis. This is a serious problem for the argument I've made so far in this book.

If firms can disarm intermediary-owners, then the political theory would only explain the *speed* with which an economy got to the Berle-Means result; managers would eventually get the same result that I say politics, by distancing intermediaries from the firm, made inevitable.

Before the firm faces problem in this scenario, it is strong enough to retain earnings sufficient for its needs and gets rid of the financiers; financiers are unimportant if the firm needs no outside financing. In the most pernicious variation of this theme, the firm generates cash from internal, successful operations, but wastes it. This problem afflicted the U.S. oil industry in the 1980s, when it unwisely spent its big inventory profits from the rise in oil prices, both by diversifying into industries it understood poorly and on unprofitable exploration for new oil.[4] And many large firms that emerged at the end of the nineteenth century and the beginning of the twentieth century produced so much cash from internal operations that they did not need outside financing.[5] When growth is wise, managers might systematically do

---

nomics 242, 247 (1903); William Lazonick, Business Organization and the Myth of the Market Economy 144–45 (1991); Christine M. Cumming and Lawrence M. Sweet, Financial Structure of the G-10 Countries: How Does the United States Compare? Federal Reserve Bank of New York Quarterly Review, Winter 1987–88, at 14, 15; Loretta J. Mester, Banking and Commerce: A Dangerous Liaison? Federal Reserve Bank of Philadelphia Bulletin, May/June 1992, at 17, 21; cf. Hargreaves Parkinson, Ownership of Industry 1–2, 52–53, 102–104 (1951) (examining relationship between ownership structure and risks of industrial nationalization); John Farrar and Mark Russell, The Impact of Institutional Investment on Company Law, 5 Company Lawyer 107, 109, 114 (1984) ("[British i]nstitutional investors are worried about the political consequences of an exercise of power. They eschew public criticism and fear public intervention").

[4] Michael C. Jensen, Agency Costs of Free Cash Flow, 76 American Economic Review 323 (1986).

[5] Alfred D. Chandler, Jr., The Visible Hand—The Managerial Revolution in American Business 373, 416 (1977).

the best thing and expand; when growth is unwise, managers might systematically do the wrong thing and still expand. Although financiers with big
stock positions should be more concerned with profits than with wasteful
growth and might check these errant managers, the intermediaries will be
powerless and absent, if during a prior stage of the firm's development,
financing by retaining earnings had ended the intermediaries' role.

That scenario is not, however, inevitable. First, controlling misspent internally generated cash is not the only function of powerful intermediaries.
And even if successful managers *always* forced intermediaries out of the
boardroom, less successful ones would never get free from finance and
would, if the political blockages did not arise, have to share authority with
intermediaries.

Second, intermediaries can be big stockholders in firms financed from
internally generated cash. It is an American preconception that intermediaries only finance; some simply hold stock. *Someone* must own the stock of
the large firm; it can be held in large blocks by powerful *nonfinancing* intermediaries.

To see this, imagine now a simple firm's life cycle as this: Stage 1, growth,
with financing from external sources. Stage 2, growth, with financing from
internal sources. And Stage 3, decline, with the firm at risk of misspending
its earnings.

There is nothing in finance or economics that requires that the firm's stock
disperse in Stage 2. Nonfinancing intermediaries could own the stock and
hold it in big blocks. Moreover, there is a positive, functional role for *nonfinancing* intermediaries in this Stage 2 in coordinating industrial organization, by holding stock in suppliers and customers to smooth out their relations, and helping to bridge the relationships between the firm's managers
and its stockholders. Adding these two functions, which I explore in chapters 18 and 19, one can see intermediaries with positive roles in all stages,
first financing the firm, then helping the successful firm to coordinate its
interactions with its suppliers and customers, then later keeping an eye on
whether managers are misspending retained earnings. While the intermediaries will not always succeed in all three stages, the intermediary can indeed
have functions in all three.

In the United States, because intermediaries are not in place in Stages 1
and 2, they have to fight their way into the boardroom in Stage 3, but the
means—takeovers and activist stockholding—are expensive, disruptive, and
not always effective. The cost of that fight could deter them, but if they could
have made a contribution in an earlier stage (and captured some of the profit
from that contribution), by improving information flows between the board
and large stockholders or by helping to coordinate complex investments,
they would *already* be in the boardroom when free cash flow problems
arose.

The functions of intermediaries might implicate *which* one owned stock at each stage, but need not undermine the holding of stock in big blocks. Thus, a bank might not be interested in holding stock for its own account unless the stock were supporting financing. Mutual funds, insurers, and pension funds, however, could conceivably hold these big blocks even if the firm required no new external financing. (Ironically, American politicians conceived of financing as the only "legitimate" function for intermediaries. Hence they built laws that facilitated *this* function but undermined what could have been the intermediaries' other governance functions.)[6]

Some examples: Toyota has had little need for new financing for decades, but five intermediaries hold 20 percent of its stock. The Japanese main banks now face free cash flow and conglomeration problems that were central to the American takeovers of the 1980s; we shall see whether they reduce the waste. Historically, American founding families continued to have a say when they withdrew from active management, even in firms that did not need financiers for new financing; the families lacked the information for day-to-day management, but in crisis they intervened to protect managers or fire them.[7] Had large-scale, stock-owning American intermediaries been possible back then, then when the founding families left the scene, they might have turned over their big blocks of stock to intermediaries, which might have been inactive when results were good, but become active when results deteriorated.

DIFFERENCES IN ECONOMIC TASK

Differences in economic task between Germany and Japan on the one hand and the United States on the other hand complicate the story. Germany developed heavy industry with heavy capital needs in the late nineteenth century and early twentieth century, and since Germany was a latecomer, the best investments were well known. Entrepreneurial experimentation and capital accumulation via retained earnings were less helpful then, one might argue, than they had been in Britain and the United States, because entrepreneurs there had already done the experimenting. With a clear path available for German industry, immediate construction of externally financed large factories was sensible, and that process of external finance instead of retained earnings matched up with ownership by outside, capital-providing financiers. This "follower" argument can help explain the differences. It does better in explaining the differences, though, when one adds that political constraints supported the "follower's" preferred structure. The concentrated German structure has persisted well past the time when Ger-

[6] See, e.g., discussion of Douglas's views, supra introduction and chapter 4.

[7] Alfred D. Chandler, Jr., The United States: Seedbed of Managerial Capitalism, in Managerial Hierarchies 9, 13–14 (Alfred D. Chandler, Jr., and Herman Daems eds., 1980).

many could be said to be a latecomer, meaning that it's not today's difference in task that explains the difference in structure, but one from long ago that persists because of inertia.

ABUSES

Many U.S. financial rules were responses to financial abuses. The rules were necessary or at least useful regulation to maintain financial stability or to prevent institutions from abusing the public. Even if some of these rules overshot the needed amount of regulation, the aspiration behind many of them was to protect the public and stabilize the economy.

This is particularly true of many of the securities laws, which arose in response to insider, Wall Street manipulations of prices that bilked the public. As a matter of fairness, and to make the public confident in the bona fides of buying stock, many securities rules were a necessity. This may well be true, but for the most part we have not analyzed the politics behind the securities laws, but the politics behind other financial rules. Of the financial rules we have analyzed, the rules that have the strongest protect-the-public background are those in ERISA; it is hard to see how this was intended other than to protect the public. (The structure of who runs the pensions is another story.)

For other rules, the protect-the-public aspiration is weaker. Thus, the persistent ban on nationwide bank branching can be justified as protecting the public only with great difficulty. Indeed, the best guess is that branching restrictions have increased the cost of many financial products and destabilized the financial system, because local banks are overly dependent on a local, sometimes erratic economy.

Other rules have a mixed basis. Thus the Investment Company Act of 1940 has two relevant sets of rules. For one set, which prevents a wide range of dealing among the fund, its affiliates, and portfolio firms, I have little doubt that the principal aspiration was protective. The political content was there but minor: Since big finance was bad, the law's framers saw little to trade off between preventing self-dealing and integrating finance with industry, so they may have drawn their restrictive lines a bit more stringently than necessary.

The second set of rules, which limits the portfolio of the mutual fund, also had some protective aspiration, but here the aspirations were, in my view, more mixed. Since the funds now *can* devote *some* of their portfolio to big blocks, the argument that big blocks inevitably lead to theft becomes a compromised principle; sometimes the 1940 Act allows big blocks, sometimes it does not. Probably *no* portfolio rule is necessary here for the purpose of preventing self-dealing; instead the needed controls are those on self-dealing. Similarly, the protective justification of mandating diversification is less convincing when the fund can put all of its eggs in the same industry basket, but cannot put them in a small handful of companies.

The Glass-Steagall Act also illustrates the mixture of reasons for these laws. There are multiple justifications for Glass-Steagall's separation of investment from commercial banking. Many fall into the category of protecting a bank's retail customers from the bank's self-dealing; that is, the bank could find itself exposed to a suddenly weak company to which the bank had lent money. The bank would then sell bad securities to the public, which unwittingly would bail the bank out. No one should be naive enough to think such things have not and would not happen. The question is whether this kind of fraud exceeds other kinds of fraud and whether because many *buyers* of securities are not so naive, they anticipate the risk of fraud and they (and the selling banks) reduce its incidence. The evidence suggests that the public did *better* in the 1920s when buying commercial bank-underwritten securities than when buying other securities.[8] While interpreting historical data is always hard, it seems that the bankers' need for a reputation for probity outweighed their temptation to defraud.

The other principled justification for Glass-Steagall was to stabilize banking in the 1930s, because securities affiliates were too risky for commerical banks. The well-publicized failure of a small bank with a big name (Bank of the United States) strengthened this perception. But, there is theoretical reason to believe that bank complexes with an income stream from a securities affiliate are *more* stable than those without, and empirical evidence that banks with securities affiliates were *more* stable during the 1920s and the beginning of the Great Depression than those without securities affiliates.[9]

True, *perceptions* of abuses are what counts in politics; even if lawmakers interpreted the evidence badly, they may have perceived that safety and abuse potential required separation. At this point, how law is made becomes a matter of interpretation. In my view, honestly held perceptions are partly produced by one's ideological cast of mind. Lawmakers and an American public that dislike concentrated power have their minds more open to perceive abuses that require restraining finance than to seeing any value to strengthening it. People who feel abused by the economic system need to blame someone, and visible, powerful financial institutions can be blamed (sometimes legitimately). Interest groups could not alone get their way without either the underlying dislike of concentrated economic power or the

[8] Randall S. Kroszner and Raghuram G. Rajan, Is the Glass-Steagall Act Justified?—A Study of the U.S. Experience with Universal Banking before 1933, 84 American Economic Review (1994) (forthcoming).

[9] Donald Langevoort, Statutory Obsolescence and the Judicial Process: The Revisionist Role of the Courts in Federal Banking Regulation, 85 Michigan Law Review 672, 682 and n.31 (1987); Eugene N. White, The Regulation and Reform of the American Banking System, 1900–1929 (1983); Eugene N. White, The Political Economy of Banking Regulation, 1864–1933, 42 Journal of Economic History 33 (1982). Since the banks with securities affiliates tended to be large, their relative safety might have been due as much to their size as to their product mix.

plausibility of the public interest, abuse prevention perceptions. The fact that law and regulation is a multidimensional drama, with real (and perceived) goals of preventing abuse or stabilizing institutions as one of the dimensions, takes nothing away from the claim that politics, ideology, and interest groups are key to another dimension of that lawmaking. There are multiple factors. Politics is one of them, and an underrecognized one.

POLITICS AS UNPREDICTABLE

Multidimensional politics implicates another problem with political analysis: on some levels, it fails to yield predictions, and is untestable. True, it can make some kinds of predictions: that, for example, if the United States had not fragmented intermediaries' stockholders a different type of boardroom could have emerged in the United States. This cannot be fully tested without rerunning history, an experiment not yet feasible. Moreover, since the political inputs change (less populism then, more populism now; this interest group in dominance now, that one then), political explanations tend to look like ex post stories, not scientific predictions.

This criticism is well taken, but still misses the mark. The fact that many political theories cannot be specified and tested yet does not mean that politics is any less real in influencing outcomes. In these matters, we are like the students of the science of fluids, motion, and air currents. We know it is important, but—like them, before the science of chaos improved in recent years—we cannot yet specify, quantify, and predict.

ANTIBUSINESS IDEOLOGY AND ANTIBANKER IDEOLOGY

Americans' dislike of concentrations of economic power should have directed itself not just at finance, but also at industry. Yet American politics fragmented finance, not industry. Why did it not break up industry as well?

It was not for want of trying. American antitrust ideology *was* largely directed at big business, "to perpetuate and preserve, for its own sake and in spite of possible cost, an organization of industry in small units," according to one famous antitrust court opinion, because "great industrial consolidations are inherently undesirable, regardless of their economic results."[10] There was a "curse of bigness," and early antitrust thinkers were uninterested in inquiry into how to deliver the best quality at the lowest price to consumers; they wanted to preserve and protect small producers.[11]

[10] United States v. Aluminum Co. of America, 148 F.2d 416 (2d Cir. 1945).

[11] Thomas K. McCraw, Prophets of Regulation 80–142 (1984) (detailed inquiry into origins and nature of Brandeis's anti–big-business ideology and his successful efforts to diffuse that ideology).

Here is one explanation of why politics fragmented finance but not industry. Imagine the forces constraining the vote in 1933 of a senator from, say, Pennsylvania, who had to decide how to vote on two hypothetical bills, one that would smash up big finance (or confirm its fragmentation) and one that would smash up big business. Although Pennsylvania voters are against both big business and big finance, the senator votes against big finance, but not against big business. Why?

The senator looks to effects in Pennsylvania. Smashing up big finance is (mostly) a problem for New York's Wall Street, not (mostly) for Pennsylvanians. Smashing up big business is a Pennsylvania problem. The senator is not sure about fragmenting U.S. Steel, Pittsburgh Plate and Glass, and other big but local firms. Since industry is more evenly distributed through the country than finance, the coalition that would break up finance falls apart when trying to break up industry. Even if the average Pennsylvanian would support both smash-ups, the senator has weaker interest group support for hitting industry than for hitting finance, because more Pennsylvanians would be visibly hurt.

The weaker antibusiness sentiments find their way into the laws that get passed. The antifinance bill, like the McFadden Act, is strict and clear: a ban on branching across state lines. The antibusiness bill, like the Clayton Act, is vague: a ban on mergers only if the mergers would substantially lessen competition or tend to create a monopoly. The antitrust parallel to McFadden would be a law that banned industry from operating from more than one location, or more realistically, banned any single industrial firm from growing above a specified size. Such proposals have come up from time to time, but did not have a serious chance of passage. The financial equivalents, however, passed and became law.

Antibusiness ideology could also be weaker than antifinance ideology, because breaking up industry might be seen as more costly, for two reasons. One, maybe big finance isn't *really* efficient. Breaking it up loses little. The industrial firms, with more efficiency effects at stake, fight the breakup more than the financial firms do. Or, two, fragmenting a factory is *seen* to be more inefficient than fragmenting finance. In the popular mind, banks and finance just do not do enough. They are just middlemen. Industry really does something.

CONTRACT AND SUBSTITUTION

There is a contractarian rebuttal to the political argument. A critic might concede that politics influences ownership forms, but argue that the market adjusts to these political results swiftly and at low cost. The rebuttal that there would be market and contractual adjustments is well taken; indeed, that is one of my secondary arguments—that primary ownership forms are politically influenced, and then many secondary ownership characteristics are contractual adjustments to the primary political determinations.

But the contractual, market adjustments need not be swift and *costless*. The contractarian rebuttal depends on how perfect substitutes are. If law bans one organizational form, will the next one be just as good? For all firms? All of the time? A ban on, say, the consumption of nectarines would have small societal effects, because of their (relatively) low use and the high substitutability of oranges, grapefruits, and peaches. A ban on, say, airplane travel would induce substitute travel, more staying at home, and different living patterns, but be costly. We do not know enough about organizational forms yet, and may never know enough, to know how easily a ban of one organizational form leads to a perfect substitute or a high-cost, imperfect substitute. Without good empirical tests, a plausible assumption is that there are some, but modest losses when one organizational form is banned and there are a limited number of alternatives.

CUMULATIVE RESTRICTIONS

Institutions could have more concentrated stock portfolios than they have now, but do not. Investment companies could have a portfolio of as few as twelve stocks, but do not. Bank holding companies can own up to five percent of an industrial firm's stock, but do not. Does this mean that law has not restrained them, now or historically?

Other rules, however, raise the costs of activity, keeping institutional blocks smaller and more passive than they would otherwise be. To be effective the institution would have to form a coalition with other large holders; but, until recently, SEC shareholder communications rules have made forming coalitions difficult, and other SEC rules still disrupt coalition-building. The cumulative effect of several rules could deter institutions from what has been only a marginally profitable task anyway.

DEFECTIVE INTERMEDIARIES

This leads to one last counterpoint. Perhaps the basic problem is that intermediaries would disable operating firms often enough that their return on investing in big blocks and sharing authority with senior managers would be lower than that from being passive. Even though the normative claim that institutional involvement is a serious benefit is not central to my thesis, at least the minimal level must be satisfied—that institutional involvement will not be very costly, and might in fact be beneficial. I will discuss this in Part V. First, I look at politics in Germany and Japan, to see how one can link politics to their ownership structures.

CHAPTER 14

Political Evolution
in Germany and Japan?

EVEN IF we knew that Germany and Japan would evolve to American-style diffuse ownership (and even if we saw no American ownership trends toward concentration), the incompleteness of current corporate theories would persist. We would need to determine the degree to which politics in Germany and Japan was inducing financial evolution. Financial fragmentation could be inherent in twentieth-century democracy, rather than merely inherent in American democracy, as I hypothesized earlier. Foreign nations' political and corporate histories could have evolved together: large industry and big finance emerged abroad when nondemocratic governments kept fragmenting forces in check. Indeed, today's foreign democracies affect corporate structures, but in ways and degrees different from those in the American past.

Although my goal here is not to provide a definitive history of how German and Japanese politics affected corporate structures—a task I commend to others—even a cursory inquiry shows political forces at work, shaping the governance of the large firm. Indeed, how could it be otherwise? The movement of capital from savers to firms, and the holding of capital in firms by savers, is central in modern economies. Capital's movement and existence has to attract political attention. Interest groups see the potential for rents from how that movement and holding are regulated, and they seek to influence the rules governing the movement and the holding. Popular opinion on how capital moves or is held can be important and will influence political outcomes. Regulators see abuses that need to be remedied. These three forces will then influence the organization of financial institutions, which in turn will affect the ownership structure of the large firm.

GERMAN "POPULISM"

Political Pressure on the Banks

Deutsche Bank reviews whether to allow its employees to chair an industrial firm's board, and some German banks have sold directly held stock.

Is this part of an economic evolution? Perhaps so, but the German banks are under intense political pressure[1] from forces not unlike those in the United States that disabled powerful intermediaries. German politicians claim that the bankers' power clashes with the German "social order."[2] The Social Democrats and the market-oriented Free Democrats want to reduce banks' power.[3] Parliamentary reports attack the banks. Members of Parliament want to limit "the percentage of equity a bank could maintain in a nonbank enterprise *and cut the number of supervisory board positions a bank executive could hold.*"[4] Managers are said to want to get bankers out of supervisory boards, although they hesitate to say so publicly.[5] Executives in Germany's medium-sized firms oppose bankers' influence and want laws prohibiting German banks from owning nonbank stock.[6] Fear of powerful banks "form[s] the backdrop of many economic and political discussions. Conducted in the press, on radio, and on television, among scholars, and, most importantly, political groups, these discussions use emotion-

[1] Ferdinand Protzman, Mighty German Banks Face Curb, N.Y. Times, Nov. 7, 1989, at D1 ("parliament has begun studying steps to limit the banks' shareholdings, their seats on boards and their influence in corporate decision-making"); Terence Roth, West German Banks Face Threat of Reduced Influence in Industry: Bonn Will Consider Rules to Curb Their Holdings and Seats in Boardrooms, Wall Street Journal, July 18, 1989, at A20 ("[w]ith mainstream politics coming into play, bankers worry that they'll be forced to sell parts of their sizable equity holdings in West German industry, thus threatening their dominant position in the country's equity markets").

[2] Hans-Jacob Krümmel, German Universal Banking Scrutinized: Some Remarks Concerning the Gessler Report, 4 Journal of Banking and Finance 33 (1980); see also Der Herr des Geldes [The Money Man], Der Spiegel, Mar. 13, 1989, at 20; Die Geheimräte der Nation [The Nation's Secret Council], Industriemagazin, Apr. 1987, at 27; Horst Greiffenberg, Die Macht der Banken [The Power of the Banks], Verbraucherpolitische Hefte, Dec. 1987, at 85; Jörg Huffschmid, Demokratische Alternativen der Bankpolitik [Democratic Alternatives for the Politics of Banking], Verbraucherpolitische Hefte, Dec. 1987, at 111; Zwischen Bonn und Banken: Finanzdiplomat Hermann Abs [Between Bonn and the Banks: Financial Diplomat Hermann Abs], Der Spiegel, Nov. 3, 1965, at 10.

[3] John Dornberg, The Spreading Might of Deutsche Bank, N.Y. Times, Sept. 23, 1990, at 28.

[4] Id. at 28; see also Wolfram Eckstein, The Role of the Banks in Corporate Concentration in West Germany, 136 Zeitschrift für die gesamte Staatswissenschaft 467, 480 (1980) (Eckstein was Secretary General of the Monopoly Commission); Johannes Köndgen, Duties of Banks in Voting Their Clients' Stock, in Institutional Investors and Corporate Governance 532, 539–40 (Theodor Baums, Richard M. Buxbaum, and Klaus J. Hopt eds., 1994) (discussing parliamentary hearings).

[5] Otto Graf Lambsdorff, Das Machtgeflecht der Banken Lichten, Frankfurter Allgemeine Zeitung, Aug. 22, 1989, at 10 (leading German politician says senior managers privately tell him that they wish to see banker power reduced). When takeovers became a real possibility, however, German managers reconsidered.

[6] Bundersverband Mittelständischer Wirtschaft, Expose zur "Macht der Banken" 9 (Apr. 24, 1991) (survey conducted by German association of mid-sized businesses). Eighty-eight percent of the businesses favored restricting the banks. Obviously mid-sized business opposition could reflect interest group opposition to banker power.

laden terms such as 'bankocracy,' 'dominion of finance capital,' and similar verbal symbols."[7]

The banks have bowed to this political pressure, at least verbally.[8] After German politicians led a storm of political protest in the region where a bank-propelled takeover target operated, the bankers lowered their public profile.[9] Moreover, Deutsche Bank, Germany's largest, has stated that the political costs are too great to maintain high visibility in corporate governance—either as an owner or as a director.[10] To dampen public protest, which German bankers may believe managers could use to get American-style legal restrictions, the banks have lowered their public profile and announced that they will not fight curbs on their control over the proxy machinery.[11] Political pressures, not just economic evolution, may have induced the banks to be lax in using their stock.

True, this German "populism" has historically been weaker than the American strain: "Germany has never known anything like the fear and resentment that monopoly used to arouse in the United States. . . . Many Germans find it difficult to believe that something growing up without order and control, like a competitive market, could not be improved by applying a little discipline."[12] In the United States, antibank sentiments com-

---

[7] H. E. Büschgen, The Universal Banking System in the Federal Republic of Germany, 2 Journal of Comparative Corporate Law and Securities Regulation 1, 25 (1979).

[8] Krümmel, supra note 2, at 53 (bankers "continue with their traditional tendency to elude public controversy by a flexible attitude and not to rise against the zeitgeist, even if they are convinced they have the better arguments"); Frankfurter Allgemeine Zeitung, Aug. 19, 1989, at 11 (leading German politicians form working group to curb banker power, and some expect the banks to understand that prudent self-limitation is necessary); Fusion doch ohne Beschluß zur Bankenmacht, Frankfurter Allgemeine Zeitung, Sept. 7, 1989, at 17–18.

[9] "Once the [target's] employees protested the [proposed] deal, the politicians in southern Germany, where [the target] is based, began to send up a hue and cry [which caused Deutsche Bank to change its position and oppose the merger.]" Jackey Gold, M & A Continental Style, Financial World, Mar. 5, 1991, at 37.

[10] Role of the Financial Services Sector: Hearings Before the Task Force on the International Competitiveness of U.S. Financial Institutions of the Subcomm. on Financial Institutions Supervision, Regulation and Insurance of the House Comm. on Banking, Finance and Urban Affairs, 101st Cong., 2d Sess. 164–65 (1990). As of 1990, this statement is reflected more in Deutsche Bank's rhetoric than in its action, insofar as the number of big blocks that the banks own in Germany's one hundred largest firms has been increasing, not decreasing. See supra chapter 13, note 2 and accompanying text.

[11] Friedrich K. Kübler, Institutional Owners and Corporate Managers: A German Dilemma, 57 Brooklyn Law Review 97 (1991). American institutional restraint is similar. California's huge state pension fund apparently fears that "an organized Calpers-backed attempt to force management changes could trigger a reaction that could curb the big fund's freedom to act independently," in a fashion similar to the restraints arising from the 1980s takeovers. Randall Smith, Calpers Mulls Stakes in Funds Seeking Changes in Firms' Strategy, Governance, Wall Street Journal, Dec. 31, 1992, at A3.

[12] Henry C. Wallich, Mainsprings of the German Revival 136–37 (1955).

bined with powerful interest groups—small bankers or managers, for example—to produce laws restricting large banks, giving deposit insurance to small banks, and protecting managers from takeovers. The restraints on German banks, in contrast, are informal and self-imposed, designed to avoid formal restraints. Why has Germany not enacted the formal restraints anyway, if popular sentiment and interest groups support them? Relative weakness of both the sentiment and the interest groups is part of the answer. Political structure and *different* formal limits are also important. The German political structure dilutes the political effect of both anti–big-bank popular opinion and anti–big-bank interest groups. Citizens vote for a party, which gets a number of parliamentary seats proportionate to its percentage of the national vote.[13] Because the party is more important than the candidate, local bankers and managers (and their campaign contributions) play a less important role than they do in U.S. congressional elections.

Codetermination

Popular opinion and interest groups do formally shape the German boardroom and do dilute banker power, through codetermination, which puts employees into the boardrooms of the biggest firms. Today's codetermination rules give employees—white-collar, blue-collar, and union-represented—half of the supervisory board's seats, an outcome attributable to neither private contracting nor purely economic evolution, but to the way Parliament settled conflict. Codetermination is a counterweight to capital—its historical origins are rooted in the German Parliament's efforts to co-opt revolutionary forces after the German revolution of 1918, when the German Parliament enacted a precursor to modern codetermination.[14] During subsequent periods of social stress, Parliament expanded codetermination, most recently in 1976 when it sought to pacify unions after a wave of strikes in the 1970s.[15] While I am unaware of a probing political analysis of Germany's expansion of codetermination in 1976, I doubt that either popular opinion concerning the banks or the interest group influence of the unions was irrelevant. Employees and managers seem, I have

[13] Lewis J. Edinger, West German Politics 119–20, 149, 172 and n.6 (1986). See id. at 148 (power of German political parties "discourag[es] interest associations from supporting independent deputies and [strengthens] cohesion within the parliamentary parties. The leaders . . . can use the threat of expulsion to keep dissidents in line . . .").

[14] Thomas Raiser, The Theory of Enterprise Law in the Federal Republic of Germany, 36 American Journal of Comparative Law 111, 117 (1988); Alan Dawley, Struggles for Justice—Social Responsibility and the Liberal State 397 (1991).

[15] Alan Hyde, A Theory of Labor Legislation, 38 Buffalo Law Review 383, 411–12 (1990).

been told, to have had an implicit understanding: pensions are more weakly funded in Germany than in the United States; German managers wanted to avoid American-style funding of pensions, preferring to finance their firms by retaining cash instead of sending the cash into pensions and then being forced to go to the capital markets for financing. In return, employees got expanded governance rights.

These understandings (settling social conflict by co-opting employees into the boardroom, and, if true, trading weak pension funding for governance rights) were more than crass deals, because Germany had an ideological tradition of codetermination, dating from the nineteenth century, when religious groups championed it to soften capitalism, to foster a workplace community without socialism, to find a middle way between capitalism and socialism. While American politics fragmented capital and labor, German politics brought them together in the boardroom.[16]

Codetermination has three important effects on German corporate governance. First, codetermination makes powerful intermediaries more politically palatable in Germany than they have been in the United States, because the employees are in the boardroom as a counterweight.

Second, codetermination affects the mechanisms of corporate governance by, for example, impeding takeovers. In the 1980s, the rise of a takeover market in the United States induced popular fears that takeovers would disrupt employment. Antitakeover laws were the result, making takeovers more difficult. German codetermination has a similar effect: takeovers that would disrupt employment are difficult because the shareholders can never capture the entire supervisory board. Codetermination may also affect voting structure by encouraging countervailing big shareholding blocks; in fact, few large German firms lack a big blockholder.

Third, codetermination affects corporate governance in the supervisory board, impeding intermediaries from pushing for rapid organizational change that would disrupt employment. Bankers also know that a powerful supervisory board enhances the authority of the employees. My understanding is that the bankers have sought to weaken the supervisory board, the arena where the employees are, while hoping that the managerial board will act as the bankers wish, perhaps after consulting them outside of the boardroom.

The rhetoric of banker withdrawal from the boardroom should be considered with codetermination in mind. What if banks feared that the governance task ahead in Germany is to tighten the belts and salaries of highly paid German workers? They could also believe that the German po-

---

[16] After World War II, American labor leaders sought industrial work councils resembling German codetermination, but partly because they faced management's determined opposition to this, they shifted to focusing on higher wages and benefits instead. David Brody, Workers in Industrial America 175, 182, 188 (1980).

litical climate would not allow the bankers a visible role in firing employees or lowering salaries. Prudence would dictate a lowered profile.

German codetermination arose in a capital-poor economy that needed to induce employee commitment. Employees got governance rights and long-term employment in return for committing human "capital" and taking low wages. This economic story fits the facts, but cannot fully explain codetermination, because although *some* firms in American economic history fit that capital-poor picture, codetermined structures nearly *never* arose, and because Japan had a similar period of capital shortage and need for employee commitment, but did not develop codetermination. The most recent leap forward for codetermination was in 1976, *after* the post–World War II reconstruction, that is, after the capital-poor story was most apt. Codetermination was employees' partial, compromised political victory, when German politicians tried to co-opt a revolution from below after World War I and to reduce labor conflict and strikes in the 1970s.

Bismarck and a Stamp Tax

History helps to explain the German boardroom and the powerful German banks in another way. After Bismarck unified Germany, he sought to develop German industry by creating great banks as engines of development.[17] A statist political system facilitated a central bank that provided liquidity to the German banks' long-term investments.[18] These banks naturally expected to oversee the investments made with funds they lent and thus involved themselves in corporate governance. Happenstance helped propel the banks' stock power. The newly unified German state taxed transfers of securities. Stock owners wanted to avoid the taxes; German banks held customers' stock in the bank's name and issued receipts to the retail owners. Then, when one customer sold stock to another customer,

[17] Alexander Gerschenkron, Economic Backwardness in Historical Perspective 14–15 (1962); Rondo Cameron, Banking in the Early Stages of Industrialization (1967).

[18] Richard Tilly, Banking Institutions in Historical Perspective: Germany, Great Britain and the United States in the Nineteenth and Early Twentieth Century, 145 Zeitschrift für die gesamte Staatswissenschaft [Journal of Institutional and Theoretical Economics] 189–209 (1989). While bank-driven industrialization went forward in Germany, the Bank of England would not provide that kind of liquidity to British banks. Id. And as a result of Andrew Jackson's populist-inspired veto of the rechartering of the Second Bank of the United States, the United States in the nineteenth century had no central bank to provide bank liquidity, inducing banks to shun long-term, illiquid investments.

the banks argued that no taxable transfer occurred when the bank crossed the trade internally, because a bank was still the owner of record. The taxing authorities agreed. Thereafter, stock owners preferred to deposit stock with bigger banks, which could best match customers' sales and purchases,[19] thus giving banks control over the proxy machinery.

A Nondemocratic Past

One last aspect of German political history is relevant. For the nineteenth and most of the first half of the twentieth century, democratic politics and its fragmenting tendencies could not affect German intermediaries because Germany was not democratic. This is not to say that financial power *necessarily* clashes with democracy—democracies have concentrated industry and can also have concentrated finance—but it does mean that the features in the United States that fragmented American finance have had less time to affect German intermediaries.

The history of German corporate governance is also partly a transmission of government directions through the bank regulators to the large banks, which implement the directions and get financial protection from the government. (Japanese and German corporate governance and regulation are somewhat similar in this respect.) This statist structure, while again not necessarily at odds with democratic politics, is at odds with American democratic history and its impulse to fragment both concentrations of private economic power and centralized political power.

JAPANESE INTEREST GROUPS

Before World War II, the largest firms in Japan were the zaibatsu, which resembled the U.S. conglomerates of the 1960s, but with family rather than public ownership, at the top. The zaibatsu were tightly connected to large banks, but the families controlled the banks.[20] In 1943, the Japanese military disrupted the system by ordering managers at munitions manufacturers to follow bureaucratic orders rather than shareholder directives and by directing munitions firms to choose a main bank to facilitate the audit-

---

[19] See generally Jacob Riesser, The Great German Banks and Their Concentration, S. Doc. No. 593, 61st Cong., 2d Sess. 618–20 (Morris Jacobson trans., 1911). Riesser does not say whether the large banks lobbied for the tax result, but does say that the result was foreseen when the tax was proposed. The tax also stunted a German securities market, by adding a private cost to some trading. Richard H. Tilly, German Banking, 1850–1914: Development Assistance for the Strong, 15 Journal of European Economic History 113, 126–27 (1986).

[20] William M. Tsutsui, Banking Policy in Japan 5, 11 (1988).

ing of wartime production.[21] In 1948, orders from the Supreme Commander, Allied Powers (SCAP) destroyed that corporate system with directives to break up the zaibatsu, to distribute their stock, and to prohibit bank ownership of big blocks of stock[22] stemming from the "American belief that [democracy] not only required free elections, free speech, and due process, . . . but also the Glass-Steagall Act."[23] Little else better shows law determining corporate structure than law imposed by a military dictatorship in 1943 or law imposed by an occupying military power in 1948.

SCAP barred Japanese banks from owning more than 5 percent of another firm's stock, foreshadowing the U.S. Bank Holding Company Act of 1956. But international politics—communism in China and war in Korea—and fear of Japanese domestic instability changed SCAP's primary goal from pacifying a defeated enemy to building a stable economic ally. So SCAP loosened its grip and decided not to pursue full fragmentation; it watched as Japan fostered close relations between finance and industry. During the following decades, stock relentlessly moved from individuals to banks and insurers, and cross-ownership bound finance and industry together.

Military directives—a type of law—deeply affected modern Japanese firms' ownership structure. The wartime Japanese military orders were practical in origin, but had some anticapitalist ideology behind them. American occupation orders to force Glass-Steagall rules on Japan were not designed to make markets efficient, but to inculcate democracy, and the weaknesses now emerging in Japanese intermediaries are thus partly the delayed result of American democratic ideology.[24]

Oddly enough, American ideology also accounts for why the Japanese banks were not further weakened, but were allowed to keep their large size. SCAP initially planned to dissolve the big banks and end nationwide

---

[21] Masahiko Aoki, The Japanese Firm as a System of Attributes: A Survey and Research Agenda 17–18 (Stanford Center for Economic Policy Research Publication No. 288, 1992). Thus Japan pushed corporate borrowers toward commercial banks and limited savers' options.

[22] See generally J. Mark Ramseyer, Legal Rules in Repeated Deals: Banking in the Shadow of Defection in Japan, 20 Journal of Legal Studies 91, 99–100 and n.21 (1991).

[23] David G. Litt, Jonathan R. Macey, Geoffrey P. Miller, and Edward L. Rubin, Politics, Bureaucracies, and Financial Markets: Bank Entry into Commercial Paper Underwriting in the United States and Japan, 139 University of Pennsylvania Law Review 369, 380 (1990).

[24] Id. at 379–80. Occupation authorities in Germany imposed McFadden, although German authorities viewed it as unwise. When the occupation ended, Germany allowed geographically fragmented banks to merge, which they did. Tsutsui, supra note 20, at 55–56; Rolf Ziegler, Gerhard Reissner, and Donald Bender, Industry and Banking in the German Corporate Network, in Networks of Corporate Power: A Comparative Analysis of Ten Countries 91, 106 (Frans N. Stokman, Rolf Ziegler, and John Scott eds., 1985); Hans A. Adler, The Post-War Reorganization of the German Banking System, 63 Quarterly Journal of Economics 322 (1949).

branching, but changed its mind. Although SCAP did limit bank stock ownership to 5 percent, and did segment commercial from investment banking, the American occupation bureaucracy thought that dissolving the zaibatsu was more important than dissolving the banks; since SCAP's anti-trust analysis found that nine big banks and a fringe of smaller banks pro-vided adequate competition, it thought the American model of financial fragmentation was inapt and thus forced Japan to adopt only the Glass-Steagall rules, and not the McFadden ones.[25] In the United States, politics shattered finance, not industry; in Japan, SCAP broke up Japanese indus-try, not finance.

The incompleteness of financial fragmentation meant that with subtlety, the Japanese could overcome the American-imposed Glass-Steagall rules— by keeping their banks big, by not adopting American passivity rules, and by channeling postwar credit through the banking system. This they did; with neither interest groups nor populism to block such efforts after World War II, the political task was easy. But now, in the 1990s, the banks are doing the heavy lifting in corporate ownership, and the weaken-ing of the banks puts the system under pressure.

Although Japan effectively repealed American efforts at fragmentation by channeling credit through banks, that system faces heavy pressures in the 1990s. The American-imposed segmentation affects Japanese financial intermediaries today in ways it did not in prior decades. The stresses in-clude more than just a weak economy. Current Bank of International Set-tlements' capital standards now make bank stockholding more difficult. Japanese savers and corporate borrowers now have access to nonbank al-ternatives that they previously lacked. Interest rates, previously depressed by the government, are reaching market levels. The American Structural Impediments Initiative seeks to fray the equity ties inside the keiretsu. If these stresses lead banks to sell their stock, they could change the struc-ture of ownership and authority in the large firm.

Interest Group Infighting

To preserve concentrated ownership, Japan could restructure its interme-diaries, but fights among interest groups have stymied a complete restruc-turing.[26] Securities firms see bank underwriting of securities by commer-

---

[25] Tsutsui, supra note 20, at 41–43 (zaibatsu focus); id. at 45–48, 63, 117 (incomplete frag-mentation); id. at 49–53 (SCAP plans to dissolve large banks); id. at 52, 119 (MacArthur de-cides banks are secondary).

[26] Elliot Gewirtz and Clark Taber, Fundamental Issues in Japanese Financial System Re-form, 7 Review of Banking and Financial Services 135, 141 (1991); Litt, Macey, Miller, and Rubin, supra note 23, at 404–22; James Sterngold, A Japanese-Style "Old Boy" Network, N.Y. Times, June 7, 1991, at D1.

cial banks as dangerous;[27] commercial bankers, not surprisingly, see no danger.[28] Interest group infighting, not indecision over the best means of achieving efficiency, explains the bureaucracies' slowness in deregulation:

> [T]he walls that have divided various types of financial institutions since World War II still stand, because of the tenacity of entrenched interests. . . . City banks, for example, will be barred from making long-term loans in the Euroyen market until the long-term credit banks and trust banks receive suitable compensation, such as expanded securities powers. . . . It is the political power of these various groups rather than economic rationale that protects them. . . .[29]

Thus, the weakened Japanese commercial banks may be unable to prevent ownership fragmentation unless they get new authority to run affiliated intermediaries, which the interest groups so far have impeded. If full fragmentation does come to Japan, politics—this time, interest group politics—will play a role.

The securities firms want to preserve one part of the current system— segmentation. Managers, however, want to preserve another part—cross-holdings, which protect them from takeovers and usually give them large, friendly shareholders. If banks cannot continue their role in the keiretsu, managers want a substitute, not the unknown. Their representatives argue that "any hard-landing approach which restricts . . . cross-holding . . . risk[s] . . . demolishing the base of [the] Japanese management systems, *and will never be accepted by a national consensus and must be avoided by all means.*"[30]

The History of Fragmented Banking

Political history helps explain why the U.S. and Japanese banking systems look so different. A half-century ago, when both nations had bank crises, politics led each to react differently. Japan then had thousands of small

[27] [Japanese] Securities and Exchange Council, How Basic System Regarding Capital Market Ought to Be Reformed 17–18 (June 19, 1991) (unpublished report).

[28] [Japanese] Financial System Research Council, On a New Japanese Finance System (June 25, 1991) (unpublished report).

[29] Frances McCall Rosenbluth, Financial Politics in Contemporary Japan 94–95 (1989).

[30] Foundation for Advanced Information and Research, Japan, A Perspective on Japanese Merger and Acquisition from an International Viewpoint 23 (Sept. 1990) (unpublished report) (emphasis added); see also Ryutaro Komiya, The Japanese Economy: Trade, Industry, and Government 255–56 (1990); Michael J. Gerlach, Alliance Capitalism: The Social Organization of Japanese Business 117 (1992) (Japanese executives opposed to ending cross-holding). Changes in Japan's pension funds may create a huge emerging pool of capital. Rosenbluth, supra note 29, at 75. Whether intermediaries or managers control these funds may determine the future of Japanese corporate governance.

banks, but lacked a populist, antibank ethos: "Since the [Meiji] restoration . . . [t]here has never been any movement in Japan strong enough to produce a Sherman Act, . . . a Money Trust Investigation, a Federal Trade Commission, or a Securities and Exchange Commission such as developed in the United States. . . ."[31] During the 1927 economic crisis, many small banks were badly run and failed, while the large ones were fairly well run and stable. Depositors ran off to the government's savings system, the large banks survived, and the government encouraged mergers among the small banks,[32] thereby concentrating banking. Today, Japan no longer has thousands of small banks.[33]

The 1933 American banking crisis had a different political result. The United States, like Japan, had thousands of small banks. When many faced collapse in 1933, they pressed Congress for federal deposit insurance at the same time Glass-Steagall separation was on the agenda. The interest group impetus for extensive deposit insurance has been the political power of small country banks. They got it enacted, got it extended, and beat back attempts to get it under control. Without it, American banking would have become more concentrated as many deposits would have run off from small, weak country banks to larger, often stronger, money center banks.[34] Recognizing this, the large banks supported Glass-Steagall separation because in 1933 they were not making money in the securities business and they hoped this support would deter deposit insurance. The large banks miscalculated, however, and Congress passed Glass-Steagall *and* deposit insurance, which to this day continues to prop up thousands of small banks. Politics subsidized the small banks, and the United States still has thousands of them.

A populist, antibank ethos is historically absent in Japan.[35] This is partly because until the postwar era, Japan was not a democratic country where such opinions could much influence government decisions. But consider the current turmoil in the Japanese economy. Many firms are in mature product markets and have substantial free cash flow, which the firms can

---

[31] T. A. Bisson, Zaibatsu Dissolution in Japan 29 (1954) (quoting U.S. Department of State, Pub. No. 2628, Report of the Mission on Japanese Combines, Far Eastern Series 21 [1946]).

[32] Frances Rosenbluth, Bank Consolidation in Prewar Japan: The Market for Regulation under a Non-Sovereign Diet 10–14, 17–25 (March 1991) (unpublished manuscript).

[33] Tsutsui, supra note 20, at 3–4, 11; Juro Teranishi, Financial System and the Industrialization of Japan: 1900–1970, Banca Nazionale del Lavoro Quarterly Review, Sept. 1990, at 309, 329–30; Juro Teranishi, Availability of Safe Assets and the Process of Bank Concentration in Japan, 25 Economic Development and Cultural Change, Apr. 1977, at 447, 448–49, 462, 465, 469. Even earlier, after a nineteenth-century bond failure, the Ministry of Finance sought to make banking somewhat more concentrated. Gary Saxonhouse, Mechanisms for Technology Transfer in Japanese Economic History, 12 Managerial and Decision Economics 83, 85 (1991).

[34] See supra chapter 7.

[35] Bisson, supra note 31, at 29.

retain, freeing themselves from the bankers, who first gained influence because they were the necessary providers of now-unneeded cash for new investments. Two tests of the current structure now loom. First, will stockholding banks keep their stock, and will they induce portfolio firms to use the cash well? Second, if the banks succeed but make managers and employees unhappy, say, by ending lifetime employment, a major test of the political theory will arise. In the United States, the disadvantaged groups would try to shift decisionmaking from the market to the political arena, appealing to the legislature to redo the economic result. While in Japan that appeal might fail, politics there is not so different that we should expect disgruntled silence from those affected. We shall see.

This broad-brush picture shows political forces shaping German and Japanese corporate structures—forces that differ in both kind and strength from those that shaped American financial intermediaries and American corporate governance. The point is not that the German and Japanese systems are less affected by politics than the American one. German codetermination in the face of revolution is hardly apolitical. The Japanese decision after 1927 to concentrate the banking system was not apolitical. Nations with a feudal past can accept centralized power, and then politics affects how that power is wielded; in the United States, whether concentrated power should exist was disputed. The point is that different historical politics led to different financial structures, and different financial structures led to different corporate structures. Today, populism in Germany weakens the power of German bankers in the boardroom through formal codetermination and the informal effects of popular resentment; interest group infighting in Japan and the American-imposed legacy of partial fragmentation limit the power of Japanese bankers in industry.

CHAPTER 15

Trends in the United States

IN THE 1980s a tidal wave of mergers and leveraged buyouts tore apart and rearranged many large American firms. Today, the structure of American intermediaries and their role in corporate governance are in upheaval. Some intermediaries seek new, active roles. Regulators are also reexamining old patterns. The Treasury Department proposed ambitious plans, which stalled in Congress, to mix banking and commerce in ways that have been volatile in American history. The SEC reduced some restrictions on institutions' governance role. The 1990s trends for institutional investors may well be the result of trying to bridge the huge fault line that separated America's intermediaries from its managers.

Ownership is concentrating. True, that concentration is weak and pale, especially compared to that in Japan and Germany, but measured against an American baseline, the change is not minor. Institutions are also becoming more active, in three dimensions. They have been pressing managers at poorly performing firms more actively than before, either through direct contact or through pressure on the board. They have sought to turn back some legal impediments. And a few new-style intermediaries have emerged—Berkshire Hathaway, Corporate Partners—with Japanese-style or German-style blocks, suggesting that a new ownership pattern may be viable.

The German and Japanese systems are also changing. The German system depends on voting of proxies by banks, and there seems little economic reason for banks to make heroic transactional or political efforts on behalf of those for whom they vote proxies. The economic pressures in Japan on main bank stockholding seem great, and without other affiliated intermediaries—such as bank-controlled pensions, trusts, or mutual funds—it is hard to see how the system *in its present form* can continue. Yet unnoticed in this debate is the prospect that some American firms will evolve—weakly and oddly—toward German- and Japanese-style ownership. Functions historically moved persistently *into* American intermediaries. The next natural "stage" in American corporate finance might be intermediaries in the boardroom, or intermediaries electing directors whose loyalty runs to the intermediaries, not managers.[1] The one American inter-

---

[1] Cf. Robert Clark, The Four Stages of Capitalism, 94 Harvard Law Review 561 (1981); Ronald J. Gilson and Reinier Kraakman, Reinventing the Outside Director: An Agenda for Institutional Investors, 43 Stanford Law Review 863 (1991).

mediary vaguely like the main bank and universal bank is Berkshire Hathaway, an insurer whose big blocks—and legal authority to take them—are *recent* acquisitions.

Concentration Trends

Institutions owned only 8 percent of the stock of the largest American firms in 1950. Now they own half, but in small, *unconcentrated* blocks. The five largest holders rarely together own much more than 5% of the largest U.S. firms. The rarities are mainly the large blocks held by Berkshire Hathaway.[2] Even with their weaker holdings, some institutions have been active, seeking to elect directors, making shareholder proposals, petitioning the SEC to loosen restraints on their activity.

Aggregate concentration already makes U.S. ownership look like a pale imitation of its foreign counterparts. The top twenty-five institutional investors on average vote 16 percent of the stock of the largest twenty-five American corporations.[3] While the U.S. concentration trends tended to slow down in the early 1990s, and the U.S. concentration is a far cry from the five banks in Japan that vote 20 percent of stock, or the three in Germany that vote 40 percent, large firm ownership is no longer that of an atomized Berle-Means corporation. True, because twenty-five stockholders cannot as readily coordinate as can five, the lack of a "leader" with a big block may mean that nothing will happen. But even current concentration levels open up possibilities: they may concentrate more, or find new technologies for coordination. The United States is now in an intermediate stage, whose future is uncertain.

Activity Trends

Institutional investors have tried to affect firms. Although the activity disproportionately comes from public pension funds, the acquiescence of the nonpublic institutions, and occasionally their actions, has brought about occasional change. Institutional investors targeted General Motors, a poor performer during the early 1990s. Two large public pension funds wrote to the GM board, asking to be apprised of the procedures the board

---

[2] Coca-Cola had a five-shareholder concentration level of 20 percent, due, not surprisingly, to legal anomalies: holdings by Berkshire Hathaway, an insurance holding company operating outside the norm, and by a bank exempt from the general provisions of the Bank Holding Company Act.

[3] Carolyn Kay Brancato et al., Institutional Investor Concentration of Economic Power: A Study of Institutional Holdings and Voting Authority in U.S. Publicly Held Corporations, at tbl. 7 (Sept. 12, 1991).

planned to pick a successor to Roger Smith, the then-incumbent chairman of the board. The board rebuffed them, but the institutions persisted, apparently continuing pressure behind the scenes on GM's independent directors, leading ultimately to the explosive boardroom events of 1992, when Robert Stempel, the successor chairman to Roger Smith, resigned under pressure, a new generation of leadership was appointed to high positions, and the position of CEO and chairman of the board was split.

This split has often been recommended by corporate governance reformers in the United States, but rarely achieved. Eighty percent of American CEOs also chair their boards. Of the remaining 20 percent, most lack a truly independent chair, because the chair is often the former CEO, taking the chair's spot for a few years to ease into retirement.[4] A chair independent of management is always achieved in Germany, where the CEO cannot serve on the supervisory board, and is roughly achieved in Japan, where the CEO must meet with large stockholders in Presidents' Council meetings. GM's authority structure is flattening at the top. If the GM coup starts a trend, the U.S. corporate future may resemble the foreign corporate present.

Concentrating ownership and the hope of effective action have led institutions to focus on political activity. In Pennsylvania, institutions fought to beat back the state legislature's powerful antitakeover law, which would have had the effect of thwarting many institutional proxy efforts for Pennsylvania companies, but they were largely unsuccessful. They were more successful with the SEC, to whom they proposed a change in proxy rules to allow institutions to talk with one another without public filings. Although the Business Roundtable—a managerial lobbying group—resisted, the SEC agreed to many of the institutional proposals.

Last is the emergence in the 1980s of Berkshire Hathaway, a Nebraska insurance holding company, that obtained changes in Nebraska law in the early 1980s to enable focused investments in concentrated blocks. The blocks, frequently of 10 percent or so of a firm's stock, allow Hathaway's senior executives, usually Warren Buffett or Charles Munger, to sit on the board. In a crisis they intervene, as Salomon Brothers' management found out.

THE DIMLY LIT AMERICAN CORPORATE FUTURE?

Although the modest concentration trends of the past decades and some of the increasing institutional activity suggest that the United States is moving, however slightly, toward the corporate structures in Germany and

---

[4] Joann S. Lublin, Other Concerns Are Likely to Follow GM in Splitting Posts of Chairman and CEO, Wall Street Journal, Nov. 4, 1992, at B1, col. 3; see Ira M. Millstein, The Evolution of the Certifying Board, Business Lawyer, Aug. 1993, at 1485.

Japan, the gap will, absent an economic or corporate crisis, be wide for some time. First, to look similar, ownership and voting would have to be much more concentrated, and the concentration trend seems to have leveled off in the early 1990s. Few of the very large American firms, other than those in which Berkshire Hathaway has a stake, have a large stockholder inside the governance system; all of the Japanese firms and most of the German ones already do. The rapid rise of Berkshire Hathaway after becoming free from traditional insurance portfolio rules suggests that more large blocks are plausible. But it has not happened yet.

Second, the Japanese system has a large block of cross-holdings *by* firms (and other institutions) of their institutional owners. Cross-holdings, with several institutions and industrial firms owning one another's stock, can help to mitigate institutional opportunism; the intermediaries can watch the industrial firms, and the industrial firms can watch the intermediaries and, if need be, try to form alliances to thwart their opportunism. That kind of cross-ownership is absent in the United States. The closest parallel here to cross-holdings is that many of the emerging institutional investors are pension fund managers. But American pension funds really differ from foreign cross-holdings, because thus far corporate managers dominate pension managers, not the other way around. Power-sharing has not yet become important. Few corporate managers want their pension people to monitor others any more than the managers wish themselves to be monitored; private pension managers are rarely governance activists. Reconstruction of private pension funds—which own more than 20 percent of the American stock market—would require either a social change, such as the move from defined-benefit plans toward defined-contribution plans, which weaken managerial control, or managers who want active pension funds, either to beat back other challenges or to achieve some other goal, such as better connecting different parts of the production process. All of these are possible; none now are certain. Next, I speculate how the corporate crises of the 1980s nearly led managers to *seek* an ownership structure similar to that prevailing abroad.

CHAPTER 16

An American Crossroads

MANAGERS MIGHT have *sought* financiers with big blocks of stock and a voice in corporate governance in the mid-1980s, when managers were seeking to stabilize their firms and boardrooms against takeovers. Managers and owners were at a crossroads: in seeking stability, managers could have shut owners out, or they could have stabilized the boardroom with big blocks. Managers' first efforts to stabilize their world were attempts to beat back hostile takeovers; managers' legal defenders in the early 1980s invented financial and legal devices designed to ward off hostile takeovers. Some devices were struck down by courts, but the most potent—mainly the poison pill—were upheld and then widely used.[1] State legislatures in the later 1980s endorsed the pill and added to management's takeover defenses.

Had these transactional, judicial, and legislative defenses failed, managers would have looked for other ways to stabilize the firm at the top, and one likely way would have been to seek out "white squires": friendly firms that took large, blocking positions. Indeed, many of Berkshire Hathaway's large positions and Tisch's position in CBS came to them because the targets in a hostile takeover *wanted them* in as big stockholders to block the hostile offerors.[2] The antitakeover defenses in the Polaroid battle are illustrative of target management's creating a similar kind of big block intermediary to stymie a hostile takeover.[3] There, to thwart the takeover, Polaroid used an ESOP, an employee stock ownership plan, which, like a pension plan, is for the employees' financial benefit and owns the firm's own stock.

---

[1] Moran v. Household Management, 500 A.2d 1346 (Del. Sup. Ct. 1985). *Moran* held that a board issuing a poison pill did not breach duties to shareholders; later cases weighed whether target management had to yank the pill in the face of a tender offer at above the market's stock price.

[2] David A. Vise, CBS Loses $114 Million in Quarter, A Record, Washington Post, Nov. 13, 1985, at E1 ("Loews Corp. Chairman Laurence A. Tisch was elected to the CBS board . . . [Loews's stock ownership] is expected to bring stability to a company that has been the subject of intense takeover speculation"); Vineeta Anand, Warren Buffett Effect: A Quick Jump in Stock Prices, Investor's Daily, Aug. 23, 1991, at 8 ("In September 1987, Buffett infused $700 million into Salomon, then facing a takeover threat from Ronald Perelman. He was rewarded with two seats on the board. . . .").

[3] See Shamrock Holdings, Inc. v. Polaroid Corp., 709 F. Supp. 1311 (D. Del. 1989); see also Donovan v. Bierwirth, 754 F.2d 1049 (2d Cir. 1985) (Grumman management tries to expand ESOP to fight takeover).

If enough of the stock were in the ESOP and the ESOP stock stood against the takeover, the hostile takeover could not succeed. Managers do not always favor ESOPs, because an ESOP is an alternative power center, holding a big block of the firm's stock. (And by tying up employee wealth in the firm where the employee works, the employee becomes under-diversified.) Although managers often pick the ESOP trustee (and sometimes the ESOP's vote is passed through to the employee-stockholders), and hence the managers do not expect trouble in the takeover, trustees have duties (and the employee-stockholders have their own interests) that can put them at odds with the managers. But when the managers are under the takeover gun, they have found ESOPs to be better than the alternative. In the Polaroid case, by putting enough stock into presumably friendly hands, management beat back the unwanted offer.

Polaroid was not aberrational: ESOPs that put a big block of votes in managerial hands lead to a fall in stock price;[4] managers' motivation for establishing ESOPs has often been to create a shield against takeovers.[5] Managers may prefer complete autonomy, but when faced with a bigger threat to their own autonomy, they can accept a big ESOP as the lesser evil.

Managers in the 1980s were scrambling for takeover protection. If clever lawyers had not invented the poison pill and if political forces had not led legislatures to validate and to extend that takeover defense, managers would have sought alternatives. A few appeared: the "white squires" that Salomon, CBS, and a few others invited in. Others sought to turbocharge boards of directors as a substitute for takeovers.[6] If managers had not found other antitakeover techniques, there is reason to think that

---

[4] Saeyoung Chang and David Mayers, Managerial Vote Ownership and Shareholder Wealth, 32 Journal of Financial Economics 103 (1992). Even if stock prices rise with an ESOP—as happens when ESOPs give managers small voting blocks, id.—the entrenchment effect is still probably there. ESOPs should not hurt employee performance. They compensate employees indirectly out of the U.S. Treasury, because of the tax benefits (deductible to the firm, but not taxable immediately to the employee). They also affect the price of takeovers; managers' enhanced blocking ability decreased takeovers' frequency, but increased the price of those that occur. Compensation, taxation, and takeover premiums make an ESOP push up stock price, even if it entrenches the managers.

[5] Joseph R. Blasi and Douglas L. Kruse, The New Owners: The Mass Emergence of Employee Ownership in Public Companies and What It Means to American Business (1991).

[6] Winthrop Knowlton and Ira M. Millstein, Can the Board of Directors Help the American Corporation Earn the Immortality It Holds So Dear?, in the U.S. Business Corporation—An Institution in Transition 169 (1988); Ira M. Millstein, The Responsibility of the Institutional Investor in Corporate Management, in the Battle for Corporate Control: Shareholder Rights, Stakeholder Interests, and Managerial Responsibilities 67, 73 (Arnold W. Sametz and James L. Bicksler eds., 1991). A shield in the 1980s for managers from takeovers, activist boards, and activist shareholders became more threatening to managers when takeovers declined in the 1990s.

they would then have systematically sought big blockholders as takeover protection.

The origins of the Japanese cross-holdings and changes in Germany support this hypothesis. The Japanese system does not in its entirety go back deep into Japanese history; many cross-holdings between firms and financial institutions arose in the 1960s, when Japanese firms were at a crossroads, similar to that facing American firms in the 1980s. Stock, which the American authorities had distributed broadly after breaking up the zaibatsu, was not in concentrated, friendly hands. Many Japanese managers feared that joint ventures with American firms would end up with the American firm's owning the Japanese firm. At the same time, corporate Japan feared that the Japanese government would sell stock from financially distressed brokerage houses; this risk and depressed stock prices made managers fearful of American-style takeovers.[7] To prevent this, managers sought to put big blocks of their stock into friendly hands.

In Germany, the prospect of American-style takeovers arose in the 1990s, inducing Dresdner Bank, Allianz Insurance Company, and Hoechst, the huge chemical firm, to develop major cross-shareholding among themselves and others.[8] German managers have behaved inconsistently toward banker control of the proxy system. They sometimes seemed to dislike it, but acquiesced when it helped them stifle takeovers. Thus to beat back takeovers, many German firms sought and got capped voting—no shareholder may cast more than 5 percent of the votes, no matter how much stock it owns. The German firms have not sought to impose a similar cap on banks' voting their proxies. No beneficial owner can vote more than 5 percent (if the cap is at 5 percent), but the bank usually can vote all of its custodial holding in the firm with capped voting, because each custodial block is less than 5 percent. Keeping the cap off the bank's custodial votes keeps the banker powerful, presumably to managers' discomfort, but if the bankers vote with managers, it also helps to thwart takeovers, to managers' relief. This kind of stockholder "caucus" through the banks also counterbalances employees' voice on the codetermined board, which can also be a relief to managers. Managers, it seems, choose to have large influential blocks of stock controlled by financial intermediaries when they fear hostile takeovers or want to balance off employees' voices.

The analogy is obvious. Lacking American antitakeover technology, German managers retained the powerful voting blocks of the banks and through capped voting reduced the chance of another block arising. Lack-

---

[7] Jack McDonald, Origins and Implications of Cross-Holdings in Japanese Companies, at 1 (Graduate School of Business, Stanford University Technical Note No. 79, 1991).

[8] Hans Otto Eglau, Allianz/Dresdner Bank—Vermachtet und Verschachtelt [Empowered and Interconnected], Die Zeit, Aug. 16, 1991, at 19; Andrew Joncus, Continental AG Shareholders Deliver Pirelli Another Blow, Wall Street Journal Europe, July 6, 1992, at 4.

ing American antitakeover technology, Japanese managers increased cross-ownership. American CEOs would have sought big blocks, if they had feared something worse, such as a wave of takeovers, and lacked a better technology for avoiding it. Institutions or other firms with big blocks would have been a natural extension of the current boardroom, which is filled with directors who are the CEO's professional friends, usually CEOs from other firms. The difference is that these friends neither own a big piece of the firms on whose boards they sit nor are employed by firms owning a big piece.

What would have been the mechanisms bringing big-block ownership to the United States? Financial institutions might have been a source of big blocks, and managers might have sought to overcome the legal and financial barriers to the big blocks. Which financial institution would have been best for managers? In Japan, extensive cross-ownership among the firms themselves binds the firms together; one-third of the cross-owned corporate stock is among nonfinancial firms, frequently in supplier-customer relationships.[9] Presumably American firms seeking stability would have sought to trade big blocks with other firms, before seeking big blocks from potentially less friendly financial institutions.

This could have been where private pension funds would have entered as the biggest source of cross-holdings. Operating firms are poorly suited to holding large blocks of stock. They usually want to use their capital for other purposes. Moreover, American firms are taxed on their direct stock holdings: in the 1930s, Congress passed a dividends-received tax, which today imposes a net tax of roughly 10 percent on the dividends a corporation receives from another corporation. Congress passed the tax not primarily to raise revenue, but to discourage corporate complexes. The effect of the tax is that cross-holdings must yield advantages exceeding the amount payable to the tax collector. The obvious advantage to managers of using pension funds for cross-holdings is that pension funds are untaxed. With tax and capital markets considerations raising the cost of direct cross-holdings, managers would have cast their eyes on their big pension funds as the source of friendly cross-holdings.[10]

Whether large cross-holdings would have helped improve corporate governance is debatable. In the short run, cross-holdings would have insulated managers from immediate threat, meaning that the American result *might* have been mutual insulation, as the Japanese result *sometimes* is. But since the American antitakeover result was substantial insulation, there is little reason to think insulation would have been much more se-

---

[9] Yusaku Futatsugi, What Share Cross-Holdings Mean for Corporate Management, Economic Eye, Spring 1990, at 17, 18.

[10] Managers might have sought to end the tax friction had it been to their advantage to remove it.

vere. Big blocks as antitakeover devices might have led the blockholder to take seats on the insulated board and later take action if performance weakened.

The doctrinal and other barriers to big blocks, real though they are, would, I believe, have fallen quickly had a united phalanx of CEOs and institutions both wanted them to fall. Could that still happen?

Maybe. In the early 1990s, the SEC changed the proxy rules, despite managerial opposition, to allow for a greater shareholder voice. Shareholders can denounce managers or their policies in a public round robin, making managers uncomfortable. Institutional investors now have other plausible ways to coordinate themselves to pressure managers.[11] If managers cannot take the heat and cannot stymie the institutions with new legal or social barriers, then they will seek the next best alternative, which might well be to try to select who their stockholders will be,[12] ask them to take large positions as semipermanent owners, and invite them into the boardroom. If that happens, we will see that the legal barriers are weak, and that when the public is uninterested, legislatures can repeal legal barriers quickly if they get in the way of managers and institutions united to push them aside. And the ownership structure prevailing in Germany and Japan, a structure that now seems alien, distant, and strange to American managers and financiers, would come quickly to the American public firm.

[11] John C. Wilcox, A Proxy Solicitor's Perspective on the New Communications Rules, Corp. Guide (P-H) ¶4.1, at 1 (Feb. 15, 1993).

[12] David Greising, Hunting Investors Who Will Go the Distance, Business Week, Nov. 9, 1992, at 101, 102.

Part V

POLICY RECOMMENDATIONS

IS CONCENTRATED ownership beneficial? Is foreign corporate governance a source of competitive advantage? Although my basic goal in this book is to show that we need a political theory to fully explain corporate forms, the next obvious inquiry is normative: should U.S. firms have a more concentrated ownership structure? While the analysis here is complex, the bottom line is simple: there is not enough evidence to support using law to *force* concentrated ownership structures, but there are enough tantalizing possibilities that we should permit them, by loosening some American restrictions.

Neither I nor anyone else will offer a corporate governance silver bullet to cure whatever ills afflict American industry: corporate governance—even if we knew how to achieve the perfect system—is not the key to economic performance and competitiveness. While extremely pathological governance, such as that prevailing in the former Soviet Union and Eastern Europe for most of this century, will disable firms, within the range of differences about which we are speaking, macroeconomic policies, competition, industry structure, and the education and motivation of managers and employees affect competitiveness and productivity more than governance alone does. Good overall performance will be difficult to trace to governance; conversely, poor performance does not mean that governance is the problem.

Corporate governance should matter least in highly competitive markets with little fixed, long-term capital; managers who seriously err will be out of business. Although corporate governance is rarely primary, it does matter when the other means of accountability are weak, as in concentrated markets of firms with heavy capital; managers who err there will not face the consequences of error immediately, either because oligopoly provides slack, or because with heavy, long-lived capital in place, the firm can slowly waste away. Since many firms have long-term, fixed capital, and some U.S. markets are still oligopolistic, governance, although secondary, is rarely irrelevant. Governance can be seen as competition's assistant; good governance speeds along competitive adaptation; bad governance slows it down.

Institutional strength has obvious defects. It creates severe conflicts of interest, particularly if the institution sells something to the firm in which it owns stock. It could deteriorate into mutual managerial self-protection and might dampen entrepreneurial leadership; committees are not entrepreneurs. Some of the bans on institutional blocks were due to perceptions, particularly during the New Deal, that institutions abused their power when they had it. Even if these perceptions were exaggerated, they were not made up, and there is no guarantee that institutions would not abuse power if allowed to have it. Hence, were there deregulation, it would have to be cautious, slow, and with an eye on the downside risks, not just the upside potential.

And enhanced institutional power may lead to calls for enhanced government involvement in economic planning, which has tended not to work well in the United States, and may yet prove to work poorly abroad. These imponderables are so large that any policy conclusion must be tentative and theoretical, showing only that there are benefits that might offset the obvious costs. In the next three chapters I analyze three roles for institutions in corporate governance: (1) holding managers accountable; (2) combating the stock markets' supposed short-term tendencies; and (3) coordinating the long-term relational investments of corporations that need to do business together.

In the end the normative story is simple: since no corporate governance form seems obviously superior for all firms at all times, we ought to allow competition among governance systems. A society does not have to choose between securities markets and institutional influence. Some firms can use one, others another. The two can compete. By discouraging alternatives to the Berle-Means format, American law and political history have discouraged this competition.

CHAPTER 17

Managers as the Problem?

INSTITUTIONS ARE UNFIT to run enterprises; the hopes for them must be more modest. The model institutional overseer would not micromanage the firm from day to day, but be ready to make changes during crisis and hold the managers accountable during the interim. Enhanced institutional voice could improve managerial performance, not by directing day-to-day operations, but rather (1) by enhancing managerial accountability, (2) by personifying shareholders (which could make managerial disloyalty psychologically harder), and (3) by improving the flow of information *to* senior managers from outside the firm.

In this chapter, we analyze the basics: making managers more accountable. This matters most for big firms that have large sunk organizational and physical capital and compete in imperfect product markets. For these firms, the other mechanisms of managerial control—product market and capital market competition, for example—are weak, and internal controls become more important. Upheavals in the boardrooms at GM, Sears, American Express, Westinghouse, Kodak, and IBM show that once-strong firms can slowly fail without product markets quickly forcing improvement. Had these boardrooms been better structured to have directors and managers see what was coming, the slide might have been arrested earlier than it was.

Boardroom problems did *not* create these firms' problems; changing markets, technologies, and regulations did. But governance—how those at the top of the firm react—could, were it better, have influenced whether those firms handled adversity well and prospered, or weakened. Derivatively, governance influenced whether the firms employees continued to make a good living, whether the firm's communities were stable, and whether the firm's customers had to find new suppliers.

ACCOUNTABILITY

American managers have often not been held accountable for their performance. Allowing enhanced institutional voice could increase that accountability; it could work if the institutions did not become overlords. Managers, who would tell institutions (or more accurately, tell the institutions' boardroom representatives) what the firm was doing, would have much autonomy; institutions would not direct them. Managers' obligation to justify their plans and results to institutions with an economic interest in the firm, would make managers more accountable. Anyone who has had to justify plans and actions to knowledgeable people knows that it clarifies and improves work, even when one knows both that one's job is secure and that those knowledgeable people will not redirect one's plans.

Institutions would know the firm and its internal workings so that in the event of a crisis, they would not need time to move up the learning curve, but could get involved immediately. Managers would have their chance, and if they failed, the intermediaries would intervene. Managers, seeking to maintain their autonomy, would try to avoid the crises that lead to institutional intervention.

Accountability is the most visible potential benefit of an enhanced voice for shareholders, but suffers from an obvious defect. Whatever problems afflict managers might merely be "kicked upstairs" and afflict the institutions. Firms' costs in aligning managers with stockholders would be transformed to the institutions' costs in aligning their boardroom agents with their own owners' goals. A shift to institutions as overlords would shift all of the managers' defects. A partial shift to empowered but usually noninterventionist institutions would, in this view, merely mean that the problems would shift only partly. This defect is one more reason why alternative structures will not be a silver bullet to cure industrial ills.

Still, there is theory to tell us that the movement of agency problems from one place (the firm) to another (the institution) need not be a wash, without economic benefit, because *internal* governance mechanisms can improve performance. Organizations can separate management and control functions internally by (1) using a hierarchy in which a subordinate initiates and a superior ratifies and monitors; (2) using a board that seriously reviews top managers; and (3) mutual monitoring across decisionmakers who do not jointly make the decision.[1] Increasing institutional voice has the potential to make each of these "internal" improvements. While a board of directors could provide all these functions—and often does—the theory behind enhanced institutional voice here is that by coupling the directors' formal duties with an economic interest (the stock held by their "backers"), directors would perform these functions better.

This kind of "loose" oversight corresponds to that in the German and Japanese structures. Contrary to conventional wisdom, bank ownership in Germany and Japan did not regularly shift control from managers to banks, but led to power-sharing. Day to day, the banker-shareholders do

---

[1] Michael C. Jensen and Clifford W. Smith, Stockholder, Manager and Creditor Interests: Applications of Agency Theory, in Recent Advances in Corporate Finance 93 (Edward I. Altman and Marti G. Subrahmanyan eds., 1985).

not run the firm; they intervene in crises and try to hold managers account-able in the interim. German supervisory boards meet only a few times a year, usually without a searching agenda, and Japanese monthly Presi-dents' Council meetings involve so many firms that no one firm will usu-ally be the focus of attention. Although neither arrangement facilitates a detailed review of senior managers, they both enable timely crisis manage-ment and big-picture, ongoing review. Moreover, in neither nation does a single intermediary often hold a dominating voting block; to oust manag-ers, several big owners must coalesce. Without a new dominating interme-diary, there does not have to be a new, focused sore point in governance.

Although mutual protection could make monitoring meaningless, the data on executive turnover show that German and Japanese ownership does not deter removal of executives when performance slackens; involun-tary resignations increase when the Japanese economy weakens.[2] This be-lies assertions that the big stockholders insulate managers from removal. The question remains whether these removals occur fast enough or in the right circumstances, and whether the removals actually improve corporate performance. Although the foreign results suggest some improvement in accountability, they are hardly dispositive, and whether or not the foreign structures improve managerial performance without creating greater eco-nomic costs is not determinative for what the United States needs to do.

PERSONIFYING SHAREHOLDERS

American managers owe fiduciary duties to an abstraction, a faceless stock market. Personification could improve performance. Loyalty to real people may motivate better than legally mandated loyalty to an abstraction. That is, if CEOs and senior managers must constantly interact with people from stockholding institutions, they should feel greater peer pressure, guilt about shirking, more camaraderie, and more empathy toward stockholding institutions, whom they would start to see as coworkers. These psychologi-cal shifts could improve performance.[3] A distant analog: Sociologists found that few Americans soldiers in World War II fought "for freedom," "for the American way," or "against aggression"; motivation came not from these abstract ideals, but from loyalty to peers in the platoon and fear of embarrassment in front of them.[4] Perhaps such loyalty and fear of embar-

[2] See supra chapter 11.

[3] See Eugene Kandel and Edward P. Lazear, Peer Pressure and Partnerships, 100 Journal of Political Economy 801 (1992). The risk, of course, is that personification could lead to a fail-ure to hold managers accountable for their mistakes.

[4] John Keegan, The Face of Battle 50–53, 72–73 (1976). While this is a male-oriented anal-ogy, I suspect some of this sociology is not just for males.

rassment can motive senior managers. Moreover, CEOs may more willingly hurt an anonymous stockholder, whose needs are not vivid and present, than they would hurt a cohort. Isolated CEOs, on the other hand, could see shareholders not as friendly institutions expecting a profit, but as too distant to merit loyalty or respect.

IMPROVING DECISIONS

Increased managerial accountability is not the only benefit. Organizational theory suggests that complexity reduces an individual's ability both to comprehend all that is necessary and to avoid bias from outmoded experience. In a modern, complex economic system, information is dispersed; no individual or staff can have all the information needed for decisionmaking. Networks can do better, the theory goes, than any one individual CEO or any one headquarters, neither of which can, for firms in technologically complex and fast-moving industries, assimilate all the information needed for critical decisions. The problem here is neither that the CEO will be systematically uninformed of technological change nor that the institutions will be systematically better informed, but that building informational networks—institutional and industrial boardroom representatives with knowledge of what is happening elsewhere—could improve the flow of information *into* the firm. Moreover, since a decisionmaker's biases are often invisible to the decisionmaker, a single individual will do worse than a network of decisionmaking, which reduces error,[5] similar to the way that the members of a good law firm with many high-quality people in overlapping fields can cooperate, converse, and get the job done better than a lawyer of equal quality working alone.

This helps explain why institutional voice may not just replace one problem with another problem, as in the case of the conglomerate headquarters, which monitored managers in the subsidiaries but then became a problem because the headquarters people began building a bigger empire, which eventually exceeded the headquarters' monitoring ability. Rather than replacing the CEO with a new centralized decisionmaking authority, enhanced institutional voice could improve the firm because institutions could use big blocks to get more interested parties to participate in the decisionmaking at the top. Better information would flow to the top of the firm.

The problems of misinformation and bias can be generalized. Market transactions have costs; command and hierarchy replace market costs with organizational costs. Relative cost determines organizational structure;

---

[5] See Raaj K. Sah, Fallibility in Human Organizations and Political Systems, 5 Journal of Economic Perspectives 67, 69–71 (1991).

firms arise when a hierarchical structure provides a more efficient means of organizing than transactions in the marketplace.[6] A mixed system of partial integration would permit hybrids that in theory could perform better than either pure type.

Changing underlying economic conditions could now make hybrids more important than they once were. Increasing complexity of information is one. New theories of firm organization describe command and control hierarchy as poorly adapted to today's continual information shifts and technological changes.[7] Although the American pyramid of decisionmaking worked well when mass production of slowly changing products was typical, the difficulties of producing today's complex products in rapidly changing markets may make a different, flatter authority structure at the top better.

———

The point is neither that more accountability is needed for all American managers, that personification is a proven benefit, that the foreign firms are working better, that all American industry has now moved into a state of informational complexity where networks can bring better decision-making to the top, nor that institutions would not create any new problems. The point is that there are enough possibilities in enhancing managerial performance that we should want to see how competition among organizational forms works out. The Berle-Means firm is good at some tasks, and concentrated ownership might be good at others. One form may be especially good at entrepreneurial innovation, and the other might be good at steady, incremental improvements to known technologies. Competition in organizational forms in the same economy, in the same culture, would let each prosper where it works best.

[6] Oliver E. Williamson, Markets and Hierarchies: Analysis and Antitrust Implications 82–105 (1975); R. H. Coase, The Nature of the Firm, 4 Economica (n.s.) 386 (1937).

[7] Peter F. Drucker, The Coming of the New Organization, Harvard Business Review, Jan.–Feb. 1988, at 45, 53.

CHAPTER 18

Short-Term Finance as the Problem?

THUS FAR we have treated managers as the problem and enhanced institutional voice as a possible solution. But maybe managers are doing just fine, but *institutions* are the problem. And perhaps concentrated ownership is a partial solution to the *institutional* problem.

Managers complain that the short-term bias of a stock market of furious traders makes it hard for managers to concentrate on the long term. Hence, managers must spurn the long term and underinvest in building up their organizations and their employees. While this sounds true to many, it has theoretical problems. Even furiously trading shareholders include buyers as well as sellers. Buyers are interested in what price they will get for their stock when they sell it. So, today's buyer is interested in what tomorrow's buyer will pay, who is interested in what the next day's buyer will pay, and so on. Since each buyer is dependent on the price to be garnered in some distant long run, each buyer is interested in the long-run price, even if he or she will not be the long-run owner. There must be something more complex to support the short-term argument than furious trading alone.

And there is one, at least in theory, tied to fragmented ownership. Information does not always flow costlessly and accurately from inside the firm to the firm's stockholders. When information is complex, proprietary, or "soft" (i.e., difficult to quantify), the insiders in the firm can understand it, yet *be unable to explain it* to the outsiders. Stockholders with small holdings cannot spend much in understanding complex, technological information, so they might ignore it. And managers with good but *proprietary* information would not want to reveal it to the stock market, and consequently to competitors, so the stock market never gets it.

That is, what if there are economies of scale in getting the information and judgment needed to accurately assess a firm's long-term outlook, because accuracy requires staff, expertise, and time spent inside the boardroom? If so, a large holding might be needed to spread the information costs.

Moreover, what if analytic evaluation required personal evaluation, from confidential conversations in the boardroom? Large blocks of stock would facilitate the flow of soft, technological information from the firm to the large blockholder. If securities analysts sometimes undervalue long-term research and development when they cannot understand it, then so might managers. "Soft" information about the quality of middle management may be available to those who sit regularly in the boardroom, but be hard for a distant stockholder to detect. If securities analysts undervalue long-term investments in the firm's employees' skills—human capital— because they cannot tell whether they are profitable or just a program to make managers feel good, then managers might avoid such human investments.

Consider how hard it is to convey soft long-term information to a distant market; dispersed investors cannot cheaply distinguish egoistic empire-building from a high net present value project, a wasteful training program from valuable investments in employees' skills. And managers are wary of revealing proprietary information to many short-term shareholders;[1] without good information, even highly paid, technically competent analysts cannot evaluate the long-term R & D policies. In contrast, financial analysts with generic skills can easily evaluate short-term financial data.

Managers might not get "credit" (salary raises in the last few years of their career, short-term stock options, etc.) if they improve the firm in ways that stockholders cannot see. Unable to get "credit," managers may forsake investments whose evaluation requires complex, proprietary, or "soft" information, and then they might blame the stock market and seek to insulate themselves from it. In theory, concentrated ownership structures could improve the flow of information from inside the firm to large shareholders, thus helping to deter such short-term possibilities. Size would give the stockholder an economy of scale over which to spread the costs of time and personnel in acquiring and evaluating complex information. Size and boardroom presence would give the stockholder a reason to keep proprietary information secret; it would be hurting its own large stock position to let the secrets out. The large shareholder would protect secrets *and* protect managers from outsiders who would second-guess truly profitable long-run investments. And some evaluations of technical, complex, long-term information need constant private interaction, in which a motivated board of stable stockholders asks for predictions and sees how they play out over years. Distant shareholders with small blocks cannot readily be part of that kind of an ongoing evaluation.

True, these informational problems challenge faith in the informational efficiency of American securities markets; the claim that these problems exist thus far lacks a strong empirical backup. But in theory the stock market could efficiently evaluate information already in the public domain, but be unable to accurately process soft, technological, and proprietary information not out there in public markets. Long-term investments could be especially susceptible to this problem, requiring inside evaluation of

[1] Oliver Williamson, Markets and Hierarchies: Analysis and Antitrust Implications 35–37, 97–98 (1975).

technological and proprietary information to allow the investor to form a good opinion of the payoff. If the investor is unable either to form a solid opinion or to diversify the risk, then the investor will need a higher return; a higher return will bias investors and managers toward shorter-term projects that outsiders can evaluate better (if only because they already show some returns and those returns will not change much during the remaining life of the project) than the informationally deficient long-term projects (over whose life returns might change a great deal). A financial system's lack of big blockholders on the inside of those major firms susceptible to this problem could in theory be a reason for the short-term horizons said to afflict financial institutions and industrial managers.

I suggested this potential benefit of big blocks several years ago,[2] and others have made similar and stronger analyses.[3] But it is unproven, perhaps because current econometric techniques do not easily measure these problems. The potential, albeit unproven, benefits of concentrated ownership here is in reducing theoretical defects of the institutions, not of the managers.

THE POLITICAL BENEFITS OF THE ISSUE

Short-termism was a debater's weapon in the 1980s. Short-sighted financiers propelled takeovers, it was said, often by defenders of managers, compelling managers to manage for the short term; some managers' policy program was to stop takeovers, and they used the rhetoric (perhaps quite sincerely) of short-termism: for managers to manage for the long-term, they had to be free from takeover pressures, as, they said, were managers in German and Japanese industry. Major academic projects then sought to inquire into the causes of a short-term bias.

The antitakeover claim, and it is a plausible one, but only in some special settings, went that managers really knew that (1) the firm was best managed independently, and (2) projects in the pipeline had a high payoff that the market did not recognize and that managers, for proprietary reasons, could not disclose. A bidder, who might have known about the high-value projects but not understood that the firm could be best run independently, would bid for the company, putting managers in a quandary about

[2] Mark J. Roe, A Political Theory of American Corporate Finance, 91 Columbia Law Review 10, 55–56 (1991).

[3] Michael E. Porter, Capital Choices—Changing the Way America Invests in Industry (1992) (research report presented to the Council on Competitiveness and co-sponsored by the Harvard Business School). See also Jeremy C. Stein, Takeover Threats and Managerial Myopia, 96 Journal of Political Economy 61, 74–78 (1988); Jeremy C. Stein, Efficient Capital Markets, Inefficient Firms: A Model of Myopic Corporate Behavior, 104 Quarterly Journal of Economics 655 (1989).

how to react. Their disclosure of the confidential information would not raise the price of the company's stock, because the effects would offset each other: disclosure would raise the price because the projects would be seen to be stellar, and lower it when analysts realized that competitors would now also take these projects on. Unable to defend against takeovers in such settings, managers might ditch these kinds of long-term projects. (This antitakeover justification also has theoretical problems. Managers could have *signaled* their belief in the firm's long-term strength *without* revealing the complex, proprietary project. They could have changed their own compensation packages so that they were paid more for getting good long-term results and less in the immediate future. That move could have made stock market professionals more confident in managers' assertions that the managers had strong long-term projects in the pipeline but could not reveal their nature.)

Although the evidence, weak though it may be, is that the German and Japanese boardrooms are as sensitive to stock price and earnings movements as U.S. boardrooms,[4] stopping short-termism as the rhetorical cover for reconstructing financial institutions has rhetorical, political advantages. Managers want to stop it; politicians do, too. Were reformers to rely on the rhetoric of managerial accountability, that rhetoric would induce opposition; the rhetoric of industrial hybrids (discussed in the next chapter) would be too complex in a political debate. But the rhetoric of anti–short-termism, like the rhetoric of patriotism, is simple and widely supported.

IMPROVING LOAN MARKETS

Concentrated stock ownership can improve financial markets by other means. Lenders may buy stock in their debtors to help protect their loans and provide a secondary information channel to support their loans. Lenders know that a crisis could arise and want to be able to influence the firm; stock may work more quickly than loan covenants and bankruptcy. Borrowers may also *prefer* that lenders own stock to reduce *lender* opportunism: First, a lender's threat not to roll over a short-term loan unless the debtor grants concessions is less credible when carrying out the threat would reduce the value of the stock the lender holds. Second, because lenders want loan repayment, and are less concerned with maximizing firm value,

[4] Steven N. Kaplan, Top Executives, Turnover and Firm Performance in Germany (September 1993) (unpublished manuscript); Steven Kaplan and Bernadette A. Minton, Outside Activity in Japanese Companies: Determinants and Managerial Implications (August 1993) (unpublished manuscript); Steven Kaplan, Top Executive Rewards and Firm Performance: A Comparison of Japan and the U.S. (August 1993) (unpublished manuscript); Randall Morck and Masao Nakamura, Banks and Corporate Control in Japan (Sept. 1, 1992) (unpublished manuscript).

they tend to induce firms toward conservative strategies. When they also hold stock, they should tend to want "sensible" risk-taking, not unmitigated conservatism.

Similarly, when creditors also have large stock positions, workouts and recapitalizations to avoid a complicated and costly bankruptcy proceeding are probably easier. The lenders have multiple information channels, and in the right configurations, lender-debtor conflict is reduced if the lenders have stock positions, because they can "internalize" the conflict.

MONITORING BY MULTIPLE INTERMEDIARIES

"Improving" information has a dark role as well. Insider trading—the trading of stock when the trader has special information—helps to explain why German banks buy stock, or at least what happens once they own it, because without insider-trading laws, bank officers can and do trade on inside information from firms. Moreover, the influence from stock may yield mutual self-protection: The stockholding lender may induce the portfolio firm to borrow on terms unfavorable to the firm; in return the bankers promise to protect management from ouster.[5]

One would have to measure whether these costs outweigh any benefits of enhancing accountability and deterring short-run finance. Since we have no such measurements now, we cannot know whether change will be good. But there are theoretical reasons why concentrated stockholding, if properly constructed, would not be highly risky. The easiest image of concentration is the concentration produced by a single large blockholder, but the better structure may well be that produced by multiple intermediaries, who can deter opportunism by monitoring one another, impel action in a way that a single blockholder might not, and facilitate power-sharing, not domination.

Multiple Blocks Checking One Another

Multiple intermediaries give managers the power to form a countercoalition against the opportunistic intermediary that is looking for side payments. A true managerial crisis inside the firm, however, should unite the stockholders—all will want to end the crisis—but the opportunist may have trouble acting alone, because it lacks enough stock to do so. True, a financial cartel might try to exploit the firm, but it would face several problems: because the members would have different financial interests (public

---

[5] See Edward Rock, The Logic and Uncertain Significance of Institutional Investor Activism, 79 Georgetown Law Journal 445 (1991).

pension plans would not try to exploit companies in the same way that insurance companies might), they would face bargaining problems in coming up with a common plan, they would attract legal attention, and if such financial cartels became common, they would attract political attention as well.

For this reason, some debate in the United States about public pension funds misses the mark. Critics of enhanced institutional voice argue that the most active institutions, public pension funds, have conflicts that will disable them in corporate governance. They will have a politicized agenda—asking firms to invest in the pension fund's home state or to adopt social investing norms before there is a political consensus—that will diminish the value of the firm. While these critics have identified a factor, they have not identified an important one, because they have not tied the debilities of public pension funds to ownership structure. Public pension funds now only own 10 percent of the American stock market. Generally a single public plan does not own a big block in a single portfolio company. They cannot themselves control a firm's actions even if they were to act in concert, because 10 percent is not enough; they must form a coalition with other investors, or at least be sure that a countercoalition will not form. Thus were a public pension fund to insist that a firm build unprofitable factories in the fund's home state, managers would have no trouble assembling a countercoalition. Since public pension funds would know that such a countercoalition could form, they would not often try to force decisions detrimental to the firm. Rather, they would usually have to seek corporate governance actions that appealed to a *majority* of all shareholders.

The more serious risk is not that the public pension funds will seek politicized decisions, but that managers can create conflicts to quiet them. That is, private pension funds will not lead, but they will sometimes follow if the public pension funds identify a serious firm malady. Incumbent managers may try to neutralize the activist public pension fund with a side payment, such as an extra factory in the home state (or a threat to close down the one already there), or by direct political attacks on the pension plan. Given today's ownership structure, the risk is more that managers could use home-state investments to neutralize useful governance forays than that public pension plans could alone foist a social action agenda on corporate America.

Multiple Blocks Impelling Action

Why don't American financial intermediaries, some of which can own some stock, go to the law's limits in stockholding? Isolated blocks, even big ones with 5 percent of the portfolio firm, are precarious because management may isolate, outmaneuver, and destroy them, as essentially happened when H. Ross Perot assembled a 6 percent block in GM and then became vocal in his criticism. (Perot's personality and maneuvering over the price of GM's buyout of Perot's stock were also factors.) In the United States a single 5 percent block does emerge here and there, but managers still have the upper hand in times of conflict. Even a half-dozen institutions with 5 percent blocks would have to coordinate their activities, which U.S. securities regulation has tended to deter. Thus, some "unleashed" American institutions should rationally refuse to hold the maximum permitted by American law because they know that in times of crisis they will need a critical mass of other large blockholders, a critical mass they lack.

This also shows some of the weaknesses in the German and Japanese ownership structures. The German banks' big voting blocks usually come from brokerage stock, for which the banks are unlikely to make heroic efforts in monitoring managers at the underlying firm. Each Japanese bank owns no more than 5 percent of an industrial firm's stock, a position that would be too weak to wrest control from managers in the United States. A German bank's typical directly owned position, while often larger than 5 percent, is usually alone still too small to yield control; only with brokerage stock or alliances with other stockholders can the bank get control. The German bank's *motivation* for involvement may come from the bank's directly owned stock; its *means* may require the brokerage stock. Directly owned stock gives the institutional owner a financial *incentive* to act; ancillary, backup stock bulks up voting power and provides the *means*. But as pressures, political and otherwise, mount on the German banks to unload their directly owned stock, the system may weaken further. For example, if political pressure on German banks leads them to reduce their amount of directly held stock while retaining their brokerage stock, they may face reduced incentives to act responsibly.

Multiple blocks may induce intermediaries to act in a way that a *single* isolated blockholder might not. The multiple blocks may solve the weakness problem without creating a dominating block that recentralizes authority in a dominating intermediary. Because the intermediaries have differing private agendas, a coalition for side payments may be difficult to maintain, but a weak firm could induce a coalition among a handful of powerful intermediaries.

———

Once again, we have theoretical, unproven benefits. Managers may not be the problem; institutions and their possible short-term propensities might be. With small blocks, far from the boardroom, the institutions might be unable to process complex, proprietary, and soft information. Managers, knowing they will get little "credit" for projects with these informational problems, underinvest, and American industry suffers. Multiple, powerful but not dominating, intermediaries might mitigate both the problem of institutional opportunism and the possible problem of short-term horizons.

Industrial Organization as the Problem?

LET US now shift from financiers, short-term thinking, and monitoring of managers to the organization of industrial production. A recurrent task in organizing industry is to coordinate long-term investments, especially simultaneous long-term investments by suppliers and customers. A supplier considers a massive investment in new machinery to make a good that only a specific customer can use. But what will stop the customer from reneging or extorting concessions from the supplier later on, after the supplier builds the specific machines? Although a detailed contract between the supplier and the specific customer may protect the supplier, many ways that the customer can exploit the supplier are unforeseeable. Vague promises from a customer to act in good faith are often not enough. Multiple cross-holdings of stock, however, may mitigate opportunism. If the customer tries to mulct the supplier after the supplier has committed itself, a coalition of stockholders could intervene to stop the opportunism. When a half-dozen suppliers and customers must simultaneously make such commitments, industrial coordination becomes important. Cross-ownership as coordination helps to explain keiretsu cross-ownership in Japan, where one-third of the stock is cross-owned, often between suppliers and their customers,[1] as I have analyzed elsewhere with Ronald Gilson.[2]

To coordinate complex investments under potential opportunism, the parties have a continuum of choices between pure contract and pure organization. At the idealized contractual pole, one party becomes the organizer and writes highly specific contracts with the other suppliers and customers; these contracts specify the terms on which the organizer can buy goods and services from the others. Every future circumstance must be specified to prevent anyone from acting opportunistically. In this idealized contracting, the organizer anticipates every contingency, and courts will enforce these perfect contracts without friction. This kind of a contractual "firm" is a loose connection of suppliers and customers, linked through a nexus of arm's-length, highly specific contracts. At the idealized organiza-

---

[1] Yusaku Futatsugi, What Share Cross-Holdings Mean for Corporate Management, Economic Eye, Spring 1990, at 17, 18. Industrial ownership of stock is also significant in Germany.

[2] Ronald J. Gilson and Mark J. Roe, Understanding the Japanese Keiretsu: Overlaps Between Corporate Governance and Industrial Organization, 102 Yale Law Journal 871 (1993).

tional pole of the continuum, contracts are not specified; the organizer buys up, or builds by itself, all of the necessary supplier factories, assembly factories, and distribution systems. The firm vertically integrates.[3]

Perfect contracting is afflicted by limited foresight—no one can anticipate everything that could go wrong—and by the threat of opportunism—the party on the other side may be unfair when unforeseen circumstances give him or her an advantage; the combination of the two makes relation-specific investments under neoclassical contracting difficult. Perfect contracting becomes impossible. But the other extreme, vertical integration, has problems too. Organizing production within a single firm reduces the contracting problem, but increases the concentrated capital and managerial expertise required, exacerbating the Berle-Means problem of scattered shareholders and powerful managers. Substituting internal ownership for market procurement—making rather than buying—means that the firm must build internal incentives and monitoring to avoid organizational opportunism.

Partial cross-ownership with contracts would be a hybrid, in the middle of the continuum. Contracts could be written as well as they could be, and cross-ownership would reduce opportunism. When the unforeseen occurred, a single opportunist could not easily bilk the others in this hybrid quasi-firm, because the others could form an ownership coalition, takeover the opportunist firm, and kick out its opportunistic managers. Equity here would serve a purpose beyond being the residual risk bearer and the actor in the firm most interested in managerial accountability. Equity would encourage relation-specific investments and reduce opportunism.[4]

Financiers come back into the picture in two ways. First, a financier's investment in a long-term loan, or a short-term loan that each side expects to be rolled over, resembles a supplier's investment in complex machinery for a specific customer. The borrower may renege on the loan by increasing the level of risk, or the lender may renege by refusing to roll over the loan at a critical juncture. In the United States, detailed loan agreements mitigate these problems. Cross-ownership could also limit borrower-lender opportunism and thereby facilitate trade in capital.

In both supplier-customer relationships and lender-borrower relationships, the relational commitment is made credible by the plausibility that a

---

[3] Gilson and Roe, supra note 2, at 884–85; Oliver E. Williamson, The Economic Institutions of Capitalism 69 (1985); Oliver D. Hart, Incomplete Contracts and the Theory of the Firm, 4 Journal of Law, Economics and Organization 119, 120 (1988); Benjamin Klein, Robert G. Crawford, and Armen A. Alchian, Vertical Integration, Appropriable Rents, and the Competitive Contracting Process, 21 Journal of Law and Economics 297 (1978). Carl Kester analyzes Japanese contractual relations in W. Carl Kester, Japanese Takeovers: The Global Contest for Corporate Control (1991).

[4] See Gilson and Roe, supra note 2, at 887.

coalition will form to control the opportunist. The coalition of stockholders will oust the opportunistic managers or make them change their direction.

The second role here for a financial intermediary is to strengthen these industrial, customer-supplier relationships by owning big, influential blocks in *both* the customer and the supplier. Industrial firms often do not want to commit their own capital to cross-ownership. Moreover, they need an outsider to prevent the cross-owners from becoming only a mutual protection society, in which each sloughs off and does nothing about the other's problems. The intermediary with stock in both can become an arbitrator, an escrow agent for the supplier-customer relationship; the supplier firm can become a source of information for the intermediary about the customer firm, and the intermediary as stockholder will have the motivation to use that information wisely.

Relational contracting problems overlap with corporate governance problems. When suppliers and customers own each other's stock and trade goods, when lenders and borrowers own each other's stock and make loans, or when intermediaries invest in suppliers and customers simultaneously, these multiple relationships (1) double the stockholders' sources of information, because the stockholder gets stock-related information from, say, sitting in the boardroom atop the firm's hierarchy and gets industrial information as a customer of the firm; (2) double the stockholders' incentives to participate in the governance of the firm, since a failing investment is also a failing supplier; and (3) double the stockholders' means of intervention, because the stockholder can use organizational controls as a stockholder and customer controls as a customer who might stop buying, allowing for both exit and voice. Whether or not this model describes the realities in Japan, where there is extensive cross-ownership among suppliers, customers, and their bankers, it is a useful one for understanding the potential for enhanced stockholder presence in the United States.

An American example of vertical integration illustrates the potential value of class-ownership. In 1919, GM needed auto bodies. Fisher Body manufactured them and needed a big customer. To build the kind that GM needed, Fisher had to invest in specific body-building assets, which Fisher was unwilling to do without assured purchases from GM. Without contract protection for Fisher, GM could threaten to abandon Fisher once Fisher built the GM-specific plants, forcing Fisher to lower its price, because the GM-specific plants would be useless if GM went elsewhere. Once Fisher made the specific investments for GM auto bodies, GM could squeeze Fisher's price down to Fisher's variable costs (plus the value of Fisher assets that could be redeployed away from GM's bodies).

To protect Fisher, GM agreed to purchase its requirements of the specific body type for ten years from Fisher. But this agreement would then have allowed Fisher to exploit GM: GM was making an open-ended commitment to buy its requirements of the specified auto body only from Fisher. What would stop Fisher from raising its price? Price might be specified in a contract, but over ten years costs could change, making a specified price impossible. To protect GM, Fisher agreed to a formula by which the price would be calculated at Fisher's variable costs plus 17.6 percent, with the 17.6 percent presumably representing the expected value of the specific assets to which Fisher was committing.

An unexpectedly rapid run-up in demand for Fisher-type auto bodies made it worthwhile for Fisher to exploit the contract's formula to hold up GM. From an integrated perspective of GM and Fisher working together, Fisher should have built new capital-intensive plants next to GM, but Fisher refused to build them and wanted to be paid under the contract formula. Capital-intensive plants had become cheaper than the labor-intensive means Fisher used, but capital-intensive production disadvantaged Fisher under the contract. Eventually GM bought up all of Fisher's stock, making it part of GM's large, vertically integrated firm.[5]

Fisher's unexpected ability to exploit GM might have been mitigated by extensive cross-ownership. Fisher would have been 5 percent owned by GM, 5 percent owned by a steel firm, 5 percent owned by an automotive paint and fabric firm (DuPont), and 20 percent owned by a coalition of banks, one of which would have been a "main bank" for this network. In such a setting, Fisher could not have readily exploited the unexpected loophole because a coalition of owners could have displaced Fisher's senior management. GM and Fisher might not have even bothered with the detail they put into the contract, a contract that ex post turned out to be insufficiently detailed.

The end result for the GM–Fisher Body problem was complete vertical integration, raising a problem for this organizational model: why is vertical integration not a general solution for investments in relation-specific assets? Why shouldn't related firms facing this problem *always* choose vertical integration—complete, not partial ownership—as a full solution, just as GM did?

Although there is no complete rebuttal, one hypothesis—suggested by GM's subsequent history—is that something else must be traded off. First, complete vertical integration raises the agency problems endemic to large organizational structures, requiring costly investments in internal monitoring; employees and managers also can behave opportunistically. GM's bloated bureaucracy and poor performance in the 1980s and early 1990s may have been due to "excess" vertical integration eventually taking its toll. Second, the cross-holding/cross-exchange structure differs from com-

[5] The basic facts for this illustration come from Benjamin Klein, Vertical Integration as Organizational Ownership: The Fisher Body–General Motors Relationship Revisited, 4 Journal of Law, Economics and Organization 199, 200–02 (1988).

plete vertical integration, because it allows some resort to contracting. The trading relationship inside the cross-owned enterprise need not be exclusive; each member could sell to, or buy from, outsiders. The picture of total organizational authority at the central headquarters changes as well; the somewhat separate organizations lack the sharply tapered pyramid of authority typical of GM and other large American vertically integrated firms. Lastly, one weakness of complete vertical integration is that if the relational failure is at the top—that is, if the division performs, but the enterprise as a whole slackens—the division cannot easily detach itself from the slackers and migrate to a high-performance company. With partial cross-ownership, that kind of migration—and the incentives it provides others in the organization—is possible.

American heavy industry, such as auto- and steelmaking, has been hard hit by international competition in the past few decades and seems to have serious governance problems. The cross-ownership prescription might fit here. If each is slow to develop new technologies and production methods, cross-ownership among relational suppliers might speed adaptation. Thus if new steel technologies, say, minimills, are to be located near new auto plants having innovative production technologies, cross-ownership might function well. Each cross-owner would double its interest in the other's prosperity: steel firms will want a better customer and a better portfolio firm. Information that the firms gather about each other while adapting the production process together may make each a more valuable stockholder to the other. Moreover, in view of the historical American mistrust of powerful financiers; this industrial-organization basis for cross-ownership by other firms could prove politically more durable than pure financial power alone.

———

The roles for big shareholders outlined in the last three chapters mark a firm's life cycle. (See chapter 13's discussion of retained earnings.) In Stage 1, when a firm takes off, external venture capital and securities markets finance the firm; the entrepreneur might be in control, but the firm needs funds from financiers, who could easily play a role in corporate governance.

In Stage 2, growth is steady, and the firm can finance itself from internal sources. The entrepreneur might disappear as a controlling stockholder; managers and institutions could share authority. The firm could use an influx of new information and relational investments; *partial* integration with capital owners (who no longer are supplying *new* capital) and cross-ownership between suppliers and customers could help it organize production. Integration with capital owners could be functional even if they do not supply capital, if they enhance accountability, enhance the information channels going into the top of the firm, blunt short-term impulses from the stock market, and help coordinate smaller nimbler firms.

In Stage 3, the firms decline because of internal decay or technological shocks that make their production or marketing outmoded. If the decline is slow, retained earnings could sustain the firm, but make reinvestment in current technology unwise. Although the firm must change, incumbent managers and employees might resist, making traditional corporate governance—shareholders disciplining managers—matter. If the decline is fast, the firm hits a crisis and risks bankruptcy with yet more disruption. The firm needs change agents, particularly when the external forces—a changing economy or changing technologies—demand that the firm adjust. Change is hard, particularly for those on the inside. Financial intermediaries may be more adept than managers in limiting the waste at this stage, but they will not be there unless they had a role to play in Stage 2. If they were not there already, they would have to fight their way in via costly and disruptive takeovers and proxy battles, or shareholder activism. If many firms have these tensions, the tensions will generate social conflict that moves into the political arena, as seen in Germany's codetermination laws, U.S. antitakeover laws, and some U.S. portfolio rules. The rules set when this social conflict becomes political conflict then influence the kinds of organizational structures permissible for new firms rising elsewhere in the economy.

CHAPTER 20

Counterpoint II

THE ISSUE of industrial organization leads to another issue. Can one identify the superiority or inferiority of institutional voice by comparing the performance of national economies where it is strong with the performance of those where it is weak?

AMERICAN COMPETITIVE SUPERIORITY

In the end, enhanced institutional voice in the United States must be justified in American terms, not by using the foreign systems as blueprints. But the post–World War II successes of Germany and Japan with different governance systems pique our curiosity. Might they have a better system? This possibility, vivid until the German and Japanese economic setbacks of the early 1990s, probably led some people to associate foreign success with the foreign differences.

There is a debater's superficially strong rebuttal to this association, as I briefly noted in chapter 2. It goes like this: After World War II, the United States was superior as an economic competitor to Germany and Japan, and the United States then had the same corporate governance system as it does now. Does this detract from the importance of looking at corporate governance weaknesses in the United States? Does it mean that poor corporate governance cannot help explain the country's recent problems or the foreign nations' successes, because each nation had the same governance system forty years ago, when the United States was strong and the others weak? Different governance structures may mask the real reasons for foreign successes: weaker entrenched interest groups,[1] or better-educated and better-motivated employees, or better macroeconomic policies, or success just from catching up by copying more advanced economies.

Many factors explained American economic superiority over Germany and Japan in 1945, including military superiority. It is logically possible that American corporate governance had a few problems then and has a few now but because governance is a secondary economic feature, it did not drag down the American economy. For many decades, large-scale

[1] See Mancur Olson, The Rise and Decline of Nations (1982).

American industry had two critical, complementary advantages over much industry abroad: economies of scale and workably competitive structure. The American market was (and is still today) so large that it could support two or three firms, and hence workable, albeit oligopolistic, competition, at the highest economies of scale in even the heaviest of industries; no other market in the world could do both. Economies of scale in a small nation meant monopoly; competition often meant inefficient scale. The United States could get both scale and competition, so if some details of organization at the top and in the boardroom were not for the best, no matter, because scale and competition were so important and might allow for profits that would hide a few defects in organization. And returns to shareholders would look good when oligopolistic competition kept price a bit above marginal cost. (Oligopoly may have led to selection of managers who would not fight hard against the other oligopolists. What CEOs did at industry meetings might have been more important than what they did inside the firm. Their organization could have had slack—governance mattered—but oligopoly profits hid any organizational problems. And in the 1950s and 1960s, there was little international competition that would highlight any organizational defects.)

As the only continental free-trade area with a stable government, a good work force, and rich natural resources, the United States was likely to have had a strong economy then even if its boardrooms were weak. These advantages are no longer exclusive to the United States. A common market in Europe and a globalized marketplace allow foreign firms economies of scale in a competitive market. Secondary matters, such as corporate governance, have become visible. Stress from international competition has revealed weaknesses in some American firms, pressed American firms to change, and led us to wonder whether secondary economic features in the United States, such as corporate governance, could be improved.[2] The existence, persistence, and (until the early 1990s) success of some rival foreign firms has eroded a few American competitive advantages, taken away some of the shareholders' oligopolistic profits, and raised the question of whether the American system is as sound in all dimensions as we have thought.

There is another debater's rebuttal. American productivity today is the highest in the world; those fearing a U.S. economic decline point not to the country's absolute level of productivity, but to its rate of gain, which for several years lagged behind that of some other nations in some industries. But again, neither the continuing productivity lead nor the lagging rate of increase tell us much about corporate governance. Education

[2] In this sense, international competition mirrors Tiebout's model of state competition as a means of providing efficient regulation. See Charles M. Tiebout, A Pure Theory of Local Expenditures, 64 Journal of Political Economy 416, 419–20 (1956).

levels, employee motivation, macroeconomic policies, the wisdom of government fiscal policies, and many other elements are more important than governance. Product market competition is usually more critical than organizational competition, and, despite some trade barriers, American firms are subject to more of it than most international rivals. But that should not stop us from seeing whether we can make incremental improvements in the U.S. boardrooms.

In the end, it does not matter whether American firms are catching up to foreign firms or extending their lead. Foreign differences do not give us a model; they only tell us that differences are possible. The issue is whether the American system can be improved, not whether it's better or worse overall than any foreign system.

ANTITRUST

Antitrust considerations militate against any wholesale concentration of financial industries. The foreign systems are so concentrated that they would for the United States be serious antitrust problems, and rightly so. But, to use a debater's rhetoric, there is a lot of room between the highly fragmented American system, with, for example, twelve thousand banks, and Germany's more centralized system, with three or four major insurers and banks (and a large fringe of small institutions). A nation could have somewhat more powerful financial institutions than the United States does without coming anywhere near the handful of majors in Germany or Japan that would be a serious antitrust concern.

THE ADVANTAGES OF AMERICAN SECURITIES MARKETS

An advantage of the U.S. financial system is its high flexibility. Large organizational structures might stagnate, but entrepreneurs set up new firms and, through the securities and venture capital markets, can often get financing to be viable. In a centralized financial system, the central players may be unwilling to finance new ventures because of monopolistic reasons, or because they fail to see the advantages of the innovation. The U.S. system may excel at big-leap improvements, because whole new structures can be quickly built by American entrepreneurs, venture capital financing, and a vibrant securities market. Foreign bank-centered systems may in contrast have the commitment needed to constantly spur adaptive, incremental improvement of known technologies, but be less able to construct whole new industries. Moreover, because American-style takeovers are possible (although much reduced since the 1980s), organizational change is more likely than in the still more closed foreign systems.

That the U.S. securities markets excel in flexibility but lag in commitment seems true, but misses the point about policy recommendations. It would be a mistake to list the advantages and disadvantages of the varying systems, weigh them, and announce a winner. It would also be a mistake to examine the advantages and disadvantages, and then announce that since one cannot find one system clearly superior to the others, we ought to stay with the American system and the laws that promote it.

Such analyses are faulty because they exclude an important middle ground: we ought to seek *competition* among organizational forms. Securities-based flexibility beats institutional-based commitment sometimes; other times it is the other way around. *Some* institutional investors would never become corporate governance players with boardroom seats; some would. Competition between the two forms, especially competition in the same national society, should bring out the best of both. If big blocks usually turn out to be unprofitable, they usually will not be pursued. If *no* institutional investor will give up liquidity for boardroom seats, then we may have wasted our time in permitting them that decision, but only then would we know whether liquidity is more important to *all* institutions than is influence. In this sense, the who-is-better comparative inquiry is misguided; a society might be able to adopt *both* organizational forms and have a competitive advantage. Even if today's U.S. securities-based system is superior, it might be improved, and I see no reason why we should not try to take the incremental gains for those firms that can profit from them and leave behind the losses, if we can.

The who-is-better argument can be seen in another way. Any normative comparison with the foreign systems also suffers from the fact that Japanese, and perhaps German, firms may maximize size, not profits.[3] When the firms have monopoly power, or when economic expansion is warranted, this may maximize social wealth (but be detrimental to shareholder wealth). Moreover, as German firms have stumbled, German media have reported unhappiness with supervisory boards that failed to avoid crises due to incompetence and directors' failure to devote enough time to their duties, complaints often heard about American boards.[4] Because one-third of the cross-holdings in Japan are held by industrial firms, which are as interested in their own sales as in profits from owning stock, and because employees' representatives make up half of the German board and are as interested in jobs as in profits, belt-tightening and downsizing would not be easy. If so, the foreign systems may work well when economic determinants impel expansion, but not when expansion is no longer warranted.

[3] Alan S. Blinder, Profit Maximization and International Competition, in 5 AMEX Bank Review Prize Essays 37 (Richard O'Brien ed., 1991).

[4] Peter Christ, Räte-Republik, Manager Magazin, Aug. 1993, at 3 (editorial); Walter Hildebrand, Andreas Nölting, and Winfried Wilhelm, Club der Amateure ["Amateurs' Club"], Manager Magazin, Aug. 1993, at 32.

The employees' presence on the board may make downsizing more legitimate to rank-and-file employees when the board acts, but it may take
more time for the board to act. The U.S. system may be more adaptable
and, when the pluses and minuses are added up, superior. Not only does
the American securities market finance entrepreneurs, but in the bigger established firms, American managers own more stock than do their foreign
counterparts, and securities markets can themselves help to correct the
problems of distant shareholders: when old structures ossify, the securities
markets eventually finance new entry and competition.

Each system has strengths and weaknesses, with U.S.-style venture capital and securities markets excelling at finding and initially developing new
technologies, and other systems better at other tasks. An economy with
several organizational forms may do better than an economy with only
one, because organizational variety increases the possibility of successful
adaptation.

THE FAILURE OF THE AMERICAN CONGLOMERATE

Let us shift back to the role of institutional voice in making managers
more accountable. Has the owner-as-monitor arrangement already been
tried in the United States, and did it fail? Was the conglomerate movement of the 1960s and 1970s—now largely discredited as going too far—
functionally the same as institutional block ownership? In large part, yes.
The managers of the conglomerate were said to run a mini–capital market,
pulling cash away from the managers of subsidiaries no longer in growing
industries, sending that cash into the subsidiaries in growing industries,
and monitoring the managers of all of them.[5]

First, however, let me note that while the conglomerate's limits might
make the normative inquiry here a dead end, the political inquiry might
help explain the phenomenon. Conglomerates emerged, were overused,
and then dipped back down to being only one of the many usable organizational forms, partly because American politics tended to preclude another
alternative, that of concentrated institutional ownership.

The prescriptive element here is, however, not completely defeated by
invoking conglomerates. The conglomerates' appearance differs from enhanced institutional ownership, because the conglomerate typically owned
100 percent of many companies, while the institutional owners would typically have large blocks, but lack total ownership.

At least in theory, the difference could be more than one of form. First,
the conglomerate does not set up a partial linkage between external capi-

---

[5] Oliver Williamson, The Economics of Discretionary Behavior: Managerial Objectives in
a Theory of the Firm 43–48 (1964).

tal markets and the firm, as would enhanced institutional ownership and boardroom presence. To the extent the problem to be remedied by linkage is inadequate information processing by the institutional investors in the American stock market, leading to short-term evaluations and discounting of complex, technological information, the conglomerate helped to create this linkage, but only by *eliminating* the outside market price entirely, not by controlling it. Thus institutional blockholders might function better if they could get outside stock price signals, which they could use to question managers. But the institutions could choose to ignore those stock price signals if, after discussion, they thought that the managers' program made sense. Sometimes outside signals are useful, sometimes not, but the conglomerate could not get them for a wholly owned subsidiary.

Consider the simplest monitoring mechanism. The monitor does nothing until it receives a signal of substandard performance; then it tries to identify whether managerial missteps caused the poor results. If those missteps are likely to continue, the monitor would require early retirement of the senior managers and promotion of the next rung of managers.

Where does the conglomerate monitor get signals of faulty performance in its subsidiary? Principally from accounting data (and internal financial data available to insiders). Yet the outside blockholder could get those *and* other signals. Before the accounting numbers showed a decline, the stock price set by traders should register the market's expectations of future trouble, triggering blockholder action. A financial monitor could be beneficial even if it did no more than filter out poor market signals (that is, the "short-term" ones) but force managers to listen to a few of the good ones; conglomerates owning 100 percent of a subsidiary lack the benefit of market signals.

Second, division managers lack the same call on capital owners that a company president of a smaller company with a few big stockholders would have; that CEO can call the stockholders for help in a way that the CEO of a Berle-Means firm cannot. Moreover, there are psychological differences. The senior managers at an independent firm may be more entrepreneurial and independent than the officers of a division or wholly owned subsidiary of the large conglomerate.

Third, *one* conglomerate headquarters directs all of the subsidiaries. An advantage of enhanced institutional voice is that it could link suppliers and customers, without absolute control or a stultifying bureaucracy. The conglomerate tends to have unrelated businesses, and the control from headquarters is absolute. Moreover, the incentives of the headquarters planner in the conglomerate should differ from those of the outside financial institution. The outsider as a financial manager should be less susceptible to the urge to build an empire, since he or she doesn't get to command that empire from day to day.

Hybrids stronger than either of their forebears, amalgams stronger than any of their constituents are not unheard of in biology, chemistry, or, I suspect, corporate governance. But if an amalgam of partial control, marketplace signaling, and partial integration of finance and industry (or of different levels of industry) would have been so superior, why did the American conglomerates not become amalgams, owning only part of their companies?

One possibility is that such a format would have had only modest advantages. Another is that perhaps the conglomerate would have evolved in such a way, if it could have done so. But once the portfolio of the conglomerate was 40 percent devoted to partial ownership, the conglomerate would have become a presumptive investment company, subject to the panoply of regulation under the Investment Company Act of 1940.[6] It would have had to pay taxes on its dividend receipts from its partly owned subsidiaries, a result of tax law designed originally to discourage these complex corporate linkages,[7] and a result that defeats the raison d'être of the conglomerate, to pull funds up from the old subsidiaries at will. To avoid those taxes, it could have become a mutual fund, but then it would have had to comply with the tax law's portfolio limits and the 1940 Act's restrictions on intercompany dealing. If the private gains that the headquarters could have captured were modest, then any one of these problems could have defeated the amalgam.

Although many conglomerates became dysfunctional in excessive empire-building, perhaps they were not so bad after all. But as can happen with something new and initially successful, success turned to excess. They got too big, and too many operating managers tried to diversify their firms unwisely. Maybe conglomerates are still a good managerial tool—but in their place, only so much, only in related industries, and only if disciplined by a corporate control market. Nevertheless, we cannot yet reject the possibility that institutional monitoring would systematically fail, as the conglomerates did.

INSTITUTIONS AS THE PROBLEM: PART II

Big blockholders with boardroom presence could enhance information flows to owners. But the possibility that stockholders are less well informed than managers is not stockholders' only debility in corporate governance, and boardroom presence might exacerbate their other debilities. Stockholders, because they are diversified, can accept a single firm's risk

[6] Investment Company Act of 1940 §3(l)(3), 15 U.S.C. § 80a-3(a)(3) (1988).
[7] See supra chapter 8.

more readily than can that firm's managers, employees, customers, and suppliers. When the firm's managers, employees, customers, and suppliers have made specific investments that they can use well only with this particular firm, they will become risk averse in ways that will conflict with the pure, diversified stockholder. Diversified stockholders want to maximize their return; managers, employees, customers, and suppliers want stability. Powerful stockholders may take risks that destabilize these other interests' commitment to the firm. Although the firm could write contracts with managers, employees, customers, and suppliers to foster stability, these contracts are hard to write with specificity. Thus it is plausible to argue that shareholders' role in corporate governance should be kept weak.

There is no sure counter to this argument. The foreign stockholder-cum-lender model reduces this conflict because the lender also wants stability. Similarly, the industrial organization model outlined in chapter 19, in which customers and suppliers are stockholders, has stockholder-customers that want stability.

Odd as it might at first seem, the pure equity holder with no other entanglements with the firm—without being a manager, lender, or supplier—may have the biggest conflict with the firm's other key players. A firm with conflicted players (stockholder and lender, stockholder and supplier, stockholder and manager) may reduce the tension between diversified stockholders and those who have made specific investments to deal with this firm (in training for employees, in equipment for suppliers and customers, in learning this firm's culture for managers). These players will find it hard to recoup these specific investments when change devalues them; but with "conflicted" players at the top who value stability the firm will move forward, but slowly.

For some firms, again odd as it might seem, *multiple* conflicts in the boardroom may minimize the *aggregate* tensions. The collateral relationships stabilize the firm in the face of demands for immediate change, reducing the basic tension of stockholders versus employee and managers. Although the collateral conflicts risk side deals, the presence of *multiple* parties means that no single one of them can totally impose its preference, or get huge side payments. Thus it may be no accident that Germany, which gives employees a strong voice in the boardroom, also has stockholder-lenders with a strong voice in the boardroom. Stockholding is concentrated in Japan as well, but these stockholders are also lenders, and suppliers and customers also have large stockholdings. Their conflicts align their interests—roughly and imprecisely to be sure—with the interests of employees and managers with firm specific investments. They all want growth but with stability.

Thus we can imagine two contrasting systems: One model, which the American system approaches, eliminates as many conflicts and collateral dealings as possible. Not only must representatives with collateral interests be eliminated from the boardroom, but the unidimensional interest of the stockholder must also be barred, because the goals of the pure stockholder conflict with those of the other key players in the firm. A second model, which American laws have tended to undermine, allows multiple conflicts in the governance structure. The multiple conflicts reduce the severity of pure self-dealing, but allow a trade-off between pure profit maximization and stability in the organization.

The theoretical bases for legal change are weak, but present. There is little empirical work that is directly useful. There is a basis for recommending expansion of the legal options available to managers and owners in structuring their relationships, but no compelling evidence that it is desirable to require or encourage change via regulation or taxation.

That the prescriptive case is debatable actually strengthens the political theory. After all, the evolutionary economic argument has strength, despite the political theory. If politics had channeled intermediaries and firms into *highly* inefficient forms, forced them to adopt *highly* dysfunctional boards of directors and ownership structures, and prevented *highly* useful ways to mitigate these inefficient structures, American industry would not have survived and prospered as well as it did. Rather, it seems that politics prodded the firms to go down one usable channel, and prevented firms from going down another usable channel. Politics thereby prevented some diversity in organizational form. The advantage of organizational diversity is similar to its advantage in genetic diversity: a changing economic environment can make some previously secondary features useful to survival. Perhaps today changes in the underlying economic circumstances make that precluded form a bit more useful than it would have been in the past.

CHAPTER 21

Changing the American Ownership Structure?

EVEN IF we could identify the best structure (which we cannot, because today's best structure is not tomorrow's and each one has distinctive pluses and minuses), there would be no reason to force reconstruction via new regulation or new taxes. We have little reason to want law that *encourages* active intermediaries and concentrated stock ownership; we do want law that *permits* more variation, allowing more competition in the United States between organizational forms.

This chapter has four parts. First, I examine how bank-based structures similar to those abroad could be permitted to compete in the United States, and I conclude that they would not function here quickly, or perhaps at all, even if permitted. Second, I examine how other financial institutions might be allowed to change their portfolios to concentrate their stockholdings. Third, I examine how, given the American path-dependent development of weak intermediaries, change in portfolio regulation may be less important than change in securities laws that inhibit *coordination* among the intermediaries holding fragmented portfolios. Fourth, I examine how and why path dependence means that legal permission may be futile: rules might change, but behavior, portfolios, and corporate structure might not.

BANK-CENTERED REFORMS:
GERMANY AND JAPAN AS BLUEPRINT?

The United States could not readily use the Japanese or German structures as a blueprint even if it wanted to, because the American path to the present yielded weak banks and strong stockholding pensions dominated by management; these cannot now be easily changed overnight. American reforms will focus more on obstacles to shareholder voice embedded in the securities laws than on obstacles to bank power.

This is not to say that banking reform is unimportant. It is, so as to better deliver financial services. Thus, early in the 1990s, the United States Treasury Department sought to repeal or modify McFadden, Glass-Steagall, and the Bank Holding Company Act. Although these reforms were intended to make for more efficient banks,[1] they would also have moved

---

[1] See Jonathan Macey and Geoffrey Miller, America's Banking System: The Origins and Future of the Current Crisis, 69 Washington University Law Quarterly 769 (1991).

U.S. bank regulation closer to that of Germany and Japan. But despite the ample reasons for interstate branching, and the lack of serious ones against it, efforts to repeal McFadden failed in the past, largely because small-town, independent bankers form a powerful lobby. That lobby might be controlled, perhaps by allowing interstate banking but *only* by buying up the small banks (not by new entry); the local bankers would reap profits from interstate branching and those profits might "buy" them into support-ing an end to the century-old ban on interstate branching.[2] Since the other historical determinant—anti–big-bank populism—is not what it used to be, the United States might sometime near the twenty-first century get the rudiments of a twentieth-century banking system.

Two problems make bank reform for *corporate governance* purposes a dead end. First, such reform would put corporate governance, the tail, ahead of financial services, the kite. Since we do not know enough about what makes banks good at corporate governance, and we know that bank-ing reform (viz. the savings and loan crisis) can be costly, reform should focus on banking's main missions, not an ancillary one. Once the main mis-sions are resolved, an ancillary one can be enhanced.

Second, institutional voice is potentially most useful for large firms. But American banks cannot take big blocks there, because the banks are not big enough. Large banks are in no shape to monitor large firms. Because fractional reserve banking is shrinking in the United States relative to other financial channels[3] and because banks are highly leveraged, even un-restricted banks will not become major direct equity players.[4] To be play-ers, they would need at least modest direct holdings and larger holdings for others' benefit, like the holdings of the German universal banks. Merg-ers between nationwide banks and mutual funds might provide this kind of a network. But even if American intermediaries wanted such big, active holdings (a few will), such a new, complex intermediary would require reg-ulation that the American system cannot yet provide; hence American reg-ulators thus far have prohibited them.

Corporate Governance as Ancillary to Financial Services

Deposit insurance makes risky any banking reform that allowed heavy stockholdings. And in deciding questions of bank size and solvency, we should not give much weight to corporate governance issues. Bank sol-

[2] Kenneth H. Bacon, Nationwide-Bank Bill Picks Up Steam as Even Opponents See Mea-sure Passing, Wall Street Journal, Feb. 25, 1994, at A3, col. 2.

[3] Steven Lipin, Bank Industry Seen Shrinking in 1990s, Survey of Executives, Regulators Finds, Wall Street Journal, Oct. 2, 1991, at A14, col. 2.

[4] Herwig Langohr and Anthony M. Santomero, The Extent of Equity Investment by Euro-

vency is too important, because American extensive deposit insurance and the too-big-to-fail doctrine (regulators save big banks because they fear financial disruption if the big ones fail) make banks and stock a volatile mixture. The biggest risk of unleashing the banks is less that they will disable industry than that they will disable themselves and pass these risks on to the public through deposit insurance.

Experimentation with banks makes sense if we could control deposit insurance (and the too-big-to-fail doctrine). Reforming deposit insurance, however, has thus far been nearly intractable—small banks have too much power. The Treasury reforms of the late 1980s were killed in Congress shortly after they were announced,[5] and although Congress did try to tie regulators' hands in paying uninsured depositors at banks that are "too big to fail,"[6] whether Congress will be able to resist the impulse to save a big failing bank has yet to be seen. In the past, the political system has allowed affected banks to appeal to politicians to stop regulators who wanted to shut down bad banks.[7] Hence, a reformed deposit insurance system should be working effectively *before* the country undertakes serious deposit insurance risks with bank stock ownership.

Some plausible but weak initiatives could begin. First, the Fed could revoke its passivity interpretations, which (as we saw in chapter 12) required banks to be passive with the stock that the Bank Holding Company Act of 1956 permits a holding company to own. Although the tenor of bank regulation and the historical separation of banking from commerce demand this interpretation, the statute's words do not. Second, the Act's 5 percent lid on stockholding should be lifted. The regulatory problem is bank solvency, not bank involvement in industry, meaning that the stock held should tie to the capitalization of the holding company and the bank subsidiary, not tie to a percentage of the portfolio firm. In its place should be

---

pean Banks, 42 Journal of Money, Credit and Banking 243 (1985). The leveraging may propel some useful monitoring.

[5] Ann Devroy and Kathleen Day, Deposit Fee Draws Wave of Protest, Washington Post, Jan. 26, 1989, at A1.

[6] The FDIC Improvement Act, which requires risk-based premiums by 1995, limits payments above the explicit insurance ceiling, encourages regulatory intervention prior to insolvency, and discourages regulators from paying uninsured depositors at banks "too big to fail," may seem to reduce the impact of congressional failure to deal with the core problem of a high ($100,000) insured amount. FDIC Improvement Act of 1991, Pub. L. 102–242, 105 Stat. 2236 (1991) (codified in scattered sections of 12 U.S.C., especially FDICIA § 141[a][1][C] [1991], 12 U.S.C. § 1823[c][4][E] [1988]). But we have yet to see how successful these reforms will be and whether regulators will be able to, and be allowed to, act swiftly and effectively.

[7] See, e.g., Perspective—S & L Scandal, Chicago Tribune, Dec. 9, 1988, at 26 (Speaker of the House Wright collected campaign contributions from the S & L and real estate lobbies, and delayed closing down insolvent S & Ls).

general financial ratio tests of the permissible use of equity by bank affiliates; whether the affiliate takes big blocks or small ones should be of less
regulatory concern. Third, since the holding company would not hold a
large stock portfolio even were it permitted to, coordination rules with the
bank complex's *other* stockholdings are important. Banks manage pension
stock, trust stock, and stock in mutual funds that the bank advises. Each
holding is small, but if coordinated with a holding company's position, the
aggregate might not be. Although most legal barriers to coordination come
from the securities laws, some Fed interpretation of the Bank Holding
Company Act could facilitate coordination.

Path Dependence:
Banks as Unprepared for a New Role

These reforms would not change corporate structure much for one key reason: banks are unready for a governance role. Governance gains would be
biggest for the biggest industrial firms, but the biggest American banks are
too small and weak, and are likely to stay that way for at least the near future until a nationwide banking system arises. Thus *allowing* interstate
banking is not the same as *having* a powerful, well-capitalized interstate
banking network; that kind of banking system would take years, possibly
decades, to develop. Today, changing technologies make the historical
bans on branching less important than they once were; computers and telecommunications may make networks of automated teller machines do
what branches and concentrated finance might once have done, making
the branching bans historically important in having kept finance small, but
no longer as influential on the costs of delivering financial services to consumers. And with fractional reserve banking weakening for economic reasons, weak banks might not take on new, complex tasks even if permitted
to do so.

Senior American bank managers lack the skills and experience to be effective. German and Japanese banks "grew up" in the boardrooms or Presidents' Councils of their nations' industry; American bankers did not and
hence are probably less knowledgeable. Different American paths to the
present might have been better, but now that the country has gone down
those paths, it is not clear that managers at the largest banks could make a
contribution. Evolution *from* today might take another path, however. Although few money center banks are in a position to take quick advantage
of changes, regional banks in good shape might use stock to be more involved in the governance of medium-sized firms, some of which will become the largest ones decades hence.

Because the big banks do not now directly hold big blocks of stock in the largest firms, and will not for the foreseeable future, the lessons from abroad, where bankers are primary, are at best general and superficial. Bankers' role here may develop more from the pension money they manage than from the modest amount of stock they would own if ownership and activity restrictions were eased. Blueprints for American reform will come from studying the American pension funds, mutual funds, insurers, boardrooms, and securities markets; the focus should be other than on banks.

THE OTHER FINANCIAL INSTITUTIONS

Banks are not the central players in the United States. Today, the big owners of stock are pension funds and mutual funds, with 31 percent and 10 percent of the stock market, respectively. They are fast growing, likely to capture an increasing part of the traded stock.

Mutual Funds

We could repeal or change the portfolio rules in the Investment Company Act of 1940 and the tax code. Buyers are best protected by adequate disclosure of the structure of the fund's portfolio. Denying an alternative investment vehicle is more likely to harm investors than to help them.

PORTFOLIO RULES

The basic concept of diversification in the 1940 Act and the tax code is well-meaning but antiquated. The bar to a fund's using many blocks of more than 5 percent of its portfolio protects little, because the mutual fund could put all of its monies into a single industry, making the fund ridiculously undiversified.

Unlike banks, mutual funds are not highly leveraged.[8] A decline in value at a large undiversified mutual fund is not as big a social problem as a decline in value of a highly leveraged bank. The decline at the mutual fund is absorbed by thousands of unlucky individuals; the absorption is smooth, the transaction costs low. The decline in value at a highly leveraged bank is absorbed by bank stockholders and the government insurance fund; the absorption of losses is bumpy, transaction costs are high, the moral hazard of excess risk-taking by insolvent banks is substantial.

[8] Investment Company Act of 1940 § 18(a)(1) and (f)(1), 15 U.S.C. § 18(a)(1) and (f)(1) (1988).

CONFLICTS OF INTEREST

Conflicts of interest cannot be ignored. But mutual funds present low levels of conflict when they do not have enough to sell to the industrial firm. They are unlike banks and insurers in that they do not have loan officers seeking to make high-interest loans. True, some mutual fund complexes want access to insider information, and some have pension plans to peddle. Some are affiliated with investment bankers, who have something to sell. And as Glass-Steagall breaks down, increasingly some are affiliated with banks, which have loans to sell. If these conflicts were serious risks, deregulation could begin with fully independent mutual funds.

Institutional ownership can *enhance* managerial power.[9] Financial institutions want to sell their products. Insurance companies and banks want to sell loans, for example. Mutual funds cannot themselves sell loans, but their investment advisors would like to manage pension plans, and corporate managers hire fund managers to run the private pension plans. In the early 1990s battle over antitakeover legislation in Pennsylvania, some mutual funds opposed the legislation. Allegations were heard that one fund dropped its opposition to the antitakeover bill when managers at a large Pennsylvania corporation switched its pension plan to the mutual fund.[10]

Deregulation could be coupled to an anti–back-scratching prohibition: a rule that no mutual fund could own more than 5 percent of a company to which the fund, or an affiliated group, sold pension services. Moreover, conflicts must be seen in context: mutual funds are susceptible to managerial influence when they are weak stockholders; they may not be if they become stronger stockholders. As the block becomes large enough, power shifts from the managers to the stockholder, who becomes more interested in making money by making the company well run rather than by selling a few dollars of services to the company.

An investor can deal with conflicts of interest of *mutual fund* managers better than she can with those of *corporate* managers. To sever her ties with conflicted and underperforming corporate managers, the shareholder must overcome a severe collective action problem. She must mount a takeover or proxy contest to get rid of the offending managers. True, she can sell her shares to someone else. But that someone else is inextricably bound to the offending managers, unless *he* can overcome the collective action problems. Since he will be bound, he will only pay for the value of the package: a pro rata interest in the firm *with these managers*. But the owner of the typical open-end fund can *redeem* her shares. She can send

---

[9] James Brickley, Ronald Lease, and Clifford Smith, Ownership Structure and Voting on Antitakeover Amendments, 20 Journal of Financial Economics 267 (1988).

[10] Gordon Crovitz, Keystone State Kapitalism, Barron's, Apr. 23, 1990, at 10.

the shares into the company, *and get her money back from the company.* The offending managers could quickly find themselves with no assets to manage. Redemption is a serious risk for sub-par mutual fund managers.

JOINT ACTIVITY

It is the *largest* public firms, those that cannot readily have a substitute for a big institutional stockholder—a rich individual, for example, or intense product market competition—that are most likely to benefit from mutual funds with big blocks. But for these firms, even the largest mutual funds might not be able to acquire big enough blocks to have influence. A *group* of financial institutions might be needed.

If there are big governance gains, they will come not from unleashing mutual funds alone, but from *networking* several intermediaries. But these linkages create the greatest risks of the very thing that fragmentation was designed to prevent: concentrations of economic power and conflicts of interest. The balance between governance gains and concentration losses probably should be shifted a bit, although we cannot say how much.

The focal point for readjusting the balance among conflicts, power, and governance would be the prohibition on joint activity with nonconflicted affiliates. These prohibitions should be *partially* lifted. Absent SEC exemption, the Investment Company Act of 1940 today bars a mutual fund owning more than 5 percent of a portfolio company from acting jointly— possibly even to go onto the portfolio firm's board—with any entity that also owns more than 5 percent of the same portfolio firm.[11] Although some SEC exemptions apply to some joint actions, the exemptions' range is unclear; the prohibition on joint activity would be dropped for affiliates that are insurance companies, other mutual funds, bank trust departments, and pension funds, as long as the other financial entities do not sell their products to the portfolio company.[12]

---

[11] Investment Company Act of 1940 § 17(a)(1)–(2), 15 U.S.C. § 17(a)(1)-(2) (1988); 17 C.F.R. § 270.17d-1 (1990); see Martin P. Kroll, The Portfolio Affiliate Problem, in Third Annual Institute on Securities Regulation 261 (Robert Mundheim and Arthur Fleischer, Jr., eds., 1972); Alan Rosenblatt and Martin E. Lybecker, Some Thoughts on the Federal Securities Laws Regulating External Investment Management Arrangements and the ALI Federal Securities Code Project, 124 University of Pennsylvania Law Review 587, 651–54 (1976); Comment, The Application of Section 17 of the Investment Company Act of 1940 to Portfolio Affiliates, 120 University of Pennsylvania Law Review 983 (1972).

[12] Rule 17a-6 moves in this direction, but insufficiently. 17 C.F.R. § 270.17a-6 (1990). And the move in the direction of exemption seems to be undercut, partially or completely, by Rule 17d-1. 17 C.F.R. § 270.17d-1 (1990). Part of the problem is substantive; if anyone acquires a pecuniary interest, presumably including just incentive compensation to a director, the exemption is unavailable. Part of the problem is simple drafting; the blanket exemptions are so opaque that it is said that few lawyers will render opinions that a joint activity is exempt.

LIQUIDITY AND INTERVAL FUNDS

Would mutual funds decline to take big blocks even if they were allowed to do so? They are not leveraged like banks, meaning they are less concerned with stock market volatility. We can find few examples in other nations of mutual funds with big blocks and boardroom presence. But one example suffices to show practicability, and there is one—Sweden, where mutual funds regularly function with five or ten big blocks of stock.[13] American investment companies could do the same.

The Swedish example illuminates an American problem. The Swedish funds are closed-end funds, which, unlike the typical American mutual fund, do *not* allow their investors to redeem out overnight. One reason why U.S. mutual funds do not take big blocks is that their redemption structure—typically overnight in practice, and within a week by law—precludes them from taking big illiquid positions. The incompatibility of big blocks and directors' seats with overnight redemption is exacerbated by regulation. Under section 16(b) of the Securities Exchange Act of 1934, a trader who either owns more than 10 percent of or goes into the boardroom of the portfolio firm, must return all trading profits, even if the trader never had any inside information. For most intermediaries, this is not much of a barrier to big blocks, because they would hold their big blocks, not trade them. But because open-end mutual funds must stand ready to redeem shares and reposition their portfolios on the basis of their own investors' demands, the interplay between section 16(b) and business-based liquidity needs makes going into the boardroom, or taking a big block of stock, quite risky.

Closed-end funds are an alternative, because they do not have the same liquidity pressures, and they are the type that takes the big blocks in Sweden. But they face two problems here. They do not discipline fund managers as well as the open-end structure does, because the assets cannot move out easily. A disgruntled investor in a closed-end fund is stuck. And persistent discounts—the trading value is usually noticeably below the net asset value of the fund, for inexplicable reasons[14]—make them unpopular.

These problems could be reduced. Business often entails trade-offs. But the 1940 Act does not allow a trade-off here. It does not yet allow the investor to buy a vehicle where the fund would take big illiquid blocks and the investors could redeem only on, say, three months' notice. Such vehicles would be particularly useful for retirement money, for which the investor has a long horizon.

---

[13] Ronald J. Gilson and Reinier Kraakman, Investment Companies as Guardian Shareholders: The Place of the MSIC in the Corporate Governance Debate, 45 Stanford Law Review 985 (1993).

[14] Reinier Kraakman, Taking Discounts Seriously: The Implications of "Discounted" Share Prices as an Acquisition Motive, 88 Columbia Law Review 891, 902–05 (1988).

The SEC staff's recent proposals to permit interval funds,[15] although not intended to enhance corporate governance, are good ones in allowing investors to trade off redemption against fund flexibility to take bigger blocks. In tandem with changes in the portfolio rules, in general joint action exemptions, and in coordination with section 16(b), they could provide another American organizational form for the ownership of stock.

Thus for mutual funds, several changes are in order. The portfolio limits, while not an absolute bar, unnecessarily raise the cost of an alternative, competitive organizational form. They should be dropped from the 1940 Act and from the tax code. The limits on joint activity should be loosened. And interval funds should be allowed.

Pension Funds

The American pension fund system is huge and now rivals the banking system in aggregate assets. The current managerial command structure for private pension funds came about largely accidentally, and now that it is here, it makes minor legal change unimportant and major legal change risky.

STRUCTURAL CHANGE

The major legal change would be to tear down the managerial command structure. Pension plans could mimic IRAs and Keogh plans; employees would direct their money to, say, Vanguard or Fidelity or Prudential, which would invest it. Plausible minimal employee protection could come from Department of Labor licensing, to protect unsophisticated investors from the thieves.[16] Just as an employee selects the bank to which the employer should send the paycheck, the employee would select the fund that would invest the pension money. With some institutions cumulating many pensions (from many employees at many companies), it is plausible that these funds would be able to take big blocks of stock and sit on boards, free from today's managerial control.

Such a change would restructure the nation's savings system for unproven corporate governance benefits, when organizing secure savings is

---

[15] Division of Investment Management, Securities and Exchange Commission, Protecting Investors: A Half Century of Investment Company Regulation 425, 442 (May 1992).

[16] One problem is that individual investors of pension money often are excessively risk averse. Individuals pick debt, not stock. Collective vehicles, with risk shared, could yield higher-equity investing.

Moreover, this could warp corporate structure, which already through tax policy favors debt over equity. The obvious answer, while we are remaking all of the country's critical financial institutions, would be to correct the debt-equity tax imbalance.

more important. After all, pensions' prime purpose is to provide old-age security, not to improve corporate governance. If corporate governance experiments were all that was on our economic agenda, then we might try such experiments—but they aren't, so we shouldn't. Although only structural change has much chance of yielding big corporate governance gains, that kind of change will have large transition costs, and may still not work well.

In chapter 9 I argued that the passive role of private pension funds is not likely to change dramatically unless one of two changes occurs. If managers perceive active pension funds to be in their own interest, the doctrinal barriers will fall quickly and pension funds' representatives will enter the boardrooms. Alternatively, unexpected social change could alter the managerial command structure. Defined-benefit plans are typically run by managers; a social shift from defined-benefit plans to defined-contribution plans could distance managers from private pensions and could change the balance of authority between managers and financiers running the pension funds. A change to defined-contribution plans is slowly occurring anyway, partly because of increasing job mobility.

DOCTRINAL CHANGE

Doctrinal changes could set the stage for structural change, but would not shift the balance very much. The doctrinal changes could include a diversification safe harbor, a clear permission to net big-block losses against big-block gains, a clear business judgment standard for portfolio construction, and enhanced scrutiny of pension funds that defer excessively to corporate managers.

But multiple problems would afflict even these simple changes, making it unclear whether change would improve matters. First, I am not sanguine that doctrinal change is important, because structure is more important. Second, some rules benefit employee-beneficiaries or the government guarantee funds; even if they overdeter corporate governance activity, they may on balance be good. Third, slight missteps in doctrinal change might produce perverse results in cutting off innovation or in fostering even greater deference to managers. Thus a safe harbor for concentrated portfolios might become the de facto standard, cutting off use of even less concentrated portfolios. Or a business judgment rule, even a narrow one applicable only to boardroom activities of pension funds with big blocks, might backfire by giving doctrinal cover that would allow pension funds to give even *more* deference to managers, especially if the managerial command structure stayed stable. Steadfast *fund* managers might *prefer* a strong fiduciary rule that they can use as an "excuse" to managers for not buckling under the managerial pressure. To remedy this, pension regulators might scrutinize pension managers more carefully if they took big blocks but deferred to managers. But this too could backfire: if the inquiries became too severe, pension managers might become even *more* reluctant to take the big blocks that would trigger such inquiries.

Moreover, we must keep in mind that the foreign comparisons weaken when we move to mutual funds and pension funds. Abroad, the banker often is simultaneously a creditor and stockholder, making it less likely to make the firm excessively risky, in a way that threatens the firm's employees. But a pure stockholder may profit at the expense of employees, managers, and creditors from the firm's excessive risk-taking. The banks' leveraged portfolio encourages it to be prudent in a way that fits the others involved in the firm; it worries about risks that threaten its loans to the firm. Lastly, large portfolio losses for a banker would trigger regulatory inquiries that would not arise if the portfolio were in a mutual fund or pension fund.

GENERAL REGULATION—
SECURITIES LAWS AND THE TAX CODE:
COORDINATION COSTS AMONG INVESTORS AND INDUSTRY

Securities Laws

I have for the most part here ignored securities laws, because my focus has been on the political and regulatory underpinnings that prevented big blocks and boardroom presence in the large public firm, and securities rules were probably neither key to the historical development of that fragmentation nor usually explicable in part by the political forces that helped produce that fragmentation. But for institutions to play a bigger role in corporate governance, they need either bigger blocks or a lower cost of coordination. Given that big blocks are not, absent crisis, a likely result for the near future, the practical focus for change will be on increased coordination. And for increased coordination, the securities laws become more important. Securities rules have become the frontline of reform, *because* ownership was fragmented.

These rules make coordination among stockholders stickier than it has to be. Until recently, ten shareholders who spoke with one another about a corporation's management risked violating the proxy rules. While some rules have loosened, more could. Mutual funds risk insider-trading liability even when they have no inside information and even when they trade in response to the flux of sales and redemptions of their own shares. While most relational investors will buy and hold, some, such as mutual funds, cannot be sure that they will be able to buy and hold. Adjusting the rule to accommodate large institutions in the boardroom makes sense.

Managers control the proxy machinery. At company expense, they solicit votes (for themselves and for major corporate changes) from scattered shareholders. Shareholders, with less information than the centralized managers, have little reason to invest in second-guessing the managers. Even if they do second-guess the managers, shareholders rarely have the economic incentive to make a countersolicitation. The solicitation will be expensive, and the shareholder will capture only a fraction of any potential gains.[17] To mitigate the cost disparity, large shareholders (or groups of smaller ones) should be allowed to make statements or nominate alternative directors through management's proxy. Current law is to the contrary: shareholders cannot get access to the managers' proxy statement to nominate directors, to oppose management proposals, or to make alternative proposals. As the votes come in, management sees how shareholders voted and can lobby the negative voters to change their mind; dissidents are blind, unaware of the results until the votes are tabulated.

Active investors have to make filings with the SEC as soon as the investors become active; to wait a few days is to court disaster. Groups that form to influence the firm must file their intentions with the SEC. (Similarly, states allow, in a residue of the antitakeover laws of the 1980s, poison pills that could be triggered when stockholders with as little as 20 percent of the firm's stock form a plan of action.) The securities laws also place substantial legal liability on the shareholder that controls the firm. Liability here is not wrong, but the notions of "control" are too wide; a group of institutions with only 10 percent of a firm's stock and a couple of directors could, unwisely, create a presumption of control.[18] These legal risks, which could lead institutional shareholders to forgo activity and anything that smacks not only of control but of influence, can be recast so as not to discourage useful activity, while still protecting shareholders generally. For example, the SEC rules could permit groups of a few shareholders (say, less than ten) to form and even vote their shares without an SEC filing when they are not seeking majority control of the firm's board; if the group solicits other shareholders with a view to control, then it would be regulated by the proxy rules, not the group-filing rules. Alternatively, the threshold for filing by a group of shareholders could be raised from the current 5 percent to, say, 20 percent.

The voting system is generally an open one: managers can find out how shareholders vote. Because private pension funds own 22 percent of the stock, open voting has obvious problems: managers, who can allocate pension money management, can see how pension managers vote. A realistic reform would require secret voting. This would not change boardroom gov-

---

[17] The best detailed list of suitable securities laws changes is Bernard S. Black, Disclosure Not Censorship: The Case for Proxy Reform, Journal of Corporation Law, Fall 1991, at 49.

[18] A. A. Sommer, Who's In Control? 21 Business Lawyer 559, 568 (1966).

ernance, because big boardroom players cannot act secretly, but it might make voting more responsible.

These securities reforms will not fully change ownership structure, nor will they in themselves allow a new, distinct organizational form to arise. But they are the kind of modest incremental adjustments that will be on the real-world calendar.

Taxes

The corporate dividends-received tax was designed to discourage complex corporate structures, but interfirm partial cross-ownership is an organizational form that might have some competitive success. Eliminating the dividends-received tax would reduce one big barrier to its arising. But again, path dependence makes a difference: cross-ownership is useful in linking *small* firms; in lieu of cross-ownership, large vertically integrated firms arose, as the GM-Fisher story shows (see chapter 19). Adding cross-ownership *after* the large firms have arisen may mistakenly encourage yet bigger firms and managerial entrenchment, not the partial decentralization and divestiture of the already big ones.

More generally, some tax rules treat institutional intermediaries that stand between the ultimate individual investor and the corporate user as separate taxable entities. To the extent that tax rules simplify and impose only one tax, private contracting can better search for the best organizational forms.

THE PROBLEM OF TRANSITION: PATH DEPENDENCE AND THE FUTILITY OF LEGAL CHANGE?

The Status Quo—Economic and Institutional Reasons

Legal change alone might not lead to structural change. Once a nation spends a century setting its institutions in place, the institutions may continue unchanged when the supporting legal buttresses are removed. Even were regulation in Germany, Japan, and the United States to be made identical, the differing structures in each might continue for quite some time.

Let us see why change might not occur even if the American rules were altered, by adopting the institution's perspective. To begin with, the social gains from involvement are probably not large. And other mechanisms substitute, albeit imperfectly, for large shareholders in the boardroom. Whatever large shareholders might accomplish in the United States is partially done by product market competition, by capital market competition, by managerial labor markets, and by incentive compensation. Even the informational roles that institutions might provide to coordinate industry and deter the short-run propensities of the stock market are alleviated by industry associations, university research, and specialized research media. Problems have already evoked responses and partial substitutes.

Second, because of free-rider effects, the private gains are even less than whatever social gains are left. The institution cannot capture all gains, and the transaction costs of transformation could exceed the private gains to a 5 percent stockholder.

Third, complex institutions are shaped by their history. Past restrictions made them what they are today; massive structural change is hard. British institutions, for example, faced some historical restrictions, but they face fewer today. Yet the institutions exercise less voice than the *current* legal limits would allow, and certainly less than the German and Japanese banks have historically exercised.[19] (True, British ownership of large firms is moderately concentrated,[20] some British institutions exercise voice, and internal controls separate the CEO from the chair of the board, all accomplishing some of what institutions might do.)

The strength of path dependence is illustrated by comparing American and British insurers: American insurers are not *now* tightly restricted, but they are inactive; until the 1980s, most big American insurers were barred from owning much stock. British insurers were never banned from owning stock, and the restraints they faced were informal. They have always owned stock and today play a restrained role in corporate governance. Thus the historical differences seem to determine the current different stockholding and governance realities. Like molten metal poured into a cast, law can shape an institution when it is first made. Pull away the cast when the metal has cooled—change the law decades later, when the institutions are set in place—and the metallic sculpture remains unchanged.

The Status Quo—Inertia

Transition is costly; if the costs of transition outweigh the gains from a superior structure change will not occur. Moreover, if there are complex economic networks, it is theoretically possible that change will not occur even

---

[19] Bernard Black, The Value of Institutional Investor Monitoring: The Empirical Evidence, 39 UCLA Law Review 895, 928 (1992) ("British . . . insurers, are quite active by American standards."); Getting Rid of the Boss, Economist, Feb. 6, 1993, at 13 ("To some extent, British [CEO's] have always had to answer to the tightly knit world of the City of London, whose old-boy networks and customs often served as a check on their worst excesses. But the [CEO's] of big American firms were true masters of all they surveyed."); supra chapter 13.

[20] Julian Franks and Colin Mayer, Corporate Control: A Synthesis of the International

if transition is less costly than the gains, because someone—presumably a government agency—must coordinate a transition in which all firms and institutions move simultaneously. Absent coordination, nothing happens. Yet with the evidence of superiority scant, there is little reason to promote that kind of governmental coordination.

For reasons that are not clear, the international pattern is that either all of a nation's large firms have concentrated institutional voice or none do. German firms' proxies are held by the big banks, and those banks or firms or families own big blocks; Japanese big firms have 20 percent of their stock owned by five banks and insurers; American big firms have distant ownership. Economic deduction suggests that firms that would benefit from concentrated ownership by financial intermediaries would have it, while firms that would not benefit from such ownership would have scattered ownership.[21] But the international results—either all one way or all the other—suggest that a tilt in the power of intermediaries in either direction leads to concentrated voting or its absence. This helps strengthen the political theory—structure depends on financial organization and regulation, not the characteristics of the firms themselves—but makes the prescriptive task harder. A nation might try to get the benefits of both arrangements by allowing both, reaping the gains from greater voice for firms where it works best and the gains from fluid stock markets where that works best. But if a slight tilt in financial regulation tilts the boardroom result all one way, those gains from diversity become hard or impossible; and this possibility is one more reason why the policy dimension for corporate governance reform may be a dead end.

This network viewpoint—rules that merely *permit* other structures would be pointless once we have the system we have, because behavior and networks are embedded and hard to change—is the best justification for policy proposals to force change by, say, a securities trading tax. The tax, which would apply to sales of securities (including normally untaxed institutions, such as pension funds) held for less than, say, six months, would take away trading strategies, forcing those owning stock to think about long-term positions. Taxation would deny the institutions liquidity, and presumably channel them into governance.

But, in my view, without solid evidence *both* that getting the new structure is worth the transition costs *and* that there are network characteristics that require simultaneous parallel changes across the board, we lack the

---

Evidence, at tbl. 2 (Nov. 1992) (unpublished manuscript) (64 percent of the two hundred largest British firms have a stockholder owning more than 5 percent).

[21] Harold Demsetz and Kenneth Lehn, The Structure of Corporate Ownership: Causes and Consequences, 93 Journal of Political Economy 1155 (1985) (describing sorting trend among American firms).

reason to *force* new organizational forms into being. Thus, although rules that merely *permit* alternative structures might be pointless, they are for now the best we can do.

The Status Quo—Political Reasons

A persuasive case for reform, backed by good data, can defeat political interest groups that would want to maintain the status quo. But since the theory and data are uncertain, and today best support only a loosening of rules that would permit organizational competition, the political problems arise again. Proposals to permit organizational competition are easy to defeat with TV sound bites—for example: Why allow an alien, un-American form of organization to slip in, when we have no reason to believe it is surely better than the fine system that we have? Powerful groups have an interest in the status quo, and they will make such arguments. Many making them will not see anything duplicitous; they will sincerely hold their view, and find the moderate position—allow competition—silly. If it is better, make it the law; if it is not, leave it to academic writings.

Managers have made such arguments in the modern context. They were instrumental in getting antitakeover laws that raised the costs of hostile takeovers. And when the SEC proposed a rollback of barriers to shareholder communication, the managers attacked, although unsuccessfully. Perhaps they lost because the rollback (allowing shareholders to talk, but not make their own unregulated proxy solicitation) was so sensible.

Moreover, incumbent *institutions* will not always welcome new organizational forms that will force them to compete or change, in ways they may not be adept. Even if there are gains from their involvement, the institutions will compete away those gains; society will be better run, but the institutions will be no more profitable. Thus, institutions who see themselves as having no competitive advantage in change would have reason to oppose it. And even if they otherwise would want change, they will see political risks. Thus key players from major financial institutions have said that they should not even get close to a major governance role, *because* of political reasons. When the possibility of insurers' being allowed to own stock and play a big role in corporate governance arose decades ago, Prudential testified that "they were shy of becoming 'partners in enterprise' *lest they be accused of extending their economic power*."[22] Bank advisers have told banks not to be active with their bank trust stock.[23]

In today's world, with banks and insurers far from the governance

---

[22] See supra chapter 6, note 68.
[23] See supra chapter 12, note 7.

picture, we should not now expect them to worry about a political reaction to corporate governance excess, but private pension funds, public
pension funds, and mutual funds, all three of which have become the
big holders of stock, have reason to worry. And we can find the leading
players for *each* of these stockholders worrying out loud about these
fears. While they may be unaware of the political origin of the separation
(although I doubt they all are unaware of it), they may be like the person who discovered she had been writing prose all her life and had not
known it.

The CEO of TIAA-CREF, the nation's largest private pension plan, says
that he is uninterested in enhanced institutional power, and that power
would induce a backlash: "It bothers me to see institutional investors
amass power in a way that I don't believe is legitimate," he said, adding
that such aggregations could prompt a backlash from the public and politicians.[24] The largest public pension plan, CalPERS, fears that "an organized Calpers-backed attempt to force management changes could trigger
a reaction that could curb the big fund's freedom to act independently," in
a fashion similar to the restraints arising from the 1980s takeovers.[25] The
general counsel to the largest mutual fund complex sees political impediments to mutual funds' having heavy involvement in corporate governance. Indeed, he examined the possibility of big-block mutual funds and
concluded that "[t]o implement their ideas on a broad scale, [those seeking
big blocks] would have to persuade Congress to relax the current limits on
institutional investors substantially." But although institutions and managers would then remain free to reject the big blocks if they found them
inefficient—the organizational competition model I have proposed here—
the mutual fund counsel predicted that "[c]orporate executives would undoubtedly oppose such a relaxation as a threat to management control, *and
they would find allies in most institutional investors*," whom he said are repelled by a German or Japanese model.[26]

The political point is twofold. First, if managers and institutions both oppose rule changes, it is hard to see where the constituency for change
would be. At least one, and probably both, would have to believe that
structural change is to their advantage. But with thin data and weak theory, that is not likely to occur soon. Second, even if rules were to change,
the institutions might not take advantage of them. On top of the private
costs of change, they see the costs of political problems.

[24] Leslie Scism, Teachers' Pension Plan to Give Firms Tough Exams, Wall Street Journal,
Oct. 6, 1993, at C1, col. 1.

[25] Randall Smith, Calpers Mulls Stakes in Funds Seeking Changes in Firms' Strategy, Governance, Wall Street Journal, Dec. 31, 1992, at A3.

[26] Robert C. Pozen, Institutional Investors: The Reluctant Activists, Harvard Business Review, Jan.–Feb. 1994, at 140, 149.

There is also a subtle, psychological bias toward the status quo: mature people often see the normal to be the world they saw when they first came of age. Today's financial leaders came of age when institutions had no governance role, and they could prefer that seemingly happier world. Add the fact that the received images of powerful institutions are foreign, and the bias can strengthen.

A key governance task is to decide how to downsize when firms are no longer fit for changing technologies. When a society's problem is the need to systematically downsize, I believe financial institutions often will hesitate, because they will fear a political reaction. Involvement with failing firms will taint the institutions with failure, and they will be blamed for the underlying problem. This taint was probably a factor in some New Deal bans and in some 1980s antitakeover laws.

Since a disproportionate amount of today's corporate restructuring involves layoffs, downsizing, and disruption, institutional investors ought to know that if they are seen as inducing this disruption, there will be a political backlash. When they are sophisticated enough not to push too hard in corporate governance, they are thereby internalizing the political theory and the politicized inhibitions about unrestrained shareholder action. Governance can matter most when firms need to downsize, and that is when the political impulses are strongest. Institutions might shy away from forcing a downsizing even if they had the requisite voting and organizational authority, and even if they were not bound by any formal restraints, because they would fear that forcing a downsizing would be likely to induce a political reaction.

Managers are situated in several markets and organizations. The internal organization of the boardroom and its relationship with institutional shareholders is only one, and perhaps not the most important. The faltering German and Japanese economies in the early 1990s tell us the obvious: that governance alone will not save firms from collapse or from change. The professional pride of managers and directors makes them try hard even if the organizational constraints acting on them are weak. Embarrassment from media attention will help correct the most egregious errors. Product markets, capital markets, managerial labor markets, employee labor markets, and corporate takeover markets constrain managers. Governance is more important when these competitive controls are weak, less important when they are strong. This is all another way of saying that corporate governance is only one dimension of competition.

Path dependence means that the immediate future for American reform is not big institutional blocks or industrial cross-ownership, but incremental improvements in the quality of boards of directors and their relationship with shareholders. Not ideal perhaps, but, given where political determinants put the American firm in the 1990s, at least imaginable.

Conclusion

THE ANALYTIC RESULT is fundamental: the modern American public corporation is not an inevitable consequence of technology that demands large inputs of capital. Technology combined with the diversification demands of investors to yield the fragmented ownership of the public firm and the shift to centralized managerial authority, but that result became inevitable only because the United States fragmented its financial intermediaries. Politics confined the terrain on which the large American enterprise could evolve. That confinement allowed the public corporation with dispersed ownership, and not some other organization, to evolve.

The fragmentation of institutional capital meant that owners' power would shift somewhere. It shifted to managers, who obtained their power partly by default: the American public would not permit large, powerful financial institutions that would share power at the top, so the power to direct large corporations further centralized in managers' hands. Managers may not be political heroes to the average voter, but they are dispersed, which makes them less visible targets than financial institutions. And managers obtained and kept some of that power because they themselves have political influence.

My argument has two steps. One, the legal system limited control by financial institutions. The limitations came in three types: (1) prohibitions—for banks and, for most of the twentieth century, the big insurers; (2) fragmentation of financial institutions—they often could not own one another and could not readily network their portfolios to assert control jointly; and (3) fragmentation of institutional portfolios. Two, these limitations were not all technical, but often have a political explanation.

I have sketched the ideas of representative actors—Woodrow Wilson, Louis Brandeis, William Douglas—and examined the political analogues, which include the Armstrong investigation, the Pujo investigation, the Pecora hearings, and surveys of public opinion. They indicate a pervasive historical mistrust of financial power. Small financial institutions and, later, managers lobbied for restrictions. These ideas, investigations, and interests resulted in laws that prohibited banks from owning stock, prohibited bank holding companies from owning influential blocks of stock in an industrial company, restricted mutual funds from buying controlling blocks of industrial companies, and prohibited and then limited insurance companies from owning stocks. As I write, just after the conservative 1980s, when popular mistrust of accumulated power on the eastern seaboard was directed more at Washington than at Wall Street, it is easy to forget the deep mistrust that once divided Main Street and Wall Street.

The political modification of the economic paradigm works on a grand scale for Eastern Europe and the former Soviet Union, where economic structures were politically determined for most of this century. Now that those structures have collapsed, politics is shaping the new ownership structures. For example, Russia has tried to privatize with a widespread voucher system, because those engineering privatization wanted to create both entrepreneurs and a mass of owners with a stake in a new system. In Poland, I understand that privatization did not put ownership in the hands of those running the old factories, partly to weaken the corrupt nomenklatura, and partly because the political demands of Polish peasants for a stake in privatization could not be avoided. Privatization experts thought, however, that they could satisfy the peasants' ownership demands and still have stock votes not be diffuse, by creating powerful mutual funds with big blocks of stock.

Savings could flow from households to large firms through powerful intermediaries that would share authority with senior managers, flattening the steep hierarchy that typifies the American firm. This has been the pattern in Germany and Japan. The foreign institutions control large blocks, but do not dominate the firm. Usually several intermediaries have blocks. The foreign structures are more like each other than like the American hierarchy. The German and Japanese fragmenting laws differ from the American ones, permitting powerful financial intermediaries that would be illegal in the United States. The German and Japanese corporate structures are no *less* politically influenced; but historically the foreign politics was different in kind and result from the American variety.

I examine Germany and Japan not to argue that they are better and should be mimicked, but to show that different systems of governance are possible, that the American-style public firm with fragmented shareholder power is not inevitable, that managers can share power with intermedaries without the corporate world's falling apart, that perhaps we could, if we wanted, change the American pattern.

American corporate reform with bite would not work well for banks. Although changes are imaginable for the other institutions, we do not know enough to mandate the right ones. Rather, we should ease up on the least useful restrictions and let economic evolution and private contracting take their course. But we should not be optimistic that much will happen of central economic importance for two reasons: we do not yet have clear evidence that institutional involvement systematically improves performance greatly, or at all; and path dependence means that institutions might not change much even if legal barriers were torn down.

A couple of years after GM's senior management rebuffed two of its large shareholders, who had wanted to discuss how to choose a new CEO, GM's board fired that new CEO. Prodded by unhappy intermediaries and media attention, the directors had become more active in prodding a declining organization to change. Similar changes swept through the boardrooms of IBM, Westinghouse, and a few other firms. These changes should be seen as intertwined with the country's history of financial fragmentation. They are new because we historically suppressed powerful intermediaries, and at least part of our corporate evolution has been to find substitutes for what was suppressed: conglomerates, outside directors, takeovers, and now active boards and stockholders.

This new shareholder activism, although isolated in a few firms, should be seen in light of this political inquiry. Financiers are today on the outside because of past political decisions. If shareholder activism becomes really important, then its regulation could spill over into politics, as it did for take-overs. Unless there is a new departure, the future's corporate governance battles will, if they turn out to be big ones, be settled by political decisions, not solely by economic efficiency.

If those struggles do indeed move into the political arena, it is hard to say how things will come out. Anti-finance "populism" is not what it once was as a political force. True, if institutions were seen as systematically squeezing firms to downsize, one would expect that the losers would appeal to political actors and get a sympathetic hearing. But if the political contest is seen as pitting responsible institutions against greedy managers, we could imagine the resulting rules as not hurting shareholder activism badly. The attention to managerial salaries in the media suggests that modern 1990s' "populism" can target managers as well as institutions. Moreover, the "high" road is not irrelevant: if institutions regularly and clearly improve firms, and if strong theory and solid evidence back up their actions, Congress and public opinion could take their side. Financial institutions face more problems when the results are mixed, the theories weak, and the evidence ambiguous.

But my conclusion here is not a political prediction. The major premise here is that we came to this juncture in corporate governance because of political decisions marked deeply by the American people's historical dislike of concentrated private economic power, and reinforced by the country's federalist organization and interest group maneuvering. There are two minor premises. One is that if history is a guide, then if shareholder activism becomes salient, it would become a political matter. The second minor premise is that while institutions in the 1990s still have a couple of strikes against them in the political arena, they do not *have* to lose the political battle.

The overall message here is less programmatic than analytic and conceptual. Politics influenced the structure of the large public firm. Firms in nations that have tolerated large pools of private economic power evolved differently than did firms in nations that have repeatedly fragmented financial institutions, their portfolios, and their ability to network blocks of stock. The firm is not isolated, but is bound to a political culture and cannot be understood as solely an economic, transaction-cost–reducing organization. It must not only be effective economically, but fit politically, because it operates not just in an economic environment, but in a political environment as well. Would-be reformers need to keep this in mind.

Structures in Germany and Japan fit their political history; structures here fit ours. It is not good enough to conclude that change in structure is sensible; the change must be politically adaptable, as well as economically astute. Moreover, the modest competitive impact of the restrictions strengthens the political thesis; if the rules scuttled a powerfully efficient, effective tool, there would be even more pressure to overcome them transactionally and politically. Because the efficiency effects are modest, the rules can and the structures can persist.

Perhaps it is all quite simple. Concentrated financial capital does not mix well with a broad-based egalitarian democracy in which interest groups can acquire great influence; one should not be surprised to see democracy influencing the structure of corporate finance. But I have tried here to inquire more deeply into the politics of the limiting legislation. The story has five elements: (1) inertia and the American federal political structure, (2) pursuit of public goals, (3) interest group politics, (4) political elites' desire to shatter economic elites, and (5) a populism that has sought to fragment power in the economy.

This history opens up two policy perspectives. A widespread academic view is that the public corporation represents the natural selection of the fittest organizational adaption to the economies of scale, difficulties of agency costs, and problems of technology. The historical demonstration suggests that the natural selection analogues are incomplete. Politics molded the modern corporation, at least in important part, and it is worthwhile for academics to begin to consider whether alternative financial and organizational forms would better resolve problems of organization. While it does not follow from the existence of political limitations that these limitations are for the worse, it is an open question whether we have achieved the best.

The second policy perspective confines the first. While I have shown to my own satisfaction that it is open as an *analytic* question whether politics allowed the best organizational configuration to control agency costs, to reduce conflicts of interest, and to reduce cartel and monopoly organization, history shows that American politics thus far has resisted enhancing the power of financial institutions. If these political forces persist, then efforts to resolve the agency problem with outside financial control must somehow defeat or elude the political restrictions.

But we need not now assess the relative strength of these political explanations. Nor need we conclude whether the restrictions are beneficial, or whether other rules could have facilitated monitoring without deterring other valuable goals. Nor need we yet fully assess how effective the new institutional activism of the 1990s will be, or whether it will generate its own political reaction, as has regularly occurred in the American past. None of this is necessary to understand the more central and until now neglected point: Politics heavily influenced corporate ownership structure. By restricting the terrain on which the large enterprise could evolve, politics created the fragmented Berle-Means corporation and the substitutes that have emerged, every bit as much as did natural laws of economy and technology. The Berle-Mean corporation arose to fit the kind of financial system that American history produced. It is an adaptation, not a necessity.

Bibliography

Government Documents

Congressional Hearings

Hearings Before Subcommittee of the House Committee on Banking and Currency. 62d Cong., 3d Sess., 1913. [Money Trust Investigation.]

Stock Exchange Practices: Hearings Before the Senate Committee on Banking and Currency. 73d Cong., 1st Sess., 1934.

Revenue Act of 1936: Confidential Hearings on H.R. 12395 Before the Senate Committee on Finance. 74th Cong., 2d Sess., 1936.

Revenue Act of 1936: Hearings Before the House Committee on Ways and Means on H.R. 12395. 74th Cong., 2d Sess., 1936.

Hearings Before the House Committee on Ways and Means on the Revenue Revision—1939. 76th Cong., 1st Sess., 1939.

Hearings on S. 3580 Before a Subcommittee of the Senate Committee on Banking and Currency. 76th Cong., 3d Sess. 1940.

Revenue Revision of 1942: Hearings Before the House Committee on Ways and Means. 77th Cong., 2d Sess., 1942.

Federal Reserve Act Amendments: Hearings Before the House Committee on Banking and Currency. 83d Cong., 2d Sess., 1954.

Control of Bank Holding Companies: Hearings Before a Subcommittee of the Senate Committee on Banking and Currency. 84th Cong., 1st Sess., 1955.

Stock Market Study (Corporate Proxy Contests): Hearings Before Senate Committee on Banking and Currency on S.879. 84th Cong., 1st Sess., 1955.

Bank Holding Company Act Amendments: Hearings Before the House Committee on Banking and Currency. 91st Cong., 1st Sess., 1969.

International Banking Act of 1976: Hearings Before the Subcommittee on Financial Institutions of the Senate Committee on Banking, Housing and Urban Affairs. 94th Cong., 2d Sess., 1976.

Role of the Financial Services Sector: Hearings Before the Task Force on the International Competitiveness of U.S. Financial Institutions of the Subcommittee on Financial Institutions Supervision, Regulation and Insurance of the House Committee on Banking, Finance and Urban Affairs. 101st Cong., 2d Sess., 1990.

Congressional Reports and Documents

House Minority Report No. 245 on H.R. 3020, House Report No. 245. 80th Cong. 1st Sess., 1947.

International Banking Act of 1978. Senate Report No. 1073. 95th Cong., 2d Sess., 1978.

Senate Committee on Banking and Currency. Senate Report No. 1455. *Stock Exchange Practices.* 73d Cong., 2d Sess., 1934.

Senate Committee on Governmental Affairs. *Structure of Corporate Concentration:*

Institutional Shareholders and Interlocking Directorates among Major U.S. Corporations, pt. 2. 96th Cong., 2d Sess., 1980. Committee print.

Senate Report No. 77. 73d Cong., 1st Sess. 1933.

Subcommittee on Domestic Finance of House Committee on Banking and Currency. Report on Bank Stock Ownership and Control. 89th Cong., 2d Sess., 1966. Committee print.

Subcommittee on Domestic Finance of House Committee on Banking and Currency. *Commercial Banks and Their Trust Activities: Emerging Influence on the American Economy*. 90th Cong., 2d Sess., 1968. Committee print.

Supplemental Views of Senators Taft, Ball, Donnell and Jenner. In [Senate] Committee on Labor and Public Welfare, Federal Labor Relations Act of 1947, Senate Report No. 105. 80th Cong., 1st Sess., 1947.

Temporary National Economic Committee. *Investigation of Concentration of Economic Power: Statement on Life Insurance*. Monograph No. 28-A. 76th Cong., 3d Sess., 1950. Committee print.

U.S. Department of the Treasury

U.S. Department of the Treasury. Modernizing the Financial System: Recommendations for Safer, More Competitive Banks. 1991.

Federal Reserve System

Board of Governors of the Federal Reserve System. Flow of Funds Accounts—First Quarter. 1993.

Federal Reserve Committee on Branch, Group, and Chain Banking. Branch Banking in the United States. 1937.

Securities and Exchange Commission

Division of Investment Management, Securities and Exchange Commission, Protecting Investors: A Half Century of Investment Company Regulation. May 1992.

SEC, Abuses and Deficiencies in the Organization and Operation of Investment Trusts and Investment Companies. House Doc. No. 270, pt. 3. 76th Cong., 1st Sess., 1939.

Wharton School of Finance and Commerce. A Study Prepared for the SEC. House Report No. 2274. 87th Cong., 2d Sess., 1962.

New York State

Governor [Cuomo]'s Task Force on Pension Fund Investment. Our Money's Worth. June 1989.

Joint Committee of the Senate and Assembly of the State of New York to Investigate and Examine into the Business and Affairs of Life Insurance Companies Doing Business in the State of New York. Report. 1906.

New York Joint Committee for Revision of Insurance Law. Public Hearings. Oct. 21, 1941.

State of New York. 1982. Report of the Executive Advisory Commission on Insurance Industry Regulatory Reform.

State of New York. Report of the Joint Legislative Committee on Insurance Rates and Regulations. 1951. Leg. Doc. No. 55.

Superintendent of Insurance of the State of New York. Forty-Second Annual Report. Pt. 2, Life, Casualty, Title, Credit and Mortgage Guarantee Insurance. 1901.

Books and Chapters of Books

Anderson, Buist. 1952. *The Armstrong Investigation in Retrospect*.

Andreades, Andreas Michael. 1909. *History of the Bank of England*.

Aoki, Masahiko. 1984. *The Economic Analysis of the Japanese Firm*.

Ballon, Robert J., and Iwao Tomita. 1988. *The Financial Behavior of Japanese Corporations*.

Baumol, William J., Steven M. Goldfeld, Lilli A. Gordon, and Michael Koehn. 1990. *The Economics of Mutual Funds Markets: Competition versus Regulation*.

Beard, Charles A. 1935. *An Economic Interpretation of the Constitution of the United States*.

Benston, George. 1990. *The Separation of Commercial and Investment Banking*.

Berle, Adolf, and Gardiner Means. 1933. *The Modern Corporation and Private Property*.

Bisson, T. A. 1954. *Zaibatsu Dissolution in Japan*.

Bittker, Boris, and James Eustice. 1987. *Federal Income Taxation of Corporations and Shareholders*. 5th ed.

Blakey, Roy G., and Gladys M. Blakey. 1940. *The Federal Income Tax*.

Blasi, Joseph R., and Douglas L. Kruse. 1991. *The New Owners: The Mass Emergence of Employee Ownership in Public Companies and What It Means to American Business*.

Blinder, Alan S. 1991. Profit Maximization and International Competition. In vol. 5 of *AMEX Bank Review Prize Essays*, edited by Richard O'Brien.

Bork, Robert. 1978. *The Antitrust Paradox*.

Brandeis, Louis. 1914. *Other People's Money—And How the Bankers Use It*.

Brimmer, Andrew F. 1962. *Life Insurance Companies in the Capital Market*.

Brinkley, Alan. 1982. *Voices of Protest, Huey Long, Father Coughlin, and the Great Depression*.

Brody, David. 1980. *Workers in Industrial America*.

Buley, R. Carlyle. 1967. *The Equitable Life Assurance Society of the United States—1859–1964*.

Bullock, Hugh. 1959. *The Story of Investment Companies*.

Bunting, David. 1987. *The Rise of Large American Corporations, 1889–1919*.

Cameron, Rondo. 1967 *Banking in the Early Stages of Industrialization*.

Carosso, Vincent P. 1987. *The Morgans: Private International Bankers 1854–1913*.

Castagnera, James O., and David A. Littell. 1992. *Federal Regulation of Employee Benefits*.

Chandler, Alfred D., Jr. 1977. *The Visible Hand—The Managerial Revolution in American Business*.

Chandler, Alfred D., Jr., and Herman Daems, eds. 1980. *Managerial Hierarchies*.

Chandler, Alfred D., Jr., and Stephen Salsburg. 1971. *Pierre S. DuPont and the Making of the Modern Corporation*.

Cleveland, Harold, and Thomas F. Huertas. 1985. *Citibank—1812–1970*.

Clough, Shepard B. 1946. *A Century of American Life Insurance*.

Danelski, David J., and Joseph S. Tulchin, eds. 1973. *Autobiographical Notes of Charles Evans Hughes*.

Dawley, Alan. 1991. *Struggles for Justice—Social Responsibility and the Liberal State*.

DeBedts, Ralph F. 1964. *The New Deal's SEC—The Formative Years*.

De Long, J. Bradford. 1991. Did J. P. Morgan's Men Add Value?—An Economist's Perspective on Financial Capitalism. In *Inside the Business Enterprise: Historical Perspectives on the Use of Information*, edited by Peter Temin.

Diamond, William. 1943. *The Economic Thought of Woodrow Wilson*.

Douglas, William O. 1940. *Democracy and Finance*.

Drucker, Peter E. 1976. *The Unseen Revolution—How Pension Fund Socialism Came to America*.

Easterbrook, Frank H., and Daniel R. Fischel. 1991. *The Economic Structure of Corporate Law*.

Edinger, Lewis J. 1986. *West German Politics*.

Federal Financial Institutions Examination Council. 1992. *Trust Assets of Financial Institutions: 1991*.

Fligstein, Neil. 1990. *The Transformation of Corporate Control*.

Frankel, Tamar. 1978. *The Regulation of Money Managers*.

Friedman, Milton. 1986. Monetary Policy: Theory and Practice. In *Central Bankers, Bureaucratic Incentives, and Monetary Policy*, edited by Eugenie Froedge Toma and Mark Toma.

Fusfeld, Daniel. 1956. *The Economic Thought of Franklin D. Roosevelt and the Origins of the New Deal*.

Gerlach, Michael L. 1989. Keiretsu Organization in the Japanese Economy. In *Politics and Productivity: The Real Story of Why Japan Works*, edited by Chalmers Johnson, Laura D'Andrea Tyson, and John Zysman.

———. *Alliance Capitalism: The Social Organization of Japanese Business*.

Gerschenkron, Alexander. 1962. *Economic Backwardness in Historical Perspective*.

Ghilarducci, Teresa. 1992. *Labor's Capital: The Economics and Politics of Private Pensions*.

Gilson, Ronald. 1986 and 1990 Supp. *The Law and Finance of Corporate Acquisitions*.

Gleick, James. 1987. *Chaos—Making a New Science*.

Graebner, William. 1980. *A History of Retirement*.

Hammond, Bray. 1957. *Banks and Politics in America from the Revolution to the Civil War*.

Harbrecht, Paul. 1959. *Pension Funds and Economic Power*.

Hardin, Russell. 1982. *Collective Action*.

Hawley, Ellis. 1966. *The New Deal and the Problem of Monopoly*.

Heller, Pauline B. 1992. *Federal Bank Holding Company Law*.

Hellwig, Martin. 1990. Banking, Financial Intermediation and Corporate Finance. In *European Financial Integration*, edited by Alberto Giovannini and Colin Mayer.

Hofstadter, Richard. 1955. *The Age of Reform—From Bryan to F.D.R.*

Ippolito, Richard. 1986. *Pensions, Economics and Public Policy*.

Jacobs, Michael T. 1991. *Short-Term America: The Causes and Cures of Our Business Myopia*.

Jensen, Michael C., and Clifford W. Smith. 1985. Stockholder, Manager and Creditor Interests: Applications of Agency Theory. In *Recent Advances in Corporate Finance*, edited by Edward I. Altman and Marti G. Subrahmanyan.

Kahneman, Daniel, Paul Slovic, and Amos Tversky, eds. 1982. *Judgment under Uncertainty: Heuristics and Biases*.

Keegan, John. 1976. *The Face of Battle*.

Keller, Morton. 1963. *The Life Insurance Enterprise, 1885–1910—A Study in the Limits of Corporate Power*.

Kennan, George. 1922. *E. H. Harriman: A Biography*.

Kester, W. Carl. 1991. *Japanese Takeovers: The Global Contest for Corporate Control*.

Knowlton, Winthrop, and Ira M. Millstein. 1988. Can the Board of Directors Help the American Corporation Earn the Immortality It Holds So Dear? In *The U.S. Business Corporation—An Institution in Transition*, edited by John R. Meyer and James M. Gustafson.

Kolko, Gabriel. 1963. *The Triumph of Conservatism: A Reinterpretation of American History, 1900–1916*.

Komiya, Ryutaro. 1990. *The Japanese Economy: Trade, Industry, and Government*. 1990.

Köndgren, Johannes. 1994. Duties of Banks in Voting Their Clients' Stock. In *Institutional Investors and Corporate Governance*, edited by Theodor Baums, Richard M. Buxbaum, and Klaus J. Hopt.

Krikorian, Betty Linn. 1991. Fiduciary Standards: Loyalty, Prudence, Voting Proxies, and Corporate Governance. In *Institutional Investing—Challenges and Responsibilities of the 21st Century*, edited by Arnold W. Sametz.

Kroll, Martin P. 1972. The Portfolio Affiliate Problem. In *Third Annual Institute on Securities Regulation*, edited by Robert Mundheim and Arthur Fleischer, Jr.

Lazonick, William. 1991. *Business Organization and the Myth of the Market Economy*.

Leuchtenburg, William F. 1963. *Franklin D. Roosevelt and the New Deal*.

Link, Arthur Stanley. 1954. *Woodrow Wilson and the Progressive Era, 1900–1917*.

Lipset, Seymour, and William Schneider. 1987. *The Confidence Gap: Business, Labor, and Government in the Public Mind*. Rev. ed.

Lipson, Ephraim. 1934. *The Economic History of England*. 2d ed.

Litan, Robert. 1987. *What Should Banks Do?*

Livingston, James. 1986. *Origins of the Federal Reserve System*.

Longstreth, Bevis. 1986. *Modern Investment Management and the Prudent Man Rule*.

Lorie, James, Peter Dodd, and Mary Kimpton. 1985. *The Stock Market: Theories and Evidence*. 2d ed.

Lorsch, Jay W., and Elizabeth MacIver. 1989. *Pawns or Potentates—The Reality of America's Corporate Boards*.

Lowenstein, Louis. 1988. *What's Wrong with Wall Street*.

McCraw, Thomas K. 1984a. *Prophets of Regulation*.

———. 1984b. The Public and Private Spheres in Historical Perspective. In *Public-Private Partnership*, edited by Harvey Brooks, Lance Liebman, and Corinne Schelling.

Millis, Harry A., and Emily Clark Brown. 1950. *From the Wagner Act to Taft-Hartley*.

Millstein, Ira M. 1991. The Responsibility of the Institutional Investor in Corporate Management. In *The Battle for Corporate Control: Shareholder Rights, Stakeholder Interests, and Managerial Responsibilities*, edited by Arnold W. Sametz and James L. Bicksler.

Moody's Bank and Finance Manual. 1989.

Moody's Manual of Industrial and Miscellaneous Securities. 1900.

New York Stock Exchange. 1990. *Listed Company Manual.*

Nisknen, William. 1971. *Bureaucracy and Representative Government.*

Noll, Roger G., and Bruce M. Owen. 1983. The Predictability of Interest Group Arguments. In *The Political Economy of Deregulation*, edited by Roger G. Noll and Bruce M. Owen.

North, Douglass. 1952. Capital Accumulation in Life Insurance between the Civil War and the Investigation of 1905. In *Men in Business*, edited by William Miller.

O'Barr, William M., and John M. Conley. 1992. *Fortune and Folly—The Wealth and Power of Institutional Investing.*

O' Driscoll, Gerald P., Jr. 1988. Deposit Insurance in Theory and Practice. In *The Financial Services Revolution: Policy Directions for the Future*, edited by Catherine England and Thomas Huertas.

Olson, Mancur. 1965. *The Logic of Collective Action.*

———. 1982. *The Rise and Decline of Nations.*

Ouchi, William G. 1984. *The M-Form Society: How American Teamwork Can Recapture the Competitive Edge.*

Paul, Randolph E. 1954. *Taxation in the United States.*

Peck, Merton J. 1988. The Large Japanese Corporation. In *The U.S. Business Corporation: An Institution in Transition*, edited by John R. Meyer and James M. Gustafson.

Pecora, Ferdinand. 1939. *Wall Street under Oath—The Story of Our Modern Money Changers.*

Pusey, Merlo. 1951. *Charles Evans Hughes.*

Ratner, Sidney. 1967. *Taxation and Democracy in America.*

Riesser, Jacob. 1911. *The Great German Banks and Their Concentration.* Translated by Morris Jacobson.

Rifkin, Jeremy, and Randy Barber. 1978. *The North Will Rise Again: Pensions, Politics and Power in the 1980s.*

Robinson, Dwight P. 1954. *Massachusetts Investors Trust—Pioneer in Open-End Investment Trusts.*

Roe, Mark J. 1993. Takeover Politics. In *The Deal Decade*, edited by Margaret Blair.

Rosenbluth, Frances McCall. 1989. *Financial Politics in Contemporary Japan.*

Rowley, Charles K., Robert D. Tollison, and Gordon Tullock. 1988. *The Political Economy of Rent-Seeking.*

Schlesinger, Arthur, Jr. 1945. *The Age of Jackson.*

———. 1957. *The Crisis of the Old Order, 1919–1933.*

———. 1960. *The Age of Roosevelt: The Politics of Upheaval.*

Seidman, J. S. 1938. *Seidman's Legislative History of Federal Income Tax Laws: 1938–1961.*

Shughart, William. 1988. A Public Choice Perspective of the Banking Act of 1933. In *The Financial Services Revolution*, edited by Catherine England and Thomas F. Huertas.

Skaggs, Neil, and Cheryl Wasserkrug. 1986. Banking Sector Influence on the Relationship of Congress to the Federal Reserve System. In *Central Bankers, Bureaucratic Incentives, and Monetary Policy*, edited by Eugenie Froedge Toma and Mark Toma.

Sklar, Martin J. 1988. *The Corporate Reconstruction of American Capitalism, 1890–1916.*

Sloan, Alfred P. 1963. *My Years with General Motors.*

Swaine, Robert T. 1946. *The Cravath Firm and Its Predecessors, 1819–1947.*

Symons, Edward L., and James J. White. 1991. *Banking Law—Teaching Materials.* 3d ed.

Temin, Peter. 1969. *The Jacksonian Economy.*

Thorelli, Hans. 1954. *The Federal Antitrust Policy.*

Thurow, Lester C. 1985. *The Zero-Sum Solution: Building a World-Class American Economy.*

Tsutsui, William M. 1988. *Banking Policy in Japan.*

Tullock, Gordon. 1988. Future Directions for Rent-Seeking Research. In *The Political Economy of Rent-Seeking*, edited by Charles K. Rowley, Robert D. Tollison, and Gordon Tullock.

Turner, Frederick Jackson. 1920. *The Frontier in American History.*

Wallich, Henry C. 1955. *Mainsprings of the German Revival.*

Wallstein, Leonard. 1928. *Some Legal Questions in Relation to Investment Trusts.*

Watson, Alan. 1984. *Sources of Law, Legal Change and Ambiguity.*

Weinstein, James. 1968. *The Corporate Ideal in the Liberal State: 1900–1918.*

Wesser, Robert. 1967. *Charles Evans Hughes: Politics and Reform in New York 1905–1910.*

White, Eugene N. 1983. *The Regulation and Reform of the American Banking System, 1900–1929.*

Wiebe, Robert H. 1967. *The Search For Order.*

Williamson, Oliver. 1964. *The Economics of Discretionary Behavior: Managerial Objectives in a Theory of the Firm.*

———. 1975. *Markets and Hierarchies: Analysis and Antitrust Implications.*

———. 1985. *The Economic Institutions of Capitalism.*

Wilson, Woodrow. 1913. *The New Freedom.*

Witte, John F. 1985. *The Politics and Development of the Federal Income Tax.*

Ziegler, Rolf, et al. 1985. Industry and Banking in the German Corporate Network. In *Networks of Corporate Power: A Comparative Analysis of Ten Countries*, edited by Frans N. Stokman et al.

Zielinski, Robert, and Nigel Holloway. 1991. *Unequal Equities: Power and Risk in Japan's Stock Market.*

Journal Articles

Abel, Andrew. 1991. The Equity Premium Puzzle. *Federal Reserve Bank of Philadelphia Monthly Review*, Sept., 3.

Adelstein, Richard P. 1989. "Islands of Conscious Power": Louis D. Brandeis and the Modern Corporation. *Business History Review* 63:614.

Adler, Hans A. 1949. The Post-War Reorganization of the German Banking System. *Quarterly Journal of Economics* 63:322.

Anderson, Charles A. 1984. Directors in Japan. *Harvard Business Review*, May–June, 30.

Bebchuk, Lucian. 1985. Toward Undistorted Choice and Equal Treatment in Corporate Takeovers. *Harvard Law Review* 98:1693.

Bell, Haughton, and Harold G. Fraine. 1952. Legal Framework, Trends, and Developments in Investment Practices of Life Insurance Companies. *Law and Contemporary Problems* 17:45.

Black, Bernard S. 1989. Bidder Overpayment in Takeovers. *Stanford Law Review* 41:597.

———. 1990. Shareholder Passivity Reexamined. *Michigan Law Review* 89:520.

———. 1991. Disclosure Not Censorship: The Case for Proxy Reform. *Journal of Corporation Law* 17:49.

———. 1992a. Next Steps in Proxy Reform. *Journal of Corporation Law* 18:1.

———. 1992b. The Value of Institutional Investor Monitoring: The Empirical Evidence. *UCLA Law Review* 39:895.

Blake, Harlan, and William Kenneth Jones. 1965. In Defense of Antitrust. *Columbia Law Review* 65:377.

Bosland, Chelcie C. 1941. The Investment Company Act of 1940 and Its Background. Part II. *Journal of Political Economy* 49:687.

Brickley, James, Ronald Lease, and Clifford Smith. 1988. Ownership Structure and Voting on Antitakeover Amendments. *Journal of Financial Economics* 20:267.

Büschgen, H. E. 1979. The Universal Banking System in the Federal Republic of Germany. *Journal of Comparative Corporate Law and Securities Regulation* 2:1.

Cable, John. 1985. Capital Market Information and Industrial Performance: The Role of West German Banks. *Economic Journal* 95:118.

Carney, William. 1990. Does Defining Constituencies Matter? *University of Cincinnati Law Review* 59:385.

Carosso, Vincent. 1970. Washington and Wall Street: The New Deal and Investment Bankers, 1933–1940. *Business History Review* 44:425.

Chang, Saeyoung, and David Mayers. 1992. Managerial Vote Ownership and Shareholder Wealth. *Journal of Financial Economics* 32:103.

Clair, Robert T., and Paula K. Tucker. 1989. Interstate Banking and the Federal Reserve: A Historical Perspective. *Federal Reserve Bank of Dallas Economic Review*, Nov., 6.

Clark, Robert C. 1976. The Soundness of Financial Intermediaries. *Yale Law Journal* 86:1.

———. 1981. The Four Stages of Capitalism. *Harvard Law Review* 94:561.

Coase, R. H. 1937, The Nature of the Firm. *Economica* (n.s.) 4:386.

Coffee, John C. 1987. The Future of Corporate Federalism: State Competition and the New Trend toward De Facto Federal Minimum Standards. *Cardozo Law Review* 8:759.

———. 1991. Liquidity versus Control: The Institutional Investor as Corporate Monitor. *Columbia Law Review* 91:1277.

Comment. 1972. The Application of Section 17 of the Investment Company Act of 1940 to Portfolio Affiliates. *University of Pennsylvania Law Review* 120:983.

Conard, Alfred F. 1984. The Supervision of Corporate Management: A Comparison of Developments in European Community and United States Law. *Michigan Law Review* 82:1459.

Cumming, Christine M., and Lawrence M. Sweet. 1987–1988. Financial Structure of the G-10 Countries: How Does the United States Compare? *Federal Reserve Bank of New York Quarterly Review*, Winter, 14.

Davis, Lance E. 1963. Capital Immobilities and Finance Capitalism: A Study of Economic Evolution in the United States 1820–1920. *Explorations in Entrepreneurial History* 1:88.

———. 1966. The Capital Markets and Industrial Concentration: The U.S. and U.K., a Comparative Study. *Economic History Review*, 2d ser., 19:255.

Davis, Shelby. 1945. Common Stock Investments by Life Insurance Companies. *Financial Analysts' Journal*, July, 3.

Demsetz, Harold, and Kenneth Lehn. 1985. The Structure of Corporate Ownership: Causes and Consequences. *Journal of Political Economy* 93:1155.

Denzau, Arthur T., and Michael C. Munger. 1986. Legislators and Interest Groups: How Unorganized Interests Get Represented. *American Political Science Review* 80:89.

Drucker, Peter F. 1988. The Coming of the New Organization. *Harvard Business Review*, Jan.–Feb., 45.

Easterbrook, Frank. 1984. Two Explanations for Dividends. *American Economic Review* 74:650.

Eckstein, Wolfram. 1980. The Role of the Banks in Corporate Concentration in West Germany. *Zeitschrift für die gesamte Staatswissenschaft* (Journal of Institutional and Theoretical Economics) 136:467.

Elkins, Stanley, and Eric McKitrick. 1954. A Meaning for Turner's Frontier. Part I. Democracy in the Old Northwest. *Political Science Quarterly* 69:321.

Enstam, Raymond A., and Harry P. Kamen. 1986. Control and the Institutional Investor. *Business Lawyer* 23:289.

Fama, Eugene F. 1980. Agency Problems and the Theory of the Firm. *Journal of Political Economy* 88:288.

Farrar, John, and Mark Russell. 1984. The Impact of Institutional Investment on Company Law. *Company Lawyer* 5:107.

Ferguson, Thomas. 1984. From Normalcy to New Deal: Industrial Structure, Party Competition, and American Public Policy in the Great Depression. *International Organization* 38:41.

Fischel, Daniel, and John H. Langbein. 1988. ERISA's Fundamental Contradiction: The Exclusive Benefit Rule. *University of Chicago Law Review* 55:1105.

Futatsugi, Yusaku. 1990. What Share Cross-Holdings Mean for Corporate Management, *Economic Eye*, Spring, 17.

Gerlach, Michael L. 1992. Twilight of the Keiretsu?—A Critical Assessment. *Journal of Japanese Studies*. 18:79.

Gewirtz, Elliot, and Clark Taber. 1991. Fundamental Issues in Japanese Financial System Reform. *Review of Banking and Financial Services* 7:135.

Gilson, Ronald J., and Reinier Kraakman. 1991. Reinventing the Outside Director: An Agenda for Institutional Investors. *Stanford Law Review* 43:863.

———. 1993. Investment Companies as Guardian Shareholders: The Place of the MSIC in the Corporate Governance Debate, *Stanford Law Review* 45:985.

Gilson, Ronald J., and Mark J. Roe. 1993. Understanding the Japanese Keiretsu: Overlaps between Corporate Governance and Industrial Organization. *Yale Law Journal* 102:871.

Golembe, Carter H. 1960. The Deposit Insurance Legislation of 1933: An Examination of Its Antecedents and Its Purposes. *Political Science Quarterly* 76:181.

Gordon, Jeffrey. 1987. The Puzzling Persistence of the Constrained Prudent Man Rule. *N.Y.U. Law Review* 52:96.

———. 1991. Corporations, Markets, and Courts. *Columbia Law Review* 91:1931.

Gormley, R. James. 1992. On the Same Side of the Table: Is Investment Company Act Rule 17d-1 Partly Invalid? *Securities Regulation Law Journal* 20:115.

Graetz, Michael J. 1987. The Troubled Marriage of Retirement Security and Tax Policies. *University of Pennsylvania Law Review* 135:851.

Grundfest, Joseph. 1990. Subordination of American Capital. *Journal of Financial Economics* 27:89.

Halpert, Stephen K. 1988. The Separation of Banking and Commerce Reconsidered. *Journal of Corporate Law* 13:481.

Hammond, Bray. 1947. Jackson, Biddle, and the Bank of the United States. *Journal of Economic History* 7:1.

Hansmann, Henry. 1988. Ownership of the Firm. *Journal of Law, Economics and Organization* 4:267.

———. 1990. When Does Worker Ownership Work? ESOPs, Law Firms, Codetermination, and Economic Democracy. *Yale Law Journal* 99:1749.

Hart, Oliver D. 1988. Incomplete Contracts and the Theory of the Firm. *Journal of Law, Economics and Organization* 4:119.

Hayes, Robert H., and William J. Abernathy. 1980. Managing Our Way to Economic Decline. *Harvard Business Review*, July–Aug., 67.

Hyde, Alan. 1990. A Theory of Labor Legislation. *Buffalo Law Review* 38:383.

———. 1992. In Defense of Employee Ownership. *Chicago-Kent Law Review* 67:159.

Jaretzki, Alfred, Jr. 1941. The Investment Company Act of 1940. *Washington University Law Quarterly* 26:303.

Jensen, Michael C. 1986. Agency Costs of Free Cash Flow. *American Economic Review* 76:323.

———. 1989. Eclipse of the Public Corporation. *Harvard Business Review*, Sept.–Oct., 61.

Jensen, Michael C., and William H. Meckling. 1976. Theory of the Firm: Managerial Behavior, Agency Costs and Ownership Structure. *Journal of Financial Economics* 3:305.

Johnson, Lyman, and David Millon. 1989. Missing the Point about State Takeover Statutes. *Michigan Law Review* 87:846.

Kallfass, Hermann H. 1988. The American Corporation and the Institutional Investor: Are There Lessons from Abroad? *Columbia Business Law Review* 3:775.

Kanda, Hideki. 1991. Politics, Formalism, and the Elusive Goal of Investor Protection: Regulation of Structured Investment Funds in Japan. *University of Pennsylvania International Law Review* 12:569.

Kandel, Eugene, and Edward P. Lazear. 1992. Peer Pressure and Partnerships. *Journal of Political Economy* 100:801.

Karmel, Roberta. 1990. Do the Capital Markets Need So Many Regulators? *N.Y. Law Journal*, Oct. 18, 3.

Karpoff, Jonathan, and Paul Malatesta. 1989. The Wealth Effects of Second-Generation State Takeover Legislation. *Journal of Financial Economics* 25:291.

Kasman, Bruce, and Anthony P. Rodrigues. 1991. Financial Liberalization and Monetary Control in Japan. *Federal Reserve Bank of New York Quarterly Review*, Autumn, 28.

Klein, Benjamin. 1988. Vertical Integration as Organizational Ownership: The Fisher Body–General Motors Relationship Revisited. *Journal of Law, Economics and Organization* 4:199.

Klein, Benjamin, Robert G. Crawford, and Armen A. Alchian. 1978. Vertical Integration, Appropriable Rents, and the Competitive Contracting Process. *Journal of Law and Economics* 21:297.

Kovaleff, Theodore P. 1978. Divorce American-Style: The Du Pont–General Motors Case, *Delaware History*, Spring–Summer, 28.

Kraakman, Reinier. 1988. Taking Discounts Seriously: The Implications of "Discounted" Share Prices as an Acquisition Motive. *Columbia Law Review* 88: 891.

Kroszner, Randall S., and Raghuram G. Rajan. 1994. Is the Glass-Steagall Act Justified?—A Study of the U.S. Experience with Universal Banking before 1933. *American Economic Review* 84:(forthcoming).

Krümmel, Hans-Jacob. 1980. German Universal Banking Scrutinized: Some Remarks Concerning the Gessler Report. *Journal of Banking and Finance* 4:33.

Kübler, Friedrich K. 1991. Institutional Owners and Corporate Managers: A German Dilemma. *Brooklyn Law Review* 57:97.

Lalonde, Robert J., and Bernard D. Meltzer. 1991. Hard Times for Unions: Another Look at the Significance of Employer Illegalities. *University of Chicago Law Review* 58:953.

Langevoort, Donald. 1987. Statutory Obsolescence and the Judicial Process: The Revisionist Role of the Courts in Federal Banking Regulation. *Michigan Law Review* 85:672.

Langohr, Herwig, and Anthony M. Santomero. 1985. The Extent of Equity Investment by European Banks. *Journal of Money, Credit and Banking* 42:243.

Lazonick, William. 1992. Controlling the Market for Corporate Control: The Historical Significance of Managerial Capitalism. *Industrial and Corporate Change* 1:445.

Levmore, Saul. 1982. Monitors and Free-Riders in Corporate and Commercial Law Settings. *Yale Law Journal* 91:49.

Lieberman, Ellen, and Jeffrey Bartell. 1990. The Rise in State Antitakeover Laws. *Review of Securities and Commodities Regulation* (Standard & Poor's) 23:149.

Lipset, Seymour Martin, and Reinhard Bendix. 1951. Social Status and Social Structure. *British Journal of Sociology* 2:233.

Lipton, Martin. 1987. Corporate Governance in the Age of Finance Corporatism. *University of Pennsylvania Law Review* 136:1.

Litt, David G., Jonathan R. Macey, Geoffrey P. Miller, and Edward L. Rubin. 1990. Politics, Bureaucracies, and Financial Markets: Bank Entry into Commercial Paper Underwriting in the United States and Japan. *University of Pennsylvania Law Review* 139:369.

Macey, Jonathan R. 1984. Special Interest Group Legislation and the Judicial Function: The Dilemma of Glass-Steagall. *Emory Law Journal* 33:1.

Macey, Jonathan R., and Geoffrey P. Miller. 1991a. Origin of the Blue Sky Laws. *Texas Law Review* 70:347.

————. 1991b. America's Banking System: The Origins and Future of the Current Crisis. *Washington University Law Quarterly* 69:769.

Maseritz, Guy. 1969. The Investment Company: A Study of Influence and Control in the Major Industrial Corporations. *Boston College Industry and Commerce Law Review* 11:1.

McCown, William, and Steve Martinie. 1988. State Regulation of Life Insurance Company Investments, *Association of Life Insurance Counsel Proceedings* 27:8.

Merkel, Philip L. 1992. Going National: The Life Insurance Industry's Campaign for Federal Regulation After the Civil War. *Business History Review* 65:528.

Mester, Loretta J. 1992. *Banking and Commerce: A Dangerous Liaison?* Federal Reserve Bank of Philadelphia Bulletin, May/June, 17.

Millstein, Ira. M. 1993. The Evolution of the Certifying Board. *Business Lawyer*, Aug., 1485.

Moore, Andrew. 1987. State Competition: Panel Response. *Cardozo Law Review* 8:779.

North, Douglass C. 1954. Life Insurance and Investment Banking at the Time of the Armstrong Investigation of 1905–1906. *Journal of Economic History* 14:209.

Note. 1935. Taxation—Taxability of Business Trust as "Association" within Meaning of Income Tax Act. *University of Pennsylvania Law Review* 84:666.

Pitofsky, Robert. 1979. The Political Content of Antitrust. *University of Pennsylvania Law Review* 127:1051.

Pound, John. 1988. Proxy Contests and the Efficiency of Shareholder Oversight. *Journal of Financial Economics* 15:237.

————. 1991. Proxy Voting and the SEC: Investor Protection versus Market Efficiency. *Journal of Financial Economics* 29:241.

Pozen, Robert C. 1994. Institutional Investors: The Reluctant Activists. *Harvard Business Review*, Jan.–Feb., 140.

Powell, Walter W. 1990. Neither Market nor Hierarchy: Network Forms of Organization. *Research on Organizational Behavior* 12:295.

Price, William H. 1909. Life Insurance Reform in New York. *American Economic Association Quarterly* 10:26.

Prowse, Stephen D. 1992. The Structure of Corporate Ownership in Japan. *Journal of Finance* 47:1121.

Raiser, Thomas. 1988. The Theory of Enterprise Law in the Federal Republic of Germany. *American Journal of Comparative Law* 36:111.

Ramseyer, J. Mark. 1991. Legal Rules in Repeated Deals: Banking. *Journal of Legal Studies* 20:91.

Randolph, Carman F. 1905. Federal Supervision of Insurance. *Columbia Law Review* 5:500.

Rock, Edward. 1991. The Logic and Uncertain Significance of Institutional Investor Activism. *Georgetown Law Journal* 79:445.

Roe, Mark J. 1990. Political and Legal Restraints on Ownership and Control of Public Companies. *Journal of Financial Economics* 27:7.

――――. 1991. A Political Theory of American Corporate Finance. *Columbia Law Review* 91:10.

Romano, Roberta. 1987. The Political Economy of Takeover Statutes. *Virginia Law Review* 73:11.

――――. 1988. The Future of Hostile Takeovers: Legislation and Public Opinion. *University of Cincinnati Law Review* 57:457.

Rosenblatt, Alan, and Martin E. Lybecker. 1976. Some Thoughts on the Federal Securities Laws Regulating External Investment Management Arrangements and the ALI Federal Securities Code Project. *University of Pennsylvania Law Review* 124:587.

Ryngaert, Michael, and Jeffry Netter. 1988. Shareholder Wealth Effects of the Ohio Antitakeover Law. *Journal of Law, Economics and Organization* 4:373.

Sah, Raaj K. 1991. Fallibility in Human Organizations and Political Systems. *Journal of Economic Perspectives* 5:67.

Samuelson, William, and Richard Zeckhauser. 1988. Status Quo Bias in Decision Making. *Journal of Risk and Uncertainty* 1:7.

Saxonhouse, Gary. 1991. Mechanisms for Technology Transfer in Japanese Economic History. *Managerial and Decision Economics* 12:83.

Sheard, Paul. 1989. The Main Bank System and Corporate Monitoring and Control in Japan. *Journal of Economic Behavior and Organization* 11:399.

Shleifer, Andrei, and Robert Vishny. 1986. Large Shareholders and Corporate Control. *Journal of Political Economy* 94:461.

Shull, Bernard. 1983. The Separation of Banking and Commerce: Origin, Development, and Implications for Antitrust. *Antitrust Bulletin* 28:255.

Smith, Clifford W., Jr., and Jerold B. Warner. 1979. On Financial Contracting: An Analysis of Bond Covenants. *Journal of Financial Economics* 7:117.

Smith, George David, and Richard Sylla. 1993. The Transformation of Financial Capitalism: An Essay on the History of American Capital Markets. *Financial Markets, Institutions and Instruments* 2:1.

Sommer, A. A., Jr. 1966. Who's in Control? *Business Lawyer* 21:559.

Sprague, O.M.W. 1903. Branch Banking in the United States. *Quarterly Journal of Economics* 17:242.

Stein, Jeremy C. 1988. Takeover Threats and Managerial Myopia. *Journal of Political Economy* 96:61.

――――. 1989. Efficient Capital Markets, Inefficient Firms: a Model of Myopic Corporate Behavior. *Quarterly Journal of Economics* 104:655.

Stelzer, Don R. 1989. The Armstrong Investigation. *Journal of the American Society of C.L.U & ChFC*, Nov., 74.

Sylla, Richard. 1992. The Progressive Era and the Political Economy of Big Government. *Critical Review* 5:531.

Symposium. 1983. Corporations and Private Property. *Journal of Law and Economics*. 26:237.

Szewczyk, Samuel, and George Tsetsekos. 1992. State Intervention in the Market for Corporate Control—The Case of Pennsylvania Senate Bill 1310. *Journal of Financial Economics* 31:3.

Teranishi, Juro. 1977. Availability of Safe Assets and the Process of Bank Concentration in Japan. *Economic Development and Cultural Change* 25:447.

Teranishi, Juro. 1990. Financial System and the Industrialization of Japan: 1900–1970. *Banca Nazionale del Lavoro Quarterly Review*, Sept., 309.

Tiebout, Charles M. 1956. A Pure Theory of Local Expenditures. *Journal of Political Economy* 64:416

Tilly, Richard H. 1986. German Banking, 1850–1914: Development Assistance for the Strong. *Journal of European Economic History* 15:113.

———. 1989. Banking Institutions in Historical Perspective: Germany, Great Britain and the United States in the Nineteenth and Early Twentieth Century. *Zeitschrift für Die Gesamte Staatswissenschaft* (Journal of Institutional and Theoretical Economics) 145:189.

Ulen, Thomas S. 1980. The Market for Regulation: The ICC from 1887 to 1920. *American Economic Review* Papers and Proceedings. 70:306.

Vagts, Detlev F. 1966. Reforming the "Modern" Corporation: Perspectives from the German. *Harvard Law Review* 80:23.

Weiler, Paul. 1983. Promises to Keep: Securing Workers' Rights to Self-Organization under the NLRA. *Harvard Law Review* 96:1769.

Weiss, Deborah. 1991. Paternalistic Pension Policy: Psychological Evidence and Economic Theory. *University of Chicago Law Review* 58:1275.

Weiss, Elliot. 1982. Defensive Responses to Tender Offers and The Williams Act's Prohibition against Manipulation. *Vanderbilt Law Review* 35:1087.

White, Eugene N. 1982. The Political Economy of Banking Regulation, 1864–1933. *Journal of Economic History* 42:33.

Wilcox, John C. 1993. A Proxy Solicitor's Perspective on the New Communications Rules. *Prentice-Hall Corporation Guide*, Feb. 15, 1.

Wilson, Woodrow. 1910. The Lawyer and the Community. *North American Review* 192:612.

Windolf, Paul. 1993. Codetermination and the Market for Corporate Control in the European Community. *Economy and Society* 22:137.

Unpublished Manuscripts, Papers, Studies, and Reports

American Law Institute. 1992. *Principles of Corporate Governance: Analysis and Recommendations* (Proposed Final Draft).

Aoki, Masahiko. 1992. The Japanese Firm as a System of Attributes: A Survey and Research Agenda. Stanford Center for Economic Policy Research Publication No. 288.

Baums, Theodor. 1991. Banks and Corporate Control. Berkeley Law and Economics Working Paper No. 9–1.

Board of Governors of the Federal Reserve System. 1990. Flow of Funds Accounts—Financial Assets and Liabilities. March. Preliminary figures.

Board of Governors of the Federal Reserve System. 1957–1980. Flow of Funds Accounts, Assets and Liabilities Outstanding.

Brancato, Carolyn Kay. 1993. Institutional Investors: A Widely Diverse Presence in Corporate Governance. Background paper prepared for Institutional Investor Project, Center for Law and Economics, Columbia Law School.

Brancato, Carolyn Kay, et al. 1991. Institutional Investor Concentration of Economic

Power: A Study of Institutional Holdings and Voting Authority in U.S. Publicly Held Corporations. Unpublished study.

Campbell, John Y., and Yasushi Hamao. 1993. Changing Patterns of Corporate Financing and the Main Bank System in Japan. World Bank unpublished paper. June.

Clyde, Paul. 1991. The Institutional Shareholder as a Monitor of Management. Unpublished manuscript.

Foundation for Advanced Information and Research. 1990. A Perspective on Japanese Merger and Acquisitions from [an] International Viewpoint. Japan. Unpublished report.

Franks, Julian, and Colin Mayer. 1992. Corporate Control: A Synthesis of the International Evidence. Unpublished manuscript.

————. 1993. The Market for Corporate Control in Germany. European Science Foundation Network in Financial Markets. Working Paper. Oct.

Heard, James, and Howard Sherman. 1987. Conflicts of Interest in the Proxy System. Investor Responsibility Research Center, Washington, D.C.

Henderson, George. n.d. History of the Insurance Investigation. Undated pamphlet, circa 1906.

Hopt, Klaus. 1993. Labor Representation on Corporate Boards—Impact and Problems for Corporate Governance and Economic Integration in Europe. Centre d'études juridiques européennes. University of Geneva, Switzerland. Sept.

Hughes, Charles Evans. 1985. Beerits Memorandum. Microfilmed on Papers of Charles Evans Hughes, Reel 140, Lib. of Cong. Photo-Duplication Service.

[Japanese] Securities and Exchange Council. 1991. How Basic System Regarding Capital Market Ought to Be Reformed. Unpublished report. June 19.

[Japanese] Financial System Research Council. 1991. On a New Japanese Finance System. Unpublished report. June 25.

Kaplan, Steven N. 1993. Top Executives, Turnover and Firm Performance in Germany. Unpublished manuscript.

Kaplan, Steven N., and Bernadette Alcamo Minton. 1992. "Outside" Intervention in Japanese Companies: Its Determinants and Its Implications for Managers. Unpublished manuscript.

McDonald, Jack. 1991. Origins and Implications of Cross-Holdings in Japanese Companies. Stanford University Graduate School of Business Technical Note No. 79.

Morck, Randall, and Masao Nakamura. 1992. Banks and Corporate Control in Japan. Unpublished manuscript.

Porter, Michael E. 1992. Capital Choices—Changing the Way America Invests in Industry. Council on Competitiveness research report.

Pound, John. 1992. The Rise of the Political Model of Corporate Governance and Corporate Control. Kennedy School of Government Working Paper.

Pushner, George M. 1993. Ownership Structure and Corporate Performance in the U.S. and Japan. Ph.D diss., Columbia University.

Ramseyer, J. Mark. 1991. Japanese Main Banks as a Regulatory Artifact: The Legal Framework. Unpublished manuscript.

————. 1993. Explicit Reasons for Implicit Contract: The Legal Logic to the Japanese Main Bank System. Unpublished manuscript.

Rose, Dwight C. 1941. Should Life Insurance Companies Be Permitted to Invest in Common Stocks? Mimeo prepared for New York Joint Legislative Committee Hearings on Life Insurance. Oct. 21.

Rosenbluth, Frances. 1991. Bank Consolidation in Prewar Japan: The Market for Regulation under a Non-Sovereign Diet. Unpublished manuscript.

Sheard, Paul. 1992. The Role of the Japanese Main Bank When Borrowing Firms Are in Financial Distress. Stanford Center for Economic Policy Research Publication No. 330. Nov.

Vista Capital Growth Fund. Prospectus. 1992.

Foreign-Language Sources

Bundesverband Mittelständischer Wirtschaft. 1991. Expose zur "Macht der Banken." Apr. 24.

Christ, Peter. 1993. Räte-Republik. *Manager Magazin.* Aug., 3.

Daiyamondo Kaisha Yoran. Various dates.

Deutscher Bundestag. 1990. Achtes Hauptgutachten der Monopolkommission. Drucksache 11/7582.

––––––. 1993. Neuntes Hauptgutachten der Monopolkommission.

Eglau, Hans. 1991. Allianz/Dresdner Bank—Vermachtet und Verschachtelt. *Die Zeit,* Aug. 16, 19.

Die FDP Will die Mineralölsteuer Erhöhen. 1989. *Frankfurter Allgemeine Zeitung,* Aug. 19, 11.

Fusion doch ohne Beschluss zur Bankenmacht. 1989. *Frankfurter Allgemeine Zeitung,* Sept. 7, 17.

Geßler, Ernst, Wolfgang Hefermehl, Ulrich Eckardt, and Bruno Kropff. 1974. *Aktiengesetz.* Vol. 2.

Die Geheimräte der Nation (The Nation's Secret Council). 1987. *Industriemagazin,* April, 27.

Gottschalk, Arno. 1988. Der Stimmrechtseinfluss der Banken in den Aktionärsversammlungen der Grossunternehmen, *WSI-Mitteilungen* 5:294.

Greiffenberg, Horst. 1987. Die Macht der Banken (The Power of the Banks), *Verbraucherpolitische Hefte,* Dec., 85.

Der Herr des Geldes (The Money Man) 1989. *Der Spiegel.* Mar. 13, 20.

Hildebrand, Walter, Andreas Nölting, and Winfried Wilhelm. Club der Amateure (Amateurs' Club) 1993. *Manager Magazin,* Aug., 32.

Huffschmid, Jörg. 1987. Demokratische Alternativen der Bankpolitik (Democratic Alternatives for the Politics of Banking), *Verbraucherpolitische Hefte,* Dec., 111.

Ito, Kunio. 1989. M & A to Kabushiki Mochiai no Honshitsu. *Kinyu Journal,* Dec., 11.

Keiretsu no Kenkyu. Various dates.

Lambsdorff, Otto Graf. 1989. Das Machtgeflecht der Banken Lichten, *Frankfurter Allgemeine Zeitung,* Aug. 22, 10.

Sprachlose Eigentümer: Aktionäre nehmen viel zu selten ihre Rechte als Inhaber von Unternehmen wahr. 1991. *Die Zeit,* June 7.

Wir Sind Gerngesehene Berater. 1989. *Der Spiegel,* Sept. 4, 45.

Zwischen Bonn und Banken: Finanzdiplomat Hermann Abs (Between Bonn and the Banks: Financial Diplomat Hermann Abs). 1965. *Der Spiegel,* Nov. 3, 10.

Magazines, Newspapers, and Newsletters

Articles

Altman, Roger, and Melissa Brown. 1986. A Competitive Liability, Ridding Wall Street of a Short-Term Bias. *New York Times*, June 1, 3.

Anand, Vineeta. 1981. Warren Buffet Effect: A Quick Jump in Stock Prices. *Investor's Daily*, Aug. 23, 8.

... And in Japan. 1993. *Fortune*, Feb. 22, 10.

Atwater, Bruce. 1991. The Governance System Is Sound. *Directors & Boards*, Spring, 17, 19.

Bacon, Kenneth H. 1991. White House Bill on Bank Law Reform Faces Hurdles as It Goes to House Panel. *Wall Street Journal*, May 14, A24.

Banker's Opinion of Insurance Bill. 1906. *American Banker*, Feb. 24, 479.

The "Buzz-Off" Defense: A Play on the Time Ruling. 1990. *M and A Dealmaking*, Mar/Apr., 7.

Cahan, Vicky, Dean Foust, and Ellyn Spragins. 1987. States vs. Raiders: Will Washington Step In? *Business Week*, Aug. 31, 56.

Caution Keynotes Company Feeling on Common Stock Bill, 1951. *National Underwriter*, Mar. 30, 1.

Chernoff, Joel. 1992. Breeden: Act Like Owners—SEC Chief Backs Larger Stakes, Larger Role for Institutions. *Pensions and Investments*, June 8, 3.

————. 1991. Business Takes Shots at Proxy Proposals. *Pensions and Investments*, Sept. 30, 4.

Coffin, Tris. 1955. Proxy Warfare May Provoke Tighter Government Rules. *Nation's Business*, July, 32.

Commissioner Pike of SEC Wants Life Companies to Buy Common Stocks. 1941. *Eastern Underwriter*, Oct. 24, 7.

Cowan, Allison. 1989. A Savvy Outsider Ventures Inside. *New York Times*, Aug. 3, D8.

Crovitz, Gordon. 1990. Keystone State Kapitalism. *Barron's*, Apr. 23, 10.

Dakin, Edwin F. 1956. Battle by Proxy—Henceforth New Ground Rules Will Govern These Contests. *Barron's*, Feb. 20, 5.

Devroy, Ann, and Kathleen Day. 1989. Deposit Fee Draws Wave of Protest. *Washington Post*, Jan. 26, A1.

Dobrzynski, Judith. 1986. More Than Ever, It's Management for the Short Term. *Business Week*, Nov. 24, 82.

————. 1991. Is Pete Wilson Trying to Mute a Shareholder Activist? *Business Week*, July 1, 29.

Dornberg, John. 1990. The Spreading Might of Deutsche Bank. *New York Times*, Sept. 23, 28.

Drucker, Peter. 1986. A Crisis of Capitalism. *Wall Street Journal*, Sept. 30, 32.

Ecker against Change of Law to Permit Companies to Buy Stocks. 1941. *Eastern Underwriter*, Oct. 24, 7.

Expropriation at Home. 1987. *Wall Street Journal*, Oct. 9, 24.

Field, Kenneth. 1942. Sees Common Stocks Unsuited for Life Companies. *Weekly Underwriter* 146:152.

Franklin, Barbara. 1990. Tough Takeover Statute—Critics Say Pennsylvania's New Law Is Extreme. *New York Law Journal*, May 3, 5.

Getting Rid of the Boss. 1993. *Economist*, Feb. 6, 13.

The Global Service 500. 1992. *Fortune*, Aug. 24, 215.

Gold, Jackey. 1991. M & A Continental Style. *Financial World*, Mar. 5, 37.

Grady Fails to Block the 6 Insurance Bills. 1906. *New York Times*, Apr. 6, 9.

Greising, David. 1992. Hunting Investors Who Will Go the Distance. *Business Week*, Nov. 9, 101.

Hansell, Saul. 1991. Despite Sharply Different Styles, NCNB, First Union and Wachovia Have Driven Each Other into the Top Tier of U.S. Banking. *Institutional Investor*, Nov., 101.

How the Insurance Companies Injure the Banks. 1905. *American Banker*, Nov. 4, 2701.

Ingrassia, Paul. 1992. Board Reform Replaces the LBO. *Wall Street Journal*, Oct. 30, 14.

Insurance Funds and Banking Capital. 1905. *American Banker*, Nov. 4, 2694.

Insurance Reform Restricts Activity: NYS Bill Would Liberalize Industry, Carves Out Banking. 1983. *American Banker*, May 10, 2.

Investment Dilemma—Trusts Forced to Choose between Drastic Reorganization and High Tax, under New Law. 1936. *Business Week*, July 11, 45.

Investment Trust Hails New Tax Act. 1936. *New York Times*, July 23, 31.

Kennedy, Joseph. 1937. Big Business, What Now? *Saturday Evening Post*, Jan. 16, 10.

Knight, Jerry. 1991. A Banking Bill That Suits No One: Special Interests All Want the Law Tailored Their Way. *The Washington Post*, Nov. 13, G1.

Langer, David. 1992. Protector Becomes the Threat to Pensions. *Pensions and Investments*, Sept. 14, 15.

Law Firm View on Impact of Paramount/Time Decision. 1990. *Insights*, May, 34.

Leviero, Anthony. 1946. Millions Paid Out by Welfare Funds. *New York Times*, May 23, 12.

Life Insurance and High Finance. 1905. *World*, Feb. 17, 6.

Life Insurance Investments in Industrial Stocks Opposed. 1941. *New York Times*, Oct. 22, 33.

Life Insurance Law Upheld by Leaders. 1929. *New York Times*, Sept. 29, 7.

Limiting Investments Discussed by Morton. 1906. *New York Times*, Mar. 10, 2.

Lipin, Steven. 1991. Bank Industry Seen Shrinking in 1990s, Survey of Executives, Regulators Finds. *Wall Street Journal*, Oct. 2, A14.

Lipton, Martin. 1990. A Long-Term Cure for Takeover Madness, *Manhattan Lawyer*, Mar., 15.

Loomis, Carol J. 1988. The New J. P. Morgans. *Time*, Feb. 29, 44.

Lorsch, Jay W. 1990. Funds Should Flex Their Muscle. *New York Times*, Feb. 11, 3.

Lublin, Joann S. 1992. Other Concerns Are Likely to Follow GM In Splitting Posts of Chairman and CEO. *Wall Street Journal*, Nov. 4, B1.

Management and Labor Join Forces to Stiff-Arm Raiders in Pennsylvania. 1990. *Corporate Control Alert*, Jan., 1.

McNamee, Mike. 1991. Just When Bank Reform Seemed Almost in the Bag. *Business Week*, Sept. 9, 51.

Minow, Nell. 1994. Do Your Duty, Retirement Managers. *New York Times*, Jan. 30, sec. 3, 11.

Miscellaneous Life News. 1906. *Spectator*, Mar. 29, 178.

Myerson, Allen R. 1993. I.R.A.'s Surging as More Worry about Pensions. *New York Times*, Apr. 15, 1.

Naylor, Bartlett. Proxmire to Seek Bank Size Limits. 1986. *American Banker*, Dec. 10, 1.

New Life Company Investments Proposed. 1951. *Weekly Underwriter*, Jan. 27, 253.

Norris, Floyd. 1992. Power behind the Windsor Fund. *New York Times*, Mar. 6, D1.

Norton, Rob. 1991. Who Owns this Company, Anyhow? *Time*, July 29, 131.

Perspective—S & L Scandal. 1988. *Chicago Tribune*, Dec. 9, 26.

Plans for Insurance Betterments Approved. 1906. *New York Times*, Jan. 6, 5.

Pound, John. 1992. After Takeovers, Quiet Diplomacy, *Wall Street Journal*, June 8, A10.

The President and Insurance. 1905. *The Spectator*, Dec. 7, 340.

Price, Margaret. 1993. Defined Contribution Popularity a Concern. *Pensions and Investments*, May 31, 3.

Protzman, Ferdinand. 1989. Mighty German Banks Face Curb. *New York Times*, Nov. 7, D1.

Pulliam, Susan. 1993. Campbell Soup Fund to Take Activist Role, *Wall Street Journal*, July 15, C1.

Roth, Terence. 1989. West German Banks Face Threat of Reduced Influence in Industry: Bonn Will Consider Rules to Curb Their Holdings and Seats in Boardrooms. *Wall Street Journal*, July 18, A20.

Salwen, Kevin G., and Joann S. Lublin. 1993. Giant Investors Flex Their Muscles More at U.S. Corporations. *Wall Street Journal*, Apr. 27, A1.

Schramm, Sabine. 1992. Markets Lift Top 1,000 Assets to $2.2 Trillion. *Pensions and Investments*, Jan. 20, 1.

Scism, Leslie. 1993. Teacher's Pension Plan to Give Firms Tough Exams. *Wall Street Journal*, Oct. 6, C1.

Smith, Randall. 1992. Calpers Mulls Stakes in Funds Seeking Changes in Firms' Strategy, Governance. *Wall Street Journal*, Dec. 31, A3.

Snyder, Arthur. 1991. Dispelling the Seeds of Doubt. *Best's Review*, Nov. 92:14.

Star, Marlene Givant. 1993. Managers Lead AmEx Coup—Investment Firms Take Up Corporate Governance Fight. *Pensions and Investments*, Feb. 8, 1.

Stark, Louis. 1947a. New Strike Looms, Coal Official Says. *New York Times*, Feb. 12, 5.

———. 1947b. Lewis Sees U.S. Powerless to Prevent Coal Strikes Unless It Goes Totalitarian. *New York Times*, Mar. 8, 1.

Sterngold, James. 1991. Japanese-Style "Old Boy" Network. *New York Times*, June 7, D1.

Top 200 Pension Funds Sponsors. 1990. *Pensions and Investments*, Jan. 20, 20.

Troy, Tom. 1988. Gov. Throws Support behind Takeover Bill. *United Press International*, Jan. 12.

Trussell, C.P. 1946. Pepper Plan Upset. *New York Times*, May 23, 1.

Vise, David A. 1985. CBS Loses $114 Million in Quarter, a Record. *Washington Post*, Nov. 13, E1.

Want Uniform Code of Insurance Laws. 1906. *New York Times*, Jan. 20, 4.

Wayne, Leslie. 1990. Pennsylvania Lends Force to Antitakeover Trend. *New York Times*, Apr. 19, A1.

———. 1992. Questions on Bank Sales of Funds. *New York Times*, Dec. 31, C1.

What Insurance Men Think of the Report. 1906. *New York Times*, Feb. 24, 2.

White, James A. 1991. Pension Officers Back Proxy-Rule Shifts. *Wall Street Journal*, Apr. 1, C1.

White, William S. 1947. Senate Votes 48–40 to Curb Union Rule of Welfare Funds. *New York Times*, May 9, 1.

Acknowledgments

Several chapters here derive from articles that I published previously:

Political and Legal Restraints on Corporate Control, 27 Journal of Financial Economics 7 (1990).

A Political Theory of American Corporate Finance, 91 Columbia Law Review 10 (1991).

Institutional Fiduciaries in the Corporate Boardroom, in Institutional Investors: Challenges and Responsibilities 292 (Irwin 1991).

Political Elements in the Creation of a Mutual Fund Industry, 139 University of Pennsylvania Law Review 1469 (1991).

Foundations of Corporate Finance: The 1906 Pacification of the Insurance Industry, 93 Columbia Law Review 639 (1993).

Understanding the Japanese Keiretsu: Overlaps Between Corporate Governance and Industrial Organization, 102 Yale Law Journal 871 (1993) (with Ronald Gilson).

Takeover Politics, in The Deal Decade 321 (Brookings Institution 1993).

Some Differences in Corporate Structure in Germany, Japan, and the United States, 102 Yale Law Journal 1927 (1993).

The Modern Corporation and Private Pensions, 41 UCLA Law Review 75 (1993).

A number of people read and commented on those articles; I thanked them then, and I thank them again, especially Bernie Black, Jeff Gordon, Victor Goldberg, and Lou Lowenstein, who commented on them all. Special thanks go to Ronald Gilson, my collaborator for an article on which chapter 19 is based, and Bevis Longstreth, both of whom read and commented on the book as a whole.

Financial support for release time came from the Bradley Foundation in 1990; the Columbia Institutional Project also supported my efforts. Two deans at Columbia Law School, Barbara Black and Lance Liebman, were generous in relieving me from administrative and other responsibilities to work on this book. Julie Gavazov and Lyn Grossman did some fine editorial work.

April 1994
Columbia Law School